D1453214

On Autobiography

Theory and History of Literature
Edited by Wlad Godzich and Jochen Schulte-Sasse

For other books in the series, see p. 290.

On Autobiography

Philippe Lejeune

Edited and with a foreword by Paul John Eakin

Translated by Katherine Leary

Theory and History of Literature, Volume 52

University of Minnesota Press, Minneapolis

The University of Minnesota Press gratefully acknowledges publication assistance provided by Indiana University.

Published by the University of Minnesota Press
2037 University Avenue Southeast, Minneapolis, MN 55414.
Printed in the United States of America.

Library of Congress Cataloging-in-Publication Data
Lejeune, Philippe, 1938-
  On autobiography.
  (Theory and history of literature ; v. 52)
  Bibliography: p.
  Includes index.
  1. Autobiography. 2. Authors, French—Biography— History and criticism.
I. Eakin, Paul John. II. Title.
III. Series.
CT25.L37 1988   920   87-38068
ISBN 0-8166-1631-0
ISBN 0-8166-1632-9 (pbk.)

Contents

Acknowledgments

Indiana University helped to launch my work on this volume through a grant from the President's Council on International Programs. With this support I was able to travel to Paris in the spring of 1985 to consult with Philippe Lejeune and with several others who know his work well, including Michel Contat, Gérard Genette, Bruno Vercier, and the late Claude Abastado. At a later stage, a second grant from Indiana University played an important part in bringing this book to publication.

I am grateful to David Bleich for encouragement to undertake this project in the first place, and to Wlad Godzich, who believed from the beginning that it should be done. I must thank Gilbert Chaitin for assistance with my own translations from the French. Finally, I want to express my appreciation to the many people at the University of Minnesota Press who worked on this volume at various points along the way, especially John Ervin, Terry Cochran, Victoria Haire, Beverly Kaemmer, and Patricia Gonzales.

P.J.E.

Foreword
Paul John Eakin

The publication in 1980 of James Olney's collection, *Autobiography: Essays The-oretical and Critical*, marks a milestone in the progress of autobiography studies toward critical maturity. Singularly omitted, however, from Olney's canon in this otherwise comprehensive and exemplary anthology is any selection from the work of Philippe Lejeune, whose range and authority as a student of autobiog-raphy are matched only by Olney himself. My aim is to address three different aspects of Lejeune's work, beginning with his concept of the autobiographical pact. The aggressiveness of Lejeune's formulations as a theorist of the genre, and the scientist aura of his carefully drawn schemata, have generated a mistaken perception of him as narrowly devoted to an intemporal formalist idealism, so I want next to consider his compelling attraction to the contingent and the referen-tial, his consuming interest in autobiography as a primary object for the cultural historian's research. As Valéry reminds us, "There is no theory that is not a frag-ment, carefully prepared, of some autobiography,"[1] and I shall conclude, accord-ingly, with some consideration of Lejeune as an autobiographer.

The Autobiographical Pact

Lejeune's study of autobiography as a genre developed in a period that, in the United States, became increasingly inhospitable to genre criticism. Some critics have claimed, moreover, that autobiography cannot properly be termed a genre at all. Thus Paul de Man, for example, complaining of the distressing sterility of generic discussions of autobiography, argued in 1979 that "empirically as well as theoretically, autobiography lends itself poorly to generic definition," and Avrom Fleishman concluded in 1983 that, since "autobiography is not generically distinguished by formal constituents, linguistic register, or audience effects," it "therefore has no history as a genre."[2] Linda H. Peterson, however, demonstrates in her recent book on Victorian autobiography that English autobiographers from Bunyan to Gosse believed themselves to be participating in a distinctive generic tradition.[3] Lejeune himself seems never to have doubted that autobiography could be approached as a genre, and he has been sustained in this belief, perhaps, by the continuing popularity of formalist criticism in France, as practiced, for example, by Gérard Genette, to whose "Discours du récit" he often alludes.[4] Both the possibilities and the pitfalls of the generic approach to autobiography are amply illustrated by the large body of work that Lejeune has devoted to this subject.

Most of the early work on French, English, and American autobiography — and I am thinking of Richard G. Lillard, Louis Kaplan, William Matthews, Roy Pascal, and Wayne Shumaker, as well as Lejeune — was devoted to the interrelated problems of formulating a definition of the genre and constituting a corpus or *répertoire* of texts.[5] Lejeune's approach to this useful practical task in *L'Autobiographie en France* was not only sensible but necessary, given that in 1971 there was no existing study of the history of autobiography in France.[6] Acknowledging autobiography to be a complex and unstable category, historically speaking, and eschewing any pretense to an essentialist or idealist objective, Lejeune proposed the following working definition of the genre: "we shall define autobiography as the retrospective prose narrative that someone writes concerning his own existence, where the focus is his individual life, in particular the story of his personality" (p. 14). The definition seems pretty straightforward, but it expresses nevertheless three of the principal biases of Lejeune as a student of autobiography: his orientation toward prose, his concern with the temporal features of narrative, and his attraction to psychology and psychoanalysis.

Like Roy Pascal and Georges May, Lejeune proceeded to emphasize that his definition was expressly intended to distinguish autobiography proper from a series of related kinds of autobiographical writing in adjacent genres, including memoirs, the autobiographical novel, the autobiographical poem, and the diary. Doubtless English readers would be quick to object to the exclusion of poetry, which would involve the refusal of a well-established tradition running from Wordsworth and Byron to Robert Lowell and John Berryman, and including Whitman, Eliot, and many others. I would agree, nevertheless, that autobiography tends generally to be a prose form, and for good reason, since narrative is above all others a temporal form and hence best suited to render the contours of our life in time.

Lejeune himself was quick to address the principal limitation of his definition, namely its failure to identify a clear line of demarcation between autobiography and the autobiographical novel. As he readily acknowledged, there is absolutely no way to distinguish between the two on the basis of internal textual evidence (p. 24).[7] Lejeune's solution to the thorny problem of establishing a boundary between factual and fictional modes of discourse was his concept of *le pacte autobiographique*. In effect, the autobiographical pact is a form of contract between author and reader in which the autobiographer explicitly commits himself or herself not to some impossible historical exactitude but rather to the sincere effort to come to terms with and to understand his or her own life.[8] The central issue of intentionality that surfaces here will continue to dog Lejeune right up to the present—witness such recent clarifications as "Le Pacte autobiographique (bis)" (1982; translated in English in the present volume as "The Autobiographical Pact [bis]") and "Autobiographie, roman et nom propre" (1984).[9] Given his insistence that autobiography is necessarily in its deepest sense a special kind of fiction, its self and its truth as much created as (re)discovered realities, and given his lively awareness that the novel has often imitated the posture of self-referential intention in all sorts of pseudo, mock, or otherwise fictive autobiographies, Lejeune concedes in *L'Autobiographie en France* that the presence of an autobiographical pact in a text, while necessary, is not enough to establish it definitively as autobiography. At this early point in his thinking, Lejeune's pact permits the reader to distinguish between autobiography and novel only on the basis of factors *external* to the text (p. 24), requiring knowledge of verifiable biographical reality to support the identity posited among author, narrator, and protagonist. In this first version of the pact, then, Lejeune is appealing to an essentially author-based criticism of autobiography. Even the most cursory reading of *L'Autobiographie en France*, however, will reveal Lejeune's obvious discomfort with the concept of sincerity, which is at once the *sine qua non* of autobiography as a genre and a "sterile problematic" (p. 84) to be avoided at all costs.

In "Le Pacte autobiographique" (1973; translated in English in the present volume as "The Autobiographical Pact"), returning to the apparently insoluble problem of establishing a distinction between autobiography and fiction, Lejeune announced a crucial modification of the position he had taken in *L'Autobiographie en France*: his discovery of the role of the proper name as "the deep subject of autobiography" (*Pacte*, p. 33; *OA*, p. 20). Taking the title page—previously overlooked—as an integral part of the text, Lejeune could now identify a *textual* criterion by which to distinguish between autobiography and fiction, namely the identity of the proper name shared by author, narrator, and protagonist. With an evident sigh of relief, he could abandon an author-based perspective that had required the reader's knowledge of a finally unknowable authorial consciousness. Putting the slippery ethic of sincerity safely behind him (or so he must have thought) as he shifted the fulcrum of the genre from the extratextual state of authorial intention to *the sign of that intention* present in the text, Lejeune was well on his way to establishing a reader-based poetics of autobiography.

The heart of Lejeune's essay on the autobiographical pact, his elaboration of his thinking about the identity of the proper name shared by author, narrator, and protagonist, offers a brilliant insight into the nature of reference in autobiography. Drawing on the distinction promoted by Emile Benveniste and Roman Jakobson between the *utterance* (*énoncé*) and the *enunciation* (*énonciation*), between the past as re-created in autobiography and the re-creation of that past in the present unfolding of the autobiographical act, Lejeune joins Olney, Barrett J. Mandel, and others in stressing that the true locus of reference in autobiography pertains not to the level of the *utterance* but to the level of the *enunciation*, the autobiographical act, where the identity of author, narrator, and protagonist is textually postulated, to be immediately grasped by the reader.[10] Unlike biography, where the resemblance of the protagonist of the narrative to the verifiable facts of the life of the historical model constitutes the decisive criterion for authenticating its structure of reference, in autobiography such resemblance is of distinctly secondary importance. Biography therefore offers a misleading analogue for the nature of reference in autobiography. Lejeune rightly focuses instead on the self-referential gesture itself as the central and determining event in the transaction of autobiographical reference.

Beginning with Benveniste's structural analysis of the functioning of the grammatical person, Lejeune applies his reasoning to the autobiographical act as follows: yes, he agrees, the "I" refers to the act of *enunciation* (" 'Ego' is he who *says* 'ego' "), but the *enunciation* is not the terminal reference in this instance; the personal pronoun refers finally to a name or to an entity susceptible of being designated by a name such that the proper name emerges as the ultimate term of the act of self-reference.[11] Ontogenetically speaking, as I have argued elsewhere, the emergence of self and the acquisition of language go hand in hand.[12] Lejeune himself seems to take precisely such an ontogenetic perspective when he observes that in the history of human development, the proper name and third-person discourse precede first-person discourse in the order of the acquisition of language. Thus the proper name becomes the mediating term between the text and the referential world that lies beyond it. The reference of the proper name to a "real person" is decisive; for Lejeune, this phrase signifies an individual whose existence is verifiable, attested to by the legal record (*Pacte*, pp. 21–23; *OA*, pp. 10–11).

Here Lejeune parts company with those contemporary theorists who take a more limited view of the possibility of reference and the existence of self beyond language, insisting on the concept of person as a linguistic structure and holding reference to be a problematical, secondary rhetorical effect. As Paul de Man put it, "is the illusion of reference not a correlation of the structure of the figure, that is to say no longer clearly and simply a referent at all but something more akin to a fiction which then, however, in its own turn, acquires a degree of referential productivity?"[13] De Man is careful to note that, in the semiological approach to literature that he advocates, "the referential function of language is not being denied – far from it; what is in question is its authority as a model for natural or phenomenal cognition." "It is therefore not *a priori* certain," he concludes, "that literature is a reliable source of information about anything but its own language." There is a special urgency in this view of language as "epistemologically highly suspect and volatile," for de Man recognizes the deep-seated human propensity "to confuse the materiality of the signifier with the materiality of what it signifies" when it comes to "the phenomenality of space, time, or especially of the self."[14]

In "The Autobiographical Pact," Lejeune's orientation toward the referentiality of autobiographical discourse is neither strictly formalist, based on an exclusively internal analysis of the features and functioning of the text, nor doggedly positivist, based on some external verification of the resemblance between the text and the person to whom it refers, for this would require a finally unobtainable knowledge of the author's inner life. Instead, Lejeune founds the poetics of autobiography upon "analysis, on the global level of *publication*, of the implicit or explicit contract proposed by the *author* to the *reader,* a contract which determines the mode of reading of the text and engenders the effects which, attributed to the text, seem to us to define it as autobiography" (*Pacte,* p. 44; *OA,* p. 29). This reader-based orientation of Lejeune's approach, which parallels the speech-act model proposed by Elizabeth Bruss, would make of autobiography "a mode of reading as much as it is a type of writing, . . . a historically variable *contractual effect*" (*Pacte,* p. 45; *OA,* p. 30), such that "the history of autobiography would be therefore, above all, a history of its mode of reading" (*Pacte,* p. 46; *OA,* p. 30).[15]

Lejeune's definition of autobiography and his concept of the autobiographical pact have already received extensive commentary, and I shall mention only one of the more controversial issues, the place of narrative in Lejeune's conception of autobiography. It was Michel Beaujour, in an essay entitled "Autobiographie et autoportrait" (1977), who first drew attention to an apparent contradiction among Lejeune's various articulations of the defining criteria of the genre. In *L'Autobiographie en France* Lejeune had boldly asserted that "autobiography is above all a *narrative*, which follows in time the *story* of an individual" (p. 33), and Beaujour points out that Lejeune had, accordingly, excluded Montaigne's *Essais* from his canon because its principal structure was logical and synthetic rather than narrative and chronological.[16] In *Lire Leiris* (1975), however, Lejeune claimed for Michel Leiris the honor of having realized "the secret project of all autobiography, the discovery of the *order* of a life," precisely by "inverting the importance and role of chronology and meaning" customarily observed in traditional or classical autobiography, thus "giving precedence to thematic order and relegating chronology to a distinctly secondary level of importance."[17] In his enthusiasm for the Freudian experimentation of Leiris, Lejeune even speaks rather extravagantly of the possibility of the ideal autobiography he would like to write himself as "a story without narrative" (p. 184; *OA*, p. 240), meaning, doubtless, "without a traditional narrative."[18] Lejeune was fed up with the straitjacket that the biographical model seemed to impose on the genre, and he offers a wonderfully funny parody of the biographical paradigm, singling out for special mockery the pretensions of the narrative of childhood: "I admire all these people who believe they are born, who seem to know what it is to be born. . . . We have the impression while reading their autobiographies, that their birth is like a piece of property that they would own in the country, or like a diploma" (p. 179; *OA*, p. 235). In "L'Ordre du récit dans *Les Mots* de Sartre" (1975; translated in English in the present volume as "The Order of Narrative in Sartre's *Les Mots*"), a companion piece to his meditations on Leiris, Lejeune praised Sartre for having grasped (as did Leiris) that the *structure* of a narrative, usually neglected by most autobiographers, could serve as a primary mode of self-representation (*Pacte*, pp. 198, 202; *OA*, pp. 71, 73).

If we juxtapose *Lire Leiris* with *L'Autobiographie en France*, as Michel Beaujour did, we seem to find a divided Lejeune, who asserts on the one hand an ideal of autobiography as "a story without narrative," and on the other a definition of the genre as a "retrospective narrative," "the story of a personality." One could infer a change of heart or a careless contradiction, but I think it would be truer to say that the disparity between these formulations points to the fundamental complexity of Lejeune's critical personality. There is a Lejeune who, as theoretician, is fascinated by the virtual possibilities of creativity in the genre, who is understandably bored by the mechanical unfolding of chronological order in conventional autobiographical narrative (*Pacte*, p. 197; *OA*, p. 70). This Lejeune is instinctively drawn to the rare examples of genuine formal experimentation in autobiography, to Sartre and Leiris, as we have seen, and to Serge Doubrovsky, who claims to have been inspired by Lejeune's concept of autobiographical pact to stretch it to the breaking point in his "*autofiction*," *Fils* (1977) (*Moi*, pp. 62–69). There is also a Lejeune who enjoys an excellent rapport with the average individual, who is a connoisseur of autobiographies published by vanity presses;[19] this is the Lejeune who rightly perceives that most autobiographies have been and always will be couched in the traditional chronological form derived from biography. I do think, nevertheless, that the theoretician in Lejeune underestimates the significance of chronology as a structure of reference in autobiographical narrative. Recent work by Paul Ricoeur, Avrom Fleishman, and Janet Varner Gunn posits a phenomenological correlation between the temporal structure of autobiography and what they take to be the essential narrativity of human experience.[20] In this sense the presence of chronology in autobiography would be a manifestation of the ineluctable temporality of human experience, a pull toward temporal structure not satisfactorily accounted for solely by appeal to biographical convention.

We might articulate the relation between the two Lejeunes I have described in terms of the relation between *story* and *discourse* in autobiographical narrative. The lesson of Leiris for Lejeune is that the true reference of *story* in autobiography is not to some comparatively remote period in the subject's past but rather to the unfolding in language of the autobiographical act itself. In this sense *story* in autobiography functions as a metaphor for *discourse*.

I would be the first to point out the limitations of my heuristic, bipartite model of Lejeune, since both tendencies often appear in close proximity within a given essay. Thus, for example, in his recent article, "Autobiographie, roman et nom propre" (1984), if he is prepared to praise the originality of Serge Doubrovsky's undertaking in *Fils*, he is also disturbed by Doubrovsky's cavalier way with referential truth. When he discovers that the identity posited by Doubrovsky's autobiographical pact is only an effect of *trompe-l'oeil*, he is obliged to recognize that Doubrovsky is essentially a novelist at heart, to be distinguished from autobiographers like Leiris who are haunted by an ethical concern for truth (*Moi*, pp. 68–69). Similarly, in the same essay, Lejeune reports that he was moved to write Jacques Lanzmann for clarification about the generic status of *Le Têtard* (1976) — autobiography or novel, "how should one read this book?" (*Moi*, p. 60).

Lejeune's struggle with the problem of sincerity at the heart of autobiography illustrates in exemplary fashion the difficulties of referential art. From as early as *L'Autobiographie en France*, we find Lejeune insisting, as a point of departure, that autobiography is necessarily a fiction produced under special circumstances (p. 30), yet without some sincere basis in referential fact autobiography risks losing its status as a distinct genre and collapsing completely into fiction. To read autobiography in the manner of Lejeune, one must be both sophisticated, alive to its imaginative art, *and* naïve, believing in the sincerity of the author's intention to present the story of "a real person concerning his own existence" (*Pacte*, p. 14; *OA*, p. 4). Accordingly, in "Autobiographie, roman et nom propre," we find Lejeune modulating from an empiricist confession of his problems as a trusting reader to a formalist promulgation of a grammar of the factors that govern the perception of a name as real in a text. Moreover, he is able to adduce documentary evidence from the readings of other critics to support his own insight into the decisive role of the proper name in determining the nature of reference in autobiography. To the extent that Lejeune is able to ground formalist criteria for generic identification in empirical fact, the essay is properly understood as an extension of the work of Norman Holland and Hans Robert Jauss, essential to the development of a reader-based poetics of autobiography as a genre.[21]

The most outspoken critics of Lejeune as a theorist of genre have not kept pace with the progressive sophistication of his development. Thus, for example, while apparently conceding the central contribution of Lejeune and Elizabeth Bruss to our understanding of autobiography as a genre, Avrom Fleishman is prepared to hang them on the issue of sincerity, failing to acknowledge that both are concerned not with an interiority of intention, but with modes of behavior displayed in the demonstrable features of literary texts.[22] Adopting the preemptive strategy that he identifies as one of his most characteristic modes as a critic, Lejeune himself presents in "The Autobiographical Pact (bis)" (1982) the most comprehensive and searching analysis that his performance as a theoretician of autobiography has yet received. He opens with a playful self-portrait (in the manner of La Bruyère) as *Autopact*, acknowledging his own responsibility for his reputation as a dogmatic formalist. Conceding refinements on several points connected with his original definition of autobiography and the autobiographical pact, he is, nevertheless, engaged in a process of fine-tuning. He remains faithful to his concept of the pact, reaffirming on the one hand his belief in the confession of identity that establishes autobiography's very existence as a referential art (*Moi*, p. 21; *OA*, p. 125), and on the other, his belief in the crucial importance of excluding by his definition anything that would paralyze the reader's trust in reference (*Moi*, p. 26; *OA*, p. 128). Like his critics, Lejeune is well aware that the motivating force of the genre for both autobiographers and their readers is a matter of ideology; the last words of *L'Autobiographie en France* are "the myth of the SELF" (p. 105).

At the very heart of "The Autobiographical Pact (bis)," Lejeune, true to his model, makes his own pact with the reader, a confession of faith in autobiography, in reference, in the self. Because I think Lejeune captures here the state of mind of many who persevere in the study of autobiography despite full knowledge of the vexing theoretical problems it poses as a genre, I shall quote the passage at some length:

> It's better to get on with the confessions: yes, I have been fooled. I believe that we can promise to tell the truth; I believe in the transparency of language, and in the existence of a complete subject who expresses himself through it; . . . I believe in the Holy Ghost of the first person. And who doesn't believe in it? But of course it also happens that I believe the contrary, or at least claim to believe it. Whence the fascination that *Roland Barthes par Roland Barthes* (*Roland Barthes by Roland Barthes*, 1975) has held for me; it seems to be the anti-*Pact* par excellence . . . "In the field of the subject, there is no referent . . . " We *indeed know* all this; we are not so dumb, but, once this precaution has been taken, we go on as if we did not know it. Telling the truth about the self, constituting the self as complete subject—it is a fantasy. In spite of the fact that autobiography is impossible, this in no way prevents it from existing. (*Moi*, pp. 30–31; *OA*, p. 131)

Let us be quite clear: belief and disbelief in the fully constituted subject can both be construed as matters of ideology. The interest of Lejeune's position resides in his willingness to concede the fictive status of the self and then to proceed with its functioning as experiential fact. While the most extreme deconstructionists would theorize belief in the self out of existence, Lejeune joins Elizabeth Bruss,

Georges Gusdorf, Karl J. Weintraub, and others in accepting such belief as a fact of contemporary cultural experience with demonstrable practical consequences for autobiography, which has become one of the most characteristic mediums for its expression.[23]

Je est un autre

Although Lejeune has maintained a continuing interest in problems of generic definition in all his books on autobiography, from *L'Autobiographie en France* (1971) right up to his most recent, *Moi aussi* (1986), he has devoted himself increasingly to a set of historical and cultural issues not typically predicated by the formalist theorizing and explication of his early work. It is regrettable that the most extended commentary on Lejeune in English to date, Michael Ryan's review of *Le Pacte autobiographique* (1975) for *Diacritics* in 1980, perpetuates the image of Lejeune as the proponent of a narrow formalist idealism, completely missing the social and historical dimension of his approach to autobiography. To be sure, the prescriptive strain in Lejeune's work, especially in the earlier essays, invites such treatment; Ryan's review, however, grossly misrepresents Lejeune's views, as when he comments, "Like the legal subject of bourgeois law, Lejeune's autobiographical subject has no historical, social, or class content."[24] In the final essay in the volume, "Autobiographie et histoire littéraire" (translated in English in the present volume as "Autobiography and Literary History"), which Ryan ignores, Lejeune himself subjects the apparently normative function of his own definition of autobiography—and those of Richard Lillard, Barrett J. Mandel, Francis R. Hart, and William Howarth—to a searching critique. He presents his work as a theorist of genre in the context of genre criticism in general, which should be devoted, he urges, not to the construction of some absolute, intemporal classification of genres but to the description of the laws governing the functioning of historical systems of genres as they evolve over time. Thus he rejects the antihistorical idealism of Northrop Frye, for example, whose theory of genres postulates the existence of an immanent structure in literature, in favor of the relativist stance of Elizabeth Bruss, who demonstrates that the autobiographical pact is a variable theoretically independent of the formal textual features with which it is often associated. Accordingly, the projects of research on autobiography that Lejeune proposes here follow Hans Robert Jauss and his concept of the shifting horizon of expectation that governs the generic recognition of literary works at any given time; they involve the systematic synchronic study of the functioning of one of the systems of reading in a given period through examination of reception and response preserved in surviving historical documents.

Since 1975, however, Lejeune's program of research on autobiography has developed along lines rather different from the program announced in "Autobiography and Literary History." Not only has his concern shifted from *reception* to *production* of texts in both the nineteenth and twentieth centuries, but his basic assumptions about autobiography and autobiographers have radically altered as well. Lejeune himself traces this shift in perspective to his detailed explication of a three-minute sequence from the film *Sartre par lui-même* (1976), directed by Alexandre Astruc and Michel Contat. The difference between Sartre's autobiographical discourse in *Les Mots* and in the filmed interview brought home the importance of the distinction between the written and the spoken, the consequences of medium for the study of genre. It is, perhaps, hardly surprising that when Sartre related his life in the filmed interview, he spoke in a colloquial manner that suggested his kinship with the man in the street: "Ça s'est fait comme ça" ("that's the way it happened"), he commented, speaking of the break with his mother that marked a turning point in his adolescence. The impact of this performance on Lejeune, however, suggests the extent to which his study of autobiography had been governed by what he came to recognize later on as an essentially elitist attitude.[25]

In the years following Lejeune's work on this film, study of the classic written text by the canonized great writer would be displaced by his exploration of autobiographical self-expression in a wide range of media by increasingly ordinary and even illiterate individuals. This shift in emphasis is readily apparent in Lejeune's next book, *Je est un autre: L'autobiographie, de la littérature aux médias* (1980): while traditional formalist studies of rhetorical structure ("Le Récit d'enfance ironique: Vallès" [1976]; translated in English in the present volume as "The Ironic Narrative of Childhood: Vallès") and generic definition ("L'Autobiographie à la troisième personne" [1977]; translated in English in the present volume as "Autobiography in the Third Person") continue to appear, most of the collection is devoted to a broad-based study of autobiographical self-expression as a pervasive social and cultural phenomenon. The title itself, moreover, captures the consequences of Lejeune's altered perspective in capsule form: the autobiographical "I" had indeed become someone else, not only literally, as with collaborative autobiography, but also more generally, in the sense that the self in question now might well prove to be someone who would never have figured in the select company of one hundred French autobiographers he had chosen for the canon published in *L'Autobiographie en France* in 1971. This new, egalitarian individual might not be a writer at all, but rather, in Sartre's concluding formula for his identity in *Les Mots*, "a whole man, composed of all men and as good as all of them and no better than any." As Lejeune put it later on, quoting this line, "Why privilege Sartre?" (*Moi*, p. 32; *OA*, p. 132). And literature, he might have added.

The result is a book in which peasants and artisans, Mémé Santerre and Gaston Lucas, figure cheek by jowl with writers like Jules Vallès, Victor Hugo, and Sartre, a book in which the object of study originally restricted by Lejeune to the "retrospective prose narrative that someone writes concerning his own existence" has been drastically redefined to admit the manifold and heterogeneous modes of referential self-expression that are currently practiced in contemporary culture. "Someone" might well include someone else, a ghostwriter, say, or oral historian, while the "prose narrative" in question might in fact be a transcript of oral discourse, broadcast on the radio or presented in film. The ownership implicit in the phrase "his own life," moreover, was now frequently a subject of litigation. The founding referential claim posited by Lejeune's autobiographical pact no longer provided an apodictic basis for generic identification; the very *autos* and *graphein* of the genre were now in question, and problem cases abounded.

Lejeune unpacked these ambiguities in his discussion of authorship and authority in the long final section of the book devoted to "L'Autobiographie de ceux qui n'écrivent pas" (translated in English in the present volume as "The Autobiography of Those Who Do Not Write"), his paradoxical formula for collaborative autobiography. Now prepared to affirm that "a person is always *several* people when he is writing, even all alone, even his own life" (*Je*, p. 235; *OA*, p. 188),[26] he seized on collaborative autobiography, which necessarily subverts the concepts of the unified author and person, as an opportunity to disclose the individualist ideology that has sustained most autobiographical practice and criticism in Western culture since the time of Rousseau. Adopting a sociological perspective, inspired in part by Pierre Bourdieu's analysis of the mechanisms of exchange in an economy of symbolic goods,[27] Lejeune demonstrates the cultural relativity of a concept like that of the author when it comes to collaborative autobiography. The notion of "the man who 'held the pen,' " to cite Jean Starobinski's phrase,[28] has been widely received as a prominent component of the identity of the classic autobiographer, and most of the individuals studied by scholars and critics so far, moreover, have been writers. In collaborative autobiography, however, the fact that someone has written the text does not necessarily determine that individual as its "author" in the published product. In the case of the ghost-written autobiography, for example, the writer rarely claims the strategic place reserved for the author's signature, which becomes in effect an attribute of the featured subject whose fame or notoriety claim the attention of the public (*Je*, p. 247; *OA*, p. 195); by contrast, in the case of the autobiography of an unknown (and often illiterate) individual gathered by a journalist or oral historian working in the field, the writer proclaims authorship in the signature as a guarantee that the subject "has written *nothing*," and this avowal in turn functions as a guarantee of the product's authenticity, that "what has been written is a faithful image of what [the subject] said" (*Je*, p. 248; *OA*, p. 196).

The test of authorship as a marker for the generic identification of a text is completely transformed by the circumstances of collaborative autobiography. The question no longer concerns the behavior of the author (whether or not the author signs his own name, or signs his name at all) but rather the author's very identity. The relation between the featured self and the writer of his or her story requires negotiation; sometimes it is settled in the writer's conscience, and sometimes in the courts. In any case, Lejeune's analysis exposes the role of class in the exercise of power in which the act of writing is necessarily implicated. The politics of autobiography is most strikingly displayed in the current vogue of the lives of common people collected by journalists and oral historians, lives that gain access to the printed word only through an intermediary belonging to the dominant class that controls the production and consumption of such texts (*Je*, p. 268; *OA*, p. 209). Lejeune has a lively sense of the ambiguities involved in transactions of this kind, for to the extent that the system of communication in question serves to promote the values and ideology of the dominant (literate) class (*Je*, p. 252; *OA*, p. 198), even the most apparently disinterested enthnographic project may not be free of the taint of exploitation. A collaboration ostensibly devoted to the preservation of autobiographical data that might otherwise perish may nonetheless entail a fundamental condescension that possesses the potential for voyeurism and violation (*Je*, p. 269; *OA*, p. 210). Thus it is by no means clear that the illiterate individual (peasant, artisan, worker) has in fact been enfranchised through such ethnographic intervention, achieving "authority" over his or her own life in the spirit if not the letter of the author's signature.

In *Je est un autre* Lejeune singles out *Gaston Lucas, serrurier, chronique de l'anti-héros* (1976), by Adélaïde Blasquez, as a masterpiece of ethnographic truthtelling, because it steers an artful middle course between fidelity to the ragged incoherence of the subject's unretouched spoken discourse, on the one hand, and surrender to irresponsible fictionalizing in the interest of producing a readable narrative, on the other (*Je*, pp. 299–301). In a more recent essay, however, "Ethnologie et littérature: *Gaston Lucas, serrurier*" (1985), Lejeune reviews the history of his own contacts with Blasquez in order to reveal the complexities of the ethnographic encounter, which becomes a kind of distorting mirror in which the traditional problems of the autobiographical pact are reflected in a new and disconcerting fashion. The initial shock of his first interview with Blasquez is the revelation that the documentary value of her book is impossible to verify, for she erased each taped interview with Lucas as soon as she made a transcription, and, what is more, felt free to alter his language to suit the purpose of her narrative (*Moi*, pp. 275, 276). It is true that later, when she discovers a tape intact, Lejeune listens and recognizes the voice of the Gaston on the tape as *identical* to the voice he attributed to Gaston in his imagination while reading the book (*Moi*, p. 277). Despite this apparent vindication of a novelistic approach to referential truth, Lejeune's interviews with Blasquez introduce him to a fractured world of multiple selves that would seem to defy the power of any referential pact to unify and structure.

For example, there is the Adélaïde Blasquez whose voice he hears on the tape, struggling to heighten the political consciousness of Gaston in order to adapt him to fit her own leftist sympathies. Then there is the Adélaïde he meets in person, who expresses her impatience with the repetitious discourse of her troublesome subject. Finally, there is the Adélaïde of the published book, who has erased her own presence from the body of the text, leaving a preface in which she characterizes her collaboration with Gaston in glowing, egalitarian terms that mask the power relations implicit in the proceedings (*Moi*, pp. 277–78). These last are communicated decisively to Lejeune later, when her publisher decides to videotape an interview with her and she invites Lejeune to be her interlocutor. When he suggests that the publisher should complement this interview with another featuring Gaston, Blasquez replies that in the context of the book, what the living Gaston has to say is without value; he doesn't exist in himself, for it is the written Gaston that counts, an individual who has acquired, thanks to her art, the consistency and truth of a character in a novel.

What, then, becomes of the referential premise of the narrative, for the guarantee of its ethnographic value is precisely that there is only one Gaston, faithfully represented? What is the obligation of the writer to the personal integrity of his or her subject and story? How is it possible to honor the obligation to referential truth without determining first whose is the truth to be told? (*Moi*, pp. 283–84). Lejeune is scrupulous to add that these delicate considerations of moral responsibility also apply to his own presentation of his meetings with Blasquez; noting, however, that she, unlike Gaston, knows how to write and hence possesses the power to answer his commentary with one of her own, he lets himself off the hook (*Moi*, pp. 289–90).[29] In *Je est un autre* and related pieces, which expand the frontiers of the study of autobiography from a narrowly literary to a broadly social and cultural context, Lejeune explodes the structures of medium and person that have traditionally defined the genre. He has not, however, left the old problems of the autobiographical act behind him: identity, sincerity, the pact — all the familiar issues that attend the solitary individual writing the story of his or her life — seem destined to crop up willy-nilly whenever it is a question of telling the truth about the self.

The Trashcan of History

In the late 1970s, at about the same time that Lejeune began the study of contemporary modes of autobiographical self-expression that would culminate in *Je est un autre*, he began to devote himself to compiling an exhaustive inventory or "*répertoire*" of all the autobiographies written in France in the nineteenth century. In "La Cote Ln 27" (1984), he presents a retrospective rationale for this vast program of research, which has the potential to occupy him (and any others who might enlist) for years to come. Like the *répertoire* he offered in *L'Autobiographie en France* in 1971, this one is to be annotated; unlike its predecessor, however, which he now terms "an [overly] purified and literary corpus" (*Moi*, p. 259), too selective to represent the actual history of the genre, this one is to be a broadly inclusive canon, as exhaustive as the surviving documents themselves permit. The purpose of the project is twofold, at once literary and historical. Because of its egalitarian nature, the *répertoire*, once constructed, will permit an anatomy of the "micro-forms" of autobiographical discourse that can be said to have achieved popular currency, a grammar of the building blocks of personal narrative. At the same time the *répertoire* will enlarge the historian's knowledge of what the social atom, the individual, is living, feeling, doing, thinking, at a given moment in the unfolding of culture (*Moi*, p. 270). Although such a project might seem to resemble those of Wilhelm Dilthey and Georg Misch, Lejeune is careful to stress that he regards the texts in his corpus not as ancillary sources of historical information but rather as primary social *facts* in their own right (*Moi*, p. 258).[30] The social history that Lejeune envisages, then, is first and foremost that of the history of discourse, and autobiography must be conceptualized, accordingly, not as some absolute literary essence but instead as historically variable, belonging as it does to constantly changing networks of social practice in which the life of the individual receives articulation.

Something of the scale of Lejeune's program of historical research is suggested by the dimensions of the stack that serves as home base for the literature of *individual biography* in the Bibliothèque Nationale. *La Cote Ln27* comprises more than 94,000 items, and autobiography as defined by Lejeune makes up only a tiny fraction of this vast jumble of texts. To the winnowing of this daunting mass of material, Lejeune brings a truly Balzacian energy, noting that his present catholic attitude toward the literature of autobiography has shifted radically from the elitist literary stance that informed his early work. Whereas before he would have recoiled from the mediocrity of *La Cote Ln27* with a fastidious "What a mess; it's a disgusting heap of trash," he now approaches the same archival dump with the "gourmandise" of a ragpicker licking his lips: "This is real trash!" (*Moi*, pp. 257–58). If I savor this passage, it is because it epitomizes Lejeune's passion for the referential in its raw factuality, a passion that sets him apart from all but a very few of those who concern themselves with autobiography today. Whereas most critics instinctively gravitate to the study of literary masterworks (and I include myself), only a few take care to remind us that autobiography is nothing if not a referential art. Thus James M. Cox justly complains, "There is a distinct tiresomeness about the ease with which literary critics assure themselves that 'mere' fact has little to do with the art of autobiography."[31] But not Lejeune, attracted as he is to the life of the ordinary individual, especially in its bourgeois, familial manifestation, delighting in "the filthy twaddle" of nineteenth-century cultural pretension that Sartre mercilessly parodies in *Les Mots*, the boring success, the petty failure, the banality of self-concept, the conventionality of life story.

Adopting membership in a social group as the only possible organizing principle for the otherwise baffling heterogeneity of his corpus of nineteenth-century French autobiography, Lejeune has published four sections of his *répertoire* to date, the lives of businessmen, industrialists, and financiers in "Autobiographie et histoire sociale au XIXe siècle" (1982; translated in English in the present volume as "Autobiography and Social History in the Nineteenth Century"), the lives of schoolteachers in "Les Instituteurs du XIXe siècle racontent leur vie" (1985), the lives of criminals in "Crime et testament: Les Autobiographies de criminels au XIXe siècle" (1986), and the lives of homosexuals in "Autobiographie et homosexualité en France au XIXe siècle."[32] In these pieces his research typically centers on problems of generic definition, archival information, the publication and reception of texts, and substantive social and cultural issues, followed by an annotated corpus of autobiographies belonging to the social group under study.

Lejeune has characterized his motivation for this research as that of the "populist novelist" (*Moi*, p. 258), a latter-day Balzac or Zola, and in *Calicot* (1984), the recently published autobiography of his great-grandfather, Xavier-Edouard Lejeune, Lejeune prints an installment of the hitherto unpublished "novel" of nineteenth-century French social history, demonstrating the potential richness that single items in the *répertoire* may be expected to yield in the time to come. Believing as he does that "every person carries within himself a rough draft, perpetually reshaped, of the story of his life" (*Moi*, p. 32; *OA*, p.132), Lejeune regards *Calicot* as an exemplary instance of "naïve" autobiography, "a monument made from the materials of everyday life, constructed with infinite patience, in solitude, by an unknown individual"[33] — the antithesis, in a word, of the innovative art practiced by Sartre and Leiris.

If it is true, as Karl J. Weintraub argues in "Autobiography and Historical Consciousness," that the concept of the self is derived from models supplied by the ambient culture, it becomes necessary to determine how such models of self and of life story function and evolve in a culture, and Lejeune's historical research for the *Cote Ln27* project and for *Calicot* bears directly on this question.[34] Whereas traditional autobiography is largely predicated on a belief in the autonomous self, the fully constituted subject who preexists the language into which he casts his story, Lejeune contends that this individualist ideology blinds us to the fact that both self and life story are culturally determined constructs (*Je*, p. 242; *OA*, p. 192). The private speech of the individual engaged in the autobiographical act is, accordingly, derived from a public discourse structured by class, code, and convention.

Thus, adopting the perspective of the historian of discourse, Lejeune observes, paradoxically, that the documentary reference of popular autobiographical texts does not consist in the deliberate creation of a faithful copy of the real (as the correspondence theory informing the publicity of such texts proposes) but rather in the unwitting imitation of common narrative forms that constitute the lingua franca of verisimilitude at a given moment in the life of a culture (*Je*, p. 208).

In his work on the *Cote Ln27*, for example, Lejeune has been obliged to resituate nineteenth-century autobiography in the larger context of the biography of the period with which it is classified: to perform research on *individual biography* at the Bibliothèque Nationale is to observe generic markers evolving at the level of the common denominator, to learn what modes of discourse were associated with life stories, to decode the significance of characteristic formulas for a title, and so forth. Again, preparing his great-grandfather's autobiography for publication, Lejeune was led to identify three cultural sources for the style of self-presentation in *Calicot*: the art of composition that Xavier-Edouard Lejeune learned in a Montmartre grammar school from 1856 to 1858, the romantic novels of Victor Hugo, Eugène Sue, Alexandre Dumas, and others that he devoured in his adolescence, and especially the newspapers of the period that he read assiduously, clipped extensively, and occasionally even recopied (*Moi*, pp. 199–200). Both the performance of the autobiographical act and the narrative that it typically produces easily lend themselves to a belief in the possibility of self-creation, an individualist, Romantic solution to the mystery of origins that masks the agency of cultural institutions at work in the language of life history, determining our stories and our selves. For the historian of discourse, the self who writes is written.

Lejeune brings to the study of the contemporary production of French autobiography the same insatiable ethnographic curiosity that characterizes his work on French autobiography in the nineteenth century. Since 1972 he has kept a record of the personal narratives published in France, and in 1984 the first installment appeared of what he hopes will be a biennial "Bibliographie des études en langue française sur la littérature personnelle et les récits de vie."[35] Always on the lookout for the characteristic or representative feature of the production of autobiographical narrative—how does autobiographical discourse exist in France today? who engages in it? who reads it? where does it come from?—Lejeune has examined the perennial flow of autobiographies from vanity presses and the current popularity of manuals that instruct the reader in the writing of autobiography.[36]

It is just possible that Lejeune's work as a historian of discourse may help to answer the large-scale questions that the referential nature of autobiography invariably prompts its most searching readers to ask. Avrom Fleishman is one of these, and he formulates the problem of the ontology of the genre as follows: "One does not sit down to write an autobiography without a narrative language in which to compose the sentences of one's life story. Where do the expressions of that language, the supplement of one's 'natural' language, come from?" Drawing on Paul Ricoeur's phenomenological conception of narrative, Fleishman suggests that life itself may be "already structured as a narrative,"[37] whereas Lejeune's approach to the origins of autobiographical discourse, as we have seen, tends to be sociological in nature. Will Lejeune's research into the lives of common, ordinary people and the common forms of life story yield an answer to Fleishman's question, or will his scrabbling in the textual detritus of the *Cote Ln27* and the vanity press turn up only a mess of pottage?[38] As far as Lejeune is concerned, he is content to proceed at a cautious and measured pace, publishing local results as he goes along, while resisting the pull toward a global level of generalization that would be unwarranted by his (comparatively) meager samples to date. The first volume of Michel Foucault's *Histoire de la sexualité* (1976–84), for example, makes him uneasy in this regard, for he believes that Foucault relies heavily on large-scale assertions without adducing enough supporting evidence.[39] It is, perhaps, too soon to pass judgment on the benefits that the history of discourse can be expected to bring to the study of autobiography, but at the very least such an approach offers a useful corrective to the tendency of theorists of the genre to generalize prescriptively on the basis of a limited canon of literary masterpieces.

Reading and Writing the Self

A few years ago, in a closely reasoned essay, Jonathan Loesberg grappled with the problem of the generic definition of autobiography, demonstrating the circularity and indeterminacy that result from the troublesome implication of its texts in an elusive, finally unknowable, extratextual reality. In particular he indicted the criticism of autobiography for its characteristic tendency to run afoul of referentiality, attributing to the author what can only be the problems of the reader.[40] Loesberg may well deconstruct the critic's preoccupation with the author's relation to the text, with intention, with sincerity, yet this deconstruction in no way prevents such readings from being enacted. On the contrary, this recurring pattern in the criticism testifies to the fact that the critic's concern with reference, with the author and the author's intention, is built into the very structure of autobiography considered as a figure of reading. The principal limitation of Loesberg's otherwise illuminating analysis stems from his heuristic insistence on distinguishing author and reader as discrete entities, whereas it is, I suspect, precisely an author's instinctive *readerly* knowledge of the effect of autobiographical narrative that would lead him or her to exploit its potential for reference to endow that principal referent, the self, with a reality it might not otherwise enjoy. That is to say, if the premise of autobiographical referentiality that we can move from knowledge of the text to knowledge of the self proves to be a fiction, the text becomes paradoxically not less precious but more: in making the text the autobiographer constructs a self that would not otherwise exist. Moreover, in the specular reciprocity of the world of autobiography the author as reader is matched by the reader as author, for the reader's involvement in authorial consciousness, which seems to be intrinsic to the functioning of the autobiographical text, is ultimately self-referential; the reader, perhaps especially the critic, is potentially an autobiographer himself or herself.

Certainly this is true of Lejeune, whose inveterate practice of featuring a meticulous, blow-by-blow account of his response to a text in much of the criticism he writes has taken on an increasingly autobiographical cast in recent years.[41] The formalist persona of the reader-critic in the early work has been supplanted, as the title of his most recent book suggests, by *moi aussi* (me too). The publication of *Lire Leiris: Autobiographie et langage* in 1975 marks a turning point in this progressive disclosure of the autobiographical self performing the critical analyses ostensibly devoted to the revelation of the selves of others — Proust, Rousseau, Sartre, Leiris. The autobiographical import of *Lire Leiris* was noted in two perceptive reviews by Jean-Michel Olivier and Claude Mauriac. In his aptly titled essay, "Lire Lejeune," the most elaborate commentary on Lejeune's work to be published to date, Olivier argued that reader Lejeune discovers at the very heart of the desire to read a desire to speak himself, so that the initial project to read Leiris becomes a projection of the reader into the text he is in the process of reading. Olivier's term for Lejeune's deliberately self-reflexive style of criticism is *l'autobiocritique*. Similarly convinced of the autobiographical nature of *Lire Leiris*, Claude Mauriac, himself an autobiographer, recognized the book as a self-portrait, and he called on Lejeune to abandon the discretion of his indirect, derivative approach to self-revelation in favor of a bold, frontal engagement in pure autobiography. Although I suspect that the *autobiocritique* displayed in *Lire Leiris* and *Moi aussi* will continue to remain Lejeune's preferred public mode of self-expression for the time to come, by his own testimony he has been answering — in private and for many years — Mauriac's call to autobiography (*Moi*, pp. 181–82).[42]

Confirming the insights of Olivier and Mauriac, in "The Autobiographical Pact (bis)" Lejeune places confession at the heart of the autobiographical domain, and, as if to demonstrate the extent to which the criticism of autobiography is likely itself to be an autobiographical enterprise, he proceeds to a double confession of his own, his belief in the subject (which I quoted earlier) and his concomitant desire to write his autobiography: "I chose to work, academically, *on* autobiography, because in a parallel direction I wanted to work *on* my own autobiography" (*Moi*, p. 31; *OA*, p. 132) It is worth noting, in this connection, how frequently critics have been drawn to give an autobiographical account of their involvement with autobiography — Roy Pascal would be a prominent example of this strain of crypto-autobiography that often motivates study of the genre. Unlike Pascal, however, who remains at the threshold in his book *Design and Truth in Autobiography*, recognizing that he is impelled to write about autobiography by "an insistent moral pressure" that he identifies with "a state of mind from which autobiography springs,"[43] Lejeune crossed over into autobiography itself, as he announced in the "Epilogue" to *Lire Leiris* (1975; translated in English in the present volume as "Epilogue").

Lejeune explicitly presents the "Epilogue" as a fragment of autobiography, and the presence of the familiar generic markers of Lejeune's own model – the confession, the secret, the quest for origins – supports this identification. The "Epilogue" constitutes, in effect, Lejeune's first published autobiographical pact, concerned as it is with the birth of his own autobiographical discourse and with the assertion of identity, especially if we grasp the extent to which Leiris functions in the critical narrative in the body of the book as a surrogate for Lejeune himself, or at least a "prodigious" and "prodigal" father (p. 183; *OA*, pp. 238–39). As Lejeune put it, *Lire Leiris* meant "read oneself here" ("*s'y lire*") (p. 181; *OA*, p. 237), to read oneself in the text. Acknowledging that his earliest attempts to write about himself had demonstrated the inadequacy of traditional autobiographical narrative derived from biography, and that his subsequent recourse to the strategies of the novel and the diary had also ended in failure, Lejeune credits Leiris with showing him the way to the kind of autobiography he too could write. In the excitement of his discovery of a new language and form, he repudiated the notion of autobiography as an act of genuine communication between author and reader (pp. 175–76; *OA*, pp. 232–33): the "I" of Leiris became an " 'I' without referent" (p. 177; *OA*, p. 234), and Lejeune proposes to himself to write "a story without narrative" (p. 184; *OA*, p. 240). This paradoxical notion inspired by Leiris points to an autobiography in which *story* is subsumed by *discourse*, in which the free association of language unfolding moment by moment during the autobiographical act supplants the conventional model of autobiography as a transparent rendering of a recoverable past.

Not surprisingly, Lejeune's conception of his autobiography seems to have changed as he has changed, and in "Mémoire familiale" (1984) (*Moi*, pp. 183–92), in which he discusses his recent preoccupation with the history of the Lejeunes, he expressly distances himself from the narcissism of the psychoanalytic, associative model he embraced with such fervor during the period of his work on Leiris. When he reviews his project of reconstructing the collective memory of his family in order to place himself and his life story in the context of those who preceded him, it becomes clear that *story* is back in the saddle again, armed this time with a tape recorder and an apparently boundless appetite for archival research. Although he rejected the traditional biographical narrative at the bidding of his surrogate father Leiris, his subsequent inquiry into family history led him to the discovery of another surrogate father-autobiographer in his great-grandfather Xavier-Edouard Lejeune, and his editorial commentaries in *Calicot* place a premium on referential truth, undoing the fictions of his ancestor even as he publishes them.

To assemble the available evidence concerning Lejeune's practice of autobiography – the published fragments in the "Epilogue" to *Lire Leiris* together with the commentaries there and in "Postscriptum à *Lire Leiris*" (1986; *Moi*, pp. 164–77) and "En famille" (1984, 1985; *Moi*, pp. 181–202) – is to recognize how various it has been. It would be hard to say whether his shifting allegiances to referential fact and imaginative art, to narrative and to language, are mutually contradictory or complementary, and Lejeune himself shows no inclination to opt for one mode at the expense of another. To the contrary, he reports the attraction he feels toward Claude Mauriac's autobiography, *Le Temps immobile* (1974–84), which experiments with a kind of temporal montage, juxtaposing writings dating from all periods of his life (*Moi*, pp. 126–27). The appeal of Mauriac is instructive, for whereas the traditional, correspondence model of autobiographical reference tends to subordinate the text to that which it is presumably about, for Lejeune, following Leiris, the creation of the text is primary; autobiography is literally a writing; and the corollary of this textualization of the genre is a performative conception of the content of a life story in which the relevant events are equivalent to the cumulative series of a writer's engagements in the autobiographical act.[44]

This writerly, Leirisian bias notwithstanding, Lejeune's practice as a critic of the autobiographical writing of others amply testifies not only to his belief in the referential dimension of such texts but specifically to his conception of the content to which they characteristically refer: if autobiography is properly conceived as the performance of a kind of writing, its subtext is the confession of sexuality.[45] Olivier has remarked on the veritable obsession with the secret in Lejeune's criticism, and the secret usually proves to be some aspect of infantile sexuality as conceptualized in the classic Freudian paradigm of the Oedipal family drama.[46] Confession of desire in Proust and Rousseau concerns masturbation and maternal love; again, Lejeune detects repressed desire for the mother in Sartre, and repressed desire for the father in Leiris.[47] Lejeune's analyses suggest that it is in the very nature of desire that there is always a sexual secret to be confessed, and what fascinates him, what he anatomizes again and again in intricate detail, are the ingenious strategies of denial and repression that refuse confession yet confess nonetheless in the very act of refusal. If confession is central to Lejeune's conception of autobiography, if the impulse to confess, to articulate desire, proceeds by indirection through the impulse to conceal and repress, and if, moreover, Lejeune affirms that he has approached confession himself mostly by indirection through analysis of confession in others (*Moi*, p. 166), what, then, may we infer about the autobiography he has yet to publish?

The history of Lejeune's engagement with autobiographical writing seems to have paralleled his shifting attitude toward psychoanalysis, and indeed the most important published fragments of his autobiography, the "Epilogue" to *Lire Leiris* and the "Postscriptum à *Lire Leiris*," concern psychoanalysis both as method and as content for autobiographical self-revelation. Lejeune's earliest exposition of the relation between autobiography and psychoanalysis, the long concluding section in *L'Autobiographie en France*, is also his most balanced assessment: distinguishing carefully between autobiography on the one hand and autoanalysis and psychoanalysis on the other, he concludes that psychoanalysis has not fulfilled its

original promise of providing a theoretical basis for the autobiographical enterprise. Lejeune is careful in this respect to note that Leiris's practice of a psychoanalytically inspired autobiography constitutes a literary rather than a clinical
application of Freudian analysis (pp. 91–104). In support of his negative finding
with regard to the contribution of psychoanalysis to autobiography, he includes
in an appendix extracts from an essay by Bernard Pingaud, "L'Ecriture et la cure,"
which argues that writing is a nontherapeutic act, and hence, I should add, unsuited to the project of confessional autobiography formulated by Lejeune: functioning as a defense mechanism, it reveals no secret but constitutes one itself (pp.
257–62). A few years later, however, Leiris had cast his spell, prompting
Lejeune in the "Epilogue" to conceive of the autobiographical act as an analogue
to the psychoanalytic encounter, in which the analysand "knows that the moment
when he speaks is the center of his story, in the sense that everything is repeated
here" (p. 179; *OA*, p. 236).

The euphoria of the Leirisian moment, which Lejeune seems to have experienced as a release from literary constraint and psychological inhibition, ena-
bling the free-associative (and imitative) style of autobiographical writing illustrated in the "Epilogue" ("prodigal" and "prodigious" father) was relatively
short-lived, as he recently revealed in the "Postscriptum à *Lire Leiris*" (1986). The
subject of the "Postscriptum," which relates Lejeune's face-to-face meeting with
Leiris in 1976, focuses on the clinical experience of psychoanalysis, both Leiris's
and Lejeune's, which emerges as the prototype for the autobiographical act conceived as confession.[48] As far as Leiris's analysis is concerned, Lejeune is frankly
disappointed: Leiris is portrayed as surprisingly naïve, psychoanalytically speaking, someone who never understood the Freudian conception of dream work,
someone who openly repudiated free association, someone who was visibly
shocked by Lejeune's suggestion that he could have wished "to be his father's
wife" (*Moi*, p. 175). Leiris himself was also disappointed by his analysis, which
seems only to have reenforced his resistance (*Moi*, p. 170), for he emerged from
it without having discovered anything, without having attained knowledge of an
origin or a secret (*Moi*, p. 173). For Leiris, and for Lejeune as well, the possibility of self-revelation through analysis is both threat and lure, and Lejeune dis-
cerns in his obsessive curiosity to get at the substance of Leiris's analysis a screen
for his desire to come to terms with his own. Ironically, he reports that his own
analysis, hitherto concealed as a kind of guilty secret, was just as disappointing
as Leiris's; its meager discoveries really didn't amount to much (*Moi*, p. 166).
The upshot of the "Postscriptum" is to discredit analysis as a paradigm for confessional autobiography; with characteristic self-mockery he writes, "I saw myself
advance stealthily toward a trivial confession" (*Moi*, p. 167). From this perspective, the paradoxical innovations proclaimed in the "Epilogue," the " 'I' without
referent," the "story without narrative," show as evasions, wishful formulas for
the confession of a confession in which nothing is confessed. Janus-faced, psy-

choanalytic autobiography shifts from liberation to repression: "writing," he now acknowledged, "is only the dream of a solution" (*Moi*, p. 164). The "Postscriptum" seems to announce Lejeune's farewell to autobiography, at least to the psychoanalytic confessional model he has embraced so far.[49]

Lejeune's own sense of his reluctance to confess may indicate that the publication of his autobiography is unlikely to occur soon or even ever. Moreover, given the high expectations his current reputation as a theorist of the genre would naturally generate concerning such a text, he is understandably skittish about getting it into print. In a revealing moment in the "Postscriptum," he characterizes his ambivalent stance toward Leiris in terms that could apply with equal justice to his own stance as autobiographer: "I was torn between contradictory fears and hopes, both equally chimerical; fear of the anger of a Noah, whose cloak I would have stripped away, desire to see my commentaries confirmed" (*Moi*, p. 165). Oedipal fear of the father and desire for his exposure may also stand for Lejeune's simultaneous attraction to and repulsion from the autobiographical act itself, angry Noah a double for Narcissus unveiled. Interestingly, he now entertains the idea of having others assist him in the performance of the autobiographical act, doing for him what he may not be prepared to do for himself, as in his project to record his parents in a series of taped interviews on the subject of his childhood (*Moi*, p. 185), or again, at the end of the "Postscriptum," in his dare to some future critic to play the Lejeune to his own Leiris, sneaking up on him unaware in his autobiographical discourse to catch him (Noah once more) in the act (*Moi*, p. 177). Whatever his own autobiography may turn out to be, and whether or not he ever lays aside his protective mantle of defensive and ironic self-consciousness, I think that Philippe Lejeune has done as much as anyone to enlarge our appreciation of the literature of autobiography, whether speculating as a theorist about what the genre might become in the hands of genius, or, as a historian, rooting in the trashcan of reference to see what it has been most of the time.

I. Autobiography: Theory of the Genre and Analysis of Discourse

Chapter 1
The Autobiographical Pact

Is it possible to define autobiography?

I had tried to do just that in *Autobiographie en France* (*Autobiography in France*),[1] so as to be in a position to develop a coherent corpus of texts. But my definition left a number of theoretical problems unaddressed. While trying to find stricter criteria, I felt the need to refine and clarify this definition. I inevitably encountered along my way the classical discussions to which the genre of autobiography always gives rise: the relations of biography and autobiography, and the relations of the novel and autobiography. These problems are irritating because of the endless repetition of arguments, the vagueness that surrounds the vocabulary that is used, and the confusion of problematics borrowed from unrelated fields. Through a new attempt at a definition, then, it is the very terms of the problematic of the genre that I intend to clarify. In wanting to provide clarity, we run two risks: that of seeming to be caught up in an endless repetition of the obvious (because it is necessary to start from the very beginning), and that, on the contrary, of appearing to want to complicate things by using distinctions that are too subtle. I will not avoid the first; as for the second, I will try to base my distinctions on reason.

I had devised my definition not by placing myself *sub specie aeternitatis*, and examining the "things-in-themselves" that would be the texts, but by putting myself in the place of the reader of today who attempts to distinguish some sort of order within a mass of *published* texts, whose common subject is that they recount someone's life. The situation of the "definer" is thus doubly relativized and specified: *historically*, this definition does not claim to cover more than a period of two centuries (since 1770) and deals only with European literature; this does not mean that the existence of a personal literature before 1770 or outside Europe must be denied, but simply that our way of thinking about autobiography today becomes anachronistic or not very pertinent outside this area. *Textually*, I begin from the position of the reader: it is not a question of starting from within the mind of the author, which indeed poses a problem, nor is it one of establishing the canons of a literary genre. By taking as the starting point the position of the reader, (which is mine, the only one I know well), I have the chance to understand more clearly how the texts function (the differences in how they function) since they were written for us, readers, and in reading them, it is we who make them function. It is thus by the series of oppositions between the different texts, which are available for reading, that I have tried to define autobiography.

In its modified form, the definition of autobiography would be:

DEFINITION: *Retrospective prose narrative written by a real person concerning his own existence, where the focus is his individual life, in particular the story of his personality.*

The definition brings into play elements belonging to four different categories:

1. *Form of language*
   a. narrative
   b. in prose
2. *Subject treated*: individual life, story of a personality
3. *Situation of the author*: the author (whose name refers to a real person) and the narrator are identical
4. *Position of the narrator*
   a. the narrator and the principal character are identical
   b. retrospective point of view of the narrative

Any work that fulfills all the conditions indicated in each of the categories is an autobiography. Genres closely related to autobiography do not meet all these requirements. Those requirements that are not met are listed here according to genres:

—memoirs: (2)
—biography: (4a)
—personal novel: (3)
—autobiographical poem: (1b)
—journal / diary: (4b)
—self-portrait or essay: (1a and 4b).

It is obvious that the different categories are not all equally restrictive: certain conditions can be met for the most part without being satisfied completely. The text must be *mainly* a narrative, but we know how important *discourse* is in autobiographical narration. The perspective is *mainly* retrospective; this does not exclude some sections from taking the form of the self-portrait, a journal of the work or of the contemporary present of the composition, and some very complex temporal structures. The subject must be *primarily* individual life, the genesis of the personality; but the chronicle and social or political history can also be part of the narrative. It is a question here of proportion, or rather of hierarchy: some transitions with other genres of personal literature work quite naturally (memoirs, diary, essay), and a certain latitude is left to the classifier in the examination of particular cases.

On the other hand, two of the conditions are a question of all or nothing, and they are of course the conditions that oppose autobiography (but at the same time the other types of personal literature) to biography and the personal novel: these are conditions (3) and (4a). Here, there is neither transition nor latitude. An identity is, or is not. It is impossible to speak of degrees, and all doubt leads to a negative conclusion.

In order for there to be autobiography (and personal literature in general), the *author*, the *narrator*, and the *protagonist* must be identical. But this "identity" raises a number of problems, which I will try, if not to resolve, then at least to formulate clearly in the sections that follow:

— How can the identity of the narrator and the protagonist be expressed in the text? (*I, You, He*)
— In the narrative written "in the first person," how is the identity of the author and the protagonist-narrator shown? (*I, the Undersigned*) Here we have the opportunity to contrast autobiography with the novel.
— Is there not confusion, in most of the arguments concerning autobiography, between the notion of *identity* and that of *resemblance*? (*Exact Copy*) Here we will have occasion to contrast autobiography with biography.
— The difficulties encountered in these analyses will lead me, in the last two sections of this chapter (*Autobiographical Space* and *Reading Contract*), to try to shift the basis of the problem.

I, You, He

The identity of the *narrator* and the *principal character* that is assumed in autobiography is marked most often by the use of the first person. This is what Gérard Genette calls "autodiegetic" narration in his classification of narrative "voices," a classification he establishes from works of fiction.[2] But he states quite clearly that there can be narrative "in the first person" without the narrator being the same person as the principal character. This is what he calls in broad terms "homodiegetic" narration. We need only continue this reasoning to see that in the reverse order there can be identity of the narrator and the principal character without the first person being used.

It is necessary, then, to point out two different criteria: that of the grammatical person, and that of the identity of the individuals to whom the aspects of the grammatical person refer. This elementary distinction is forgotten because of the polysemy of the word "person"; it is masked in practice by the conjunctions that *almost always* come between a given grammatical person and a given relation of identity or a given type of narration. But it is only "almost always"; the undeniable exceptions compel us to rethink the definitions.

Indeed, by bringing up the problem of the *author*, autobiography brings to light phenomena that fiction leaves in doubt: in particular the fact that there can be identity of the narrator and the principal character in the case of narration "in the third person." This identity, no longer being established within the text by the use of "I," is established indirectly, but without any ambiguity, by the double equation: author = narrator, and author = character, from which it is deduced that narrator = character even if the narrator remains implicit. This procedure is consistent, to the letter, with the root meaning of the word "autobiography": it is a biography, written by the person involved, but as a simple biography.

This procedure could be used for very diverse reasons and could bring about very different *effects*. Talking about oneself in the third person can imply either tremendous conceit (this is the case with Caesar's *Commentaries* or with the comparable texts of General De Gaulle), or a certain kind of humility (this is the case with certain early religious autobiographies, in which the autobiographer calls himself "the servant of God"). In the two cases the narrator assumes, vis-à-vis the character that he was, either a distancing from the perspective of history or a distancing from the perspective of God, i.e., of eternity, and introduces in his narration a transcendence with which, in the final analysis, he identifies. We can imagine the totally different effects—of contingency, of dividing, or of ironic distancing—that the same procedure might produce. This is true of the book by Henry Adams, *The Education of Henry Adams*, in which the author relates in the third person the quasi-Socratic quest of a young American in search of an education—himself. In all the examples given above, the third person is used throughout the narration. There do exist some autobiographies in which one part of the text refers to the principal character in the third person, while in the remainder of the text the narrator and this principal character are confused in the first person; this is the case with *Le Traître*, in which André Gorz expresses the uncertainty of his own identity through tricks of voice. Claude Roy, in *Nous (Us)*, uses this procedure more tritely in order to place an episode of his love life at a modest distance.[3] The existence of these bilingual texts, true Rosetta Stones of identity, is of great import: it confirms the possibility of autobiographic narration "in the third person."

Even if we remain within the personal register (first and second persons), it is obvious that it is possible to write without using the first person. What would prevent me from writing my life's story and calling myself "you"? In the realm of fiction, such a thing was done by Michel Butor in *La Modification*, and by Georges Perec in *Un Homme qui dort (A Man Who Is Sleeping)*. I am not aware of any autobiographies that have been written entirely in this way; but this method appears somewhat fleetingly in the *speeches (discours)* that the narrator addresses to the person that he was, either to cheer him up if he's in a bad mood, or to lecture him or repudiate him.[4] There is certainly a distance from this point to a narrative, but such a thing is possible. This type of narrative would show clearly, at the level of enunciation, the difference between the subject of the enunciation and the subject of the utterance treated as addressee of the narrative.

These uses of the third and second persons are rare in autobiography, but they keep us from confusing the grammatical problems of person with the problems of identity. We could also imagine a diagram with dual access conceived in this way:

grammatical person → / identity ↓	I	YOU	HE
narrator = principal character	classical autobiography (autodiegetic)	autobiography in the 2nd person	autobiography in the 3rd person
narrator ≠ principal character	biography in the 1st person (witness narrative) (homodiegetic)	biography addressed to the model	classical biography (heterodiegetic)

Remarks on the diagram

1. By "grammatical person," we must understand here the person used in a privileged manner throughout the narrative. It is obvious that the "I" is not understood without a "you" (the reader), but the latter remains generally implicit; in

the opposite direction, the "you" supposes an "I," equally implicit; and narration in the third person may include intrusions of the narrator in the first person.

2. The examples given here are all borrowed from the gamut of referential narratives that are biography and autobiography; we could also fill up the diagram with examples of fiction. I indicate the categories of G. Genette in the three corresponding blocks; we see that they do not cover all possible cases.

3. The case of biography addressed in the model is that of academic discourses, where the person whose life is told is addressed, before an audience who is the true addressee, just as in an autobiography told in the second person, if such existed, the addressee (formerly oneself) would be there to receive a discourse that would be presented to the reader.

It is necessary, starting with exceptional cases, to dissociate the problem of the person from that of identity. This dissociation allows us to understand the complexity of existing or possible models of autobiography. It is also characteristic of this dissociation to shake the certainties that exist with regard to the possibility of giving a "textual" definition of autobiography. For the moment, having brought up the exception, let's go back to the most frequent case: the classic autobiography "in the first person" (autodiegetic narration); our purpose is to discover new uncertainties, aimed this time at the manner in which the identity of the *author* and the *narrator-character* is established.

I, the Undersigned

Let's suppose, then, that all autobiographies are written in the first person, as the great refrain of the autobiographers — I — leads us to believe. Thus Rousseau: "I, I alone"; Stendhal: "Put *I* with *me* and you have repetition"; Thyde Monnier: *Moi (I)* (autobiography in four volumes); Claude Roy: *Moi, je (Me, I);* and so on. Even in this case the following question is still being asked: how does the identity of the author and the narrator manifest itself? For an autobiographer, it is natural to wonder quite simply: "Who am I?" But since I am the reader, it is no less natural for me to ask the question differently: who is "I?" — i.e., who is it who *says* "Who am I?"

You will excuse me for mentioning, before going on with the analysis, some elementary notions of linguistics. But, in this area, the simplest things are the ones that are most quickly forgotten: they seem natural and disappear in the illusion that they engender. I will begin with some of Benveniste's analyses, even if I end up with conclusions slightly different from his.[5]

The "first person" is defined through articulation on two levels:

1. *Reference*: the personal pronouns (I/you) have real reference only within discourse, in the very act of enunciation. Benveniste points out that there is no

such concept as "I." The "I" refers, each time, to the person who is speaking and whom we identify *by the very fact* that he is speaking.

2. *Utterance*: the first-person personal pronouns mark the *identity* of the subject of the enunciation and of the subject of the utterance.

Thus, if someone says: "I was born the . . . ," the use of the pronoun "I" results, through the articulation of these two levels, in our identifying the person who is speaking with the one who is being born. At least this is the total effect obtained. We are not necessarily led to believe here that the types of "equations" established on these two levels are the same. At the level of reference (speech as it refers to its own enunciation), identity is immediate; it is instantaneously understood and accepted by the addressee as a *fact;* at the level of utterance, it is a question of a simple relationship . . . uttered, i.e., of one assertion like another, that we can believe or not, and so on. Moreover, the example that I have used gives us some idea of the problems raised: is it really the same person, the baby who is born in such and such a clinic, in an era of which I have no memory whatsoever — and *me?* It is important to clearly differentiate these two relationships, blurred in the use of the pronoun "I"; we will see later that it is our failure to make such a distinction that causes the greatest confusion in the problematic of autobiography (see *Exact Copy,* below). Setting aside for the moment the problems of utterance, I will limit myself to thinking about enunciation.

The situation of *oral* discourse is the starting point of the analyses of Benveniste. In this situation, we might think that the reference of the "I" poses no problem: "I," it is the person who is speaking — and me, in my position as interlocutor or listener, I have no difficulty in identifying this person. Nevertheless, there exist two series of oral situations in which this identification can pose a problem.

1. *Quotation*, which is discourse within discourse. The first person of the second discourse (quoted) refers to a situation of enunciation itself expressed in the first discourse. Different signs, dashes, quotation marks, etc., differentiate the inserted (quoted) discourses, when we are dealing with written discourses. Intonation plays an analogous role in oral discourse. But these signs become blurred, or faded, and uncertainty appears: this is the case in *re*-quotation/*re*-citation and in a more general way in the theater. When Berma plays *Phèdre*, who is saying "I"? The theatrical situation can certainly perform the function of quotation marks, pointing out the fictitious character of the person who says "I." But here, our head starts to swim because the idea crosses the minds of even the most naïve of us that it is not the individual who defines the "I," but perhaps the "I," the individual, that is to say, the individual exists only in discourse. Let's avoid chaos for the moment. What we are touching upon here, in autobiography, are problems related to the difference between the autobiographical novel and autobiography. But also, in terms of autobiography itself, we find evidence that the first person is a role.

2. *Oral from a distance*, which takes place in the moment, as in a telephone

conversation, any conversation through a door or at night. There is no other way to identify the individual except through aspects of voice: who's there? — me — who, me? Here, dialogue is still possible that might lead to identification. Let the voice be delayed in time (recording), or even, in the moment, one-way conversation (radio), and we cannot identify it. We now go back to the case of writing.

Up to this point, I have tried to follow Benveniste, simply by imagining everything that, in an oral situation, might succeed in restoring the identity of the undetermined individual. That the "I" refers to the enunciation, no one is trying to deny. But the enunciation is not the last term of the reference: it poses in its turn a problem of *identity*, which, in direct oral communication, we resolve instinctively from some extralinguistic facts. When oral communication is confused, identity is a problem. But, in written communication, unless s/he wants to remain anonymous (which does happen!), the person who formulates the discourse must allow his/her identification within this speech by using something besides physical signs, like the postmark, writing or spelling peculiarities.

Benveniste indicates (p. 226) that there is no such concept as "I" — quite an accurate remark if we add that there is no such concept as "he" either, and that, in general terms, no personal, possessive, demonstrative, pronoun, etc., has ever *referred* to a concept, but simply exercises a function, which consists in referring to a noun or to an entity that can be designated by a noun. Accordingly, we will propose to qualify his analysis by the following two propositions:

1. The personal pronoun "I" refers to the speaker at the moment of discourse when the "I" appears; but this speaker is himself capable of being designated by a noun (whether we are talking about a common noun, determined in different ways, or about a proper noun).

2. The opposition *concept/no concept* takes its meaning from the opposition of common noun and proper noun (not from common noun and personal pronoun).

Benveniste thus justifies, economically, the use of this first person, which has reference only in its own enunciation: "If each speaker, in order to express the feeling he has of his irreducible subjectivity, made use of a distinct identifying 'signal' (in the sense in which each radio transmitting station has its own call letters), there would be as many languages as individuals and communication would become absolutely impossible" (p. 220). A strange hypothesis, since Benveniste seems to forget here that this distinct signal *exists*, and it is the lexical category of proper names (those proper names that designate people): there are almost as many proper names as there are individuals. Naturally, this is not an aspect of verb conjugation, and Benveniste is right in emphasizing the economic function of the "I"; but, in forgetting to articulate it in the lexical category of names of people, he renders incomprehensible the fact that each one, utilizing the "I," does not lose himself for all that in anonymity and is always capable of enunciating what is irreducible in naming himself.

It is in the *proper name* that person and discourse are linked even before being joined in the first person, as the order of language acquisition by children shows. The child talks about himself in the third person while calling himself by his first name, long before he understands that he too can use the first person. Next each of them calls himself "I" in speaking; but for each one, this "I" refers to a single name, which he will always be able to express. All the identifications (easy, difficult, or undetermined) suggested above from oral situations inevitably result in transforming the first person into a proper name.[6]

Each time that oral discourse is necessary, the return to the proper name is accomplished. This is the *presentation*, made by the person involved or by a third party (the word "presentation" itself is suggestive by its inaccuracy: physical presence is not sufficient to define the speaker; there is complete presence only through naming). Similarly in written discourse, the *signature* designates the enunciator, as the address does the addressee.[7]

It is thus in relation to the *proper name* that we are able to situate the problems of autobiography. In printed texts, responsibility for all enunciation is assumed by a person who is in the habit of placing his *name* on the cover of the book, and on the flyleaf, above or below the title of the volume. The entire existence of the person we call the *author* is summed up by this name: the only mark in the text of an unquestionable world-beyond-the-text, referring to a real person, which requires that we thus attribute to him, in the final analysis, the responsibility for the production of the whole written text. In many cases, the presence of the author in the text is reduced to this single name. But the place assigned to this name is essential: it is linked, by a social convention, to the pledge of responsibility of a *real person*. I understand by these words, which figure in my definition of autobiography, a person whose existence is certified by vital statistics and is verifiable. Certainly, the reader is not going to verify this, and he may very well not know who this person is. But his existence is beyond question: exceptions and breaches of trust serve only to emphasize the general credence accorded this type of social contract.[8]

An author is not a person. He is a person who writes and publishes. Straddling the world-beyond-the-text and the text, he is the connection between the two. The author is defined as simultaneously a socially responsible real person and the producer of a discourse. For the reader, who does not know the real person, all the while believing in his existence, the author is defined as the person capable of producing this discourse, and so he imagines what he is like from what he produces. Perhaps one is an author only with his second book, when the proper name inscribed on the cover becomes the "common factor" of at least two different texts and thus gives the idea of a person who cannot be reduced to any of his texts in particular, and who, capable of producing others, surpasses them all. This, we will see, is very important for the reading of autobiographies: if the autobiography is a first book, its author is thus unknown, even if he relates his own story in the book. He lacks, in the eyes of the reader, that sign of reality which is the previous production *of other texts* (nonautobiographical), indispensable to that which we will call "the autobiographical space."

The author is, then, the name of a person, identical, taking upon himself a series of different published texts. He draws his reality from the list of his other works which figure often in the front of the book: "By the same author." Autobiography (narrative recounting the life of the author) supposes that there is *identity of name* between the author (such as he figures, by his name, on the cover), the narrator of the story, and the character who is being talked about. What we have here is a very simple criterion, which defines at the same time as autobiography all the other genres of personal literature (journal, self-portrait, essay).

An objection comes to mind at once: what about pseudonyms? An easy objection to avoid, as soon as we have defined pseudonym and distinguished it from the name of a fictional character.

A pseudonym is a name that is different from the one found in vital statistics, which a real person uses in order to *publish* all or part of his writings. The pseudonym is the name of an *author*. It is not exactly a false name, but a pen name, a second name, exactly like the one a religious assumes upon taking orders. To be sure, the use of a pseudonym can sometimes cover up deceptions or be imposed for reasons of discretion; but it has to do most often with isolated productions, and almost never with a work being passed off as the autobiography of an *author*. Literary pseudonyms are in general neither mysteries nor hoaxes. The second name is as authentic as the first; it simply signals this second birth which is the published writing. Writing his autobiography, the author under his pen name will himself explain its origin; thus Raymond Abellio explains that he is calling himself Georges Soulès, and why he has chosen his pseudonym.[9] The pseudonym is simply a differentiation, a division of the name, which changes nothing in the identity.

We must not confuse *pseudonym*, defined in this way as the name of an *author* (*noted on the cover of the book*), with the *name* attributed to a fictional person *within the book* (even if this person has the status of narrator and assumes the whole of the text production), because this person is himself designated as fictitious by the simple fact that he is incapable of being the *author* of the *book*. Let me give a very simple example: "Colette" is the pseudonym of a real person (Gabrielle-Sidonie Colette), *author* of a series of narratives; Claudine is the name of a fictitious heroine, narrator of the stories that have her name for a title. If the *Claudines* cannot be accepted as autobiographies, it is quite obviously for the second reason, not at all for the first.

In the case of the fictitious name (i.e., different from that of the author) given to a character who tells his life story, the reader has reason to think that the story lived by the character is precisely that of the author: by cross-checking with other texts, or by delving into external news items, or even by reading the narrative whose fictional appearance rings false (as when someone tells you: "What happened to a very good friend of mine was . . . " and proceeds to tell you the story of this friend with a completely personal conviction). We would have all the reasons in the world to think that the story is exactly the same; nonetheless, the text produced in this way is not an autobiography. The latter supposes first of all an *identity claimed* at the level of enunciation, and absolutely secondarily, a *resemblance* produced at the level of the utterance.

These texts would therefore fall into the category of "autobiographical novel." This is how I will refer to all fictional texts in which the reader has reason to suspect, from the resemblances that he thinks he sees, that there is identity of author and *protagonist*, whereas the author has chosen to deny this identity, or at least not to affirm it. So defined, the autobiographical novel includes personal narratives (identity of narrator and protagonist) as well as "impersonal" narratives (protagonists designated in the third person); it is defined at the level of its contents. Unlike autobiography, it involves *degrees*. The "resemblance" assumed by the reader can be anything from a fuzzy "family likeness" between the protagonist and the author, to the quasi-transparency that makes us say that he is "the spitting image." Thus, concerning *L'Année du crabe* (1972) by Olivier Todd, one critic has written that "the entire book admits to being obsessively autobiographical behind the transparent pseudonyms."[10] Autobiography does not include degrees: it is all or nothing.

We see, in these distinctions, how important it is to use a clearly defined vocabulary. The critic was talking about "pseudonym" for the name of the hero: for me, pseudonym is good only for the author's name. The hero can resemble the author as much as he wants; as long as he does not have his name, there is in effect nothing. The case of *L'Année du crabe* is exemplary from this point of view. The subtitle of the book is *Novel*: Olivier Todd's hero is named Ross. But on page 4, a publisher's note assures the reader that Todd is Ross. A clever advertising trick, but one that changes nothing. If Ross is Todd, why does he have another name? If it was he, how come he does not *say* so? It matters little whether he coquettishly allows us to guess it, or that the reader guesses it in spite of him. Autobiography is not a guessing game: it is in fact exactly the opposite. What is missing here is the essential, what I call the *autobiographical pact*.

Turning back from the first person to the proper name, I am therefore prompted to rectify what I wrote in *Autobiography in France*: "How to distinguish autobiography from the autobiographical novel? We must admit that, if we remain on the level of analysis within the text, there is *no difference*. All the methods that autobiography uses to convince us of the authenticity of its narrative can be imitated by the novel, and often have been imitated." This is accurate as long as we limit ourselves to the text minus the title page; as soon as we include the latter in the text, with the name of the author, we make use of a general textual criterion, the identity ("identicalness") of the *name* (author-narrator-protagonist). The autobiographical pact is the affirmation in the text of this identity, referring back in the final analysis to the *name* of the author on the cover.

The autobiographical pact comes in very diverse forms; but all of them demonstrate their intention to honor his/her *signature*. The reader might be able to quibble over resemblance, but never over identity ("identicalness"). We know all too well how much each of us values his/her name.

An autobiographical work of fiction can be "exact," the protagonist resembling the author; an autobiography can be "inexact," the protagonist presented differing from the author. These are questions of fact—let's still put aside the question of knowing *who* will be the judge of the resemblance, and how—which have no bearing on questions of *right*, that is to say, on the type of contract entered into between the author and the reader. We see, moreover, the importance of the contract, in that it actually determines the attitude of the reader: if the identity is not stated positively (as in fiction), the reader will attempt to establish resemblances, in spite of the author; if it is positively stated (as in autobiography), the reader will want to look for differences (errors, deformations, etc.). Confronted with what looks like an autobiographical narrative, the reader often tends to think of himself as a detective, that is to say, to look for breaches of contract (whatever the contract). It is here that the myth of the novel being "truer" than the autobiography originates: when we think we have discovered something through the text, in spite of the author, we always accord it more truth and more profundity. If Olivier Todd had presented *L'Année du Crabe* as his autobiography, perhaps our critic would have been sensitive to the faults, to the gaps, to the manipulations of his narrative—namely to the fact that all questions of *fidelity* (problem of "resemblance") depend ultimately upon the question of *authenticity* (problem of identity), which is itself expressed with regard to the proper name.

The *identity of name* between author, narrator, and protagonist can be established in two ways:

1. *Implicitly*, at the level of the author-narrator connection, in the case of the *autobiographical pact*; the latter can take two forms: (a) the use of *titles* leaving no doubt about the fact that the first person refers to the name of the author (*Story of My Life, Autobiography*, etc.); (b) *initial section* of the text where the narrator enters into a contract vis-à-vis the reader by acting as if he were the author, in such a way that the reader has no doubt that the "I" refers to the name shown on the cover, even though the name is not repeated in the text.

2. *In an obvious way*, at the level of the name that the narrator-protagonist is given in the narrative itself, and which is the same as that of the author on the cover.

Identity has to be established in at least one of these two ways; this is often accomplished by both of them at the same time.

Parallel to the autobiographical pact, we could place the *fictional pact*, which would itself have two aspects: *obvious practice of nonidentity* (the author and the protagonist do not have the same name), *affirmation of fictitiousness* (in general it is the subtitle *novel* which today performs this function on the cover; it should be noted that *novel*, in current terminology, implies fictional pact, whereas *narrative* [*récit*] is, itself, indeterminate and compatible with the autobiographical pact). Some people will object perhaps that the novel has the capability of *imitating* the autobiographical pact: is not the eighteenth-century novel composed precisely by imitating the different forms of personal literature (memoirs, letters, and, in the nineteenth century, diary)? But this objection does not hold—if we consider that this imitation cannot go back as far as the final term—namely the *name* of the *author*. We can always pretend to record, to publish the autobiography of someone we are trying to pass off as real; as long as this someone is not the *author*, who alone is responsible for the *book*, there is in effect nothing. Only cases of literary fraud therefore would escape this test: they are extremely rare—and this rarity is not due to respect for someone else's name or to the fear of penalties. Who would prevent me from writing the autobiography of an imaginary character and to publish it under his equally imaginary name? It is exactly this, in a slightly different domain, that MacPherson did for Ossian! This is rare, because few authors are capable of renouncing *their own name*. Witness the fact that even the fraud of Ossian was short-lived, since we know who its author is, since MacPherson couldn't keep his name (as adapter) from being included in the title!

Once these definitions are in place, we can classify all the possible cases by bringing into play two criteria: the relationship of the name of the protagonist and the name of the author, the nature of the pact concluded by the author. For each of these criteria, three situations are possible. The protagonist (1) has a name that is different from that of the author; (2) has no name; (3) has the same name as the author; the pact is (1) fictional; (2) absent; (3) autobiographical. In articulating these two criteria, we obtain theoretically nine combinations; actually only seven are possible, the coexistence of the identity of the name and the fictional pact, and that of the difference of name and the autobiographical pact being excluded by definition.

The accompanying chart gives the pattern of possible combinations; the numbers indicated are those of the description that follows; in each box, at the bottom, is the effect that the combination produces on the reader. It goes without saying that this chart is applied only to "autodiegetic" narratives.

1. *Name of the protagonist ≠ name of the author.* This fact alone excludes the possibility of autobiography. It matters little, from then on, whether or not there is, in addition, affirmation that the work is fiction (1a or 1b). Whether the story is presented as true (autobiographical manuscript that the author-publisher would have found in an attic, etc.) or whether it is presented as fiction (and believed to be true, attributed to the author, by the reader)—in any case, there is no identity of author, narrator, and hero.

protagonist's name / Pact ↓	≠ author's name	= 0	= author's name
fictional	1a NOVEL	2a NOVEL	
= 0	1b NOVEL	2b indeterminate	3a AUTOBIO- GRAPHY
autobiographical		2c AUTOBIO- GRAPHY	3b AUTOBIO- GRAPHY

2. *Name of the protagonist = O.* This is the most complex case, because it is indeterminate. Everything depends, then, on the pact concluded by the author. Three cases are possible:

a. *Fictional pact* (the "fictional" nature of the book is indicated on the cover page). The autodiegetic narrative is thus attributed to a fictitious narrator. It's a case that must happen infrequently—no example comes immediately to mind. We might be tempted to evoke *Remembrance of Things Past*, but for two reasons that fiction does not correspond exactly to this case: on the one hand, the fictional pact is not clearly indicated at the beginning of the book, with the result that innumerable readers have made the mistake of confusing the author Proust with the narrator; on the other hand, it is true that the narrator-protagonist has no name—except one single time, when in the same utterance it is suggested to us as a hypothesis that we give the narrator the same first name as the author (an utterance that can only be attributed to the author, because how would a fictitious narrator know the name of his author?), and when it is thus pointed out to us that the author is not the narrator. This bizarre intrusion on the part of the author functions both as fictional pact and as autobiographical clue, and sets the text in an ambiguous space.[11]

b. *Pact = 0.* Not only does the protagonist not have a name, but the author does not conclude any pact—neither autobiographical nor fictional. The indetermination is total. Example: *Mother and Child*, by Charles-Louis Philippe. Even though the secondary characters in this narrative have names, the mother and child have no family name, and the child has no first name. We can certainly suppose that it is about Mme. Philippe and her son, but this is not written anywhere. Moreover, the narration is ambiguous (does it concern a general hymn to childhood or the story of one particular child?), the place and time are quite vague, and we do not know who the adult is who is talking about this childhood. The reader, according to his mood, will be able to read it in the register that he wants.

c. *Autobiographical pact.* The protagonist does not have a name in the narrative, but the author has declared explicitly in an initial pact that he is identical to the narrator (and thus to the protagonist, since the narrative is autodiegetic). Example: *Histoire de mes idées* (*Story of My Ideas*), by Edgar Quinet; the pact, included in the title, is clarified in a long preface, signed Edgar Quinet. The name does not appear one single time in the narrative, but, because of the pact, "I" always refers to Quinet.

3. *Name of the protagonist = name of the author.* This fact alone excludes the possibility of fiction. Even if the story is, historically, completely false, it will be on the order of the *lie* (which is an "autobiographical" category) and not of fiction. We can distinguish two cases:

a. *Pact = 0* (let's understand by pact the pact of the title or the prefatory pact). The reader establishes the author-narrator-protagonist identity, although it is not the object of any solemn declaration. Example: *Les Mots* (*The Words*), by Jean-Paul Sartre. Neither the title nor the beginning indicates that this is an autobiography. Someone is telling the story of a family. On page 13 the narrator intervenes explicitly for the first time in the narrative ("*He intrigues me: I know* that he remained a bachelor," or "She loved him, *I believe*"); on page 14, in the story, appears Doctor *Sartre*, who, on page 15, has a grandson: "me." From the name, we thus grasp the identity of the protagonist, of the narrator, and of the author whose name is displayed above the title: Jean-Paul Sartre. And, that it indeed concerns the famous author, and not a homonym, is proved by the text itself, whose narrator takes credit on page 54 for *Les Mouches* (*The Flies*), *Les Chemins de la liberté* (*Roads to Freedom*), and *Les Séquestrés d'Altona* (*The Condemned of Altona*), and on page 251, *La Nausée* (*Nausea*). The story will even give us the most diverse aspects of this name, from the dreaming about fame: "That little Sartre knows his business. France does not realize what she would be losing if he passed away" (p. 92), to the familiar (and familial) deformations of the first name: "André feels that Poulou puts on airs" (p. 224).

We might consider this criterion perfectly contingent. The occurrence of the proper name in the narrative takes place long after the beginning of the book, in reference to a minor episode that we really feel could disappear from the text without changing its general appearance. Thus in the autobiography of J. Green, *Partir avant le jour* (*Leave Before Day*, Grasset, 1963), it is only on page 107, in an anecdote on giving away prizes, that the name appears. At times even this irruption of the name into the text is unique and allusive. This is the case in *L'Age d'homme* (*Manhood*), where Michel is read behind "Micheline";[12] the fact remains that almost always, he appears. Naturally, in general, the autobiographical pact does not mention the name: our name is so obvious to us, and it will appear on the cover. Because of this ineluctable character of the name, it never is the object of a solemn declaration (the *author*, by the very fact that he is the author, always assumes that he is more or less known to the reader), yet it always ends up reappearing in the story. After all, this name itself can be given in plain language, or, insofar as it almost always has to do with an author's name, it can be implied by the attribution that the narrator makes to himself of the author's works (if Quinet does not name himself, he names his works, which amounts to the same thing).

b. *Autobiographical pact.* This is the most frequent case (because very often, so as not to appear in a formal way at the beginning of the book, the pact nevertheless appears scattered and repeated throughout the text). Example: *Les Confessions de Jean-Jacques Rousseau* (*The Confessions of Jean-Jacques Rousseau*); the pact already appears in the title, is developed in the preamble, and confirmed throughout the text by the use of "Rousseau" and of "Jean-Jacques."

Here, then, I will call "autobiographies" the texts that enter into cases 2c, 3a, 3b; as for the rest, we read the texts falling into cases 1a, 1b, 2a as novels; and, according to our mood, category 2b (but without our overlooking the fact that it is *we* who are choosing).

In this type of classification, consideration of borderline cases is always instructive and says more than the description of what is a matter of course. Are the solutions that I declare impossible really so? Two fields are to be explored here: first, the problem of the two blackened squares in the chart above; next, the problem of the anonymous *author*.

— *The blackened squares.* (a) Can the hero of a novel declared as such have the same name as the author? Nothing would prevent such a thing from existing, and it is perhaps an internal contradiction from which some interesting effects could be drawn. But, in practice, no example of such a study comes to mind. And if the case does present itself, the reader is under the impression that a mistake has been made. Thus the autobiography of Maurice Sachs, *Le Sabbat* (*The Sabbath*), had been published in 1946 by Correa, with the subtitle *Souvenirs d'une jeunesse orageuse* (*Memories of a Stormy Childhood*); it was republished in 1960 by Gallimard (and again in 1971 in the collection Livre de Poche) with the subtitle *Novel*: because the story is told by Sachs using his own name (he even gives his real name — Ettinghausen — in addition to his pseudonym), and since the responsibility for the subtitle is clearly the publisher's, the reader picks up on the error. (b) In the *stated* autobiography, can the protagonist have a name different from that of the author (the question of the pseudonym aside)? This is hardly ever seen;[13] and if, by some artistic effect, an autobiographer chose this formula, the reader would always have doubts: isn't he reading a novel, quite simply? We see in these two cases that if the internal contradiction was voluntarily chosen by the author, it would never result in a text that we would read as an autobiography;

nor really as a novel either; but in a Pirandellian game of ambiguity. To my knowledge, it is a game that we practically never play *seriously*.

In the above chart, the ascending diagonal, which includes the two blackened squares and the central square, marks out a zone of indetermination (from "neither one nor the other" in the central square to "the two together" in the blackened squares).

— *The anonymous author*. This chart assumes that the author has a name; a tenth case should therefore be considered: the case of the anonymous author. But this case (with the subdivisions that it would engender depending on whether the protagonist has a name or not, and that a *publisher* concludes in the place of the absent author such and such a pact with the reader) — this case is also excluded by definition, as the author of an autobiography cannot be anonymous. If the disappearance of the author's name is due to an accidental phenomenon (the manuscript found in an attic, unpublished and not signed), there are two possibilities: either the narrator states his name someplace in the text, and an elementary historical study lets us know if this has to do with a real person, given that by definition an autobiography recounts a dated and situated story; or else the narrator-protagonist does not give his name, and we are dealing either with a text that is part of category 2b or else with a simple fiction. If the anonymity is intentional (a published text), the reader is in a state of legitimate mistrust. The text can appear to be authentic, to give all sorts of verifiable and likely particulars, to ring true — it remains that all this can be counterfeited. At best, this would be a sort of extreme case, analogous to category 2b. Everything rests, then, on the decision of the reader. We will have an idea about the complexity of the problem in reading, for example, the *Mémoires d'un vicaire de campagne, écrits par lui-même* (*Memoirs of a Country Priest, Written by Himself*) (1841), attributed to Father Epineau, whose ecclesiastical office would have forced him to remain provisionally anonymous.[14]

Surely by asserting that it is impossible to write an anonymous autobiography, I am only stating a corollary to my definition, and not "proving" it. Everyone is free to assert that it is possible, but then it will be necessary to start with another definition. We see that here, everything depends, on the one hand, on the link that I establish, through the notion of *author*, between the person and the name; on the other hand, on the fact that I have chosen the perspective of the reader in defining autobiography. For any reader, a text in the autobiographical style, which is claimed by no one, and a work of fiction are as much alike as two drops of water.

But I think that this definition, far from being arbitrary, brings out the essential point. What defines autobiography for the one who is reading is above all a contract of identity that is sealed by the proper name. And this is true also for the one who is writing the text. If I write the story of my life without mentioning my name in it, how will my reader know that it was *I*? It is impossible for the autobiographical vocation and the passion for anonymity to coexist in the same person.

The distinctions proposed here, the attention paid to the proper name, have, then, a great importance on the practical level as criteria for classification; on the theoretical level, they impose several series of reflections whose features I will only mention.

1. *Author and person*. Autobiography is a literary genre which, by its very content, best marks the confusion of author and person, confusion on which is founded the whole practice and problematic of Western literature since the end of the eighteenth century. Whence the kind of *passion for the proper name*, which exceeds simple "author's vanity," since through such passion it is the person him/herself who claims existence. The deep subject of autobiography is the proper name. We think about those sketches by Hugo, displaying his own name in gigantic letters across a countryside in chiaroscuro. The desire for fame and eternity so cruelly demystified by Sartre in *Les Mots* rests entirely on the *proper name* become author's name. Do we imagine the possibility of an *anonymous* literature today? Valéry was already pondering over it fifty years ago. But it doesn't seem that he thought about practicing it himself, since he ended up in the Academy. Having achieved his reputation, he could dream about anonymity. The *Tel Quel* group, by calling into question the notion of author (replacing it by that of "scripteur"), heads in the same direction but does not pursue the thing any further.

2. *Person and language*. We saw earlier that we could legitimately wonder, with regard to the "first person," if it was the psychological person (conceived naïvely as being outside language) who was expressing himself by making use of the grammatical person as an instrument, or if the psychological person was not an *effect* of the enunciation itself. The word "person" contributes to the ambiguity. If there is no one outside of language, since language is other people, we would have to arrive at the idea that autobiographical discourse, far from referring, as each person imagines it, to the "I" minted in a series of proper names, would be, on the contrary, an alienated discourse, a mythological voice by which we would all be controlled. Naturally, autobiographers are in general farthest from the problems of the Beckettian hero of *L'Innommable* (*The Unnameable*) wondering who is saying "I" in him; but this anxiety shows on the surface in some books, such as *Le Traître* (*The Traitor*) by Gorz—or rather in the kind of transcription that Sartre did of it (*Des rats et des hommes* [*Of Rats and Men*]). Under the name "vampire," Sartre designates these voices that control us. The autobiographical voice is undoubtedly part of them. Thus would open up—all psychology and mystique of the individual demystified—an analysis of the discourse of subjectivity and individuality as the myth of our civilization. Moreover, each of us indeed feels the danger of this indetermination of the first person, and it is no accident if we try to neutralize it by grounding it in the proper name.

3. *Proper name and proper body.* The acquisition of the proper name is no doubt as important a stage in the story of the individual as the mirror stage. This acquisition escapes memory and autobiography, which can recount only these second and inverse baptisms that are for a child the accusations that freeze him in a role through a qualifier: "thief" for Genet, "yid" for Albert Cohen (*O vous, frères humains* [*You, Human Brothers*], 1972). The name received and assumed first — the father's name — and especially the Christian name that distinguishes you from it, are no doubt essential basic principles in the story of *me*. Witness the fact that the name is never indifferent, whether we adore it or we detest it, whether we accept that we owe it to others or we prefer to receive it only from the self. This can go on to a generalized system of displacements, as it does with Stendhal;[15] to an increase in the value of the first name, as in Jean-Jacques (Rousseau); and, in a more banal way, to all those games of chance, to parlor games or to private games on those few letters in which each of us thinks instinctively that the essence of his being is registered. Plays on spelling and meaning: of the unhappiness in being named François Nourissier, for example;[16] plays on sex: Michel or Micheline Leiris (see note 12). The presence of a name in the voice of those who have pronounced it: "Oh Rousseau, I thought you were a good fellow," said Marion. Infantile meditation on the arbitrariness of the name, and search for a second name that is essential, as with Jacques Madaule.[17] History of the name itself, established often quite tediously for the reader in those preambles in the form of a family tree.

When we try, then, to distinguish fiction from autobiography, to determine what it is that the "I" refers to in personal accounts, there is no need to go back to an impossible world-beyond-the-text; the text itself offers this last word at the very end, the proper name of the author, which is both textual and unquestionably referential. If this reference is beyond doubt, it is because it is based on two social institutions: vital statistics (agreement internalized by each of us from early childhood) and the publishing contract; there is, then, no reason to doubt identity.

Exact Copy

Identity is not resemblance.

Identity is a *fact* immediately grasped — accepted or refused, at the level of enunciation; resemblance is a *relationship* subject to infinite discussions and nuances, established from the utterance.

Identity is defined starting with three terms: author, narrator, and protagonist. Narrator and protagonist are the figures to whom the subject of the enunciation and the subject of the utterance refer *within the text;* the author, represented at the edge of the text by his name, is the referent to whom the subject of enunciation refers by reason of the autobiographical pact.

As soon as it becomes a matter of *resemblance*, we are obliged to introduce a fourth symmetrical term on the side of utterance, an extratextual referent that we could call the prototype, or better yet, the *model*.

My reflections on identity have led me to distinguish especially the autobiographical novel from autobiography; for resemblance, it is the opposition with *biography* that is going to have to be specified. In the two cases, moreover, vocabulary is the source of errors: "autobiographical novel" is too close to the word "autobiography," itself too close to the word "biography," for some confusions not to arise. Is not autobiography, as its name indicates, the biography of a person written by him/herself? We thus have a tendency to consider it a particular case of biography, and to apply to it the "historicizing" problematic of this genre. Many autobiographers, amateur or established writers, fall naively into this trap—probably because this illusion is necessary to the functioning of the genre.

As opposed to all forms of fiction, biography and autobiography are *referential* texts: exactly like scientific or historical discourse, they claim to provide information about a "reality" exterior to the text, and so to submit to a test of *verification*. Their aim is not simple verisimilitude, but resemblance to the truth. Not "the effect of the real," but the image of the real. All referential texts thus entail what I will call a "referential pact," implicit or explicit, in which are included a definition of the field of the real that is involved and a statement of the modes and the degree of resemblance to which the text lays claim.

The referential pact, in the case of autobiography, is in general coextensive with the autobiographical pact, difficult to dissociate, exactly, like the subject of enunciation and that of utterance in the first person. The formula for it would not be "I, the undersigned" either, but "I swear to tell the truth, the whole truth, and nothing but the truth." The oath rarely takes such an abrupt and total form; it is a supplementary proof of honesty to restrict it to the *possible* (the truth such as it appears to me, inasmuch as I can know it, etc., making allowances for lapses of memory, errors, involuntary distortions, etc.), and to indicate explicitly the *field* to which this oath applies (the truth about such and such an aspect of my life, not committing myself in any way about some other aspect).

We see what makes this pact look like the one that any historian, geographer, or journalist draws up with his/her reader; but we must be naïve not to see, at the same time, the differences. We are not talking about practical difficulties with the test of *verification* in the case of autobiography, since autobiography tells us precisely—here is the advantage of its narrative—what it alone can tell us. Biographical study easily allows us to gather other information and to determine the degree of the narrative's accuracy. This is not where the difference lies; it lies in the rather paradoxical fact that this accuracy has no essential importance. In autobiography, it is indispensable that the referential pact be *drawn up*, and that it be *kept*; but it is not necessary that the result be on the order of strict resemblance.

The referential pact can be, according to the criteria of the reader, badly kept, without the referential value of the text disappearing (on the contrary) — this is not the case for historical and journalistic texts.

This apparent paradox is due naturally to the confusion that I have maintained up to this point, following the example of most authors and critics, between biography and autobiography. To clear it up, it is necessary to restore this fourth term that is the *model*.

By "model," I understand the real that the utterance claims to *resemble*. How can a text "resemble" a life — that is a question the biographers rarely ask themselves and that they always assume is resolved implicitly. The "resemblance" can be found on two levels: in the negative mode — and at the level of the elements of the narrative — the criterion of *accuracy* intervenes; in the positive mode — and at the level of the whole of the narrative — what we will call *fidelity* intervenes. Accuracy involves *information*, fidelity *meaning*. That meaning can be produced only by narrative techniques and by the intervention of a system of explication involving the ideology of the historian does not prevent the biographer from imagining that it is on the same level as accuracy, in a relationship of resemblance with the extratextual reality to which the entire text refers. Thus Sartre declares shamelessly that his biography of Flaubert is a "true novel."[18] The model, in biography, is thus the life of a man "such as it was."

In order to represent the biographical undertaking, we can construct the accompanying diagram, in which the division into *columns* differentiates the text and the world-beyond-the-text, and the division into *rows* the subject of enunciation and the subject of utterance. Included inside the line separating the text from the world-beyond-the-text is the author, in the marginal position represented by his name on the cover of the book.

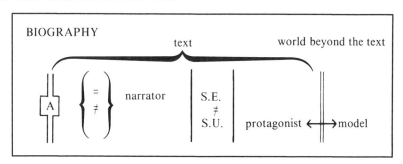

Abbreviations:	A = Author
	S.E.= Subject of the enunciation
	S.U. = Subject of the utterance

Relationships:	= identical to
	≠ not identical to
	↔ resemblance

Commentary on the diagram. In biography, author and narrator are sometimes linked by a relationship of *identity.* This relationship can remain implicit or vague, or can be made explicit, for example, in a preface (for example, that of *L'Idiot de la famille* [*The Idiot of the Family*], where the biographer, Sartre, explains that he has some accounts to settle with his model, Flaubert). It can also happen that no identity relationship is established between author and narrator. What is important is that if the narrator uses the first person, it is never to talk about the protagonist of the story—this is someone else. Consequently, as soon as the narrator is involved, the principal mode of the narrative is the third person, what G. Genette calls heterodiegetic narration. The relationship of the protagonist (in the text) to the model (referent in the world-beyond-the-text) is certainly first of all a relationship of identity, but it is especially one of *"resemblance."* As a matter of fact, in the case of the subject of utterance, the identity relationship does not have the same *value* as it does for the subject of enunciation. It is simply a given of the utterance on the same level as the others; it proves nothing; it itself needs to be proved through resemblance.

We notice already here what is going to fundamentally oppose biography and autobiography; it is the hierarchical organization of the relationships of resemblance and identity. In biography, it is resemblance that must ground identity; in autobiography, it is identity that grounds resemblance. Identity is the real starting point of autobiography; resemblance, the impossible horizon of biography. The different function of resemblance in the two systems thereby is explained.

This becomes obvious as soon as we outline the diagram that corresponds to autobiography:

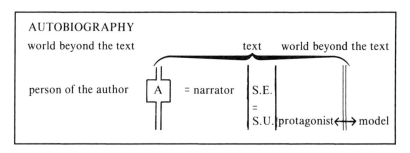

The personal narrative (autodiegetic) seems here to be absolutely irreducible to the impersonal narrative (heterodiegetic).

Indeed, in personal narrative, what does the "equal" (=) sign that is found between the subject of enunciation and that of utterance signify? It really implies *identity;* and that identity, in turn, involves a certain form of resemblance. Resemblance with whom? If we are talking about a narrative written exclusively in the past, like biography, resemblance of the protagonist to the model could be looked at exclusively as a verifiable relationship between protagonist and model; but all narrative in the first person implies that the protagonist, even if some distant adventures about him are being told, is also at the same time the *real* person who produces the narration: the subject of the utterance is double because it is inseparable from the subject of enunciation; in a way, it becomes single again only when the narrator talks about his own present narration, never in the other direction, to designate a protagonist untainted by any real narrator.

We realize, then, that the relationship designated by "=" is not at all a *simple* relationship, but rather a *relationship of relationships;* it signifies that the narrator is to the protagonist (past or present) what the author is to the model. This implies that the ultimate expression of truth (if we reason in terms of resemblance) can no longer be the being-in-itself of the past (if indeed such a thing exists), but being-for-itself, manifested in the present of the enunciation. It also implies that in his relationship to the story (remote or quasi-contemporary) of the protagonist, the narrator is mistaken, lies, forgets, or distorts—and error, lie, lapse of memory, or distortion will, if we distinguish them, take on the value of aspects, among others, of an enunciation, which, itself, remains authentic. Let's call authenticity that inner relationship characteristic of the first person in the personal narrative; it will be confused neither with identity, which refers to the proper name, nor with resemblance, which assumes a judgment of similitude between two different images, made by a third person.

This detour was necessary in order to grasp the inadequacy of the diagram on autobiography. The illusion is that held by all those who start off from the problematic of biography in order to think about autobiography. While constructing the diagram on biography, I had been prompted, because of the nonidentity of the protagonist and the narrator, to distinguish *two "sides"* for the extratextual reference, placing the author on the left and the model to the right. The fact that we are concerned with *simple* relationships of identity on the side of the author, and of resemblance on the side of the model, allows a linear presentation. For autobiography, the "reference" is made on one side alone (confusion of author and model) and the relationship that articulates identity and resemblance is in fact a relationship of relationships which cannot be represented linearly.

We would thus have the two following formulas:

Biography: A is or is not N; P resembles M.

Autobiography: N is to P as A is to M.

(A = author; N = narrator; P = protagonist; M = model)

Since autobiography is a referential genre, it is naturally subject at the same time to the order of resemblance at the level of the model, but this is only a secondary characteristic. The fact that *we* believed that resemblance is not obtained is incidental from the moment when we are sure that it has been certified. What matters is less the resemblance of "Rousseau at the age of sixteen," represented in the text of the *Confessions*, with the Rousseau of 1728, "such as he was," than the double effort of Rousseau around 1764 to *paint*: 1) his relationship to the past; 2) this past such as it was, with the intention of changing nothing therein.

In the case of identity, the borderline and exceptional case, which confirms the rule, was that of *fraud*. In the case of resemblance, this will be *mythomania* — that is to say, not the errors, the distortions, the interpretations consubstantial with the elaboration of personal myth in all autobiography, but the substitution of an obviously *made-up* story, and one *totally* unrelated to life; as for fraud, it is extremely rare, and the referential character attributed to narrative is thus easily called into question by a survey of literary history. But, disqualified as autobiography, the narrative will retain its full interest as phantasm, at the level of its utterance, and the falsehood of the autobiographcal pact, as behavior, will still reveal for us, at the level of enunciation, a subject that is, despite everything, intentionally autobiographical and one that we will continue to assume beyond the trumped-up subject. Thus we come back to analyze on another level, no longer the biography-autobiography, but the novel-autobiography relationship, to define what we could call *autobiographical space*, and the effects of *contrast* that it engenders.

Autobiographical Space

We must now show on what naïve illusion rests the widespread theory according to which the novel is truer (more profound, more authentic) than the autobiography. This commonplace, like all commonplaces, has no single author; each one, in turn, speaks the commonplace with his own voice. Thus André Gide: "Memoirs are never more than half sincere, however great the concern for truth may be: everything is always more complicated than we say it is. Perhaps we even come closer to the truth in the novel."[19] Or François Mauriac: "It is looking much further back for excuses, limiting myself to one single chapter of my memoirs. Is not the true reason for my laziness that our novels express the essential part of ourself? Only fiction does not lie: it half-opens a hidden door on a man's life, through which slips, out of all control, his unknown soul."[20]

Albert Thibaudet gave the commonplace the academic form of the "parallel," an ideal dissertation subject, opposing the novel (profound and varied) and the autobiography (superficial and schematic).[21]

I will demonstrate the illusion starting with the formulation proposed by Gide, only because his work furnishes an incomparable area for demonstration. Rest assured, I have no intention of defending the autobiographical genre, and establishing the truth of the contrary proposition, namely that autobiography would be the most truthful, the most profound, and so on. To invert Thibaudet's proposition would be of no interest, except to show that right side up or upside down, it is always *the same* proposition.

Indeed, at the very moment when in *appearance* Gide and Mauriac depreciate the autobiographical genre and glorify the novel, *in reality* they are drawing something very different than drawing a more or less questionable scholarly parallel: they designate the autobiographical space in which they want us to read the whole of their work. Far from being a condemnation of autobiography, these often quoted sentences are in reality an indirect form of the autobiographical pact. Indeed they establish the nature of the ultimate truth to which their texts aspire. In these judgments, the reader forgets all too often that autobiography is understood on two levels: at the same time that it is one of the two *terms* of the comparison, it is the *criterion* that is used in the comparison. What is this "*truth*" that the novel makes more accessible than autobiography does, except the personal, individual, intimate truth of the author, that is to say, the truth to which any autobiographical project aspires? So we might say, it is as autobiography that the novel is declared the truer.

The reader is thus invited to read novels not only as *fictions* referring to a truth of "human nature," but also as revealing *phantasms* of the individual. I will call this indirect form of the autobiographical pact *the phantasmatic pact*.

If hypocrisy is a homage that vice pays to virtue, these judgments are in reality a homage that the novel pays to autobiography. If the novel is truer than autobiography, why are Gide, Mauriac, and many others not happy with writing novels? In posing the question in this way, everything becomes clear: if they had not *also* written and published autobiographical texts, even "inadequate" ones, no one would ever have seen the nature of the truth that it was necessary to look for in their novels. Thus these declarations are perhaps involuntary but very effective tricks: we escape accusations of vanity and egocentrism when we seem so aware of the limitations and insufficiencies of our autobiography; and no one notices that, by the same movement, we extend on the contrary the autobiographical pact, in an *indirect* form, to the whole of what we have written. Double blow.

Double blow, or rather double vision – double writing, the effect, if I can risk this neologism, of *stereography*.

Posed in this way, the nature of the problem changes completely. It is no longer necessary to know which of the two, autobiography or novel, would be truer. It is neither one nor the other; autobiography will lack complexity, ambiguity, etc.; the novel, accuracy. So it would be one, then the other? Rather, one *in relation* to the other. What becomes revealing is the space in which the two categories of texts are inscribed, and which is reducible to neither of the two. This effect of contrast obtained by this procedure is the creation, for the reader, of an "autobiographical space."

From this point of view, the works of Gide and Mauriac are typical. Both have organized, for different reasons, a spectacular failure of their autobiography, thus forcing their audience into reading all the rest of their narrative production in the autobiographical register. When I talk about failure, it is not a question of making a value judgment on admirable (Gide) or estimable (Mauriac) texts, but simply of echoing their own statements, and of establishing that they have *chosen* to leave their autobiography incomplete, fragmented, full of holes and open.[22]

This form of indirect pact is becoming increasingly widespread. Formerly it was the reader who, despite the denials of the author, took the initiative and the responsibility for this type of reading; today, on the contrary, authors and publishers start off from the beginning in this direction. It is revealing that Sartre himself, who at one time thought about continuing *Les Mots* in fictional form, reverted to Gide's formula: "It would be time finally for me to tell the truth. But I could tell it only in a work of fiction," and that in this way he clarified the reading contract that he would have suggested to his reader:

At the time I was thinking of writing a story in which I would present in an indirect manner everything that I had previously intended to say in a kind of political testament. The testament would have been a continuation of my autobiography, but I had decided not to write it. The fictional element of the story I was considering would have been minimal; I would have created a character about whom the reader would have been forced to say: *"The man presented here is Sartre."*

This does not mean that for the reader there would have been an overlapping of the character and the author, but that the best way of understanding the character would have been to look for what came to him from me.[23]

All these games, which show clearly the predominance of the autobiographical project, are found again, to varying degrees, in many modern writers. And this game can itself be naturally imitated within a novel. This is what Jacques Laurent did in *Les Bêtises* (*Nonsense*, Grasset, 1971), by giving us to read both the fictional text that his protagonist would have written, then different "autobiographical" texts of the same protagonist. If Jacques Laurent ever publishes his own autobiography, the texts of *Les Bêtises* will take on a dizzying "contrast."

Reading Contract

At the end of this reflection, a brief balance sheet allows us to take note of a displacement of the problem:

—*Negative side*: certain points remain blurred and unsatisfying. For example, we might ask ourselves how the identity of the author and the narrator can be established in the autobiographical pact when the name is not repeated (see above p. 16); we might remain skeptical in view of the distinctions I suggested earlier in *Exact Copy*. That section and the one entitled *I, the Undersigned*, look only at the case of autobiography in autodiegetic narration, whereas I have stressed that other formulas of narration were *possible*: will the established distinctions hold, in the case of autobiography in the third person?

— *Positive side*: on the other hand, my analyses have seemed fruitful to me each time that, going beyond the apparent structures of the text, they prompted me to question the positions of the *author* and the *reader*. "Social contract" of the proper name and the publication, autobiographical "pact," fictional "pact," referential "pact," phantasmatic "pact" — all the expressions used refer back to the idea that the autobiographical genre is a *contractual* genre. The difficulty I had come up against in my first attempt derived from what I was searching for in vain — on the level of structures, modes, and narrative voices — clear criteria to ground a difference that any reader nevertheless experiences. The notion of "autobiographical pact" that I had so elaborated was still wavering, for want of seeing that an essential element of the contract was the proper name. That something so evident was not apparent to me, shows that this type of contract is implicit, and, appearing grounded on the nature of things, barely invites reflection.

The problematic of autobiography proposed here is thus not grounded on a relationship, established from the outside, between the extratextual and the text — because such a relationship could only be one of resemblance, and would prove nothing. Neither is it grounded on an internal analysis of the functioning of the text, of the structure, or of aspects of the published text; but upon analysis, on the global level of *publication*, of the implicit or explicit contract proposed by the *author* to the *reader*, a contract which determines the mode of reading of the text and engenders the effects which, attributed to the text, seem to us to define it as autobiography.

The level of analysis utilized is therefore that of the *publication/published* relationship, which would be parallel, on the level of the printed text, to the *enunciation/utterance* relationship, on the level of oral communication. In order to go on, this study of author/reader contracts, of implicit or explicit codes of publication — on that fringe of the printed text which, in reality, *controls* the entire reading (author's name, title, subtitle, name of the collection, name of the publisher, even including the ambiguous game of prefaces) — this inquiry would have to take on a historical dimension that I have not given to it here.[24] The variations in these codes over time (due both to changes in the attitude of authors and readers, and to technical or commercial problems of the publishing business) would make it seem much more clearly that we are dealing with codes, and not with "natural" or universal things. Since the seventeenth century, for example, conventions concerning anonymity or the use of the pseudonym have changed a great deal; plays on the allegations of reality in works of fiction are no longer practiced today in the same way that they were in the eighteenth century;[25] on the other hand, readers have become accustomed to feel the presence of the author (of his unconscious) even behind productions that do not seem autobiographical, so much have phantasmic pacts created new habits of reading.

It is at this global level that autobiography is defined: it is a mode of reading as much as it is a type of writing; it is a historically variable *contractual effect*. The present study is based on the types of contract currently in use. Whence come its relativity and the absurdity that there would be in wanting it to be universal; whence come also the difficulties encountered in this undertaking of definition. I wanted to make explicit in a clear, coherent, and exhaustive system (which takes all cases into account) the fundamental criteria of a corpus (that of autobiography) made up in reality according to multiple criteria, variable in time and according to individuals and often noncoherent between them. To succeed in giving a clear and complete formula of autobiography would be, in reality, to fail. While reading this chapter in which I have tried to push exactness as far as possible, one will have often felt that this exactness was becoming arbitrary, inadequate for an object perhaps more within the scope of Chinese logic such as Borges describes it, than within that of Cartesian logic.

When all is said and done, this study would seem to me, then, to be itself more a document to study (the attempt of a twentieth-century reader to rationalize and clarify his criteria of reading) rather than a "scientific" text: a document to assign to the file of a scientific history of literary *communication*.

The history of autobiography would be therefore, above all, a history of its mode of reading: comparative history where we would be able to bring into dialogue the reading contracts proposed by different types of texts (because it would be of no use to study autobiography all by itself, since contracts, like signs, make sense only through the play of opposition), and the different types of readings really practiced on these texts. If autobiography is defined by something outside the text, it is not on this side, by an unverifiable resemblance to a real person, but on the other side, by the type of reading it engenders, the credence it exudes, and the qualities that are manifested in the critical response to autobiographies.

Chapter 2
Autobiography in the Third Person

The I calls itself I *or* you *or* he. *There are these three persons in me. The Trinity. The one who addresses the* I *in the familiar "you" form; the one who treats him as* Him.

Paul Valéry

Bertolt Brecht used to suggest to actors that they transpose their role to the third person and into the past. These exercises were limited to rehearsals, and intended to encourage distancing. Autobiographers are actors too. And some of them really take this game seriously, in front of their public. But since they are at the same time the authors of the role they are interpreting, the procedure has a totally different function for them. It helps them to express their problems of identity and at the same time to captivate their readers.

These sophisticated games, and after all they are rather infrequent, are revealing *borderline cases*: they bring out into the open what is ordinarily implicit in the use of "persons." My plan here is to study, thanks to them, "the use of personal pronouns in autobiography," as Michel Butor would say. To use them as examples of "grammar" in order to clarify autobiographical narration with all the problems of pact, voice, and perspective that it brings up.[1]

We will still be concerned with modern autobiographical texts. The third person, certainly, has been used formerly in historical memoirs like those of Caesar, in religious autobiographies (where the author calls himself "the servant of God"), and in aristocratic memoirs of the seventeenth century, like those of the president de Thou. It is still used today in some related genres, brief genres, very strongly coded, and related to publishing strategies, like the preface, the publisher's blurb, and the biographical notice written by the author. I will at times make allusion to these. But I have chosen to remain within a coherent whole: the use of figures always depends in the final analysis on the reading contract and on the "horizons of expectation" of the genre.

31

I will present successively two different situations: *autobiography in the third person*, which can seem like the simple realization of a figure of enunciation; and *autobiography with a fictional narrator*, which is based on a more complicated system.

Persons and Person

The Soft Pedal

If I sit down at my table to write this study, and I write: "He sat down at his table to write . . . ," the meaning of this sentence will depend above all on the reading contract that I will propose to my reader. It is this contract that will define the genre (with the attitudes of reading that it implies) and establish, eventually, the relationships of identity that order the deciphering of personal pronouns and of the enunciation. It would be the same if I wrote: "I've just sat down at my table to write."

This contract, which informs the reading, is already what is guiding the writing (even if it might happen that between the writing and the publication, I change the contract). I can choose, for example: fiction, whose reading is independent from what the reader knows about the author; autobiographical fiction, in which the reader is invited to an ambiguous reading; autobiography, in which referential reading and attitude of communication are combined. I will imagine here that I am writing my sentence (my text) and that it is being read strictly autobiographically: the person my text is talking about is I, the author of the text, and what is said is guaranteed to be accurate, exact, to be taken in the literal sense. It turns out simply that instead of talking about myself in the first person, I am talking about myself in the third. Thus Michel Leiris switches into the third person in order to substantiate a statement of failure:

> Sadness not diminished by the idea that, all things being useless, what he had been able to do was of no importance, he told himself that not very much in his life was worth holding onto.[2]

Far from reading this as a simple statement about a character (which it would be if it were a page out of a novel), the reader perceives the erasing of the enunciation as a fact of enunciation. Recourse to the system of the story and to the "non-person" that is the third person functions here like a *figure of enunciation* within a text that we continue to read as discourse in the first person. The author talks about himself *as if* it were someone else who was talking about him, or as if he were talking about someone else. This *as if* concerns enunciation alone: utterance continues to be subjected to the strict and proper rules of the autobiographical contract. Whereas if I were using the same grammatical presentation in an autobiographical fiction, utterance itself would be taken in the perspective of a phantasmatic pact ("this has meaning in relation to me, but is not I").

This *figure* gives contrast and tension to the text: we feel it; I feel it myself while writing, like an unnatural ellipsis of enunciation. We constantly expect the artificial order of exclusion of the first person to cease, exactly like, when we read a lipogram, we watch for the return of the forbidden letter. At the very moment when I am writing, I mold my sentences through a sort of scouring and transposition of personal discourse: I write to myself while making myself keep quiet, or more exactly, by depressing the soft pedal. All I would have to do is lift my foot in order to restore resonance.

This use of the third person can be understood as a "figure," as opposed to the proper, or literal, meaning of the third person, which is the use of the "nonperson" in talking about the person who is neither the addressor nor the addressee of discourse. But this figure must not be understood as an indirect manner of talking about the self, which would be used in contrast to the "direct" character of the first person. It is another way of achieving, in the form of a *splitting*, what the first person achieves in the form of a *confusion*: the inescapable duality of the grammatical "person." Saying "I" is more customary (hence more "natural") than saying "he" when one talks about himself, but it is not simpler.

The Instances of the "I"

We would be almost tempted to say that "I" is itself . . . a figure. Or at least that it has all the complexities of one. In order to recognize this, we need only take the expanded formula that Benveniste has proposed: "I" is "the person who is uttering the present instance of the discourse containing *I*."[3] Going from this formula to "I" supposes a double displacement:

— With regard to enunciation, the deictic ("the present instance of discourse") slips from the enunciation to the speaker. This is what the customary formula of prefaces "in the third person" also reveals: "he who writes these lines";

— The subject of the utterance ("the individual") is represented by the subject of the enunciation. We are made to understand that the person we are talking about is "the same" as the one who is speaking. This "identity" is to be taken in its literal sense only in one single case, that of performative utterances. Everywhere else, it is a more or less approximate figure, and the "nonperson" thus finds himself being both represented and masked by the person.

By unfolding the pronoun "I" (or "you") in this way, we inevitably come up against the problem of *identity*. Who is this "individual" Benveniste is talking about in his formula? It is difficult to remain on a level of strictly grammatical description; any slightly advanced analysis of the play of pronouns and persons in enunciation is faced with the dizzying necessity of constructing a theory of the subject. "Identity" is a *constant relationship* between the one and the many. Linguistically, this problem of identity appears on two levels:

— At the lexical level, it is "resolved" by the class of "proper names," to which in the final analysis the personal pronouns refer. The name is the guarantor of the unity of our multiplicity: it federates our complexity in the moment and our change in time. The subject of enunciation and that of utterance are indeed "the same," since they have the same name! Here we are given substance and unity. The dizziness would only return if we realize that we are perhaps only . . . our own homonym, or that if we were aware of the "arbitrariness" of the name (which would therefore be defined only by the intersection of utterances where it appears) . . .

— At the level of enunciation, the problem of identity is often masked by a tendency to substantivize pronouns and to personalize roles in a situation of "communication." It is very reassuring to conceive of the addressor and the addressee as persons who would start to communicate with one another. But this is playing on the double meaning of the word "person." The distribution of the roles of enunciation such as Benveniste describes them is not only a system of social rules; it is part of all utilization of language. Any speaking subject carries within himself that double split of addressor and addressee, and of enunciation and utterance. He rests fundamentally on a *split*. Or rather he does not "rest" there (which would imply a paradoxical stability), but he functions thanks to this split. "The individual is a dialogue," said Valéry. Communication is therefore a "dialogue of dialogues"; and any theory of enunciation would have to restate as a function of this hypothesis that each "role" already contains the set of roles, which can go on to infinity.

From these thoughts, we can formulate the idea that when an autobiographer talks to us about himself in the third person or talks to *himself* about himself in the second, this is no doubt a figure with regard to accepted usages, but that this figure arranges a return to a fundamental situation, which we find tolerable only if we imagine that it is figurative. In general, these gaps, these divisions, these encounters are both expressed and masked by the use of a single "I."

The first person, such as it is used in autobiography, often leaves the identity of the addressee uncertain. Internal dialogue and literary communication merge. We become aware of this when the autobiography unfolds the enunciation by writing its text "in the second person."[4] The use of this process proves, on the one hand, the copresence in enunciation of an "I" (that has become implicit), of a "you," and of a "he" (hidden under the "you"), all three referring to the same individual. It also proves, on the other hand, the double character of the addressee: if I talk to myself while saying to myself "you," at the same time I display this unfolded enunciation to a third party, the eventual listener or reader.[5] The latter takes part in a discourse intended for him, even if he himself is no longer addressed. Enunciation is dramatized; it can only be unfolded in this way because imaginary footlights guarantee its unity and its relationship to its ultimate addressee. Now this dramatization already exists implicitly in many autobiographical texts in the "I": the reader can just as well believe that "I" speak to him directly, or that "I" show him how he talks to *himself*. In reality, the addressee is always more or less double, but according to the choice of the pronoun, one of his faces is out in front and masks in part the other.

The "I" (like the "you") masks, on the other hand, the gap that exists between the subject of enunciation and that of utterance. This gap can be minimal when the text settles itself in a coherent way in the register of discourse. It can increase beyond measure when there is narration. This is true of the autobiographical text, which rests on an articulation and a permanent coming and going between discourse and story. The inherent duality in the narrative voice is found to correspond to some gaps of perspective, between the narrator and the hero: gaps of information, gaps of appreciation, which are the source of all the plays of focusing and of voice characteristic of this type of narrative (restrictions of field to the protagonist or intrusions of the narrator, lyric or ironic settings, etc.). These gaps or these tensions are otherwise really masked, or at least equalized by the use of the first person, which proposes a unique signifier whose level of functioning (enunciation/utterance) and reference (at the level of the utterance) change continually. If the autobiographical narrator ever uses other figures in a combined manner, like the narrative present and the indirect free style, he will be able to create rather bewildering plays of confrontation between what he was and what he is, under the pretense of an apparently singular "I."[6]

Naturally we are not really fooled by this unity, no more than we are by the "alterity" in the case of autodiegetic narration in the third person. It remains, however, that the first person is as it were a "lexicalized" figure; it has usage going for it; it functions according to a logic of self-referential evidence which in general masks its complexity, its figurative and indirect character for the speaker and the listener. The naïve and trusting use of the first person ("me, I") is the rule; the critical reflection is a secondary phenomenon that grafts onto this first usage. And this critical reflection is arduous, so much does the "I" always tend to recombine in our eyes the fictitious unity that it imposes as signifier.

The first person always conceals, then, a secret third person, and in this sense all autobiography is by definition indirect. But in the autobiographies "in the third person" that I am going to present, this indirect character is acknowledged; it draws attention to itself in a provocative way: the procedure comes across as being artificial because it shatters the illusory effect of the first person, which is to make the indirect be taken for the direct. And because the explanation of the third person involves an occultation of the true narrator, who disappears into the implicit, or is replaced by a figurative narrator, or even by a fictitious narrator.

Everything happens as if, in autobiography, no combination of the system of persons in enunciation could satisfactorily "totally express" the person. Or rather, to say things less naïvely, all the imaginable combinations reveal more or less clearly what is the distinctive feature of the person: the tension between impossible unity and intolerable division, and the fundamental split that makes of the speaking subject a creature of flight.

Figures

From One Code To The Other

Within the framework of an autobiography, which is by definition "autodiegetic," the use of the third person induces a play of figures that are not fundamentally different from those that accompany the use of the first. When, under the guise of the first person, we pretend to have the child we once were speak, while making that child seem to take responsibility for the contents of a sarcastic analysis made by an adult (combination of the voice of the child and the perspective of the adult), we create a figure of enunciation as complicated and more Machiavellian than when we dissociate ourself from the person we were (or are) while pretending to talk about ourself as if we were another person. In reality, we are never neither really someone else, nor really the same person. The figures of the third person provide a gamut of solutions in which it is the distancing that is put out in front, but always to express an articulation (a tension) between identity and difference.

We come to know these figures through the *transformation* of utterances "in the first person." Most often the *rules* of the transformation remain implicit. But sometimes the author clarifies them in part in a sort of reading contract to the second degree, included in the autobiographical text and preceding a section in the third person. So it is in Daniel Guérin's *L'Autobiographie de jeunesse* (*Autobiography of Youth*): after having related his entire youth "in the first person," the author adds an appendix entitled "A la recherche de clés sexologiques" ("The Search for Sexological Clues") in which he summarizes his own narrative *as if* he were a doctor studying a case. Here is the text of this supplementary contract grafted onto the first:

> Having completed the autobiographical narrative, I would like— although the carnal obsession is not, by far, its only theme—to try to sketch a "balance-sheet" of its sexual components. I am going to proceed as if I were a practician who would have been given the confession of one of his patients and who would try to analyse it in order to sift out the sexological clues. Therefore we will talk now about the sexual dissident in the third person.[7]

A summary of the book follows in which he talks about the "patient," about "our young man," by systematically adopting the present tense used in the genre of the case study or of the biographical summary, but without changing any of the information and the interpretation already presented in the first narrative. Each transformation is thus inscribed in the framework of the *figurative passage from one genre to another*. This passage is achieved so much more easily because the lead-off genre (autobiography) and the finishing genres (biography, novel) already have many common traits, and because throughout their history, they have been developed by reciprocal grafts and exchanges. Autobiography such as it is practiced today owes much to the biographical model, and undoubtedly also to the novel, both in its most traditional aspects and in its newest refinements. The majority of games in which contemporary autobiographers indulge are the timid echo of the investigations of modern novelists into narrative voice and focalization. Justified timidity: in fiction, one risks nothing, one can break identity and put it back together, allow oneself all points of view, give oneself any means. The autobiographer finds himself confronted with the limitations and constraints of a real situation, and can neither deny the unity of his "I," nor go beyond his limitations. He can only pretend.

What type of effect does this figurative shift engender in a biographical or fictional presentation of the self? It would be tempting, but ultimately fruitless, to introduce here a psychological hypothesis that would make the use of this procedure a "behavior" subject to a single diagnosis: the most diverse strategies have laid siege to this "figure," and this would be to fall into a form of mythology rather than to substantivize "the third person" in this way.[8] This distancing procedure is extremely complex: it brings into play the transformation of one or several parameters of enunciation and can result in rather different effects. It is therefore necessary to distinguish the factors, and, for each factor, to imagine the possible solutions.

The three principal factors are: the reference of the third person; the transpositions of voice, of perspective, and of time; finally the very extension of the use of the figure and its eventual articulation with the "normal" usage of the first person.

Reference. There are three ways in which to specify that the third person refers to the author of the text:

1. Use of a periphrasis indicating explicitly that the third person will carry out the functions of the first: "he who is writing these lines" (ritual formula of prefaces in the third person); "he who is speaking to you" (figure used locally in a discourse). This solution implies that the formula is taken up again periodically, in order to avoid confusions and refer, each time that it is necesssary, the "he" to the enunciation (name of the author, presence of the speaker). It is very awkward and is practiced in brief and heavily coded texts like the preface.

2. Use of a "he" without explicit reference. It is therefore the context that imposes the identification of the protagonist talked about with the author and that

makes us understand that we are dealing with a figurative enunciation. This is the situation in texts where a systematic blending of the first and third persons is organized. Depending on the situation, the mime can refer to the tradition of the psychological novel or to that of biography, each of which is, moreover, closely related to the other.

3. Use of the proper name itself. This procedure, at the same time that it dissipates all ambiguity, accentuates the figurative character of enunciation (at least in our civilization, where the custom is not to talk about oneself by naming oneself constantly). It can correspond to very diverse intentions and effects: figure of majesty, serious (or humorous) use of the biographical presentation, imitation of the psychological novel, beginning of the formation of a "double." The name is open to presentations referring to social codes and to different literary genres: first name alone, first name and last name, last name alone, or preceded by "Mr.," literary pseudonym rather than a last name, last name preceded by a title, and so on. One can also designate oneself by simple initials. Or even use a fictitious name, one of those little names that we give ourselves in private; or a name that already makes you a character in a novel: for example, Gide refers to himself in his journal as "Fabrice," or "X."[9] So we are on the frontier of fiction, but it is a matter of a "fictitious fiction," if I might say, since it is simply mimed within a text that continues to pass itself off as autobiography.

Transpositions. Transpositions are difficult to analyze. It is necessary first of all, while trusting in the effect of the reading, to restore a potential text to the first person in order to compare it to the text in the third person from which it is derived. This procedure of going back and forth is not always possible, insofar as the figurative use of the presentation in the third person allows some changes of perspective, and the establishing of intermediary postures (as is true in the "fictions" that I will analyze later). Even when the text is "reversible," the types of transformation are varied and their effects complex.

The simplest case is that of a potential text presenting itself as a self-portrait or a private journal, written in the same system of discourse. The author informs the reader that he has such and such a view of himself, elaborates the descriptions of his behavior or of his character. The effect of the passage from "I" to "he" will depend on two factors: the contents of the utterances in the first person, and the tenses that are used (tenses of discourse or tenses of the story).

Two different effects of distancing are obtained depending on whether the utterance does or does not bring about the effects of enunciation. To transpose a "I believe that," "I remember," or any number of other expressions, to the third person comes down to transforming an effect of enunciation into a simple related utterance, a sort of narrative of words in indirect free style assumed by a new narrator who places himself between the first and us. The autobiographer observes his own discourse instead of assuming it directly; he steps back a little and in reality splits himself as narrator. We have the impression that he is speaking to us, as it were, in "simultaneous translation." Even if he doesn't add one word, he produces an effect of unvoicing and of stepping back (an effect whose functions can be very diverse: protection, self-irony, solemnity). If the potential text does not bring about an effect of clear enunciation (that is to say, if the "I" carries out especially the function of a "he"), the transposition doesn't produce the effect of a splitting of the speaker, but more simply of a change of position in a speaker who talks about himself *as if* he were someone else. In one case the enunciation splits, in the other it distances.

These effects can be combined, and we shift easily from quoting the discourse of the person involved to miming biographical discourse. Moreover, between the two exists a large recovery zone, the autobiographical text often already being itself a translation "in the first person" of the conventional biographical text. Barthes had indeed shown that from one side of the recovery zone, *for the focalization*, certain elements were not transposable from a narrative in the third person to a narrative in the first; from the other side, in reverse order, *for the enunciation*, certain elements are transposable only at the cost of a total change of effect.[10]

It is only by detailed explication of texts, where enunciation, perspective, and the system of tenses would be treated as independent variables, that we could establish the gamut of possible transpositions. Autobiography in the third person provides a marvelous field of study, since by definition (by *contract*) it forces the reader, at least implicitly, to carry out an operation of translation, since all the procedures are used in a figurative manner. Better: it happens that the texts we are concerned with are presented as *bilingual* texts, juxtaposing utterances to analogous contents written sometimes in the first person, sometimes in the third person, so that the grammarian would not even have "potential" texts to restore in order to make comparisons. This is the case in *Frêle Bruit* by Michel Leiris,[11] and especially in *Roland Barthes* by Roland Barthes.[12]

I will cite three examples of transposition used by Barthes. The first muffles its own discourse while still retaining a self-referential element of the enunciation ("here"); the second implies an internal focalization so that we ought to experience it as the transposition of a personal discourse; the third resembles the mime of discourse that someone else could hold on him or on his texts:

> Writing a certain text, he experiences a guilty emotion of jargon, as if he could not escape from a mad discourse no matter how individual he made his utterance; and what if all his life *he had chosen the wrong language*? He is all the more readily overcome by this panic here (in U.) where, staying home at night, he watches television a good deal: here is continually represented (remonstrated) a public language from which he is separated.

He more or less remembers the order in which he wrote these fragments; but where did that order come from? In the course of what classification, of what succession? He no longer remembers.

It frequently seems that he regards sociality simplistically: as an enormous and perpetual friction of languages (discourses, fictions, image-
systems, reasonings, systems, sciences) and desires (impulses, injuries,
resentments, etc.). Then what does "reality" become in such a philosophy?[13]

In the case of a split in enunciation, the narrator, who is the intermediary between the narrator of the potential text and us, remains a plain formal authority
(as is a translator); he does not appear through a discourse that is different from
the repeated and textually noticeable discourse. On the other hand, as soon as
there is what I call distancing of the narrator, that is to say, miming of the forms
of another's discourse on oneself, the authority of the narrator can take on the consistency of a role, in order to express himself in a coherent discourse, where the
cleavage of the enunciation corresponds to a gap in perspective. This gap can
have nothing of the fictitious about it and can be simply that which exists between
an aged autobiographer-narrator and the life of the protagonist that he was, a gap
that is the basis for the majority of autobiographies in the first person. This is
something like what happens in *The Education of Henry Adams*, where the narrator maintains a rich pedogogical and sarcastic discourse in order to present and
comment upon the story of his hero (himself), without using the first person either
to assume his discourse or to name his protagonist.

But it can happen that the posture of the narrator emerges in the form of an
explicitly personal discourse in opposition to the contemporary protagonist rejected in the nonperson. The reader will thus have the impression of being in the
presence of a disturbing split personality, if something is presented in a serious
manner; or else—and this is the most frequent case—the impression of a game
that is difficult to manage without foundering in the ridiculous or without emphasizing precisely what we are pretending to avoid, narcissism. Gide gets out
of it by making the action move toward fiction when he confides to us his impres-
sions of his travelling companion Fabrice (himself):

Although he is too taciturn, I like traveling with Fabrice. He says, and
I believe him, that at forty-eight he feels infinitely younger than he was
at twenty. He enjoys that rare faculty of starting off anew at each
turning-point in his life and of remaining faithful to himself by never
resembling anything less than he does himself.

One of Fabrice's most disconcerting intellectual peculiarities for his
neighbors (I mean for his companion of the present moment, whoever
he might be) was to break away from himself constantly.—From him-

self? No, I have expressed it badly: Rather, to break away from circumstances.[14]

Claude Roy, at the beginning of the last volume of his autobiography, uses a similar procedure, but without recourse to a fictitious name. The confrontation represented in this way is situated in the past:

It had been then almost forty years that Claude Roy lived with Claude Roy. Little by little I had almost managed to get along with him. I had taken the time. Now I knew his idiosyncrasies, his pleasures, his anxieties, his impulses, his whims. I had come to know him as if he had made me. Not well enough, happily, to be bored with him already: he had more than one curve in his bag, that catchall. Enough resourcefulness to often catch me off guard . . .

What continued to interest me about this *alter ego*, of whom I didn't really know whether he used my name or if I used his in common practice, was also that reserve of indignation that he still maintained at an age when men have in general cooled down, become resigned and "set in their ways" . . .

There were other things for which I faulted Claude Roy. Less serious. Often contradictory. For example, I had a grudge against him for having become on the one hand an ironic scalded cat, always weighing the pros of some and the cons of others, unproductive to the end out of perplexity. And for having stayed, on the other hand, sentimental, naïve in politics often to the point of being a sucker.[15]

All these effects are also related to another variable: the system of tenses. If the potential text is written in the tenses of speech, we can preserve them (as Barthes does in the three fragments cited above), but we can also transpose them to the tenses of the story. A page of personal meditation having to do with the present of the narrator is in this way transformed into a page from a classical psychological novel (or at least, in the cases that I am studying, *seems* to be changed). We play at talking about ourself as if we were the hero of a work of fiction, by changing the "code." Thus Gide-Fabrice:

Michel's soul offered Fabrice rapturous perspectives, which were still clouded, it seemed to him, by the morning mists. To dissipate them the rays of a first love were needed. It was of this, not of the love itself, that Fabrice felt he might be jealous. He would have liked to suffice; tried to convince himself that he might have sufficed; he grieved to think that he would not suffice.[16]

Or Barthes:

He did not seek out an exclusive relationship (possession, jealousy, scenes); nor did he seek out a generalized, communal relationship; what he wanted was, each time, a privileged relationship, marked by a perceptible difference, brought to the condition of a kind of absolutely singular affective inflection, like that of a voice with an incomparable timbre; and paradoxically, he saw no obstacle to multiplying this privileged relationship: nothing but privileges, in short.[17]

We can, by means of this transposition, introduce some shifts in perspective between the supposed narrator and the protagonist, of whom we will then say: "he didn't understand that . . . ,"[18] which is difficult to translate into the first person of the present tense, at least literally.

Finally we would have to imagine the cases in which the potential text is already in the historical tenses: then the problem is to determine whether we are dealing with a pure narrative, or if a discourse is mingled with history. We saw earlier some examples of the problems posed by the different ways that "I" as narrator and "I" as protagonist are treated.

Extension. These effects depend on one last factor, the extension of the use of these figures, that is to say, the relationship with context. Three situations are possible:

1. Systematic use of the third person. This is true for all texts in which the author simply slips into the place of a heterodiegetic narrator in well-coded genres like historical memoirs, prefaces, and biographical notices.[19] There is then only one grammatical figure related to some contractual effects that are not very open to personal variations: discretion and solemnity of the preface, objectivity of the historical narrative or of the biographical notice. But within the framework of a genre like autobiography, whose conventions are diametrically opposed, the use of the third person produces, on the contrary, a striking effect: we read the text from the perspective of the convention that it violates. For this, the reader must remember the convention. If the text is written entirely in the third person, only the title (or a preface) is left to impose an autobiographical reading. And if it is a long text, the reader runs the risk of forgetting it. This explains why there are so few modern autobiographies written *entirely* in the third person. We can hardly cite any but the one written by Henry Adams (*The Education of Henry Adams*) and Norman Mailer's story, *The Armies of the Night* (1968). In the French language, there does not exist, it seems, an equivalent endeavor.[20] The third person is almost always used in a contrastive and local manner in texts that also use the first person. This contrast ensures the effectiveness of the figure. It can involve either an exceptional use of the third person or a deliberate alternation between the third and first person.

2. Exceptional use of the third person. We can, for the length of a sentence, treat ourself as "He" in order to distance ourself. Stendhal, rereading his journal,

writes in the margin: "This man is to be thrown out the window."[21] In *Les Mots* (*The Words*), Sartre repudiates his past in this way: "In 1936 and 1945, the individual who bears my name was treated badly: does that concern me? I hold him responsible for the insults he swallowed: the fool wasn't even able to command respect."[22] Reactions of humor. The third person can also be used for short intervals (a few pages) for reasons of modesty or for quick mirror games. It is in this way that Claude Roy distances an episode of his love life, [23] and that Gide tries, in several pages of his journal, to show himself from the side as if he were using a three-way mirror. But when Gide wants to describe more fully, after starting off in the third person, he *modulates* and returns to the first person. We see this in the following passage, which introduces a very long spiritual examination of conscience:

> Spiritualistic to an unbelievable degree, he never went to pray, or weep, or meditate over the tomb of his parents. For that goes far back, that disregard for matter which keeps it from holding his attention. It is as if he did not believe in it. I say "he," but that "he" is I. No logic in this; it is instinctive and spontaneous. I can find no better example of it than this: when at Cuverville I was present at the lugubrious delivery of my sister-in-law.[24]

Episodic, these uses alter nothing in the structure of the text or the work. It is not the same for certain uses, scarcely more extensive, but which correspond this time to a process of composition.

3. Alternate use of the third and first person. A system of oscillation and of indecision makes it possible to elude what is inevitably artificial or partial in each of the two presentations. If "I"and "he" hide one another reciprocally, is it not best to let them be unmasked one by the other while systematically alternating their use? This is the plan that underlies some of the texts from which I have drawn my examples; it corresponds visibly to contemporary anxieties and, sometimes, to a reflection on some modern theories of personality. But the matter is more easily imagined than realized. Claude Roy and Michel Leiris use the process in a relatively unobtrusive manner, one to open and close his narrative, the other to stress the last part of it. The only French works that have organized this alternation in a dizzying and systematic manner are *Le Traître* (*The Traitor*) (1958) by André Gorz and *Roland Barthes* (1975) by Roland Barthes, one in the shadow of Sartre, the other on the fringe of Lacan. In the two cases, the text no longer supports a classical and reassuring reading; it is constantly broken by brutal skids (in Gorz), or by a perpetual coming and going made possible by the fragmentary composition (in Barthes). These breaks and glistenings, which are moreover theorized within each of the two texts, are related to the impossible expression of identity, and to contortions, anxious in Gorz, euphoric in Barthes, of lucidity.

Elasticity. These games naturally have their limits, inscribed in the conditions of their functioning. To display openly the multiplicity of postures usually hidden by the pronoun "I" is only possible if identity continues to be postulated in the final analysis by the reading contract. The more the autobiographer "does the splits," the more it becomes necessary, on another level, for this contract, in relation to which (within which) there is a split, to be established. We cannot escape the problem of identity, but only displace it, and stage it as a problem.

The reader will inevitably experience this staging, when it is grounded on processes contrary to the conventions of the genre, as a pleasant artifice or as a pathetic game, as a pretense; it reveals to him precisely that the autobiographer cannot *seriously* do what he sets out to do. The splitting in two can only be figurative (just as the unity can only be mythical). The reader will attribute all the plays of enunciation to one single speaker, all the plays of focalization suggesting that the autobiographer sees himself as someone else to an internal comedy performed in private, even if the scene mimes the intrusion of a glance coming from the audience. Now we are really in the audience, and we witness the ventriloquy games, the performances in front of a three-way mirror, of someone, of another person who remains locked in his identity, even if he sets all its elasticity in motion.

Barthes's self-portrait is likely to remain a canonical example for the study of these problems. Barthes sought the maximum elasticity, for fear of staying trapped in his "imaginary." He himself writes a critical book about himself, in a collection of ambiguous status: the rule of the game requires that the critic reconstruct "so and so by himself," by proceeding with a montage of texts;[25] but this self-portrait is in a situation of dependence in relation to the discourse of the critic. What will happen if the author "himself" slips into this role of critic? This is what Barthes has attempted: he rereads his own works pencil in hand, watches himself, rewrites himself, tries to escape from the weight of the "I" through ceaseless variations on the personal pronouns (he is in turn "I," "you," "he," "R.B."), theorizing and criticizing this practice as he goes along.[26] He detaches himself not only as protagonist but as narrator ("all this must be considered as if spoken by a character in a novel," p. 119), encroaches upon the role of the reader, and ends up writing a review of his own book in a journal that lends itself to the game.[27] In the end (and even if he anticipates it and says it beforehand), this game of flight from his "imaginary" turns out simply to become in our eyes his imaginary's essential characteristic.

The elasticity of the "I" has its limits. If the game were no longer a game, the coherence of the "I" would be broken, the conditions of communication and of writing would disappear. Can one really talk about oneself as if one were another person, place oneself at the window in order to watch oneself pass by in the street? These are the same problems that I am going to meet up with again in presenting more sophisticated methods, which were germinal in some of the situations I have already analyzed. Gide was pretending to watch "Fabrice"; he could just as easily have invented a "Fabrice" who would watch Gide. Proposing a fictitious narrator's account of himself could thus correspond either to a triumphant narcissism that humorously proclaims his identity or to the anxieties of a paranoic who seeks to rebuild it.

Fictitious Fictions

Points of View on the Self

One could not write an autobiography without elaborating and communicating a point of view on the self. This point of view may include some *gaps* between the perspective of the narrator and that of the protagonist; may be complex or ambiguous; may integrate, in order to retrieve or modify it, the image that the author believes others have of him. But, as complex or twisted as this point of view is, it will carry in the final analysis the mark of the author. We do not really know how to get out of the self; that is to say, to represent, equally with our own, a point of view different from our own. Articulating two really different points of view on the same individual is possible only outside the boundaries of an autobiographical project:

—either, for the author, within the framework of a novel, but it is then at the cost of reality (omniscience and "nonfocalization" are possible only in fiction);

—or in reality, but it is then at the cost of the autobiographical situation. The elementary type of these "dialogues" of points of view is the correspondence between two people read by a third, the confrontation of autobiographical texts written by different people, or the collection by an ethnographer of life accounts of several people belonging to the same family or to the same milieu.[28] It is from this type of situation that biographers are able to adopt the attitude of omniscient narrators.

Is it possible to go against what seems to be an inherent inevitability in the position of the autobiographer? We can imagine two types of attempts to abolish this limit, but these can only be a question of approximations or appearances.

Approximations, on the side of reality: we can imagine taking charge from the beginning and organizing on our own this confrontation of witnesses that in general is established after the fact and in spite of those concerned. This would be to imagine a "common autobiographical project." But the sole fact that two people start out in such an undertaking assumes some related points of view, a fundamental complicity and a sort of "collective narcissism." The texts that they will produce will reflect in fact an internal differentiation of a single point of view. Nevertheless, there are very few examples of it, and always in situations of fraternal, conjugal or friendly symbiosis. The Goncourt brothers write their journal together: they say "we" and act as if they were one single person. Two spouses can sum up their life by exchanging a series of letters (but they do so only through the screen of fiction).[29] Two old friends can keep parallel journals, but the project will be "common" only for one of the two: that is what happened for André Gide and the "La Petite Dame." Unknown to Gide, the latter began to make note of everything that she observed about him in a journal, comparable to his, that she kept from 1918 to 1951. In this way she achieved a system of very Gidian "shifts," which even Gide imitated while doing the portrait of his traveling companion Fabrice, the glance of a critical, but accessory, *alter ego*.[30] The existence of truly antagonistic points of view excludes *a priori* the possibility of a common project of *overlapping* autobiographies.

Simulacra, on the side of fiction: because if one seeks to make someone else's point of view part of his autobiography, it could only be in an imaginary way, by restoring the other as a character in the novel; these games or these fantasies will translate, in the eyes of the reader, the idea that the autobiographer has of the idea the other can have of him.

It is with the presentation of some of these "fictitious fictions" that I will end this chapter. We are not concerned with genuine fictions, that is to say, with autobiographical novels governed in their entirety by a fictional pact. The general system remains that of autobiography; it is only on the level of one of the postures of the narrative (the character of the narrator) that a sort of game is grafted: the autobiographer tries to imagine what would happen if *someone else* was telling his story or sketching his portrait. He isn't looking to represent, by mimicking the discourse that is being put forth on someone else, the gaps of his internal perspective, but to recover the discourse that others are capable of holding on him, in order to impose on them, when all said and done, the image of himself which seems real to him.

The texts constructed according to this system are rare and have some differences between them; the only thing they have in common is that the use of this figure always involves the whole of the work and determines its entire composition. Two types of such texts exist: one borrows the forms of the eyewitness account, the other those of the dialogue.

Fictitious Witness

The canonical example of the first type is *The Autobiography of Alice B. Toklas* by Gertrude Stein.[31] What you have to do is imagine how one of your close friends would be able to tell your life's story: one takes the pen in his stead and writes down his account. Naturally, there is no fraud here; the reader is warned of the rule of the game: right away Gertrude Stein makes herself known as her secretary's autobiographer; and it is because the reader keeps in mind that this is a condition of the contract that he can savor the humor and the virtuosity of the exercise. If he was inclined to forget it, the final sentences of the book would remind him: Alice Toklas admits that, since she does not have the time to write her autobigraphy, Gertrude Stein offered to write it in her place. "And she has and this is it," concludes the narrator. It is true that the initial indication is ambiguous, all the more since Alice Toklas was not an imaginary person, but the very real companion of Stein. This wavering is part of the game of affectation characteristic of this type of procedure.

The game is twofold: at the same time fictional and autobiographical. On the fictional side, we are concerned with building the character of the witness, with inventing a perspective for him, with making up a style for him, so that he will be consistent enough to sustain the whole narration; we enjoy creating the freshness of "another" perspective on ourselves. To tell the truth, this game can seem rather condescending to the reader: this "other" is your subordinate, is defined only in relation to you, and you attribute to him a candid and admiring view of you. The construction of the fictitious posture of the "witness" is finally only the alibi for a presentation of the self: this detour by the witness justifies the "field restrictions" (we are not forced to talk about what has escaped the attention of the other; we can model this social figure while leaving in the shadow the entire personal domain), and it provides a humorous way of singing your own praises without someone being able to accuse you of naïveté in pride. When all is said and done, far from corresponding to an internal splitting in two or a social uneasiness, this type of game is an astute way to achieve a form of self-hagiography that neutralizes or paralyzes criticism. The reader must be captivated by the double reading proposed to him by the enunciation of the "witness" as fictitious authority and as autobiographical relay.

At least such is the game practiced by Stein. It is difficult to generalize from one single example. It is indeed evident that this type of strategy can be realized in other contexts: the dizzying construct set up by Barthes undoubtedly fulfills this function of protection better. Also evident is that the fiction of the "witness" could be used in a more critical perspective but would always be suspected of affectation.

Can we, following Gertrude Stein, reuse this procedure without falling into plagiarism? This is what Jean-Jacques Gautier has tried to do recently in *Cher Untel*.[32] Aline Moussart, secretary of the writer "So-and-So," keeps her journal; little by little she traces there the portrait of the writer all the while recounting her own story, and the story of her dealings with him. At the end of her journal, she comes up with the idea of suggesting to "So-and-So" that he publish the present manuscript under his name and pass off this journal as fiction. Gautier's attempt differs from Gertrude Stein's on two essential points. First, Aline is in a conflicting relationship with the writer; she is thus led to sketch a more delicately shaded portrait of him; and as a character in a novel she has more of a personal life than Alice Toklas, even if she has less style. Especially, the whole of the game is not presented as an autobiography, but as a novel. It is true that the fictional veil is retained: So-and-So is not Gautier, but he has published exactly the same books. This is a classic procedure of autobiographical fiction, where an identity is suggested while allowing the shadow of a doubt to hover.

Fictitious Dialogue

The second type is very different: it is no longer a question of constructing a point of view on the self, but of *destroying* one of them. The text is presented as an answer to a discourse that has already been uttered, and that must be recovered in order to be dissolved. We are going to imitate it in order to respond to it. For this, within the framework of an autobiographical text presented as such, we fictitiously reenact a *trial*, setting the scene and making the roles of prosecution and defense enter into dialogue; things indeed go in favor of the autobiographer who little by little makes his true image triumph.

This is what Rousseau did in the dialogues entitled *Rousseau juge de Jean-Jacques*.[33] The autobiographical narrative of the *Confessions* had been composed to answer the accusations hurled against him, but Rousseau has the impression of remaining misunderstood and persecuted by an elusive plot. These secret enemies keep silent, work in the shadow. Obsessed by this mute and indirect accusation, Rousseau himself wants to try to call up this accusation, to bring it into the light of day in order to be able finally to refute it and get rid of it. In the prologue, "On the Subject and Form of This Writing," he explains his strategy. He suggests to us the dialogue of two fictitious characters: one, named "Rousseau," admires the books of Jean-Jacques Rousseau, but does not know the man; the second character, named "the Frenchman," knows the author but has not read his books. "Rousseau" has difficulty believing all the bad things that "the Frenchman" says about Jean-Jacques. Their dialogue brings to the forefront the misunderstanding that is the fragile foundation of this trial. To clear the matter up, "Rousseau" is going to visit Jean-Jacques while "the Frenchman" reads the author's works. This double confrontation reestablishes the truth about the character of Jean-Jacques and allows us to understand the plot of which he is the victim.

The author, in the prologue, explains the form he has chosen:

> The dialogue form having seemed to me the most appropriate to discuss the pros and cons, I have chosen it for this reason. I have taken the liberty in these conversations of taking back my family name that the public judged fitting to take away from me, and I have called myself as a third party, following their example, by my baptismal name to which they were happy to reduce me.[34]

Here we have one of the oldest strategies in polemical literature: fictitious dialogue attributed to real characters, or attributed to fictitious characters, but bearing on real people. One of the two concerned parties claims the right to reconstruct the discourse of the other in order to integrate it into a setting over which the first has complete control. Since Plato, this game has been played a great deal. We find it in diverse forms in *Les Provinciales*, the *Critique de l'Ecole des femmes*, and the *Interviews imaginaires* by Gide. In the autobiographical register, this is something like what the Spaniard Torres Villarroel has done in his *Correo del otro mundo* (*Postman from the Other World*), where he combines the method of the "dream" and that of the dialogue to settle his account with his enemies and put together a flattering picture of himself from different perspectives.[35]

But what Rousseau has attempted is more complicated. Recourse to this method of dialogue is for him a solution of despair, and the game is perfectly serious, so serious that readers can be discouraged by the total lack of humor, the insistence, the repetitions, and the paranoic appearance of this setting. Such seriousness makes the *Dialogues* examplary of the point of view that interests me: Rousseau has attempted the impossible in earnest; he has pursued as far as possible what the others are doing without believing it very much. On the one hand, he puts himself inside others in order to understand how they see him; on the other hand, he puts himself outside his self in order to see that self as if he were someone else. In the two cases, the game is, when all is said and done, a fake. But it is only when all is said and done, and not right away—in spite of Rousseau and not intentionally. Rare are the autobiographers who have played this game both ways (putting oneself in others, putting oneself outside the self) with such an "elasticity," while attempting the big split in order to be others and someone else at the same time. It is worth the effort to follow Rousseau in this double "madness":

—On the one hand, he wants to reconstruct the real point of view others have of him. It is no longer a question, as in polemical literature, of having a good time by caricaturing the adversary in order to crush him. Rousseau attempts to construct another person who is as much like him as possible, someone that he himself can believe in, who is not a simple puppet. But the manner in which he has constructed this other person reveals precisely that it is impossible for him (Rousseau) to imagine him. It would not be right to judge Rousseau severely; thus his adversaries can only be wicked men or fools. Others will therefore divide themselves into two bodies. One, irredeemable, is the group of "Gentlemen" who organize the plot and intentionally lie to mislead the public. With them, no dialogue is possible. The other, redeemable, is a Frenchman who is their dupe but who is, deep down, an honest man, and who, by a suitable maieutic, is going to be brought back to the truth, that is to say, to the point of view that Jean-Jacques has of himself. Pathetic fake: this Frenchman is a fake custom-made "other." To hide this truth from himself, Rousseau ascribes to him all the opinions of other real people and makes it convenient for him to put up (for three hundred pages) a great resistance to the evidence, to which he only gives in little by little.[36]

—On the other hand, since he makes the effort to put himself "in the place of others," Rousseau would be within his right to demand the same. But, impartial, he does not want to impose his point of view on himself (this is what he already did in the *Confessions*). He is going to give a lesson in objectivity. Instead of proposing his inner evidence, he shows how he would set about to know Jean-Jacques if he were someone else. This is the fictitious role of this "Rousseau," who decides to go pay a visit to Jean-Jacques in order to sound him out and form an opinion. The most surprising passage of the *Dialogues* is the long narrative of this visit,[37] "Rousseau" observing the behavior of Jean-Jacques while listening to his remarks, and constructing little by little an "objective" portrait that the reader can naturally take only as a self-portrait, even though he expresses himself through the fictitious voice of a homodiegetic witness. The vertigo reaches its peak when "Rousseau" begins to quote a speech that Jean-Jacques supposedly made to him.[38] This direct speech (which failed in the *Confessions*) appears to us as no more than a view at the end of inverted opera glasses, at the bottom of a sort of funnel, quoted by a fictitious "Rousseau," himself the pedagogical puppet of . . . Jean-Jacques Rousseau. We hear a muffled voice that sends out a pathetic call for the response of another person — another person who would be a *real* other person.

He reread what he had written.

Is it reasonable to study such a rare phenomenon? He had scarcely been able to gather a few examples drawn from a dozen books — when each year, hundreds of autobiographies candidly written "in the first person" flood the market. But this corpus would have been meager only if he had wanted to make us believe in the existence of a genre, the "autobiography in the third person." Well, his purpose was the reverse. In his eyes the analysis of these borderline cases was simply a kind of wedge to shatter the cohesion, in part imaginary, that is granted to "genres." By dissociating the different factors, we notice that the effect produced came only from their combination and from their hierarchical organization on the genre's horizon of expectation.

We could, from this type of untangling, distinguish and formulate more clearly some theoretical problems that the "normal" functioning of genres tends to confuse or to conceal — multiple, divergent problems sending the inquiry off on very different paths.

For the "persons," he dreamed of continuing the work undertaken by Valéry in his *Cahiers* (*Notebooks*).[39] Valéry seemed to him to have the knack of placing himself from the very first at the heart of the problem, at the spot where the linguistic subject and the psychological subject are articulated, paving the way where Lacan, Benveniste, and many others have since joined in. It remained to draw the conclusions for the autobiographical narrative, as much for enunciation as for communication. And maybe in particular for a poetic of reception (what becomes of the "I," "you," etc., for me who is listening or is reading?). This question was related, laterally, to that of the contract.

Throughout his study, as a matter of fact, he had analyzed the articulation of the elements of the autobiographical contract, but a question was left hanging: what difference is there between the figures and "fictitious fictions" used within an autobiographical text, and the system of the autobiographical novel? Is there a continuous transition from one to the other? Couldn't he pursue the question by comparing two equally overwhelming texts, *Roland Barthes* by Roland Barthes, on the autobiographical side, and, *La Mise à mort* (*Put to Death*, 1965) by Aragon, on the fictional side, where the games of splitting in two and mirrors overflow the universe of fiction and invade the reading contract itself?

After all, the margin between fiction and autobiography seems thinner than ever to him. Where the analysis distinguishes, reality often presents a continuous spectrum. Especially today, when so many fictional texts are, from the very first, offered to readers within the framework of an autobiographical space, and the most conscientious autobiographers are no longer able to put the genre into practice except in the form of parody or game. But it happened that he was asked, as if his role had been to settle the matter, in the face of such an ambiguous text: "And that, does that enter into your definition?" *His* definition, which was the dictionary's and everybody's, was the reason he had been taken for Aristotle—unless it was for La Palice. It had been, and remains for him, the point of departure of a many-sided and open investigation aiming for clarity and precision, without too much simplification. And not a ridiculous point of arrival.

A crossroads of problems, then. He hesitated, then chose to explore another strategy, an equally subtle one, which consists in the interweaving of the voice of the adult narrator with the voice of the child whose presence he seeks to restore.

He sat down at his table to write.

Chapter 3
The Ironic Narrative of Childhood: Vallès

"I am six years old, and my buttocks are peeling off."
Who is speaking? Is it the voice of a child, that of an adult? of an adult mimicking the voice of a child and transforming a witty remark into a word or expression said naïvely by a child but which seems funny or poetic to adults? This voice belongs to Ernest Pitou, narrator and hero of *Le Testament d'un blagueur* (*The Testament of a Joker*, 1869). The strength of this opening is due, as far as the word game goes, to our uncertainty about the origin of the enunciation. By writing this sentence, Vallès accomplishes a small revolution: he finally finds the method that is going to allow him to talk about his childhood, a method that he will perfect some years later while composing *L'Enfant* (*The Child*, 1879); and he offers a solution (among others that are possible) to one of the fundamental problems of a genre that is developed during this second half of the nineteenth century, the narrative of childhood.[1]

In the classical autobiographical narrative, it is the voice of the adult narrator that dominates and organizes the text; although he stages the perspective of the child, he hardly lets him speak. This is completely natural: childhood appears only through the memory of the adult. We talk about it, eventually we make it speak a little bit, but it does not speak directly. To reconstruct the spoken word of the child, and eventually delegate the function of narration to him, we must abandon the code of autobiographic verisimilitude (of the "natural") and enter the space of fiction. So it will no longer be a question of remembering, but of making up a childlike voice, this dependent on the effects that such a voice can produce on a reader rather than on a concern for fidelity to a childlike enunciation that, in any case, has never existed in this form.

Vallès did not come up with this voice right away. In the "Lettre de Junius" ("Letter from Junius", 1861), in the chronicles of *La Rue* (*The Street*, 1866), he vented his rancor against a tyrannical education and his nostalgia for the country in the most traditional way, as an adult who ponders over good and bad memories. It is only in 1869, under cover of a hasty satirical sketch that he is asked to do, that he muffles the discourse of the adult and tries to construct a new narrative voice. Two tricks of presentation allow him to relegate the discourse of the narrator to the background. Ernest Pitou is dead, and it is his executor who submits his memoirs in his place; and in the memoirs themselves, the narrator has left his memories "in bit and pieces," by imitating the layout of a journal. The way is clear for another voice to settle in.[2]

Whose voice? Can a child really say: "I am six years old and my buttocks are peeling off"? We need only put the sentence back in the historical past tense to convince ourselves that the responsibility for it rests rather with an adult narrator: "I was six years old and my buttocks were peeling off." In reality, the effect produced by Vallès is the result of the blending of two voices. The sentence seems to begin like a perfectly plausible childlike enunciation – "I was six years old" – and continues through a stylistic shortcut which connotes more the enunciation of an adult, but which, on our impetus, we can first experience as a word or expression said naïvely by a child but which seems funny or poetic to adults. The indecisiveness has been made possible by the use of the narrative present, which has given us the illusion of a direct enunciation. This insidious mixture of two voices produces a troubling and suggestive effect on the reader, an effect that is not produced by the transcription into the past that I have given it (where we laugh at a play on words, but "between adults"), and that would not be produced by a narration in the present either, but "in the third person," which would give, in the style of *Poil de Carotte*: "Ernest is six years old and his buttocks are peeling off."

The brief analysis of this little sentence shows the complexity of the problems posed by this new type of narration. It suggests also a method of study: vary the factors in order to distinguish which factor, or which combination of factors, is responsible for the effect produced. This supposes that we are relying on a theoretical analysis of the whole of the system. My purpose is to construct such an analysis here, a sort of study of "applied poetics" that can be used as a reference and a working tool for the reading of Vallès, and as a point of departure for a reflection on the genre of the narrative of childhood.

My analysis – if we leave out the first section (Eclipse of the Narrator) – will focus both on *Le Testament d'un blagueur* and on *L'Enfant*. I will show how, with *L'Enfant*, Vallès has reintroduced the shadow of the classical narrator, and the effects he has drawn from it.

I will take my examples from *L'Enfant*. But the use of the examples is tricky:

often the element one wants to illustrate is associated with others in the chosen sentence, and the effect produced by the sentence always depends upon its context. Accordingly, I have preferred to have my reader hear the narrative voice of *L'Enfant* first by giving him an excerpt of some length to read. I will not comment upon this excerpt. I offer it to the reader rather as a sample upon which he himself will be able to practice verifying, or rectifying, my analysis. This text, taken from chapter 6, presents almost all of the problems I will study (except that of "narration in the second degree"); furthermore, on the thematic level, it gives a rather complete picture of the book.

I go into the furrows up to my knees, during the plowing season: I roll around in the grass at the time that they are making hay, I cheep like the quails that fly away, I do somersaults like the little ones who fall out of the nests when the plow goes by.

Oh! what good times I have had in a meadow, at the edge of a stream bordered with yellow flowers whose stem was trembling in the water, with white pebbles at the bottom, and which carried off bouquets of leaves and branches of golden elder trees that I used to throw into the current! . . .

My mother doesn't like me to stay like this, silent, mouth wide open watching the water flow.

She's right, I'm wasting my time.

"Instead of taking your Latin grammar to learn your lessons!" Then, getting upset, showing concern:

"If it's possible, all stained with green, heels all full of mud . . . We buy you new shoes so you can do this to them! Let's go, back to the house, and you won't go out tonight!"

I know full well that shoes get ruined in the fields and that you have to put on your clogs, but that's not what my mother wants! My mother makes me get an education, she doesn't want me to be a country person like she is!

My mother wants her Jacques to be a *Gentleman*.

Has she made him coats with olive-shaped buttons, bought a top hat, put on trouser straps, so he'll fall into the manure again, go back to the stables to put on clogs!

Oh yes! I would prefer clogs! I like the odor of Florimond the plowman much more than that of Mr. Sother, the teacher in level eight: I'd rather make bales of hay than read my grammar, and prowl around in the stables than loaf around studying.

I only enjoy knotting the sheafs, digging up stones, tying sticks, carrying wood!

Maybe I was born to be a servant!

It's awful! yes, I was born to be a servant! I see it! I feel it!!!

My God! Don't let my mother know anything about it!

I would accept being Pierrouni the little cowherd, and going, a branch in my hand, a green apple in my teeth, to lead the animals into the pasture, near the blackberries, not far from the orchard.

There are wild red roses in the bushes, and up above a bearded spot, which is a nest, there are creatures of the good Lord, like little beans that fly, and in the flowers, green flies that seem drunk.

They let Pierrouni go around all unbuttoned, when it's hot, and have his hair a mess when he wants to.

They're not always telling him:

"Leave your hands alone, now what have you done to your tie? – stand up straight. – Are you hunchbacked? – He's hunchbacked! – Button your jacket. – Turn up your pants. – What have you done with the olive-shaped button? The button there, to the left, the greenest one? – Ah! that child will be the death of me!"

Method

I have chosen to go through one by one all the stages that lead from the narrator's voice to that of the "protagonist." This progressive unfolding is a convenient process of presentation, but naturally it has its limits.

First, because the analytical procedure seems to go in the opposite direction of Vallès's practice. Where I differentiate, Vallès does his best to confuse. What I am going to separate like the steps of a flight of stairs is in fact a continuous and reversible slope. Vallès exploits all the situations where the basic oppositions of classical narrative are apparently neutralized, in order to create a perpetual "dissolve" or a "double exposure" between the two voices. Moreover, the narrative voice changes at almost every sentence or every paragraph: not only does the text become unpredictable, but the normal speed of reading makes a sort of magnetism take place. The text goes more quickly than the reader: hardly has the latter identified the "voice" of a sentence than the following sentence compels him to "adapt" differently. Out of inertia, the different positions of the narrative voice end up being superimposed in the reader's consciousness.

These effects of transition or of confusion are so subtle that different readers will at first not agree on the interpretation of one and the same passage, or rather on its "attribution." The reader often has a tendency to reduce the ambiguity instead of analyzing it; he wants to know clearly "which of the two is speaking"; whereas "to see clearly," in this case, is rather to analyze by what methods, in what proportion, and according to what hierarchy, and in view of what effect, are the two voices confused. The spectral analysis of the enunciation will perhaps allow us to understand how the different tones of the narrative are produced.

Above all, I am going to conduct an analysis whose main feature will inevitably be simple, but I will have to continually *recombine* the methods used in order to understand the effects produced by Vallès. His art, as a matter of fact, is due not to the systematic use of such and such a method, like the narrative present or the "interior monologue," but to the systematic articulation of four elements, each of which, taken separately, has rather limited and very traditional effects, but which contain the seed of some unexploited possibilities that their association with the other elements is going to reveal. These four elements are:

1. The use of narrative "in the first person," where the same pronoun "I" designates the adult narrator and the protagonist, the subject of the enunciation and that of the utterance.[3]

2. The use of the "narrative present," a figure that introduces an apparent disruption in the distinction between story and discourse, and between anteriority and simultaneity.

3. The indirect free style, which organizes the integration (and eventually the confusion) of two different enunciations.

4. The use in a written narrative of features characteristic of orality, and the blend of levels of language.

It is the *intensive* and *combined* use of the last three elements in an autodiegetic narrative which allowed Vallès to create such surprising and modern effects. To be certain of this, I conducted a quick comparison with other narratives of childhood, those found at the beginning of contemporary novels like *Histoire d'un homme du peuple* (*Story of a Man of the People*, 1865) by Erckmann-Chatrian, the *Mémoires d'un orphelin* (*Memoirs of an Orphan*, 1865) by Xavier Marmier, and *Le Petit Chose* (*Little What's His Name*, 1868) by Alphonse Daudet: the narrative present, the indirect free style, the features characteristic of orality are used here in a discrete and punctual manner, and there is never any association between them. Consequently, all these narratives without any ambiguity make one dominant voice heard, that of the narrator, and produce, at best, the type of contrast characteristic of classic autobiographical narrative.

It is exactly the eclipse of the narrator, such as it is practiced in *Le Testament d'un blagueur*, that will allow Vallès to play on the combination of elements presented above.

The Eclipse of the Narrator

In novels written in the form of memoirs, it is normal for the narrator to be discreet about his present situation and about his personality: he makes use especially of an alibi of paradoxical narration, both retrospective in regard to voice and contemporary in regard to perspective. The majority of classic autodiegetic fictions effect in this way a filtering in the functions of the autobiographical narrator, according to measurements that can vary. If he forbids his narrator all anticipation, the author ends up cheating — as in *Sans Famille* (*Without Family*), where Hector Malot combines the retrospective voice with a form of suspense that it renders, if not impossible, at least unlikely.[4] But whatever the measurement and its function, the autodiegetic narrator of the personal novel openly exercises his functions as narrator to varying degrees, and in particular his function of narration.[5]

In *Le Testament d'un blagueur*, Vallès attempts a sort of eclipse of the retrospective narrator. He does not suppress him, but sets it up so most of his footprints are half-erased; their perception is made difficult, it is clouded by the interference of another source of enunciation: discourse or narrative seeming to come from the protagonist. At the beginning of the text, an "editor" usurps the narrator's function in order to present his testament in his place. In the testament itself:

— The narrator abstains from all references to the situation of enunciation and all discourse addressed to the "narratee": he seems to renounce his function of communication.

— The discontinuous structure of the text makes him also seem to abstain from exercising his administrative function. He exercises it, however, and does so through the play of subtitles, which are uninterpretable in the hypothesis of a narration coming from the protagonist. In *L'Enfant*, the dividing up into chapters, the titles and subtitles, and the blank spaces that separate the groups of paragraphs will function in the same way as signs of the narrator.

— The narrator exercises the function of testimony very little, and if he rarely does without the function of commentary, this is not immediately perceptible, for two reasons. First because it often proceeds by the indirect means of an ironic enunciation. Next because the use of tenses in the narrative masks the presence of commentary as it masks the very practice of narration; this is due especially to the extensive use of the narrative present.

The Narrative Present

The narrative present, or historical present, is a very classical narrative *figure*. It functions in a context in which the narrator normally uses one of the two systems at his disposal to recount a past story: that of discourse, centered on the present, where this story will be told in the compound past tense [*passé composé*] and in the imperfect; and that of history, where it will be told in the (literary) past tense [*passé simple*] and in the imperfect. The figure of the narrative present consists in a momentary ellipsis of all marks of time, whether these marks be those that oppose story to discourse, those that oppose in the system of discourse the moment of enunciation to that of utterance, or those that, in each system, are utilized for contrast (the opposition of the simple and compound past with the imperfect). This zero degree of time produces different effects according to the context in which it is used. Most often it is utilized to create a specific effect of contrast, in the framework of a narrative of anecdotes. The signs marking the relationship of the narrator to the story are suddenly missing, so that the story seems to "burst" the diegetic screen, to hold its narrator back in order to move to center stage. Of course, we are dealing here with a figure, with a "manner of speaking" that does not fool us: everything happens *as if* the story were becoming contemporaneous with its narration (effect no. 1).

Can we use this figure in the long run? In the classical narrative, this is hardly ever seen; in the long run, as a matter of fact, we lose sight of the context, and the effect of external contrast disappears; on the other hand, the narrative present excludes all internal contrast. Consequently, platitude and monotony would result. Even in Vallès's newspaper articles, the narrative present remains caught up in a contrastive and broken system.[6]

Nevertheless, the principal innovation brought to the narrative of childhood in *Le Testament d'un blagueur* seems to be the extensive use of the narrative present. If it escapes monotony, it is because it is associated with other methods and is utilized as a means of transition and of confusion. The general tone that the present provides functions as a sort of surface glossing which in reality hides two different sources of enunciation, and seemingly blurs the hierarchy of the levels of the text. Thus it is in this passage from *L'Enfant*, where identical forms of the present sometimes hide narrative present, sometimes an indirect free style relating the thoughts of the child:

> I'm sobbing, I'm suffocating: my mother reappears and pushes me into the closet where I sleep, where I'm afraid every night.
>
> I might be five years old and think I'm a parricide. It's not my fault however!
>
> Did I force my father to make that wagon? Wouldn't I have preferred to bleed myself and that he no longer be in pain?
>
> Yes—and I scratch my hands so I'll hurt too.
>
> It's because mama loves my father so much! That's why she's so worked up.
>
> They made me learn to read from a book where it is written, in big letters, that we must obey our mother and father: my mother was right to beat me.[7]

When the narrative present is, as here, associated with the use of the first person, with the practice of a segmented narration that imitates oral discourse,[8] with the choice of a perspective that is often that of the child, and with the use of the indirect free style, a reversal effect is produced that is contrary to effect no. 1, an effect from which we protect ourselves with more difficulty than we do from the first—probably because everything happens *as if* the enunciation was becoming contemporaneous with the story, and it was therefore the doing of the protagonist (effect no. 2).

We imagine, for example, that in spite of the presence of the signs of the narrator, the reader might find it hard to determine who is narrating the following episode:

Le Fer-à-cheval . . .
I am going there with my cousin Henriette.
She's coming here to see Pierre André, the harness-maker of the suburbs.
He's from Farreyrolles, as she is, and she has to give him some news about his family, private news that I can't know; because they turn away to confide in one another and she whispers the news in his ear.
I see him there leaning over; and their cheeks are touching. When Henriette comes back, she is pensive and doesn't speak.[9]

We are all the more tempted to effect this shifting of the narrator's voice into the protagonist's because the latter is constantly being integrated into the narrative by the indirect means of the indirect free style.

The Indirect Free Style

The indirect free style is also a narrative *figure*, grounded in part on elliptical phenomena. Its function is to integrate a speech, told within the speech that produces it, by creating a kind of "dissolve" by means of which the two enunciations are going to be superimposed. In the direct style, the repeated utterance would be quoted in its real text, without transformation, but it would be clearly separated from the speech that repeats it by quotation marks or dashes, no confusion being possible. In the indirect free style, the repeated utterance is integrated into the speech of the narrator by ellipsis of any introductive method: it agrees, for the person and the tense, with the speech that repeats it, but it keeps its syntax and vocabulary.[10] In this way overlapping of the two enunciations is obtained: we hear one voice that speaks within another. This voice is not quoted; it is in some way *mimed*.

In the classical narrative, the figure of indirect free style is used in a limited way, in a sentence, a paragraph; the second enunciation appears only fleetingly through the first enunciation. It is a method of economy, which can simply be used in the "dissolve" of the narration or be used in view of pathetic or ironic effects. The economy can be the source of ambiguity. If the second enunciation is not distinguished stylistically from the first, the reader might wonder if the narrator is imitating the reflections of a protagonist or if he is explaining his own.

Uncertainty will increase if other methods are combined with the indirect free style. In the autodiegetic narrative, the narrator and the protagonist are both "I," and all distinction related to the mark of the person disappears. According to the context, we might be uncertain whether indirect free style is being used, and sometimes take for an enunciation coming from the narrator alone that which is the transposition of the thoughts of the protagonist. How should we read the last sentence of chapter xvi of *L'Enfant*: "My father had lied to me"? As information on the father given by the narrator to the reader, accompanied by a harsh judgment of the adult? Quite obviously the principal information bears not upon the father's lie, but on the scandalizing discovery the child has made about him; we are involved, then, in an elliptical transposition in indirect free style of "my father lied to me."

Furthermore, if in an autodiegetic narrative the narrator systematically uses the narrative present, all distinction related to the mark of tense is going to disappear, and we will be even uncertain whether there is indirect free style, but by leaning this time in the other direction, in attributing to the protagonist the entire reponsibility for the enunciation. Indeed, in a speech that uses indirect free style in an autodiegetic narration told in the narrative present, all distinction of tense and person becoming impossible, there is no longer, on this level, any difference between a speech in indirect free style repeating an utterance of the principal character and that of the utterance itself. We then find ourselves faced with a speech repeated in *direct free style*.[11]

And if this speech develops at any length, there will be a great temptation to talk about an "interior monologue" of the character. In *Le Testament d'un blagueur* and in *L'Enfant*, Vallès has often made use of this method: we think we hear "live" the reflections that the child was having *in petto*.

Candies, I don't care, if they give them to me one by one as a reward, when I'm good. I like them when I've had too many.[12]

Are we really dealing here with an interior monologue? Certainly not. What defines the interior monologue is its autonomy: as in the theater, the speech of the protagonist must be presented independently of all other enunciation.[13] Here, on the contrary, the enunciation remains *double*: the reader can never forget that this "monologue," if it is interior, is primarily within the voice of the narrator, that it is part of a system of ventriloquy. This is not a child who is speaking, but an adult who turns his voice into a child's. The speech that seems to come from the protagonist is in fact a mimed speech, around which and in which floats the diffuse and insidious presence of the narrator: we remain in the domain of the "as if."

Apparently absent, the narrator reveals himself at the same time in a contextual and stylistic manner. Contextual: even when it is rather developed, this "monologue" rarely unfolds in a continuous way: brief fragments of monologue alternate with narrative passages, and they are caught up in an exchange between the two voices, with some "sheddings" of voices, some breaks and contrasts which serve to remind us that the narrator is an adult. Stylistic: in the indirect free style, the syntax and vocabulary of mimed speech are in general completely respected, but the narrator can also *blend* the characteristic traits of the language of the child with others that could only be attributed to the adult. In this way we will find blended into infantile speech, information that makes sense only within the framework of a communication between a narrator and a reader: the use of syntactic turns characteristic of written language and the literary register; exaggerations in which are clearly shown the intention to produce such and such an effect; the use of a vocabulary with ironic or pathetic connotations entering into the strategy of the adult narrator.

This duplicity of enunciation is particularly evident in the narrative of childhood, because the two sources of utterance are relatively distant from one another: the perspective, value judgments, and attitudes of the child in question and of the adult narrator are different. Vallès makes use of this gap to achieve ironic or pathetic effects, by playing on the contrast between the candor, the ignorance, or the resignation of the child, and the revolt, the insinuations, or the ironies of the adult who addresses, above the head of the child (and through his "speech"), a reader who must not be fooled.[14]

In the Trilogy, the more the autobiographical narrative of Jacques Vingtras progresses, the more the protagonist matures and progressively rejoins the presumed positions of the narrator. The gap between the two sources diminishes, and the reader might be tempted to believe that when we get to *L'Insurgé* (*The Rebel*), the two sources coincide, and that we can treat the monologue of the protagonist like a direct discourse referring back to a single source of enunciation. Such is not the case. Even if the effects produced change, structurally the monologue remains caught up in a double enunciation that gives us to the end the impression of a made-up voice that mimes itself.

The insertion of the indirect free style into the narration in the first degree reminds the reader of the adult's presence. But is the narration always in the first degree? Indeed that indirect free style can itself serve as a support and alibi for a narration in the second degree, which will thus be blended into the narration in the first degree, and will establish a permanent uncertainty as to the origin of the narrative.

Narration in the Second Degree

Among the thoughts of the protagonist that the narrator relates in the indirect free style in the present, some "retrospective" thoughts can be found, the protagonist recalling and relating what happened to him the night before, "the other day," recently, or what happens to him constantly in the present. If ever these evocations are consistent, the protagonist is going to find himself locally transformed into a sort of narrator in the second degree:

> The other day they gave us as a subject—"Themistocles addressing the Greeks." I have found nothing, nothing, nothing![15]

The protagonist sees himself temporarily entrusted with the narration of his own story—an artificial delegation since it is impossible for us to know why and to whom the child is narrating. The narrator does not need to justify the procedure, and he indeed knows that in the final analysis the responsibility for this mimed narration will be attributed to him, which is part of the game of indirect free style in the present. But at first sight the reader can be deceived: he has before his eyes not only thoughts or speech of the protagonist, but a narration that makes the narrator's useless, that seems to take the place of it rather than taking turns. We will surprise even the protagonist-narrator in the second degree using modalizing expressions ("I believe") or fragments of autobiographical discourse which would only make sense (verisimilitude) if he were really telling someone:

> But he, himself! (oh! I'm selling a family secret!) I have seen that his exercises, for the examination, were also done in bits and pieces.(Ibid)

From the moment when the protagonist performs a function of narration, he has at his disposal the same palette of tenses as a narrator in the first degree—with this slight difference that his situation (fictional) leads him to use the tenses of discourse much more often (the compound past and the present with all of its values). How will the reader be able to distinguish, in regard to such a sentence or such a paragraph in the present, if it is a question of a narrative present of the narrator in the first degree, or of a present of the narrator in the second degree, which the laws of concordance of the indirect free style in the narrative present allow to remain as such? He will have to make up his mind according to other signs, the pace of the narration, the syntax, the perspective; but these signs will themselves often be either indifferent (allowing one *or* the other reading) or contradictory (imposing at the same time the one *and* the other reading).

If this second immediately retrospective narration is generalized, one will have the impression of reading a kind of private journal, the second narrator being displaced parallel to the story.[16] But this is only one impression, because this second narrator does not write (someone writes for him) and doesn't really speak either (to whom, when would he speak?). His narration is integrated into the narration in the first degree that controls his reading, and which alone is capable of ensuring its unity and coherence. All the remarks that I was making about contextual and stylistic signs of the first narrator in the indirect free style are equally applicable to this narration in the second degree, which we could legitimately call an *indirect free narration*.

The Voice of the Protagonist

Finally, at the bottom of this ladder, we must place the voice of the protagonist, such as it appears "live," that is to say, in passages of dialogue. But the symmetry that I am establishing in this way is rather artificial: the voice of the protagonist in dialogues does not have the same status, is not perceived in the same manner, as the one that is expressed by the indirect free style. When we take inventory of the child's speeches that are quoted directly in *L'Enfant*, we see that their quantity is insignificant: the dialogues repeated by the narrator are almost all *heard* dialogues whose dominant voices are those of the mother, the father, and other adults, in the midst of which the child's voice makes itself heard sporadically and weakly: questions or candid remarks, beginnings of protestations quickly stifled. These tenuous bits of very elementary language that emerge in the conversations quoted contrast in quantity and in tone with the sophisticated development of the "subconversation" in the indirect free style that represents what the child is thinking without being able to say it, at the same time that the value judgments of the adult are reflected there. Formerly stifled, the voice of the narrator-protagonist overflows today in a derisive subconversation through which he takes vengeance for the oppression and redeems himself from the submission that was his.

The analytical process to which I have just submitted myself does not correspond to the immediate experience of the reader, who is placed before a constantly unstable and ambiguous enunciation. I have, in the course of the analysis, indicated how variations and confusions are realized. My remaining task is to touch on two more general methods through which the uncertainty of the origin of the enunciation is produced.

Ironic Enunciation

An ironic utterance is an utterance through which we say something other than what we are thinking by making it understood that we are thinking something different from what we are saying. It functions like a subversion of the other's discourse: we borrow from the adversary the literality of his utterances, but we introduce a shifting of context, of style or of tone, which renders them virtually absurd, shocking, or ridiculous, and which explains implicitly the total disagreement of the speaker. Irony is a dangerous and tricky weapon: dangerous because it robs the other of his language, it "vitiates" his speech, which he will no longer be able to use with the same effectiveness; and, at the same time, the assailant is out of reach, since all he does is repeat what the other says and so can, ironically, plead innocent. The adversary is led to "commit suicide with his own tongue." Irony is a tricky weapon also because its subtlety, the extreme economy of the method, is such that if the reader is inattentive or unaccustomed to deciphering rhetorical figures, he will take the feigned submission to the speech of the other for a real submission. When we speak, intonation eliminates these errors. In writing, the confusion is produced more easily; it could be avoided only through a change in typography (we could invent ironic characters, like italic characters) which, explaining the distancing, would render it less effective.

The principal targets of the narrator are the experiences and the ideology of the family and the school. Sometimes, the narrator attacks directly, for example, in reassuming on his own behalf the speech of the mother and turning it against the child. Thus, when the coat to be worn at the prize-giving is being made:

No, Jacques, it isn't ready. Your mother is proud of you: your mother loves you and wants to prove it to you.

Do you think that she'll let you put your coat on without adding a touch of beauty, a patch, a tassel, a trifle on the lapel, on the back, on the cuffs of the sleeves! You don't know your mother, Jacques![17]

But most often, the game is played not by two, but by three: the ironic criticism passes indirectly through the imitation of an infantile enunciation. Therefore, an interference is produced between the functioning of the ironic enunciation and that of the indirect free style.[18] How are the two directions of ironic discourse going to be divided in the tiering of indirect free discourse? The child spends his time taking over the mother's speech or that of the school (both of which function in this way like the speech of the superego), and the narrator takes over and mimes this speech of the child. This results in a certain number of quite unacceptable utterances, of the type: "My mother did well to beat me," "I am no doubt a bad son," "Are we a family of idiots?" and so on.

The interpretation of this irony is tricky. The first solution would consist of attributing to the protagonist the literal meaning of the utterance, and to the adult narrator the ironic distancing; in this case, the alienated child would interiorize and take over on his own behalf the speech of the superego which condemns him, and the narrator by formulating and explaining this acceptance would make it intolerable for the reader. And it is a fact that the speech of the superego must continue to count for the child being talked about, to weigh heavily even on his private reactions. But it is absolutely impossible for his relationship to the superego to take the form of the candid and total acceptance suggested by the ironic utterance; too many other signs in context show us a divided and more and more lucid child. The second solution consists, then, of attributing to the child both the literal meaning and the ironic distancing: the lucid child will take revenge on the superego by an ironic reprise of this discourse, and the adult narrator would content himself with transmitting this reaction to us. As a matter of fact, the child is often shown on the verge of revolt, of escape, or of transgression. But it appears rather improbable that his revolt could be explained by the ironic utterances that we are reading—first because the ironic methods that are used are complicated and culturally marked; on the other hand, this irony supposes a third party in relation to which it is constructed, a third party that exists at the level of the narrator (he is the reader) and not at the level of the "interior monologue" of the child. And so each of the two solutions has a shadow of verisimilitude, but is proved to be unacceptable upon reflection. And neither can we attribute the whole of the method to the narrator (although, of course, this is the only right solution), since we come to know all of this through the voice of the child. We can naturally look at this reluctance that holds us back as a reflection of the uncertainty and contradictions of the child wedged between submission and revolt, a not very glorious overlap from which the adult narrator would redeem himself by transforming it, at his level, into an ironic process.[19]

This analysis should be nuanced: the balance of candor and lucidity evolves through *L'Enfant*, and the calculations on "the verisimilitude" of such and such an attitude will vary according to the passages and the contexts. But it has another limit, because it assumes that the whole text must be read like a realistic novel. Now we are not sure that this is indeed the contract suggested by the author, nor that it is the aesthetics of the text.

Verisimilitude and Coherence

The reading of the enunciation is made tricky by the uncertainty or rather the constant variation of the reading contract. The narrative of *L'Enfant* is written at the same time on two different horizons of expectation: on the one hand, the realistic autobiographical novel, in which a narrator remembers and attempts to put back together as faithfully as possible the personal childhood experience; on the other hand, farce, the satirical sketch in the tradition of the fabliaux of the Middle Ages and of the Molièresque comedy, in which the characters are no more than the means of a demonstration and are conceived according to the effect to be produced. The eventual candor of the child will take on a different value according to the passage: sometimes the reader will be able to bring up the question of verisimilitude, and work out the balance of candor and lucidity; sometimes he will clearly be faced with a false naïveté, the childlike character becoming the simple prop in the ironic demonstration found in Pascal and Voltaire,[20] or a farcical puppet as in Molière.[21] Recognizing the code of these genres, the reader will laugh by parenthesizing all calculation on the realism of the scene.

But this formulation is too simple. It implies that the text of *L'Enfant* could be divided into clear-cut zones of realism and of farce. Now it is at best a question of a passing predominance of one or the other; in reality the two attitudes are constantly associated, the rather realistic scenes often being broken by ironic effects or by beginnings of farce, and the farcical scenes being subtly grounded on realistic points of departure, on the utilization of credible reactions and on childlike language. Through this game of blending between different (and even contradictory) expectations and attitudes of reading, Vallès composes a "vacillating" and unpredictable text which keeps the reader at the highest degree of attention and emotion: the impression of "personal experience" that the text provides originates from here. It is due less to the realistic evocation of a childlike word that is spoken, than to this game of voice, to these methods of fusion, of reluctance, and of shifting between the spoken word of the child and that of the adult.

From *Le Testament d'un blagueur* to *L'Enfant*

In the course of this theoretical unfolding, I have analyzed what *Le Testament* and *L'Enfant* had in common. But they also present some differences.

Although the narration of *Le Testament d'un blagueur* is revolutionary in relation to that of the "Lettre de Junius" ("Letter from Junius"), it retains a certain inflexibility owing to the systematic utilization of these new methods: since the text appears from the very start to be a satire, there is hardly any uncertainty about the type of reading to practice; the very broad use of the narrative present produces a monotonous effect, a lack of contrast; finally, the mimed "voice" of the child undoubtedly overshadows the implicit voice of the adult. Monotony and monochord — to those reproaches, others must be added concerning composition. Naturally, it is in relation to *L'Enfant* that these characteristics of *Le Testament* appear to be insufficiencies; it can thus seem unfair to mark the limits of a still lively and very new text, all the more so because some exceptions and false notes (traces of autobiographical discourses, discordances of tense) indicate the course that Vallès will take in 1876.

In *L'Enfant*, the narration is assumed explicitly by a fictional retrospective narrator, Jacques Vingtras. From the first sentence appears the discourse of the autobiographical narrator which had been eliminated in *Le Testament*, modification all the more spectacular since it is precisely the initial anecdote of *Le Testament* that is picked up again:

Testament: I am six years old and my buttocks are peeling off.
   My mother says that you musn't spoil children, and she whips me every morning . . .
L'Enfant: Have I been nourished by my mother? Is it a peasant woman who gave me her milk? I have no idea. Whatever the breast that suckled me, I remember no caress from the time when I was a little child: I have not been pampered, patted, kissed; I've been whipped a lot.
   My mother says that you musn't spoil children, and she whips me every morning . . .

Into a narration which, for the most part, remains consistent with the system of *Le Testament*, Vallès reintroduces classical methods that this narration seems precisely to exclude: the use of autobiographical discourse and the utilization of historical tenses. This return of the classical narrator into a text that functions through the eclipse of the narrator, far from being a regression, is on the contrary the sign of a new revolution. From now on Vallès systematically transgresses the constitutive oppositions of the classical narrative. The law of the organization of the text is no longer coherence or verisimilitude, but the search for maximal intensity through a deliberate game of bursting the conventional expectations.

Autobiographical Discourse

Most of the elements of classical autobiographical discourse can be spotted in *L'Enfant*. But they do not function at all as they do in an autobiographical text:

— They are somewhat reduced in number; the frequency of the autobiographical narrator's interventions diminishes regularly as we get farther along in the book, and becomes practically nonexistent toward the end. The explicit presence of this narrator seems linked to the narrative of infancy; the two are subsequently blurred, the function of commentary shifting toward the protagonist insofar as he becomes responsible for a second narration.

— These elements do not form between them a coherent and regular chain; it is not they that together become part of the narrative as is true of classical autobiography.

— They do not really end up constituting the narrator as a protagonist, whose identity and personality could be grasped. It is impossible to know who "Jacques Vingtras adult" is, where he is in his life. This is all the more striking for us because in reading the letters written by Vallès to Malot, we have an idea of what the discourse of a really autobiographical narrator could have been.[22]

The elements of autobiographical discourse (principally the discourse certifying the strength and the tonality of "memory") are utilized outside the laws of ordinary perspective, in a narrative that has abandoned the concern for verisimilitude. From time to time it is especially a question of making the voice of the adult heard in order to recall his existence and impose a double reading of utterances that seem to come from the child, to engender the system of oscillation and uncertainty between the two voices. The elements of autobiographical discourse are arranged like splashes of color (timbres of voice) in a sort of montage or *collage*. We can think about certain cubist montages in which fragments of image constructed according to the ordinary laws of perspective are inserted in a comprehensive structure that does not respect them.

The System of Tenses

In *L'Enfant*, some long sequences are related in historical tenses (literary past/imperfect), as in the "Lettre de Junius" and in chronicles. Is it a step backward? No. As with autobiographical discourse, we notice an important deviation in relation to the practices of the classical narrative. The sequences related in historical tenses are relatively few if we compare them with the sequences in the narrative present or with those that the narrator in the second degree takes charge of. These sequences no longer form a coherent and regular chain; they do not structure the text. In a way, we might even tend to believe that the proportions and the hierarchical organizations are the reverse of those of the classical narrative: the "contrast" would be obtained through the intermittent passage in historical tenses in a narrative whose fundamental sign would be the present. But is it a question of "contrast," or of its contrary, the "placing at a distance"? In reality, we have the impression that Vallès decided to take no account of the laws of opposition which ground the system of tenses in the narrative — as if he were avenging himself on the sacrosanct rules of the "concordance of tenses" displayed in Latin grammars. His narration is based on a deliberate practice of *discordance*, the permanent oscillation between three regimes, that of the narrative present (with all the ambiguities and transitions that it allows), that of retrospective narration in tenses of discourse (spoken past/imperfect), and that of narration in historical tenses (literary past/imperfect). We enter into a regime of *instability* and *unpredictability*; the changes of the system, the perpetual "sheddings," can certainly, in each instance, be given a shadow of justification (distancing, change of tone, and so on). But in the long run, we see indeed that they obey a general law of variation and of modulation between incompatible systems.

   L'Enfant can be read neither as a diary nor as a monologue contemporary with events, nor as a retrospective narrative, nor even as a realistic montage articulating the two perspectives in a coherent way. Vallès constructs a strange voice for himself that defies all verisimilitude and whose essential law is the search for intensity. This intensity is not that which would come from a faithful rendering of the childish "personal experience," or from the written reproduction of an "oral" discourse; it is founded on the continual transgression of basic oppositions of the written classical narrative. This search for expressiveness seems less to herald, as is sometimes said, the interior monologue (which remains subject to the laws of verisimilitude and coherence), than the practices of Céline in *Voyage au bout de la nuit* (*Journey to the End of the Night*) and in *Mort à crédit* (*Death on the Installment Plan*). It is a question of obtaining an effect of variety and maximum contrast through a system of oscillation between the simultaneous and the retrospective, through a mixing of several systems of incompatible tenses, through a constant blending of the familiar register and the most literary register, all transgressions which make the narration striking at the same time that they make the narrating authority *irretrievable*.[23] The blends of voices between the narrator and the hero appear less like the articulation of two chronologically different cases, than like the result of the work within a voice that mimes, reverses its mimes, jeers, plays naïve, a *made-up* voice that no longer makes any "natural" (that is to say, believable) sound but that perhaps invents a new form of the natural.

Chapter 4
The Order of Narrative
in Sartre's *Les Mots*

The Order of Narrative in Autobiography

What order should a person follow in telling his life story?

This question is almost always eluded, resolved in advance, as if it were not even asked. Nine of ten autobiographies inevitably begin at the moment of birth and will then follow what is called "chronological order." Inevitably the autobiographer also experiences, at least for the narrative of childhood, a certain difficulty in respecting this order: his memories are poorly dated, and he is afraid of confusing periods of time; his memory plays tricks on him—the forgetfulness, the memory that returns after the fact, the document that is found later and contradicts the memory, and so on. Scrupulously, the narrator informs the reader of these difficulties. He derives from this the twofold advantage of seeming to be sincere and careful about accuracy, and of exploiting the richness and poetic vagueness of his inner life. The most experienced of the literary fall into these naïve affectations. Besides, this is what gives a certain charm to these stereotyped clichés. Writing one's autobiography is a little like falling in love for the first time: we are thrilled to discover that *amour* [love] rhymes with *toujours* [forever], *mémoire* [memory] with *passoire* [strainer]. But once this scene has been played, the disparities or the inaccuracies thus excused, the autobiographer does not seriously question the order of his narrative again. Either he wanders at the mercy of his memory, without managing to find the order that structures it: too often this "fidelity" to memory, which does not always go along with any serious quest, is a solution of facility which can, moreover, compromise the relationship with

70

the reader, and turn to chatter. Or else he sets out to follow, as best he can, the passage of time day in and day out, convinced that this order is the way things really are.

However, the contradiction that the order of memory brings about ought to lead to questioning the "natural" status implicitly granted chronological order. The very idea of a "natural narrative" is absurd; at the most, there is conventional or believable narrative, and we know that, in every work, it is the form that determines the content. If autobiographers really wanted, as they often pretend, to convey what is singularly theirs (either as an individual or as a representative type of a group or of a moment of history), shouldn't they first reflect on what structure to give the text? Experience shows that the expression of singularity is generally considered a problem of *content* (exceptional character of the information provided), or a problem of *style* (work of expression, of the play on intonations, and of the attitude of the narrator toward the hero and the reader), but very rarely as a problem of the *structure* of the text.

There are several obvious reasons for this: verisimilitude, convention, facility. Any original inquiry into the structure of the narrative awakens the mistrust of the reader, who perceives something contrived, whereas the use of traditional narrative gives him the impression that this is a personal experience. Studies of the modern novel are useless for autobiography: life continues to resemble Balzac. Undoubtedly because at a certain level (that level on which the easiest communication with others takes place), we live our life like a historical serial: it is chronology that rules all our relationships with other people, from love life to social accomplishments, and ends up claiming to rule all our relationships with ourselves. We are constituted as subjects only in relation to others, and it is natural that chronology, the basis of our story, maintains an essential place in the narrative of life.[1]

In this way that we have of looking at and recounting our life, the fictional model plays an important role, but it does so especially in the degraded form that is the very ambiguous genre of *biography*, that is to say, the narrative of the life of someone who existed, composed by a narrator who passes himself off as a historian. We suspect biography of error, of partiality, of deformation; never do we suspect the very form of its narrative, and its order, to be already, by their simple existence, an interpretation. Witness the fact that there does not exist, at least in France, any serious study of this literary genre as such, nor of the vision of the world that the narrative structures that it uses traditionally imply.[2]

But, you might say, what other narrative order could be used? Can a life story be narrated other than in its unfolding?

How is it, then, we could answer, that certain autobiographers complain about the limits that the traditional technique of chronological order seem to impose on them?[3] And is it not perfectly possible that a text, while referring in the final analysis to the chronological order of classical biography, is itself constructed in another order? From *The Sound and the Fury* to *La Modification* (*The Modification*) or *Histoire* (*Story*), there is no lack of examples. Why do such studies barely interest autobiographers?

The chronological effects that autobiographers allow themselves always have as their terrain the relationship of the *present* of the writing, and the *past* narrated by the writing.[4] It is on this level that all structural effects are found. If the time of the writing has lasted only a few months, as was the case of Stendhal with *La Vie de Henry Brulard* (*The Life of Henry Brulard*), we get a sort of journal of the writing of the narrative; if it has lasted several dozen years, as in the case of Chateaubriand, we get a much more complex composition: having themselves become a part of the story being told, the different tenses of writing allow us to organize a narrative in which the order of tense has gone up and down the thread of the order of the text many times. We have here the invention of an original form of narrative, expressing a certain vision of the world.[5]

But research works—excluding those on the tense of the writing—that deal with the order of exposition of different moments of the past are extremely rare. By research, I do not mean the methods traditionally used in chronological narrative, like dramatic anticipation, explanatory flashback, or recapitulative sequences;[6] these breaches of chronological order, after all, indeed show that this order is unnatural, since we are incessantly obliged to violate it in order to understand the *meaning* of a life story. Up to and including chronological order, it is *meaning* finally that organizes the narrative.

Even when the autobiographer believes that the historical linear order is inadequate, he falls back on solutions that are scarcely better, like the essay that breaks down the narrative into sections that have headings, or the reduction of the narrative into juxtaposed linear series: this is the way that Simone de Beauvoir proceeds in *Tout compte fait* (*All Said and Done*).[7] Such an easy solution shows that the autobiographer is rather unaware of the problems of the genre that is being used. When we hear an autobiographer complain about the limits and inadequacies of the genre, which do not allow him to express the complexity of his story or the depth of his feelings, we have to read these passages as a confession of his conformity. Who forces him to use the ready-made mold of the linear narrative? Why doesn't he just invent the form that suits his experience?

Most attempts at breaking out of this mold do not get beyond the stage of intention or of vague desire - for example, some of the attempts at stretching chronological order, as Claude Roy tried to do it in *Moi, Je* (*Me, I*). The only inclusive attempt that I am familiar with is the one by Mikhail Zochtchenko, who in *Avant le lever du soleil* (*Before Sunrise*)[8] tried to narrate his youth the other way around, by going progressively back in time from youth to adolescence, from there to childhood, to infancy, to the impossible memory of birth. He could naturally follow this order only by abandoning the linked narrative, and by composing his book, a little like Jules Vallès in *L'Enfant*, through the juxtaposition of brief scenes. This backward search, both humorous and pathetic, nevertheless leaves the reader unsatisfied: the method is exploited in too garish a manner, and based upon a rather elementary and ultimately unfruitful Pavlovian psychological theory. It is nonetheless fascinating, despite the relative failure of Zochtchenko, because it symbolizes two of the fundamental facts of autobiographical narrative: 1) that the most general order in which the narrative can take place is that of the *inquiry*, and that it is practically the only really "natural" order (that is to say, it is indissolubly linked to the very situation in which the autobiographical narrative is produced); but this order is masked in general by the fact that almost all narrators choose to conduct their inquiry by following the chronological order of the story; 2) that the final object of any autobiographical endeavor is the impossible quest of birth, evidence that the systematic use of the order of biography masks as well. How many authors, blinded by tradition, begin by stating as a fact that which is indeed the problem of birth: "I was born the . . . "

As interesting as it is, Zochtchenko's attempt remains on the order of method; it seems like an improvised technique, mechanically applied. It does not seem to express an elaborated vision of the world, or result from a controlled work of writing. Reversing an order is still following it. That leaves *intention*.

Actually, a narrative form is not improvised. At the moment when we pick up the pen to write our life story, everything has already been played out; thus if we question ourselves for the first time about what form to give the narrative, we will fall again, after some naïve reflections, into traditional methods believed to be original. The very rare autobiographers who have succeeded in inventing a new narrative order are those who have tackled autobiography after having spent part of their life, of their work as a writer, in research or in attempts that have made them question all that the methods of traditional biography *imply*, and who have formed a new vision of human beings and a new practice of writing. Because they do not rely on such previous research, almost all autobiographers end up falling back, after some qualms, some complaints, or some attempts at innovation, into the rut of chronology, which corresponds in reality to their vision of the world.

Among modern writers, only Michel Leiris[9] and Jean-Paul Sartre have found themselves in the situation of inventing new structures of narrative, because they were undoubtedly the only ones who not only grasped that the biographical narrative was not to be used as a matter of course, but who gave sufficient thought to the idea that a renewal of the autobiographical narrative implied a general renewal of anthropology, and of models of description and explanation of humans.

For Sartre, actually, autobiography has meaning only in relation to a new anthropology. It is not simply a matter of applying a general theory to his own life, but of modifying that theory by this very application. In his *Plaidoyer pour les intellectuels* (*A Plea for Intellectuals*),[10] Sartre clearly shows the dialectical aspect of his investigation. He is not a scientist who studies an object. He himself and the methods he uses are the product of the society he is studying; his investigation must therefore effect a kind of permanent round trip. To dissipate the effects of the dominant ideology, "a passing from the inquiry through the singularity of the inquirer" is necessary. Autobiography is thus one moment of a dialectical inquiry, a moment of vertigo and of metamorphosis. Through this critical turning back on the self, a new beginning for the investigation is made possible.

In 1964, this revolutionary role of *Les Mots* (*The Words*) was not clearly apparent to the general public. They enjoyed reading this brilliant narrative; they liked believing that Sartre was making amends and returning to the fold of tradition by revealing amusing childhood memories, with incisive portraits and an overflowing of plays on language that makes us think more about reversals and facets of a bourgeois style, than about the concise work of dialectics. My purpose here is not to explore all the aspects of this misunderstanding.[11] I only want to show, through a precise analysis of the order of the text, one of the methods through which Sartre made this misunderstanding possible, that is, to show how he made it possible for an original perception of human beings, which is expressed through an important renewal of the technique of biography, to be taken as a classic book of childhood memories.

Therefore each of the two sections that follows has a different purpose and approach. In the first, The Order of *Les Mots*, I try to establish, scrupulously, the order of the narrative; in order to follow the account, it is necessary to have the text of *Les Mots* fresh in your mind, or to skim through it as we go through the demonstration. A reader in a hurry can read in a single glance the result of this demonstration in the chart on pages 80–81. In the section Dialectics and Temporality, on the contrary, I outline in broader terms, and in a more synthetic manner, the conclusions I draw from this analysis of the text.

The Order of *Les Mots*

Les Mots is an autobiography with an apparently traditional structure.[12] Sartre begins like everyone else with his family tree (maternal side, paternal side), his birth, the death of his father, etc., then draws us into a story of childhood that takes him through his twelfth year; after which, believing that the principal characteristics of his "neurosis" are established, he gives a brief statement about how he is situated today in relation to that childhood, and promises, for later perhaps, the story of the crisis that has allowed him to come out of it. A great many chronological indications allow us, throughout the narrative, to situate all the narrated elements. The book is divided into two sections, *Lire* (Reading) and *Ecrire* (Writing), which, of course, give a general indication of the themes treated but refer finally to chronological order, since reading always precedes writing. Sometimes the reader notices some disruptions in the chronological order, but this occurs very often in childhood memories and is justified by the need to regroup analogous things, to give explanations. When all is said and done, the reader remains convinced that a *story* is being told.

Upon examining the order of the text more closely, the reader will quickly see that the signs arranged by Sartre himself to point out the structure of the text—namely the title, the division into two parts that are themselves subtitled, and the breaking up of the text into more or less long sequences separated by blank spaces—that all these signs do not correspond entirely to the real order of the text. I will try to show that the title *Les Mots* does not cover all the material treated, that the split into two parts is in reality secondary, and that their title instead misleads the reader, and finally that the separation of the sequences is very often relevant, but not always, and that it happens to *mask* the real articulations.

In the search for the real order, we will discover:

1. That the order of the text is not to be sought on the side of chronology. Everything happens as if all the events and all the behaviors evoked in the book were quasi-contemporary. The chronological order is utilized only on secondary levels of the text.

2. That when we thought we were reading a story, we followed an analysis in which the logical links were covered up by a chronological vocabulary. The order of the book is that of a dialectic disguised in narrative order.

Chronology

The Break of 1916. One initial fundamental question is asked when we analyze *Les Mots*: isn't it a question, not of the order of the narrated elements, but of their connection with omitted events? The narrative, if there is narrative, brings us from the age of four years (first memories) to the age of eleven and a quarter years (autumn 1916). Why does he stop there? No reason is given for it in the outline of the story. All the reasons put forward concern the analysis: his neurosis has *then* become his character, such as he was *then*, such as he has remained since, and so forth. The reader can naturally wonder about this sudden halt in the narrative *before* the period of puberty, whose crises and changes in general furnish autobiographers with some rich material, and of which we know, on the psychological level, how it reactivates all the problems posed and unresolved throughout the course of infancy. On the level of psychoanalysis, is this not reducing the story of the subject to what Freud calls the "latency period": the problem of Oedipus settled before any conflict by the death of his father, and the crisis of adolescence left unmentioned? This brings to mind the great discretion with which Sartre talks about his sex life. The reader knows, on the other hand, that, in the outline of the story, the break in the narrative could be justified by a major event: the remarriage of Sartre's mother, in 1916, and his departure for La Rochelle. Everything happens as if this event, by uprooting the child from the Parisian setting and giving the family a new organization, explained the sudden interruption of the narrative at the age of eleven. But from a practical point of view, this is not the question in *Les Mots*. We will see that in reality things are more complex, but it is only through the deciphering of the *dialectical* order and of its imperfections that the significance of this chronological break can be explained.

For now, we might also notice that there are in reality two chronological breaks at the end of *Les Mots*: the autumn of 1916, and the composition of *La Nausée (Nausea)* and of *L'Etre et le Néant (Being and Nothingness)*, around 1940. Through the story of the child until the age of eleven, it is the story of the author of *La Nausée* that is the real object of the narrative. This is clearly seen on the emotional level: Sartre is not angry with himself for having *become* this mythomaniac and neurotic child between the ages of four and eleven, but for having *stayed* that way from eleven to thirty-five years of age: "Filthy twaddle: I gulped it down without quite understanding it; I still believed in it at the age of twenty "(pp. 151; 179). The brutal end of *Les Mots*, bringing 1916 and 1940 together, reveals the superimposition of the two periods: through childhood, it is the youth that is put on trial. It remains for us to understand why he remained fixed at the age of eleven for such a long time—a point that stays, for the moment, in the shadow. But for the main point, we grasp that what is presented as the story of the child, laid out in an apparently logical order, is in reality the retrospective projection of the analysis that the adult later made of his neurosis. The real break in Sartre's life is that of 1940, that is to say, the beginning of the awakening of his political consciousness.

Sartre said that he would not write the sequel to *Les Mots*.[13] We can guess why: it is because the "sequel" is implied, already narrated, in every line of this narrative; this would be unnecessary repetition. If *Les Mots* were telling a story, the break at the age of eleven would seem unjustifiable, and the reader would wait for the sequel. Can we imagine the *Mémoires d'une jeune fille rangée (Memoirs of a Dutiful Daughter)* ending at the end of chapter 1, on the threshold of puberty? Well, oddly, the reader of *Les Mots* accepts this break, without waiting for the sequel as if it were a question of a truly chronological narrative, of an ordinary biography: he indeed believes that if the story remains suspended, the analysis itself is terminated.

If the reader really wants to know what has happened in this displacement between 1916 and 1940, he knows that he can read the Foreword composed in 1960 for *Aden Arabie*,[14] which contains a sort of repetition of the analysis of *Les Mots*, applied to the youth and to the life of Sartre up to the writing of *La Nausée*: the distance between the adult who has come back from his madness and the hero is represented here through the opposition of a Nizan whom Sartre understands retrospectively and who anticipated the awakening of his own consciousness, and of a Sartre who is still the victim of the myths of his childhood.

The authentic sequel to *Les Mots* would be, on the level of analysis, the story of what made the writing of *Les Mots* possible, that is to say, of the *conversion*. *Les Mots*, as a matter of fact, is related to religious autobiographies of conversion. Backward conversion, here, that goes without saying. But it doesn't matter. The new convert examines his past mistakes in light of the truths he has conquered. This aspect of conversion narrative is seen even in the ambiguous plays on the addressee of autobiography. Who is the "narratee" of *Les Mots*? Of course, the general bourgeois reader whom Sartre addresses with a sort of aggressive complicity: the book is a settling of accounts. But at the same time, it is an argument invoking the "extenuating circumstances" intended for those who have *understood* before him, and whose ranks he has rejoined; *Les Mots* seems, then, like a sort of posthumous dialogue with Nizan.

What is lacking, therefore, is a second narrative, that of conversion itself, which is realized on two levels: the entrance into history in 1939, then, the incubation of Marxism in the 1950s. The elements or the sketches of this second narrative figure elsewhere, scattered, in a certain number of Sartre's writings, from *Qu'est-ce que la littérature?* (*What Is Literature?*) by way of the article on Maurice Merleau-Ponty (*Situations*, vol. 4), up to and including the texts on the current role of intellectuals (*Situations*, vol. 8). Before *Les Mots*, few things allowed us to imagine what Sartre's childhood was like;[15] for a second volume, on the contrary, we imagine rather well the perspective of the whole.

What technique would Sartre have employed, had he written this second narrative? The chronological order, which his entrance into history would have imposed upon him this time? Or rather, as his statements of 1970 seemed to indicate, would he have constructed a sort of theoretical genesis of his political project? A pointless question, since it seems impossible from that point on that Sartre write such a narrative. It is through other means that he now attempts to realize his project of a "political testament," through dialogues, like those he has just had with Victor and Gavi,[16] or those he is working on with Simone de Beauvoir.

Absence of Chronological Order. Strict chronological order exists in *Les Mots* only in the introduction and the conclusion of the book. The introduction (pp. 11–18; 9–18) recounts everything that precedes the first memories: history of the family, marriage of his parents, his birth, his father's death, his mother's return to the Schweitzer home; it is the child's prehistory, bringing him, thanks to the death of his father, the gift of freedom. The conclusion of the book (pp.193–214; 229–255) shows, from the age of eleven until the period when Sartre is writing, the man fixed in what he calls his "neurosis," and being liberated from it in part after 1940 by his awakening political consciousness. Moreover, it is revealing to juxtapose the beginning and the end, the passage from this empty freedom to the now characteristic neurosis; between the two is opened up the space of transformation, of the passage from one to the other: the project. This story takes up pages 19 to 192 (19 to 229), and covers approximately the period 1909–16 (from four to eleven years of age). At this very comprehensive level, chronological order is respected, and it corresponds to a coherent logical order. Instead of being divided for appearances into two equal parts, one entitled *Lire* (*Reading*), the other *Ecrire* (*Writing*), we could better imagine the book divided into three parts: the "initial situation," with which the child is confronted (pp. 11–18; 9–18): the analysis of the way in which he faces that situation, while progressively elaborating his project (pp. 19–193; 19–230): and the new inner "situation" that is its result (pp.193–214; 230–255), the fixing of the neurosis. Very dialectically, this third part sets up the possibility of a new reaction from Sartre to the situation that he has thus made for himself from the one that was made for him. This third part of *Les Mots* could therefore become in its turn the first part of the second section of the autobiography. We will see that a more concise analysis of the dialectical order leads to articulating the end in a slightly different manner.

But the middle part, which includes the essentials of the story, is not organized chronologically. In reality, all the events or feelings are treated as if they were contemporaneous, and their order of succession in the narrative does not correspond to any history, but to the inevitably successive unfolding, through analysis, of a state of simultaneity, in a sort of ideal theoretical genesis.

All the details used in the first part, *Lire*, from page 18 to page 116 (18–135), take place between 1909 and 1914, most of the memories dating from Le Goff Street, where the Schweitzers settled in 1911. Several times even the date of 1914 is not a firm cutoff point (pp. 72; 83): "Until the age of ten, I remained alone between an old man and two women"; then in 1915, admission to the Lycée Henri IV; pp. 92; 107, the questionnaire filled out in November 1915. When we draw up the complete list of the details of the text that are dated by Sartre himself, we see very quickly that there is no general chronological order in this part, and that the use of chronological order appears only within the defined sections, rather rare all the same (pp. 37–61; 40–69, the stages of the reading experience are of course presented in an order that must be chronological, although no date is given; pp. 67–72; 76–83, the scholastic career is also presented by following the course of studies, up to 1915 with admission to secondary school). In general, the elements used in the narrative are taken from any point during the 1909–14 period, with the only concern being the illustration of the phase of dialectical evolution that the child's project goes through. This technique would not be surprising, if Sartre himself were not playing, in his narration, the traditional game of sequential narrative that his whole chronology, otherwise displayed, refutes.

When we analyze the second part, *Ecrire* (pp. 116–92; 137–229), in the same way, we experience a double surprise: the first discovery that is made seems to contradict the conclusions drawn above; but the second confirms them in a striking manner. We see at first that the second part is constructed following an impeccable chronological order, practically without infringement; thus *Les Mots*, after a thematic beginning that pays little heed to dates, would finally run into a classical narrative, whose logical development would follow the order of time. But we discover at the same time with a certain astonishment that the very coherent narrative of the second part does not follow in *sequence* the events of the first part, but that it *superimposes* itself on them and occupies practically the same period: from 1912 to 1915. It is at the age of seven (1912) that the child becomes acquainted with literary writing (pp. 119–21; 139–41): from seven to eight years old (1912–13), that he writes novels on his own (pp.121–31; 141–53); at the age of eight, that his grandfather clearly explains and guides his vocation (pp.131–40; 153–65); from eight to ten years old, that the child invents his mandate (pp. 140–75; 165–209). At the end of this sequence, moreover, Sartre moves backward; the child-with-a-mandate is no more than nine years old (pp. 174; 207). We clearly see why: it has to do with connecting (pp. 176; 210) with the event of August 2, 1914. The period covered in this way is exactly the same as the one in which all the events that seemed in the first part to *lead to* the second take place. We realize, then, that if we readily believe that the beginning of the experience of reading had to *precede* the initiation into literary composition (that is to say, that the event recounted on page 43 [48], "I knew how to read," occurs prior to that of page 120 [140], "I became a versifier"), it does not follow that the second part is as a whole subsequent to the first. They are superimposed one upon the other, only slightly displaced, one toward the back (technical apprenticeship of reading, in the first part), the other toward the front. As a matter of fact, from page 175 (209), the second part brings up events that outwardly put an end to dreaming about genius: the war of 1914, and that first year at the little Lycée Henri IV (1915–16) (pp. 175–92; 209–29). But we indeed see that this sequence serves as a conclusion, in a way "as a common factor," to the strictly contemporaneous developments of the first and second parts. Thus the narrative of pages 116–75 (137–209) has exactly the same order as the sections on pages 37–61 (40–69) and 67–72 (76–83) alluded to above: it is organized *internally* in chronological order, but externally it does not maintain any chronological relationship with the other episodes. The general order of the narrative is, then, not that of a story.

It is that of a dialectical fable.

Dialectics

Having eliminated the deceptions of a disorderly chronology, the real order of the text appears: it is that of a totally a-chronological analysis, which follows not the temporal order of events, but the logical order of the bases of the neurosis. It is a theoretical and abstract genesis, a sort of analytical fable that shows, under the pretext of the narrative, the rigorous sequence of analyses. This could be summed up in a biblical type of a fable: in the beginning was freedom, and freedom floated over a situation (*Situation et liberté* [*Situation and Freedom*]); freedom was empty, and, to give it form, it made itself a child-model under the gaze of others (*Singerie* [*Copying*]); but one day freedom saw that it was naked and hollow, and it was afraid of itself and wanted to cover itself (*Nausée* [*Nausea*]); and it tried to hide behind other roles, this time internalized (*Bouderie* [*Sulking*]); but the role ended up becoming part of the character, the clothing stuck to the skin (*Folie* [*Madness*]). What the order of the narrative refers to is not therefore the story of an individual, but the dialectic order and approach brought into focus from *L'Imaginaire* (*Psychology of the Imagination*) and *L'Etre et le Néant* (*Being and Nothingness*).

Hence, it becomes easy to define the structure of the book, by abandoning, at the same time as all chronology, the deception of the division into two parts. The book is in reality divided into five periods, which I will call "Acts," believing that this structure is not without analogy to Sartrian drama (for example, *Le Diable et le Bon Dieu* [*The Devil and the Good Lord*]).

The structure of the book is presented in the accompanying chart, with page numbers given in parentheses. My text presents the justification, act by act, of this outline.

ACT I. – *SITUATION AND FREEDOM*
(11–18; 9–18)

ACT II. – *THE PRIMARY COMEDIES*
(*Copying, external usage*, 19–72; 19–83)
A.   *Family comedy* (19–36; 19–40)
     1. Comedy (19–31; 19–34)
     2. Virtual contradictions (31–36; 34–40)
     3. Resolution (36; 40)
B.   *Literary comedy* (37–72; 40–83)
     1. Comedy (37–69; 40–69)
     2. Virtual contradictions
        a. Sincerity (61–63; 69–72)
        b. True readings (63–67; 72–76)
        c. School (67–72; 76–83)
     3. Resolution (72; 83)

ACT III. – *THE AWARENESS OF EMPTINESS*
(nausea, 72–95; 83–110)

     1. Awareness of deception (72–76; 83–87)
     2. Awareness of contingency (76–81; 87–93)
     3. Ennui, anxiety of death (81–84; 93–97)
A.   *Saint* (failure of the family religion, 84–89; 97–102)

4. Failures of the comedy (89–94; 102–109)
5. Nausea in front of the mirror (94–95; 109–110)

ACT IV – *THE SECONDARY COMEDIES*
   (*sulking, internal usage*, 95–175; 110–209)

B. *Hero* (epic, precarious sulking, 95–115; 110–134)
C. *Writer* 119–75; 139–209)

   Event no. 1 (7 years old)
   Initiation to literary   →   *Period no. 1* (from 7 to 8 years)
   writing (119–21; 139–41)   Concrete practice of writing
                                          (121–31; 141–53)

   Event no. 2 (8 years)   ←   Precarious Joy (131; 153)
   Devoted to the career
   of scribbler (131–49;
          153–76)   →   *Period no. 2* (from 8 to 10 years)
                                     Reprise of the mandate in arrogance
                                          (140–75; 165–209)
                                     A. *Writer-Hero* (142–48; 167–75)
                                        Failure: absence of enemy
                                          (148–50; 175–77)
                                     B. *Writer-Saint* (150–59; 177–88)
                                        Modulation (159–62; 188–92)
                                     C. *Writer: Reputation and death*
                                          (162–74; 192–207)
                                        This remains a comedy
                                          (174–75; 207–9)

ACT V. – *MADNESS*
   (175–214; 209–55)

Stage 1. *Apparent recovery* (176–92; 209–29)
   a. The war of 1914–love of the mother
   b. Lycée at 15–camaraderie
Stage 2. *Real madness* (193–211; 229–52)
   Optimism and drive from 1916 to 1939
Stage 3. *Relative recovery* (211–14; 252–55)
   I've changed. Announcement of a second book

Act I: Situation and Freedom (pp. 11–18; 9–18). This section calls to mind the prehistory of the child, and defines the situation in the midst of which he is going to appear, as a pure *freedom*; moreover, it is with this word that the act ends. It is a kind of whirlpool at the center of which is hollowed out an empty space, a pure availability, a freedom: the child. The concept and the experience of freedom, which are at the center of Sartre's thought, are thus carried back to the origin of his story. The analysis of the disappearance of the father before the age of Oedipus functions at the same time like a sort of "insurance" taken out against Freudian psychoanalysis, and like the biographical grounding of the entire "project" of the child. The whole "setting" from the outset is intended to set freedom as an absolute origin, before all history (that is, before all memory and all consciousness). It is not at all related to an awakening of consciousness, to a reaction, that would manifest it in the midst of a story. Freedom is outside the story, the *hole* that engenders any story, that makes the existence of a story necessary — hole, emptiness, that will moreover *recur* indefinitely throughout the story, and will be, in that way, its true motor. This initial freedom must not be confused with a will that is conscious of itself; it is simply a lack, which longs to be filled, a shapeless hole, which aspires to a form. The Sartrian narrative manages to make us see this emptiness as anterior, whereas we understand fully that it resides in the inseparable experience of the movement through which it seeks to fill itself up with something. It is almost as if a Genesis narrative of the world wanted to present to us, as successive steps, the appearance of heaviness, and the event of the fall.

If this freedom is empty, it is not for all that indeterminate, it exists in situation. The satiric painting of the Schweitzer family with which the book opens allows us to anticipate the form that this initial hole would be given in order to exist.

Act II: The Primary Comedies (pp. 19–72; 19–83). This shapeless emptiness is naturally going to take its form from its milieu. Here begins the concrete application of the theory exposed in *Questions de méthode* (*Search for a Method*), of "the particular family—as a mediation between the universal class and the individual."[17] By parodying Simone de Beauvoir's formula on the female condition: "One is not born, but rather becomes, a woman,"[18] we could have Sartre say: "One is not born a child, one becomes a child."

Act II then successively presents two forms of comedy: the family comedy (pp. 19–36; 19–40), and the literary comedy (pp. 37–72; 40–83). I call these "primary" comedies, because the narrative is arranged to make us see them as naïve comedies and comedies without flaw. The child enters into the comedy of adults, in the popular roles of the goody-goody and the know-it-all; he receives from adults, in exchange, a certificate of existence. But this conduct of bad faith inspired by that of adults must be, in this first period, lived by the child in a naïve and natural way. Sartre reserves for act III (see next section) all the child's errors and all the awakenings of his consciousness. He strives hard here to restore what we could call "the good faith of bad faith" and to present (ironically) this state as a kind of paradise, to which the later awakening of consciousness will put an end.

But here again the dissociation of the comedy played out "naïvely" and the awakening of consciousness is a sort of analytical fiction, which, moreover, has trouble taking the form of a historical narrative. It is in this second act that the shifting between narrator and child seems most shocking to the reader, since, at this "level," the comedy of the child is presumed to be lived naïvely, whereas the mode of narrative adopted by the narrator always ends up making the reader believe that the "I" that the narrator is talking about was aware of his deception. There is a contradiction here between the mode of analysis and the thing analyzed, and Sartre fails to maintain the discourse of naïveté that would suppose, for this step, the comedy of the child. He gets out of it ably, by anticipating criticism (pp. 61; 69), and setting up in a crafty way a device of "preparation" for the continuation of his analysis.

Indeed, in each of the two primary comedies that I distinguish, Sartre follows the same order of presentation. First, there is a description of comedy itself (family comedy pp. 19–31; 19–34; literary comedy, pp. 37–61; 40–69). Next comes an account of what I call the potential contradictions, that is, the possibilities of rupture or of opposition, everything that could hinder or ruin the comedy. Thus for the family comedy, the potential contradictions (pp.31–36; 34–40) are Louise's denying mind, the "bad" Germans, who could have hindered or modified the comedy. Mention of these flaws, which existed, but which did not hinder the comedy, is made in order to vary and to make convincing the perfection that had been attributed to comedy at first; on the other hand, it cleverly announces act III (see below). A change of accent will suffice: the *although* will become a *because*; the minor restriction inserted inside the painting of happiness will become the major cause of the rupture. This second concessive part ends in a third, which I call resolution (in the musical sense: return to the perfect chord), a much more rapid third part, but an essential one.[19] Yet this return to harmony, after the utterance and the elimination (temporary) of contradictions, is made in the mode of derision. We return to perfection, to the ending of the comedy, but this is done to stress its emptiness. The internal dialectic of the two narratives of primary comedy is thus constructed in a dynamic way, so that the awareness of the emptiness that will be recounted in act III becomes inevitable. If Sartre fails finally to paint the good faith of an ingenuous bad faith, he makes the reader anticipate, through a cunning system of irrelevancy and shifting, the awakening of the hero's consciousness; this makes it very believable when it happens. Slyly anticipating what happens next in the analysis makes what happens next in the "narrative" indispensable.

This can be verified in the literary comedy. The narrative of literary comedy is followed by the three "potential contradictions" (pp. 61–72; 69–83): a) anticipation of the reader's critical reaction and calling into question the notion of sincerity (pp. 61–63; 69–72); b) "However, I also read real things"—which thus designates, even in the eyes of the child, all the others as false, but which at the same time varies the stifling comedy of the know-it-all, and introduces a certain credibility into the character (pp. 63–67; 72–76); c) story of academic life: school *could have* rescued him from this comedy, but the circumstances did not allow it (pp. 67–72; 76–83). Resolution: "Until the age of ten, I remained alone between an old man and two women" (pp. 72; 83). Exactly as on page 36 (40), the circle of perfection is closed again, but in a mode of derision. So the hero becomes aware of this, and his naïve comedy is going to lead to anguish.

Act III: The Awareness of Emptiness (pp. 72–84; 89–95; 83–97; 102–10). Emptiness could not be aware of itself at the beginning: it has to have tried to "fill" itself (act II), in order for it to realize that it is *hollow* (act III). The shapeless freedom of act I is at first identified with a role in order to accede to *being* it in act II – insofar as this role finally seems a simple role, and it will become aware, in anguish, of its existence. In act III, then, all the events that have some connection with what we are tempted to call "nausea" are going to be brought together. The child is uprooted from immediacy. Let us take note that this "moment" of rupture is purely mythical, and that it is illustrated through a series of events that extend from the age of five (pp. 82; 94) to the age of ten (pp. 92; 107).

The story of this intolerable awakening of the consciousness of existence takes up pages 72–84 and 89–95 (83–97, 102–10): it is understood that here I had to allow myself some leeway in the order of the text that I claim precisely to account for, relating the sequence of pages 84 to 89 (97 to 102) with the beginning of act IV. This leeway is only apparent, and I have chosen to make use of it so as to bring to light the profound exactness of the reasoning. To be faithful to the letter of the text, I would have to insert this sequence, which bears upon the failure of the religious solution, within act III; it would therefore play the same role there as the "potential contradictions" did in act II, at the same time varying and making plausible the scope of the anguish; but, also by showing the necessity of an escape, presented here as a failure, it would pave the way for act IV, which recounts the escapes that succeeded. This interlocking structure of anticipation facilitates the transition from act III to act IV.

"Nausea" begins for the child with the discovery of his own deception (pp. 72–74; 83–84) and that of adults (pp. 74–76; 85–87): here we find the same cruel analyses that the narrator was doing in act II, but now they are taken over by the child himself. Then contingency appears on the level of fate ("abandoned" by his father without a vocation and with no money) and on the level of the existence of the body (pp. 76–78; 87–89); found again here, but presented now in the register of anguish, are elements already utilized earlier in a euphoric atmosphere.[20] Next comes the admirable story of the contingency discovered in front of the granitic necessity of Mr. Simonnot (pp. 78–81; 89–93), all of it resulting in the different symptoms of nausea: boredom, the invasion of the drab and languid (pp. 81–82; 93–94), and especially the anguish of death (pp. 82–84; 94–97); I am leaving aside, then, the failure of the religious solution (pp. 84–89; 97–102). The story continues beyond this failure by imitating the dramatic ascent toward a height: "Yet things were going from bad to worse" (pp. 89; 103); three anecdotes mark the progressive fall of his career as an actor; not only is the comedy hollow, but it goes bad – the haircut transforms him into a brat (pp. 89–90; 103–4), and he suffers two failures, in 1914 and 1915 (pp. 90–94; 104–9). We end up at the height of nausea, concentrated in the horrible position of standing in front of the mirror (pp. 94–95; 109–10).

This third act is the heart of the entire book. It is there that everything comes together again before the book leads to new escapes. It is at the juncture of this third act that Sartre uses the greatest number of dramatization devices in the narrative. While reading it, we are reminded of many passages from *La Nausée*. Doesn't *Les Mots*, moreover, explain how he has become the author of *La Nausée*; and at the same time how he refuses to remain the author of *La Nausée*? Between the titles of the two books we easily imagine a dialectical cross fire: the novel *La Nausée* retrieves the real nausea by making a *word* of it; the autobiography *Les Mots* (*The Words*) tells about the nausea that the words themselves inspire in the man who was able to awaken from his long madness.

We also understand how the first title chosen by Sartre, *Jean Sans Terre* (*Jean without Property*), is justified. It corresponded exactly to that third act – and more precisely to page 76 (87), which is undoubtedly the center of gravity for the entire story ("Jean without Father," we could say).

But we have left our hero at the height of nausea. How is he going to get rid of it?

Act IV: The Secondary Comedies (pp. 95–175; 110–209). The necessity that escapes him – he is going to try to recapture it in another way. The primary comedies were, we could say, for external use: Jean-Paul was playing, *for the adults*, the child roles necessary for *their* comedy. The awakening of consciousness in act III ruins this system: the adults play their role of spectator badly; the child who is playing the role of the child sees that it is a role, and ends up playing it badly. He sees only one solution in getting out of there: he has to *interiorize* the comedy and discover the imaginary. The secondary comedies will therefore be principally for internal use; they are played behind closed doors, the author-actor playing the role of spectator at the same time. He is no longer going to play children's roles required by adults, but the adult roles (heroes) required by the child that he is. The primary comedies were more on the order of imitation; the secondary comedies will be more on the order of sulking.

Act IV is built around three possible roles: *the Saint, the Hero, the Writer*. The first two roles outwardly end up in failures. The possibility of holiness, anticipated in Act III (pp. 84–89; 97–102), is not offered to the child, because of the religious indifference of the familial setting; but it will be understood that the religious vocation missed in this way is realized under the guise of the literary vocation (pp. 150ff., 108–11; 177ff., 248–52). The role of the Hero is made the subject of the first scene of act IV (pp. 95–115; 110–34): they are "imaginary exercises" practiced in a continuous manner between the ages of six and nine, in the roles of daredevil, of avenger, etc. (pp. 97–101; 113–18); the discovery of the cinema (pp. 102–8; 118–25) feeds and inspires these heroic fantasies that extend from Griselda to Zévaco by way of Michel Strogoff (pp. 101–14; 117–33). But Sartre acknowledges the failure of this heroic sulking, which proves to be as fragile as imitation, and does not unburden the child of his contingency and of his solitude (pp. 114–15; 133–34). In light of this resurgence of nausea, a comedy that can take it becomes necessary.

We understand that the split between the two parts *Lire* and *Ecrire* corresponds, in our outline, to a certainly important articulation (since it separates the failed comedies from the only comedy that will succeed), but secondary all the same, since it is only a division within act IV.

Thus the third possible role remains, *The Writer* (pp. 119–75; 139–209), who will be a success. From page 119 (139) to the end of the book the narrative becomes, outwardly, chronological. The "role" is lived successively in two ways: as praxis, as fantasy. Each time an *event*, for which the grandfather is responsible, opens the narrative of a *period*. Here is the outline:

> *Event no. 1* initiation into literary writing at the age of seven (pp. 119–21; 139–41).
> *Period no. 1* naïve practice of writing, from seven to eight years old (pp. 121–31; 141–53).
> *Event no. 2* the grandfather speaks to the child about his vocation at the age of eight (pp. 131–40; 153–65).
> *Period no. 2* reverie on the fantasy of the writer, from eight to ten years of age (pp. 140–75; 165–209).

This is naturally only an outline, which summarizes a more complex dialectic. Event no. 1 is an act of imitation in itself, but the refusal that then opposes the grandfather to Jean-Paul's works makes him continue the comedy for himself. Period no. 1 is thus going to recount a secondary comedy that this time succeeds: beyond the humorous analysis of the techniques of plagiarism, and the reappearence of anguish—but this time on the level of an imaginary content—it must be clearly understood that, for the first time since the beginning of the book, the hero ends up, through this concrete practice of writing, in a form of plenitude (see the paragraph on pages 130–31 [153], which is exactly the opposite of the paragraph that ends act III on pages 94–95 [109–10], but also the pronouncement of the word on which the description of madness, in act V, on page 211 [252], will end).

The child is happy; he has found a form of necessity. Is the existential dialectic that gave rise to the narrative going to end there? No, because naturally that "necessity" is precarious. From this comes event no. 2 (the grandfather consecrates him an official of literature), which makes the child descend again from on high into a feeble and insipid contingency, and urges him in response to clarify, in reverie, the status that he had implicitly experienced during the concrete practice of the writing previously recounted. From whence comes, in period no. 2 (from eight to ten years of age), the permanent reverie on the myth of the Writer.

This part of the text (pp. 140–75; 165–209) is probably densest. Everything happens as if, in thirty pages, the entire analysis of *Qu'est-ce que la littérature?* on the situation of the bourgeois writer in the nineteenth century was summarized.[21] This is not a trick. It is undoubtedly here that the fertility of Sartre's method appears, showing that it is during childhood, and through the intermediary of the family, that the individual assimilates the ideology of his class. The myth of the Poet or of Fame, elaborated in the nineteenth century in response to the anguish and the contradictions of bourgeois writers, responds *also* to the anguish of the orphaned child (Sartre) in search of what he needs: he makes the myth his own and becomes, without knowing it, a bourgeois writer. The private anguish of the child (his place in the family) runs into the collective anguish of bourgeois writers (their place in society).

Under the pretence of narrative, Sartre constructs an analysis in three stages that repeats, this time within the last component of the triad (the *Writer*), the three components of the triad Saint-Hero-Writer (on page 163 [193], Sartre himself will designate these three components in this way: epic, martyrdom, death). To escape from the depressing image of the pen-pushing writer, the child first of all palms off on the writer the powers of the hero, whence the *Writer-Hero* (pp. 142–48; 167–75). Naturally, in order for the dialectic to advance, this solution must fail; from which comes a time of negative transition (pp. 148–50; 175–77: the child sees no enemy to fight, "I was back where I had started from"). As always, the grandfather is there to furnish the child with solutions *in spite of himself*, from which comes the second figure of the *Writer-Saint* — and martyr (pp. 150–59; 177–88). The third figure of the *Writer-Writer*, if I might say, is produced not by contradiction and rebounding, but by an imperceptible modulation around the idea of "death," common to *martyrdom* in the religious perspective and to *posthumous life* in the literary perspective (pp. 159–62; 188–92); the myth of the writer is thus analyzed in its specific features: the way in which the desire for glory expresses the vertigo of death (pp. 162–74; 192–207), and the conception of time and causality that this fantasy implies. These last pages are admirable, for they can be read equally as an analysis of a child's fantasy, and as a striking commentary of *Mémoires d'outre-tombe*[22] (*Memoirs from Beyond the Grave*) — or as a middle-class funeral oration.

Has the secondary comedy of the *Writer* succeeded, then? Not yet. Act IV ends with two fundamental pages (pp. 174–75; 207–9) in order to grasp the structure of the end of the book, and the linking of act IV and act V. A friend (undoubtedly

a psychoanalyst, like the one on page 19 [19], or the one on page 193 [230]) intervenes at a good time, like an associate placed in the room: "You had an even
worse attack . . . than I imagined." And Sartre here protests: his delirium remains conscious and precarious; it is a comedy that must be maintained at every
instant under pain of falling back into anguish. The fragility peculiar to comedy,
by which we are never completely fooled, and which we must therefore make every effort to continue—this finally is the trait common to all the behavior analyzed
in acts II, III, and IV: Sartre often stresses the unstable and ambiguous character
of the behavior of bad faith.[23] On the level of the construction of the narrative,
we realize that there is an easy way to put together a dialectical articulation that
is dramatic in scope—I will try to analyze it later in this chapter. For the moment,
the essential point is that the child remains suspended, in a very satisfying
comedy, but still precarious and half conscious.

As in a well-constructed play, act V must supply a surprising coup de théâtre.
By reminding us that *until this point* we are *still* in the domain of a comedy of
bad faith in part conscious, pages 174–75 (207–9) prepare us for the idea that this
surprising coup de théâtre will be *topical*.

Act V: Madness (pp. 174–214; 207–55). The surprising development is the
change of *place* of the comedy, that is to say, its passage from the conscious to
the unconscious, accompanied by a passage from the precarious to the definitive,
and from the chosen to the endured. It is the most mysterious (not to say nebulous)
aspect of the story. The reader, who was following until then a clear and explicit
logic, has the impression of suddenly witnessing a conjuring trick. Dialectics
gives way to magic. We make short work of the matter; we believe that we have
nothing to reply; but we are left with the feeling that this comedy, in passing over
into the unconscious, has brought with it whatever it was that made it move into
the unconscious in the first place. The coup de théâtre is announced dramatically
(pp. 175–76; 208–9), then realized, so to speak (pp. 193; 229–30). The act unfolds in three stages:

First Stage: Apparent Recovery (pp. 176–92; 209–29). Two events, he says,
shook what little reason he had left. The reader is surprised, since these two
events, when they are recounted, appear on the contrary to be beneficial. As for
the two events (the war of 1914, acceptance into the lycée), the narrative order
is analogous. *In the first phase*, the child is traumatized by contact with the real,
which makes his superiority and his comedy crumble: his lucubrations do not
hold up when faced with a real war; he rediscovers once again (see pp. 73; 83)
that he is an imposter, and takes refuge in a new form of sulking (the reader is
accustomed to this chain of events) (pp. 175–81; 208–15); or else, at the lycée,
in contact with other real children, he becomes acquainted, with difficulty at first,
with democracy (pp. 185–86; 220–21); but each time this contact with the real
ends up being beneficial. In a second phase, the child discovers some positive be-

havior that really fills the emptiness, and which is not an illusion: very curiously the war of 1914 runs into the *love of the mother* (pp. 182–85; 216–20), and more classically the lycée leads to camaraderie (pp. 186–93; 222–30). In short, at this stage, the child finally succeeds in establishing real relationships with *others*, and it is at this moment we are told he is crazy.

No attentive and demanding reader could accept this brutal and unjustified leap. Earlier I stressed the quite visible incoherence of the chronology; but the logical order of the narrative also presents, at least here, some flaws that we must try to understand. It is not a question of making any one judgment on the story of the individual Jean-Paul Sartre, in the name of theories different from his own. On the contrary, it is a question, in the name of the logic within the narrative, of restoring the sequence in its entirety. Indeed, "confession" texts are to be interpreted not as discourses *on* the thing confessed, but as repetition, on the level of discourse, of the so-called confessed behavior. The precise analysis of the construction of the texts, and of their flaws, allows us to prove it.

It is therefore difficult to understand how the fact that he is on good terms with his mother and discovers the joys of camaraderie can transform a child "actor" into a madman and fix a comedy in a character. Naturally, we can make up hypotheses: these two outcomes, outwardly happy, in reality deprive the neurotic of his alibis, but without relieving him of his neurosis; deprived of sustenance in day-to-day living, the neurosis takes refuge in the deep layers of the psyche (see the symptoms of split personality, pp. 182–83; 216–18), and settles itself in a character. If this was the way things were, why would Sartre not have explained it clearly? Why this brutal leap? The reader is left with the impression that there is something missing in the narrative.

We can try to restore the missing piece. What shakes in the child "the little reason that remained" (pp. 176; 209) cannot be the war of 1914 or the lycée, since each of these circumstances, while ruining his comedy, gives him back the sense of the real; it cannot be his mother's love or camaraderie, since each of these traits appears, at this stage of the evolution, to be an unhoped-for solution and actually constitutes what little reason he has left! What throws him into "madness" can therefore be only that which makes this solution impossible: a later stage, in which the mother's love will be compromised, the camaraderie ruined; an event that does not figure in the text, but that will explain that absurd and brutal *fixing* of the comedy, and under the shock, the change of *place* of the comedy, leaving the surface to penetrate the depths ("my delirium left my head and flowed into my bones" pp. 193; 230).

The very text of *Les Mots* allows us to restore these events.[24] They are named quite clearly here; as is almost always true of texts of confession, they are simply not *in their place*. They have been put aside, elsewhere. What brutally breaks the love of the mother can only be her remarriage.[25] This is mentioned only twice, on page 20 (20) ("The picture disappeared when my mother remarried.") and on page 76 (88) ("We were never in our own home, neither on the Rue le Goff nor later, when my mother remarried.")–the latter passage being essential since it justifies the initial title of the book: *Jean sans terre*. What brutally breaks the camaraderie can only be the discovery of ugliness. This is mentioned only twice, on page 91 (105) ("Anne Marie had the kindness to conceal from me the cause of her grief. I didn't learn what it was until I was twelve, and I was hit hard.") and on page 211 (252) where the founding feature of this trauma is dramatically emphasized, but where Sartre seems to say that it is subsequent to the evolution recounted in *Les Mots*, such that he reserves the account of it for the sequel to his autobiography: "when and how I served my apprenticeship to violence and discovered my ugliness–which for a long time was my negative principle, the quicklime in which the wonderful child was dissolved."

The reader of Sartre has all the more reason to suppose that these two events (displaced) are the missing piece in the entire dialectical system of *Les Mots*, that these two events echo the traumas upon which Sartre has based the analysis of Baudelaire's *project* and that of Genet, in the two biographies written before *Les Mots*. For Baudelaire, the shock of his mother's remarriage;[26] for Genet, the shock of "you are a thief" (which must echo a "you're cross-eyed and you're ugly"); in Genet's case, the very text of *Les Mots* invites comparison: the sentence on page 211 (252), "the quicklime in which the wonderful child was dissolved," recalls the sentence by Genet that Sartre used as the title of the first chapter of his biography, "the melodious child dead in me . . . "

Therefore, if we put these two elements *in their place* in the dialectical chain, everything becomes quite clear. But are these elements really missing? In this type of neurotic structure, the repressed element has two ways of executing its return: the *displacement* in the order of the text, which allows it to appear all the same in its true form, but in the wrong place; or the *disguise*, which allows it to appear all the same in its true place, but in the wrong form. Reading these two texts on the love of the mother and on camaraderie more attentively, we notice that the story of the rupture is included within the story of harmony, but with a displacement of person.

1. In the story of the love of the mother, it is the meeting of the man with the "hungry" look, who lusts after the mother and reprimands the child (pp. 184; 219): since the narrative is euphoric, this intrusion makes the bonds between mother and child tighter. In reality, undoubtedly, the opposite will occur. Otherwise how is the tone of modest but sorrowful emotion that ends this passage to be explained? In *Les Mots*, Sartre scarcely familiarizes his reader with this tone. If the catastrophe is not recounted as an event, it is presented as an affective structure of the narrative at the end of page 185 (220): up to the more or less conscious repression, as when we choke back tears: "I remember that I am a man and I look away." The narrative also "turns its head," in a temporary amnesia of the trauma.

2. In the story of camaraderie, the trauma is represented by the "supernatural"

metamorphosis of Bénard into Nizan. As a matter of fact, if we do not go along with the identification,[27] this whole passage falls into the register of anecdote, which would be very surprising in such a compact development. On the other hand, as soon as we realize that Bénard is the image of the "wonderful child," and Nizan the image of the cross-eyed child, the anecdote becomes the anticipated form of the drama of 1917 and depicts it in a hidden form, but in its logical place in the dialectical order: "There was one detail, however, that made me feel I was dealing not with Bénard but with his satanic likeness: Nizan was wall-eyed. It was too late to take this into consideration. What I had liked about that face was the embodiment of Good; I ended by liking it for its own sake. I was caught in a trap: my inclination for virtue had led me to prize the Devil" (pp. 192; 228). There is a new position in front of the mirror; it is like the end of act III (pp. 94–95; 109–10), but this time the comedy is no longer enough to get out of it. This will be madness. This madness has been repeated by Sartre, undoubtedly quite consciously (but this hinders nothing), at the level of the structure of the narrative: the deliberate leap from one stage, which blurs the tracks and places the reader before an accomplished fact — reflection on the narrative level of the internal coup d'état.

   Second Stage: Real Madness (pp. 193–211; 229–52). A new intervention by a fellow analyst ("Temperamental neurosis") is approved by Sartre this time. The change is uniquely topical: the delirium is the same, but it acts now as if it were natural. The comedies in act IV were precarious and ambiguous: the anguish always came back. The madness is complete and happy. It is necessary to get beyond it in order to fear it as madness — whereas the comedy destroyed itself from within. Madness is a block; it has this granitic and necessary quality once envied in Mr. Simonnot, it is *happy*. It is on the word "happy" that this section, such as I have divided it, ends. Sartre added, to boost his dialectic: "It was too good to last." Now, it is beautiful enough to last: from 1916 to 1940, he tells us. From within, this madness looks like happiness: what is analyzed now by Sartre is the optimism, the wrenching from the past, the exalting of progress, the dynamic projection into the future, and, finally, the inversion of the order of time. The first four acts painted a time undermined from within by an initial emptiness that recurred through all the efforts that were made to fill it; it is directed now by a later plenitude that represses the past as it goes along and draws the individual into the building of the future. Time has been turned inside out. Those of Sartre's readers who find that they too have an optimistic "character" have undoubtedly been surprised to see this individually invigorating and socially very productive dynamism qualify as madness, since, after all, it produced the writer Sartre, and they may have wondered if it is not now that Sartre is "mad," his madness consisting in believing that he was mad before. No matter. Madness is a relative notion; we have known this since Foucault and the antipsychiatrists. For Sartre, it is defined as the refusal to live the real, that is to say, the evidence of death, and social alienation. In order for the evolution to resume, a new clash with the real is necessary. *Third Stage: Relative Recovery* (pp. 211–14; 252–55). This is the narrative that promises an incredibly succinct epilogue: "I have changed." On the one hand, it promises the "awakening" that we imagine is subsequent to *La Nausée*: madness that can be cured naturally, it seems, only if it has succeeded. Sartre actually had to become again, *in the eyes of others*, a writer, in order to be able to detach himself from the myth and become just anyone again. On the other hand, he establishes in spite of everything the "permanence" of his madness. Consequently, had Sartre written a second narrative, are we to imagine that it could only have been constructed on a structure that is the symmetrical opposite of *Les Mots*, a dialectical structure in which the negative-motor element (which we try to escape and which always comes back) would have been, no longer the anguish of contingency, but the illusion of necessity. If Sartre did not write a second narrative, it is undoubtedly because he renounced literature; perhaps it is also because the evolution he was supposed to analyze had not come to an end, and because such a dialectic is impossible to construct as long as we have not reached its end. The staggering flow of the epilogue confirms this.[28] Nine years passed between the time when Sartre began *Les Mots* and the time when he went back to it again in order to publish it. Since 1964, certainly, the process of conscious awakening has continued: the crisis of 1968 confirmed Sartre in his criticism of the notion of the intellectual, but yet he continues to live out the contradictions therein.[29] Undoubtedly the latter could be surpassed only in favor of an event that has not yet taken place: revolution, the only possible coup de théâtre for a fifth act. It is from this point that everything will be cleared up. But will there still be intellectuals to write autobiographies, if they were political in nature? Meanwhile, Sartre ends his epilogue by *inverting* the terms of the prologue of Rousseau's *Confessions*, as if to lead the genre ironically back to its origins and to sign the end of bourgeois individualism: "If I relegate impossible Salvation to the proproom, what remains? A whole man, composed of all men and as good as all of them and no better than any."

Dialectics and Temporality

Dictatorship of Meaning

The diagram that I have constructed above is quite obviously only a very simplified approximation: it does not take into account, in its detail and its complexity, the dialectical progression, but simply indicates the general line of the logic of the narrative. Whereas the reader remains completely indifferent to the inconsistency of chronology, the slightest flaw in logic attracts his attention; this means that the logical order is the true order of the text.

Nevertheless, in rereading the narrative that I have taken from *Les Mots*, you will notice that I in my turn have been obliged, by force of circumstances, to tell a story, to assume continually a linear sequence along which the hero was progressing from one stage to the other, according to a dialectical diagram to be sure, but one that is realized in an actual story directed in a very banal way from a "before" toward an "after": dramatic coming to life again, alternation of events and of periods—nothing is missing here. That this story has broken with "chronology" is indeed possible, but as text, it is doubtless narrated according to the best-tested techniques, which keep the reader breathless up to the end.

The first idea that comes to mind, then, is that *Les Mots* would be a narrative of theoretical genesis, analogous to the analytical myths of origins, such as people like Condillac and Rousseau wrote them in the eighteenth century. In these fictions, the succession of the stages of an analysis through which a progressive and genetic montage of the thing studied is assembled is presented as a historical succession of the origin of the thing itself. This is how understanding is explained, by taking an inanimate statue, by giving it smell first, by showing progressively the other senses, and so on. Or current social order, by starting with a real savage, and by having him invent progressively the use of instruments, the building of houses, the family, then, with agriculture and metallurgy, property, and so forth. Or else a mad Sartre, by taking an empty freedom, by giving it a content, which sounds hollow, from whence comes the mime of an internal plenitude, which one day is fixed in madness. The analysis of the stages of a synchronic state end up seeming like an analysis of the stages of a diachronic story.

The transposition is made quite naturally. To the philosopher, it is a natural step, which the laws of language justify. Language itself is arranged in the order of time. As soon as an utterance explores several aspects of a simultaneous thing, it is must do so in a successive manner and thus displays instantaneousness in the time of the enunciation. Every utterance of a spatial contiguity is resolved in a temporal sequence. Fictional description knows these problems well, but phenomenological description does too. Let's give two examples of it, borrowed from Sartre himself. In *L'Imaginaire*, for example, Sartre shows that it is necessary to distinguish two layers in the imagining attitude, even though, in experience, everything is given "in the unity of the same consciousness": he therefore sets down the principle of a "logical and existential anteriority of constituent elements":

> But we must also remember that we can react in the second degree, love, hate, admire, etc., etc., the unreal object we have just built up, and although these feelings naturally occur with the analogue properly so called in the unity of the same consciousness, they represent,

nevertheless, different articulations with the logical and existential priority having to be granted to the constituent elements.[30]

The analysis is therefore going to unfold in sequence what is lived in unity, and introduce, within the moment, a sort of logical temporality, expressing in the vocabulary of time instantaneous relationships of structure, translating the depth or the determining function into the idea of a "logical and existential anteriority." Or else, in *Baudelaire*, he states more tritely in conclusion:

Such in its main outlines would be the portrait of Baudelaire. But the description which we have attempted is inferior to the portrait in this respect—that it is successive instead of being simultaneous.[31]

As long as the thing analyzed in this way is in the instant or simultaneity, the problem remains relatively simple. But as soon as the present state is perceived as the product of a history, the passage will be realized quickly, through the intermediary of the temporality of enunciation, from the order of the analysis of the thing in discourse, to the order of its production in reality. "The logical and existential anteriority" will tend to be represented as a historical anteriority, so much more easily that it will be given narrative anteriority. The thing will happen all the more easily if the explanatory logical diagram used to unfold the thing studied is found to be a dialectical system, because to the diachronic display will be added the appeal of the metamorphosis of articulations coming to life again, and the progression will be transformed into suspense: dialectics is naturally dramatic. Although poor chronology has the virtue of being "faithful" (but to what?), it does not have this particular appeal.

We can, with the help of this idea, attempt a first hypothesis on the relationship of chronology and dialectics in *Les Mots*. The dialectical order will have absolute priority in the construction of the narrative, and all the *dialectical articulations* will have to be represented as diagrams of *historical succession*. If chronological order is found by chance to coincide with dialectical order, it will be respected. If it is badly suited to it, it will be straightened out. And if it is not suited to it at all, it will be broken calmly without even taking the trouble to make a secret of it. Dialectical order obeys the law of the jungle, and it has the cynicism of the wolf facing the lamb: the lamb is always wrong. It might, for example, muddy the water above the point where it is drinking, exactly like an unexpected event cropping up at the age of ten can cause a reaction at the age of seven. If it is not he, then it is his brother. That is of no importance. There is dictatorship of dialectics, and chronology can only obey and tread softly. In fact, all the unexpected events between 1909 and 1916 are treated as if they belong to a vast synchrony, and the order of their entrance into the narrative depends solely on their *function* in the dialectical mechanism. The paradox is that the narrative is presented *at the same time* as entirely diachronic, and that it insists in a scrupulous and cynical way on the datings.

The natural chronological sequences taken up again in the narrative are few in number: the order of the apprenticeship of reading (does not know how to read, wants to, learns to read, reads), of literary writing, of some parts of a scholastic career—it scarcely goes any further. And chronological order is within these sequences and is scarcely concerned with the relationship of the sequences between them. What is more, the narrative impudently presents as chronological purely logical articulations surrounded by a chaos of dates. The most striking example is naturally that of the passage from the first to the second part:

> In any case, things weren't going right.
> I was saved by my grandfather. He drove me, without meaning to, into a new imposture that changed my life. (pp. 116; 135)

This dramatic moment seems to separate a "before" from an "after." Well, before, there are a considerable number of events and states that take place from 1909 to 1915; after, one event from 1912. But the reader is not surprised that the event that changes everything takes place before that which it must change. He is, throughout the book, stimulated by dramatic formulas that persuade because they are pleasant: "There was nothing. Yet things were going from bad to worse" (pp. 89; 103), or else: "It was high time: I was going to discover the inanity of my dreams" (pp. 120; 141), or: "It was too good to last" (pp. 131; 153), and so on. The reader thinks he discovers the model for this ingenuously cynical dictatorship of dialectics, on which the narrator relies, in the hero, as if, in a certain way, the adult was repeating the tricks of the child at the level of the techniques of narration, in the same way that he repeats his antics in the effects of his own style:

> . . . by moping, the inexorable martyr that I was kept alive a misunderstanding which the Holy Ghost himself seemed to have tired of. Why not tell that ravishing admirer my name? Ah, I would say to myself, she comes too late. "But since she accepts me in any case?" "Well, it's because I'm too poor." "Too poor? What about the royalties?" This objection did not faze me: I had written to Fayard instructing him to distribute the money which was due me to the poor. Nevertheless, I had to finish the story. Well then, I would pass away in my little room, abandoned by all, but serene. Mission accomplished. (pp. 161; 190–91)

Such is the narrative "fiddled over" by the child. It is moreover the law of all narrative: meaning determines events, and not the other way around. All narratives are composed starting from the end.[32] Quibbling over details serves no purpose; it is meaning that will end up being right. For the child, it is necessary that he die unknown. For the adult who is writing *Les Mots*, it is necessary that the child end up mad. If an event is troublesome, it is set aside. All the solutions that the child could find, the adult puts aside. If the comedy that he plays goes badly, he will have to find another. But if it is going well, it's the same. Sometimes it is not good enough to last; sometimes it is too good. In any case, the child must end up mad but happy: neurosis accomplished. In some articulations (for example, pp. 131–40; 153–65), it is no longer even the chronology that is broken, but the meaning of the event. If the child finds a successful solution, it is decreed too good to last. It is therefore necessary to find an event in order to break this happiness and go on to the next stage, reverie on the myth of the writer. This will be the grandfather's intervention, accepting the vocation of writer. This apparent success is then going to be dialectically shaped into catastrophe. Writer, yes, but scribbler! The reader, hindered by the subtlety of these analyses, ends up realizing that it is a matter of getting an event, that for once is on the right date, to play a role for which it was ill-prepared.

It is meaning that dictates, and never chronology: if we do not have, for the moment being talked about, materials capable of illustrating the meaning that we want to produce, we will take them two years before or three years after, while pointing this out to the reader, however: "Two striking memories remain with me, though they date from a little later" (pp. 91; 105; what matters is that they are striking). And in order to pass from the account of the Writer-Hero to the one dealing with the Writer-Martyr, a delayed event is constructed, to tell the truth, one that is rather near the Freudian after-event (with the difference, however, that the reactivation of the memory is conscious): "Two years before, in an effort to awaken me to the spirit of humanism, he had set forth certain ideas about which he no longer said a word for fear of encouraging my folly but which had remained graven in my mind. They quietly regained their virulence . . . "(pp. 150; 177).

This dictatorship of meaning is thus deployed unscrupulously. One thinks about the provocative offhandedness with which Sartre announces, at the beginning of his biography of Flaubert, questioning himself precisely about what *order* to follow: "One enters into a dead person as one does a mill." And into the child one once was in the same way. But in the mill, there is no disorder of openings that allows any path to be taken; it is the order of a gearing. It is the great mill of dialectics.

Density of Narrative

Until now, I have pretended to defend the chronological order, by displaying the different "effects" used by Sartre. It was necessary to proceed in this way in order to show the omnipotence of the dialectical order. Now we could only accuse Sartre of faking if he made a secret of it—well, he provides, on the contrary, all the chronological indications that allow us to see things clearly—and if chronological order was a sort of gold standard of the truth. But chronological order has no more truth in itself than the standard measurement registered at the Department of Weights and Measures, no more truth than the axes of the coordinates compared with the functions for which they serve as reference. But even before going through the chronological process, and showing the merits and the advantage of Sartre's technique, I would like to emphasize its effectiveness.

The dictatorship of dialectics, I have tried to show above, gives the narrative a dramatic structure that keeps the reader breathless from beginning to end. Let's admit that autobiographies that produce this effect are rare. They all overrun the opposite mark, even when the narrator intervenes in his narrative in order to dramatize it: because then, he intervenes from the outside, like a *deus ex machina*. Whereas here, the very order of the chain of elements in the narrative is enough to create this effect. It does so all the better because the rhythm of the narrative is very lively and snappy: no dead time, no monotony either; the flashing accelerations, the reversals of situation constantly renew the kind of suspense on which the book is based. The ordinary rhythm of autobiographies would instead look like that of a romantic serial: the vague expectation of the future and the premonitions are deadened by the leisure of the writing, which give the actual text the image of a weak and wavering duration, and of hazy distances. In *Les Mots*, on the contrary, the rhythm is that of a play; it obeys the imperatives of scenic representation: to deploy within a limited time, with maximum clarity, all the stages of a plan. From whence comes the clarity, but also the harshness, of the contours: they are neither remote nor vague.

At the same time that they carry the reader along, this density and this tension fascinate, that is to say, prevent the reader from having any other attitude than adhesion or refusal. The plenitude of meaning ensures that no margin is left, for example, in the interpretation of the text. (1) *All* the elements of the narrative are explicitly signifiers. Whereas often in autobiographical narratives, relevance tends to slacken, and the narrative fluctuates around clarified meanings, leaving a margin of interpretation for the reader, here the narrative is adjusted, meaning and narrative are coextensive and absolutely indissociable. (2) All these significations refer to one unique system in the midst of which they are articulated. It is impossible to uproot these significations from their function in the system, impossible to imagine another system that takes the whole of signifying elements into account—this is extremely remarkable. Quite often, insofar as autobiographers are incapable of controlling their life, they are also incapable of *closing* the structure of their text. At best, they organize the uncertainty of meaning in a system of ambiguity, and stage the *game* of interpretation: this is the case of Rousseau when faced with internal contradictions; of Gide composing, with a diabolical cunning, *Si le grain ne meurt* (*If It Die*) on the simultaneous use of a double problematic (that of sin and that of nature); of Leiris wavering over psychoanalysis. Here, there's nothing like that; the text presents itself as a whole, as an unimpaired totality. If we thought we caught sight of a flaw here, it was a flaw within the logic (the madness) of the system, and that ensures its functioning. The only retreat left to a skeptical reader who is naturally incapable of proposing another interpretation, is to see, in that perfection and that omnipresence of dialectics, a course of protection. Claude Burgelin advanced such a hypothesis in order to account for the totalizing proliferation of *L'Idiot de la famille* (*The Idiot of the Family*),[33] and it could also be used to explain the density of *Les Mots*. All the endings of the text that could lead to a psychoanalytic reflection are flawlessly blocked, either by the interventions of fellow psychoanalysts or by some small preventive developments (note pp. 48; 54).[34] But bringing such a diagnosis of "course of protection" to bear on the closing of the text, is that not itself seeking to protect oneself from a text that is perhaps declared closed only because it opens on a final truth that is difficult to sustain: namely that the neurosis is *political*?

On the whole, this dictatorship of meaning in the narrative is not at all stifling. If someone were to read our analyses without having read *Les Mots*, he would imagine at best an abstract and dry work, at worst a propaganda narrative. Anyone who has read *Les Mots* knows that it is nothing of the kind. The tremendous success of the book proves it. It is even a book that can be read without being at all familiar with Sartre's thought: at most one will be bothered by a few formulas, or will find it heavy going toward the middle of the second part. For the remainder, one will have the impression of "authentic" and of "slice of life," which the autobiographer often strives for without success. That's because, if there is no part of the narrative that is not explicitly meaningful, by the same token, there is practically no meaning that is not explained through a story (a story that can, moreover, be condensed into one word, one sentence, or extended to the dimensions of the scene or the anecdote) or through a description, a "phenomenological" mime. Meaning bursts out of the very technique of description of the concrete personal experience, where each gesture, each action, is described by defining the lines of force, the meaning of the *project* that it manifests. This quite effective technique had already been used by Sartre in one of his first narratives, *L'Enfance d'un chef* (*The Childhood of a Leader*), which is not without ressemblance to *Les Mots*: parody of the narrative of childhood, attempt to analyze the origin of a neurosis, ironic demystification of a course of bad faith.[35] Indeed the "phenomenological" description makes perceptible (and so comical) the disparity between the appearance of the action and its real function. The more compact the description, the more the gap becomes obvious: very often, it is concentrated in a witty remark, where it would be wrong to see a simple game in a segmented style. It is deception or bad faith that is aimed at and hits on target.[36]

There is therefore fusion of narrative and dialectics, as much on the level of the sentence or the paragraph—thanks to the "phenomenological" style that defines intentionality—as on the global level of the book—thanks to the dialectical articulation of all the intentions defined in this way. Sartre has, then, avoided the stumbling block of the propaganda narrative, but at the same time, he has been able to provide a neat solution to one of the classical difficulties of all childhood narratives. Aside from traumatizing events, and some historical references, the memory of our childhood is not presented naturally in the form of a story; for this reason, the autobiographer, in order to set some order, will usually have to regroup his/her memories by *themes*: academic and family life, sports, the problem of death, the problem of birth, the discovery of nature, the taste for entertainment, and so on. It is rather easy to regroup these memories, but much more difficult to articulate the groups obtained like this and avoid the disparity of juxtaposition. In general, this can be pulled off by staggering the entry of these thematic developments along a chronological development, or through purely rhetorical transitions that deceive no one. Too often, the thematic order is only the modest cover for the difficulties there are in finding an order to one's life. Sartre has succeeded in utilizing these thematic developments, in themselves almost too easy, by placing them within a rigorous dialectical order. Readers of traditional autobiographies were not confused by reading *Les Mots*, because there they found all the classic themes from childhood memories: my first books, my first memories of grade school, my contacts with death, my discovery of the cinema, and so forth, right up to the classic memories of entering high school, pictures of good pals. But they did not really notice that these little pieces were "double agents" and did not have the innocence and relative insignificance that they have in current autobiographies. Moreover, the greatest accomplishment of *Les Mots* is that it successfully reconciles the most traditional techniques of the genre of childhood memories, with a rigorous dialectical construction. If I have been able to talk about faking, it is because of the places where the "weld" remains visible. But, essentially, the book is built like a trap, because of the two simultaneous readings that it makes possible: chronological and thematic in appearance, dialectical in reality. It remains for us to find out who is caught in the trap: Sartre retrieved by bourgeois readers, or the latter snatched up in spite of themselves in a dialectical machine? The misunderstanding remains complete. *Les Mots* undoubtedly could have the corrosive power intended by Sartre only after the appearance of a second volume clarifying the last part of the story, where the excessive density and rapidity appear to the average reader like a still obscure whirlwind, and allow him to avoid having to draw his own conclusion.

New Vision of Time

By privileging meaning, at the expense of chronology, would Sartre be indifferent to temporality? Not in the least. It is now necessary to go beyond the current and naïve opposition on which I have relied since the beginning of this analysis. Too many autobiographers see in chronology the basis of temporality, whereas it is only one aspect of it. To take this aspect as the essential point, to privilege the "social settings of memory," is in reality to choose a certain conception of human beings. The habitual techniques of chronological narrative are not "neutral," simply consistent with something that would be the "nature" of things. They are based on two postulates that Sartre has as a matter of fact questioned in his phenomenology of temporality: the existence of a past in itself, and the identity of the relationship of succession and of the relationship of causality.

In the analysis that follows, naturally, I am studying Sartre's views on time, such as it appears in autobiography, for a subject who is facing his past. It is a completely different problem from the problem of time in the novel. Sartre's theories on the novel centered on the present, on a freedom that is in the process of creating itself, and that cannot know the future; these reflections, which correspond to the technical inquiries of *La Nausée* and of *Chemins de la Liberté* (*Roads to Freedom*), lose all relevance as soon as the point of view on time changes. It is no doubt because she did not understand it, that Simone de Beauvoir encountered so many difficulties in her autobiographical undertaking.

Everything happens on the whole as if the Sartrian narrative had known two "regimes": that of *fiction* centered on the present[37] (from *La Nausée* to the break in *Chemins de la liberté*), and that of *biography*, centered on the past (from the portrait of Baudelaire to the three volume opus on Flaubert, which, moreover, will itself undoubtedly remain unfinished); insofar as the technique refers to metaphysics, we might ask ourselves if the abandonment of novels and the proliferation of biographies after 1947 is not the delayed result of the awakening of political consciousness, and does not reflect the passage from the existential phenomenology of *L'Etre et le Néant*, to the much more ambitious anthropological aim of the *Critique de la raison dialectique* (*Critique of Dialectical Reason*). This is only a hypothesis. It remains that, starting with *L'Etre et le Néant*, Sartre expounds a conception of temporality that brings the habitual chronological narrative into question:

1. The existence of the past in itself, assumed by so many theories of memory and time, is condemned as an absurdity.[38] To assume a past in itself, is to cut it off from the present, and to run the risk of never being able to explain how it happens that we perceived this past. There is a past only through *my* real present. Sartre's analyses, done at a time when he was undoubtedly scarcely thinking about autobiography,[39] describe the natural situation of any autobiographer, just as of any living person. What he does, in a certain way, is to condemn the use of traditional biographical narrative, and to put aside the historicizing vision of life. Not that it is necessary to put them aside completely, because, after all, the social settings of memory are *also* part of my relationship with the past; but they are far from being the final term to which everything must refer. This idea clashes strongly with the common illusion, the illusion that is undoubtedly necessary to the autobiographical quest, however, and analogous in time to the necessary illusions of perception in space. This is clear in autobiography: each of us imagines that it is the being in itself of the past that is the object of his narrative (from which comes the concern for exactitude, the cross-checking, the construction of a

chronological story), and perceives his real relationship to this past as a hindrance (gaps of memory, confusion, distortion, and so forth), as a negative and limiting factor. This illusion (since there is a past only in this relationship) is found everywhere; I refer to André Maurois's very candid example in *Aspects de la biographie* (*Aspects of Biography*). But we will be more surprised to see that, despite her existentialist background and the knowledge she had, from 1954, of Sartre's autobiography, Simone de Beauvoir has constructed her whole autobiography on this naïve conception of the past in itself. This is seen as much in the techniques that she uses, as in her reflections on the problematic of the genre, even when she formulates them in an apparently existential vocabulary. If she criticizes chronological narrative, for example, while still continuing to use it, it is not because it betrays the being-for-me of the past, but its being in itself: she visibly imagines the past as a succession of presents, each one having its being in itself (that is to say a past and a future inside each present). From an existentialist point of view, she is right to think that each present *is* like this *when it is present* (that's why she would rather use the personal journal openly, instead of trying to disguise it in autobiography), but wrong to think that the past is made up of an addition of presents in itself, which it would be necessary to reconstitute one by one and align in chronological order. It is nevertheless what she *wants* to do, and what she complains about not being able to do:

> By imprisoning it in words, my account turns my history into a finite reality: and it is not a finite reality. Yet at the same time it scatters it abroad, breaking it up into a string of set, distinct moments, whereas in fact past, present and future were inextricably bound together in each one of them. I may write "I got ready to leave for America": but the outcome of that once-living project, its then future, has now sunk and vanished behind me, just as a plan that no longer has any vitality would disappear. Again, every stage of my life was haunted by those I had lived through earlier—my life as an adult by my childhood and adolescence, the war by the years before the war. By following the sequence of time, I put it out of my power to convey these interconnections, this dovetailing; so I failed to give my past hours their threefold dimension: they march by, devoid of life, reduced to the flatness of a never-ending present, cut off from what went before and from what came after.[40]

Reading this statement of failure, which is very clear on the apparent reasons for the failure, but blind on the profound cause (the desire for the past in itself), we understand how much, *a contrario*, Sartre's synthetic and dialectical study is justified. Simone de Beauvoir's failure was, from this point of view, foreseeable from the beginning of *Mémoires d'une jeune fille rangée*. A comparative study of the narrative technique in the first chapter of these *Mémoires*, and in *Les Mots*, shows indeed two things: *in appearance*, Simone de Beauvoir seems to utilize a dialectic analogous to Sartre's, to the point of giving her text, published before

Les Mots, but after Sartre drafted the first version of it, a look of imitation; but *in reality*, as soon as the order of the narrative is analyzed, we see that it is nothing of the kind. In *Les Mots*, the dialectic is disguised as chronology; in the *Mémoires*, it is the chronology that tries to pass itself off as a dialectic. Sartre follows the order of meaning shamelessly: he disguises the logical sequences as chronological succession; Simone de Beauvoir disguises the very wisely chronological sequence of the narrative in dialectics, and tries to make us accept as articulations of meaning the joinings of a thematic juxtaposition.

But, you might say, isn't denying all existence to the past in itself contesting the very possibility of writing an autobiography? Is there no use in being as exact, as accurate as possible, in reconstructing the past such as it was? Under the pretext that the past is only a dimension of *my* actual present, can I recount just anything? Quite obviously, *no*. But we must not confuse the demand for accuracy, which is in reality a necessary principle, but *negative* (*do not* forget, *do not* distort, etc.) and *relative* (since it refers back to the image of the past in itself such as it exists within the being-for-myself of the past), with the demand for meaning, which is the positive and first principle of the autobiographical quest, positive because this is what engenders the structure of the text and first since it has as its function to restore the being-for-myself of the past. In order for there to be autobiography, these two requirements must be met; but it is also necessary that they be hierarchized. This is what happens in *Les Mots*; all the episodes mentioned are, within the realm of the possible, dated and localized, and Sartre has scrupulously obeyed historicity; he has also sought to imagine as clearly as possible what he was *then*. But he does not believe in the least that these efforts help to tell the truth about the "past-in-itself": at best they help (him) not to make a mistake.

2. Every narrative that respects chronological order implies a certain conception of causality that is sketchy and mechanistic, and is based on the illusion of *post hoc, ergo propter hoc*: a formula that perhaps would be valid for a mechanical, linear isolated system, but is no longer valid as soon as the system becomes complex, dependent, and is no longer mechanical. Human temporality does not function like this—proved, morever, by all the instances where autobiographers stretch chronology. Even if we, like Simone de Beauvoir, wanted to find the being in itself of the past, it is not by adding up the temporality inside each moment in a linear order that we would manage to do it. Suppose that within my relationship to the past, I want in this way to look at the past in itself; I will never succeed in doing so by accumulation. Only a global, synthetic vision can apprehend temporality. It is not a question of representing the multiplicity of moments, dividing the space of life like Zenon of Elea, but of proving movement by advancing, by sifting out the law according to which movement is engendered. Autobiography, for Sartre, will not be "the story of my past," but "the story of my future," that is to say, the reconstruction of the *project*.

The Sartrian notion of project seizes temporality in its profound unity, in its law. Elaborated on the theoretical level in *L'Etre et le Néant* and taken up again in *Questions de méthode*, the notion of project has been utilized by Sartre constantly, as much in his direct relationships with others[41] as in his biographies. Man is not a causal system, but a freedom. Placed in a certain situation, he does not submit to it; he invents a way out of it, within the field of the possible. This invention of the future is not situated *in* the framework of time; it is this invention of the future that constitutes time.

All behavior that freedom invents in this way manifests a fundamental and *unique* project, elaborated in the course of childhood, and one which has become a permanent and timeless element in the story of the individual. "A life, it is a childhood dressed up in various guises."[42] To write a biography is thus to try first of all to identify this project, and to rediscover it in its origin. On the accuracy of this first step depends all verisimilitude and interest of the autobiographical or biographical narrative. Deduced from several ways of behaving that have been judged fundamental, the project is used next as a hypothesis to account for the totality of behaviors. This inductive and synthetic method might seem hazardous or chimerical: hazardous in the sense that an error at the outset is multiplied and ends up by distorting the whole (for example, if Flaubert had learned to read normally?); chimerical, in that we can see here the same type of retrospective illusion (the unique result makes us imagine that the cause was unique also); and troubling too, since freedom seems here to be only another face of necessity.[43] But there is "retrospective illusion" only in the eyes of someone who lives the chronological illusion: it is illusion against illusion; and it is shocking fatalism only if we have not understood that, for Sartre, freedom is not capricious pleasure, but the way in which human beings can contribute to the dialectics of history, can realize it.

Perceived as the sole direction of the individual's most characteristic ways of behaving, the project is thus taken as a reading hypothesis of the whole of his story. The facts, events, feelings, and ways of behaving are then perceived not as elements to be organized chronologically in order to reconstruct a story, but as *signs* to be deciphered, in order to reconstitute a project, which does not belong exclusively to any time period and which includes them all.

That the project does not belong exclusively to any time period does not mean that it has no story — wouldn't it be because the project develops within a situation, which has one itself? But its temporality could not be apprehended in a chronological way; it would therefore remain only a dust of indecipherable facts. The structure of the narrative in *Les Mots* gives us the impression of not being *successive* (despite the decoys of the presentation), but *cumulative*: not only because it is necessary to take notice of a kind of memory of the text, which is true of any narrative (a narrative is something that constitutes a memory for you; from the tenth page, the reader has become someone who believes that he is remembering); but because the dialectical order that was adopted ensures that nothing that has happened on the fundamental level is ever abolished, but that the motivating forces (freedom and anguish, that is, the fear that freedom has of itself) and the mechanisms set in motion (flight in the imitation of a necessity) continue indefinitely to reproduce themselves at every stage of composition.[44] The anguish is always there and will always be the same: every story, in each of its moments, only repeats, only modulates, the fundamental project, while offering, of course, new outcomes and new metamorphoses, while opening differently the field of possibilities, but without changing anything about the problem at the point of departure that freedom has proposed. This results in a relative indifference to the anecdotal order of succession of different events that the problems and tentative solutions in the midst of a same synchrony *manifest*, that is to say, of a broad period when we can consider *grosso modo* that the fundamental project appears within a constant figure. Of the irreversible, or rather irreducible, there is only freedom and anguish: they resurge indefinitely everywhere, which gives the text moreover the appearance of a tragedy ruled by fate; furthermore, everything being reversible and precarious, we circulate freely forward and backward, even if, for the conveniences of exposition, we use the vocabulary of irreversible and causal succession.

The main problem, in the narrative of a project, is thus the determination of broad zones which can be treated like synchronies, and their articulation with fundamental breaks, which on the one hand limit these zones, and on the other engender *all* the behaviors manifested there. In order to be *fundamental*, the project is not necessarily "chronologically" *first*. On the contrary, it will most often have the characteristic of being *central*, of being represented as a movement of reversal where the past engenders the future, occupying in the story a position that is always second, the initial and "previous" being accorded only to the situation in front of which this freedom is placed. Naturally, the problem is knowing if what looks in the dialectical analysis like a break, a moment of reversal and of reaction, is presented in the *story* like a dramatic event and experienced as irreversible (an event whose model is conversion, the bolt out of the blue, trauma), or if it is not itself coined, dissolved, elaborated progressively in the course of a more or less broad period, which we then could treat again synchronically. We see that repeated on the level of the historical appearance of the project is the same problem on the level of its development. Sartre has clearly stated at the beginning of *Saint Genet* that this question has in reality no importance at the level of the story, since it changes nothing in the nature or the existence of the project; at the level of the narrative, it is certainly more practical (that is to say, at the same time for effect, more favorable to dramaturgy, and for meaning, more faithful to the dialectic) to *represent* it by one unique and central event.[45]

We see henceforth the double treatment that dialectical narrative applies to chronological data: to *display* in a kind of logical succession (where the dialectical articulations are expressed in terms of dramatic sequences) elements taken in any order in the midst of a broad chronological period treated in synchrony—this in order to depict *ways of behaving*; to *concentrate* in one unique event all the events that manifest the points of articulation (awakening of consciousness, choices). It is, then, a general *redistribution*, which takes note of chronology in two ways: from the point of view of illusion, by borrowing its language; from the point of view of reality, on a very global level, by accounting for the fundamental meaning and the order of development of life, and by relying strongly on the breaks that are found to be simultaneously important chronological events and dialectical articulations at the level of analysis–a rare coincidence, moreover.

The entire biographical narrative thus starts off from a rather simple initial cell, from a schematic trait in which the project is summed up. G. Genette suggests that we imagine that narratives like *The Odyssey* and *A la recherche du temps perdu* (*Remembrance of Things Past*) are the monstrous expansion of an initial sentence which would be "Ulysses returns to Ithaca" or "Marcel becomes a writer."[46] Undoubtedly this is true of every narrative. The examples of G. Genette are striking, precisely because of the monstrosity of the expansion that hides the seed. Sartrian biography is fascinating, in the reverse sense, in that, up to and including his most monstrous expansions (*L'Idiot de la famille*), the seed remains visible. For *Les Mots*, the seed is, in its most simple form, a variation of the classical autobigraphical seed. Every autobiography is the expansion of the sentence: "I became myself." We would have here: "I *made* myself," which nevertheless must be stated precisely, substantiated; this would be, then, the little pseudo-biblical diagram that I proposed earlier, or the outlines or sketches that Sartre himself has traced either in *Les Mots*, or in interviews summarizing the book.[47]

As Proust's work is entirely the development of one single text, so Sartre's narrative work will seem perhaps like the development of one single structure of biography. Indeed, at the end of this investigation on the order of narrative in *Les Mots*, it is confirmed that the change made by Sartre in the traditional structure of the autobiography is only one consequence and one aspect of the revolution that he caused in biographical narrative in general, and that this manifests, by applying it phenomenologically to individuals, a new anthropology. To pursue such an inquiry, it would be necessary to extend this study of *Les Mots* to all biographical narratives written by Sartre. It seems that, in the classification of these narratives, it is perhaps not the autobiography-biography opposition that would be relevant, despite the problems posed by the use of the first person. Sartrian biographies are divided instead into two groups, according to the nature of the relationship of the narrator to the hero and the real information that he has about the story. In a first group would be found, for example, the biographical outlines of Nizan and of Merleau-Ponty, and *Les Mots*, texts which resemble one another by their density, their incisive and concrete character; they are phenomenological narratives of the fundamental project of three people that the author visited at great length and that he apprehends directly at first. In a second group, following chronological order, at the same time as the developing order of the fullness of the analysis, *Baudelaire*, *Saint Genet*, and *L'Idiot de la famille*. In these three cases, the man was at first (for Genet) or solely (for Baudelaire and Flaubert) known through his works, and the actual personal experience (in particular for infancy) largely escapes the biographer. The more information is lacking, the more analysis develops, proliferates in monstrous expansions: the less we know of it, the more we are obliged to calculate, to deduce, and to replace the singular by the universal, and the more we take pleasure in doing it. Whence the very different allure of these biographies, in which meaning is no longer "adjusted" to the narrative but floats around it. Between these two groups, privileged comparison must be established between *Saint Genet* and *Les Mots* because the dialectical order that structures them is analogous, and because both of them have, historically, the most verisimilitude (*Saint Genet* is much more believable than the *Baudelaire* or the Flaubert, perhaps simply because Sartre knew Genet and is his contemporary). The dialectical order of exposition of the project is as it were immanent in the narrative in *Les Mots*; in *Saint Genet*, scraps, pieces of narrative, are found set, utilized, integrated in an openly philosophical text; Genet, or Gustave in *L'Idiot de la famille*, often plays the role of the friend Peter who came complacently to lend his fictitious assistance to Sartre's analyses in *L'Imaginaire* and *L'Etre et le Néant*: the singular universal then becomes again very quickly universal-singular-universal. Whereas the autobiographical situation, or amico-biographical, leaves to the singular universal that singularity that makes us believe that it is authentic. Between the two series of biographies, there is the same difference as between enormous laboratory works carried out *in vitro* in fictitious conditions (enormous machine constructions built leisurely without that constraint and those limitations that any real situation involves), and an analogous work, executed *in vivo* in a real situation. The biographical act therefore engages him who is writing (if Nizan and Merleau-Ponty are dead, their relationship with Sartre is still living; and for Sartre, his life is still *in front of him*); totalization can no longer be given the facility of allowing one part of the elements to be totalized: facts, acts, ways of behaving, projects, everything is there, and can only be totaled up in a narrative.

The invention of the dialectical narrative in *Les Mots* is thus a doubly important event. From the perspective of the evolution of the autobiographical *genre*, it is one of the rare renewals of technique and of vision that we have seen in a long time. Among Sartre's works, *Les Mots* is the most "totalizing" that he ever wrote. Naturally, in order to express a judgment such as this, we must place ourselves in a posthumous perspective and one of posterity that is from now on unacquainted with his project. But that he does not write for later generations would not prevent them from reading it and from causing in the *reading* of his work a distortion that he certainly foresees. If we might say that *Les Mots* is the most *totalizing* work, it is because we find grounded here, *in one single form*, in a perfect synthesis, the two models of philosophical discourse and of narration; such fusion had been attempted many times before in different ways, in the fictions of *La Nausée* or *L'Age de raison* (*The Age of Reason*), in phenomenological descriptions, in dramatic structures, and in biographical undertakings. But in all the attempts, admirable in their genre, equilibrium was not acheived, or rather the weld remains visible. The same thing will undoubtedly happen to Sartre as happened to Rousseau. Rousseau was for his contemporaries the author of the *Discours* (*Discourse*), of *La Nouvelle Héloïse* (*The New Héloïse*), and of *L'Emile* (*Emile*), texts that are today if not unreadable (because in recent years they have become readable again), in any case read very little; he is for us above all the author and the model of the *Confessions*. Sartre was, for his contemporaries, the author of *La Nausée*, *L'Etre et le Néant*, of *Saint Genet*, of fascinating dramatic work; for posterity, he risks becoming above all the author of *Les Mots*. In 1964, *Les Mots* was perhaps a work of conflict, pamphlet as much as autobiography; its opening into a later narrative, like the actual political evolution of Sartre, still gives it all its virulence today. But it is without doubt its destiny to be a virtually posthumous book, because it is the only one to have succeeded, by its very *form*, in totalizing a life.[48]

Norman Rockwell, *Triple Self-Portrait* (1960). Original oil for the cover of the *Saturday Evening Post*, February 13, 1960. Printed by permission of the estate of Norman Rockwell. Copyright © 1960, estate of Norman Rockwell.

Chapter 5
Looking at the Self-Portrait

I do not know how to paint. I do not really know anything about painting. I go to museums. I have had love affairs with portraits. Twenty years ago, at the Pitti Palace in Florence, I was quite taken with a "Portrait of an Unknown" by Titian. It is also called "The Man with the Green Eyes," or "Grey." I have just seen it again. So precious, so fragile, that it has been put under glass. When I move toward it, I see coming toward me in the reflection of the pane of glass another unknown figure that I did not recognize at first – me.

For several years now, in the course of my visits, I have been seeking out self-portraits. Like everyone else, I have been struck by some of the series – that of Rembrandt, for example, scattered to the four corners of the world. At the same instant, at various ages, Rembrandt is looking at himself in Amsterdam, New York, Paris, Florence, in the eyes of hundreds of tourists. From one museum to another, they recognize him; he's an old friend. It's reassuring. We need to be reassured. We can never be too sure of what we're looking at in a museum.

In the presence of self-portraits, I have taken to jotting down my doubts, my mistakes, my questions. Of course, these are the same kinds of uncertainties that I have when "autobiographical" texts are in front of me. Because of my lack of competence with painting, I have left my comments, presented here, in their form of notes taken in haste, of a diary. They do not deal with painting itself, but with its *reception*. They revolve around two very simple questions: What is it that makes a self-portrait recognizable as such? What special interest can there be in looking at a self-portrait?

Three Mistakes

December 1978. New Haven, Conn., Mellon Collection. A self-portrait by Hogarth that matches another portrait painted by Hogarth and depicting one of his friends. Upon entering the room, I am convinced that the second painting is a self-portrait of Hogarth: it resembles, like two drops of water, the memory I have of another self-portrait by Hogarth (seen in London?), where he pictured himself with some type of bulldog. I recognized my mistake while consulting the labels, but I was so surprised that I wondered if perhaps an error had not been made on the labels!

Everything depends on the label. In a museum, people almost spend more time reading the labels than they do looking at the paintings. We measure out our admiration, we adjust our gaze, depending upon the author or the subject. This allows you to take on an attitude, play a particular role. To read a label, you have to move closer and lean over; the jerk who clings to the label strikes the pose of an expert who is checking something.

If this is not a self-portrait, I have to change my expression. I've gone to all this trouble for nothing, I can pack up my metaphysical anxieties. But really, how does it happen that there is no *internal* sign that allows us to distinguish a self-portrait from a portrait? Perhaps painting is unable to use the "first person" . . .

New York, Metropolitan Museum of Art. From a distance, at ten meters, I have no doubt, this is a self-portrait of El Greco. It is indeed he: stern, serious, tragic, and, of course, old (impossible to imagine him young). I move nearer, I read the label: El Greco, *Portrait of a Man.* Again a mistake. But I come even closer, and I notice that I'm not the only one to have been mistaken. *Painted about 1590–1600, this portrait of an unknown man has been mistakenly identified both as a self-portrait by El Greco and as a self-portrait of his father.* And so doubt rushes through me, a doubt that includes the label itself. Obviously, I cannot prove that this is a self-portrait, but upon what can the expert labeler rely in order to state positively that *this is not* a self-portrait? Written sources? Comparison (risky after all) with other paintings that are known (but how?) to be self-portraits? But what does it matter? The interesting thing would be not to settle this debate, but to analyze it historically. The history of *reading* a painting. Why did they believe in the past that this was a self-portrait? How is it that they could have hesitated over the author (the father or the son!) without hesitating over the genre (self-portrait)? When did things become confused? What ideological investments (or financial: is a self-portrait worth more than a portrait?) are tied to these changes in interpretation?

New York, Frick Collection. A superb self-portrait by Rembrandt, and the sketch of a self-portrait by Van Dyck. Then two other paintings, which from a distance I take to be self-portraits, this time for perfectly serious "internal" reasons. A man is depicted looking toward us, with a brush in his right hand. No luck: Frans Hals, *A Painter.* I should have suspected as much: he is holding his brush without really painting, just as a musician would have a musical instrument in his hand, to indicate his profession. And then he is holding it in his right hand (which is at the left of the painting). Well, everyone knows that the image in the mirror is inverted: your right hand is to the right of the picture, and so appears to be your left hand. I have my criterion! If the painter is painting with his left hand, it's a self-portrait; with the right, a portrait. But even here nothing is certain: left-handed painters do exist. And nothing prevents a painter from representing himself, as Velásquez did in *Las Meninas,* the way that other people must see him.

Here is another man, who is also looking toward us; he has a paper in front of him, a brush in his hand, and he is painting. The setup is typically that of the self-portrait this time. Rembrandt, *Portrait of an Artist.* And of course this artist is not Rembrandt, whose self-portrait is on the opposite wall. Portrait of a colleague (who perhaps was painting Rembrandt in the process of painting him, the colleague?). They were painting each other's portrait.

Despite the existence of left-handers and of colleagues, it remains that the representation of a man in the process of painting (on a canvas that we do not see, or whose frame we see at a slant or from the back) and who is turning, the brush raised, to look toward the spectator as if the latter were a mirror — this representation induces in the spectator the "self-portrait effect." Even if it's the label that has the last word.

But what if it were a fictitious work? I asked myself that question when beholding a bewildering painting, the *Triple Self-Portrait* of Norman Rockwell (reproduced here on p. 108). We have a *back* view of the artist, seated on a stool, leaning over in order to look at himself in a mirror posed on a chair (mirror in which we see his reflection almost (?) as he must see it himself), while his hand remains raised with the brush on the canvas that is in front of him and where his self-portrait is beginning to appear. The painter and his image in the mirror correspond to one another perfectly: same size (the painter seen from the back at full length, the full-face image and only half-length), same glasses (which hide the expression from us). The self-portrait on the canvas is much larger than life, without glasses, pleasantly stylized. The pipe he is smoking is horizontal, and not falling as it is in "reality." At the same time that it opposes "reality" (fictitious) to fiction, the *Triple Self-Portrait* articulates the three possible "degrees" of the self-portrait. On canvas, oneself painted like someone else, a mere portrait; in the mirror, a portrait of the self in the process of painting himself, leaning and turned, the palette in hand: in "reality" (that is to say, the painting we are looking at), the relationship of the first two images with the painter, a relationship that can only be visible to *someone else*, or to the self through an imaginary movement backward (unless we imagine some very complicated mirror games, which allows a person to see himself from the back in the process of looking at himself from the front). Hung to the right and to the left above the sketched canvas are two series of "origins" of the self-portrait: a sheet of sketches of the self-portrait itself (four heads and a hand holding a pipe)—this is the before-text; and on the other side, reproductions of four famous self-portraits (Dürer, Rembrandt, Picasso, Van Gogh)—this is the intertext.

When we see this painting for the first time, it appears to be, as much as a self-portrait, a sort of pedagogical and humorous exercise on the theme of the self-portrait. The triangle of props (stool, chair, easel), the couple of the eagle and the helmet "dressing" the mirror and the canvas, the book open on the chair are also there to lend . . . reflection. Rockwell draws a striking effect from the coming together of two very classical genres: the self-portrait and the "painter's studio." And what we see here is both exactly what the painter cannot see and what the onlooker of the self-portrait *imagines*.

But he doesn't imagine everything, since he would also have to imagine Rockwell painting this—which would make a "quadruple" (self)-portrait: when we see three of them, it's because there are four. I had guarded myself against this dizzying slippage (as against all kinds of infinite regression) by asking myself if the man we saw at work, quartered between the mirror and the easel, was indeed Rockwell, the author of the painting. Doesn't anything say so? Yes: the canvas on the easel is signed by him. Furthermore, in the title of the painting, "triple" has no meaning for the man who is in the painting (he has before him *only one* self-portrait); this therefore can refer only to the author himself.

And if the label was *in* the painting itself? If the proposed pact was inscribed on the canvas, tattooed, encrusted even in the painting? This could be done in two ways. Allusively, through a reminder of other works, supposedly already known, "by the same author" (which already assumes the notion of author and the existence of his mark, the signature). The painter, in his studio, identified by his own paintings, as character, and by his (double) signature, as painter of himself. Or else explicitly, through an inscription saying essentially: "I am so and so, and it is I that I am painting (or it is I that I have painted)." This seems to have been practiced in the sixteenth century, in the early years of the self-portrait, in a epoch when painters were accustomed, with portraits themselves, to inscribing the name of the model (and his age) on the canvas. I wander around the Prado, and on Dürer's self-portrait I decipher: 1498 / *Das malt Ich nach meiner gelstalt / Ich war sex und zwanzig jor alt / Albrecht Dürer*. This is quite clear. In the Uffizi, Holbein's self-portrait carries the following inscription: IOANNES HOL-

PENIUS BASILEENSIS SUI IPSIUS EFFIGIATOR AE XLV. "Self-portrait art-
ist" is, then, expressed in Latin as *sui ipsius effigiator*. It is clear, and pretty (but
is it Holbein who wrote it?). Alas, painters were quickly diverted from this clarity
of the early times; they gave up putting names on portraits. Out of discretion?
In order to clear the painting of all writing? They relied on the label, and the label
jumps constantly.
   The museum visitor is often struck by this infirmity of the painting. "From the
School of So-and-So." "Attributed to." But also "Portrait of an Unknown." Without counting the copies, admitted, and the "fakes." But this infirmity exists only
because we live, since the Renaissance, in a veritable obsession with the *author*.
Who would agree to visit a museum without proper names? — I don't know how
long they have been signing canvases. Do they have, sometimes, on the back,
other indications that allow them to be identified?
   For the self-portrait artist, the problem of identity is double (as author and as
model). But as a matter of fact, it is not a problem *for him*. If he neglects to establish that this has to do with his own portrait, it is undoubtedly because for him
(as for those close to him), such a thing is obvious! He does not think that one
hundred kilometers away, or in one hundred years, no one will be in a position
to be sure that it is indeed he. Let's supppose that Jerome Bosch painted his own
face in the middle of the right panel of *Jardin des Délices* (*Garden of Earthly
Delights*) in the fantasmagoric display of torment: everyone who knew him was
well aware of it. *Private Joke*, whose wit will not be appreciated by foreigners
and later generations (undoubtedly it didn't matter to him). An identity is an established relationship between a picture and a proper name — like those snapshots required by bureaucracies and which lose all meaning if you have not taken care
to write your name on the back.

   In museums, I look at portraits in the same way that I watch other visitors or the
attendants seated on the chairs. Of course through the supplementary filter of the
painting. But as *other people*. Sometimes the expression of the model bothers me,
as in a fantastic tale where the eyes of a painting are alive and, horror, follow
you when you move. Or else I reverse the roles and I imagine that they are the
ones who are watching us watch them. In front of official portraits and portraits
in caricature parade onlookers who are no less rigid or ridiculous than the portraits. I imagine all this in order to break away from the mortuary aspect of the
portrait (otherwise we should say: a "mortrait," a "self-mortrait").
   September 1981. I have an hour before catching my train at Victoria. I go in
to wander around the National Portrait Gallery (without equivalent in France, except for the astute exposition "The Family of Portraits" in 1979 at the Museum
of Decorative Arts). Here the fun quickly gives way to nightmare. Heads, heads,
heads. Beyond social and historical variations (changes in the function of the portrait and in the techniques of painting), monotony, frozen and stereotyped charac-

ter of the art of the portrait itself. Centering of a solitary individual in a conventional decor (no matter what the convention). Terribly distressed, I no longer see any more than resemblances. And it is here that I imagine, as Swift could have done it, the effect that a gallery of portraits of poodles and horses would produce. What bizarre obstinacy to endlessly paint and repaint, for centuries, the same thing, all those heads of animals protruding from lace collars or fabric, hair done, all dressed up, and all so profoundly serious. That's it: the seriousness of the head that is posing, and that everyone makes a big deal about. Because the portrait doesn't work without the following assumption: this individual has a social value, and, more fundamentally, man has a value. Moreover, all representations, objects as well as landscapes, are grounded on an assumption derived metonymically from the former. They work only as signs of man. Therefore, I see the self-portrait as a particular situation, somewhat irregular, in which in the middle of the most coded genre (the portrait) a spark abruptly bursts forth (which is at times only in the mind of the spectator), allowing the essence of the art to be seen in a staggering way: the self-representation of humans (and not the representation of the world), the self-portrait becoming the allegory of art itself.

A spark. Before a self-portrait, I see again, I saw again (sometimes to the point of hallucination), my own positions in front of the mirror. Actually this doesn't work for all self-portraits, and it works sometimes for ordinary portraits (for example, for *The Man with the Green Eyes* by Titian, in which I will confess, braving ridicule, I had found *my own* self-portrait). As soon as I imagine that what I see is a man looking at himself in a mirror, I see no more than his expression, and I am caught in the trap. If he has a brush in his hand, his body at an angle, and he is turning toward me, I get the immediate impression that he has just turned, thus just arrived, he too, and we find ourselves abruptly face to face, examining each other's expression, and I read in his expression the surprise of being me, or let's say of being . . . this.

It is a novel. A fantasy. Maybe everyone is not like me, does not feel this. They will tell me: how, while looking at a self-portrait of Delacroix, or of X, etc., can you identify yourself totally? Indeed yes, providing that he seems attentive. Because if I do not look like Delacroix, Delacroix doesn't either. No one looks like *himself*. Nothing in me necessarily implies the color of my eyes, the length of my nose, or any of the rest. I'm used to them, but it's a habit that does not resist the surprise of passing in front of a mirror, or a somewhat stubborn self-contemplation. When I look myself straight in the eyes, I lose my sense of identity. Brush in hand, I reconstruct myself; I fill in the gaps; I surround myself; I restore myself; I put myself back "in shape," on stage, for others, as another. But it is never very solid, there remains that spark of surprise, a flash of white in the pupil.

An anachronistic reading no doubt, unsuited to so many placid old (or modern) self-portraits in which the artist places himself without fanfare in the series of his models, so unobtrusive that without the label, really, one would never believe it. Perhaps I have also been influenced by the self-portraits of writers—sketches with the pen done without any notion of ostentation, without the premeditation and the slowness that the execution of a painting implies—physiognomy and expression trapped impromptu in the margin of a text. I am thinking of the black self-portraits of Baudelaire, of the sketches of faces and of hands that we find regularly in Valéry's *Cahiers* (*Notebooks*), of the drawings of Antonin Artaud. Anguish and questioning are read here more clearly than in many of the self-portraits of painters—but how can we not assume that the painter, too, if he has done his own portrait, has gone through this? "Me—this?"

The painter is there, brush in hand. He has painted; he will paint (on a canvas that I do not see, and which is exactly the one I am looking at). But at this moment he is not painting. He is looking at himself. And this gaze *stands for* painting. I who do not know how to paint, I find here an "existential" angle to enter (to imagine myself entering) into the activity of the artist. Likewise, the reader of Proust privileges the experience of reminiscence, which he can share with the narrator, without really understanding that it is only a metaphor of the activity, invisible but omnipresent, that separates him from the narrator: writing.

If I imagine that the canvas is a mirror, it disappears as painting. The self-portrait artist saw in his mirror a painting (to be done); I see in his painting (finished) a mirror. The painting is like a sheet of glass without silvering: the painter is behind (on the other side in relation to me), and I surprise him in the act of looking at himself. Suddenly we become . . . contemporaries. The self-portrait is the only pictorial genre that has given me the poignant feeling, which Barthes describes so well with regard to photography in *La Chambre claire* (*Camera Lucida*), of having before my eyes not an image of the past, but an impression directly inscribed by it. Illusion, of course. It is a pretty morning in the autumn of 183-; it's a little chilly, and instead of going to tramp up and down the Roman countryside, I have stayed in my studio; this man whom I see there in the mirror with his visor, and who is looking at me, and whom I am going to paint, it is I, Camille Corot.

So if the painter appears, the painting disappears. Moreover, can we paint the painting? And what are the arts, or the media, which allow a self-representation of the art, or of the artist? Music, hardly. Despite appearances, not cinema either, Elizabeth Bruss has shown. For the first person, writing is invincible. Self-sculptures? Self-busts? Yes, more deathlike still than the self-portrait (to mold oneself, to polish oneself, to cast oneself in bronze—to turn round the self) and giving the onlooker less the charms of specular hallucination. For a long time I had wondered what the self-portrait could be in photography. At thirteen years of age, when I got my first camera, one of the first things that I did was to hold the camera at arms length in front of me, turned back toward me, and shoot. Very frustrating and bizarre. I had a completely blurred moonface. Later, with delayed shutter speeds, it's a little like "go over there to see if I'm there." I didn't know how to go about it (since then I have limited myself to atrocious positions in picture-taking booths). Nevertheless, the photographic self-portrait is a widely used genre (I'll propose to call this the phauto). And much more inventive than its pictorial cousin since, accepting that a person has not seen himself, he is freer to imagine himself and to place himself on the stage, and even to play with the label in order to call anything, through metaphor, a self-portrait.

The painter is, in the self-portrait, doubly present: as character represented, and by the painting itself. For the onlooker, once the magic of the reflexive glance has evaporated, it can be difficult to establish a link between these two aspects. Illusory Rosetta Stone. Reading a writer's autobiography provides me with information about him as person and as artist; this opens a new interpretive space for a reading or a rereading of his other texts. Nothing like that occurs in painting. The encounter of the image of the painter can seem anecdotal, on the side of the character, and tautological, on the side of the painting. Chagall painted by Chagall can only be yet another Chagall. It is possible that the self-portrait is, for the onlooker, relatively *insignificant*. And far from shedding some light on the rest of the work, the self-portrait needs it, on the contrary, as background in order to produce its little ray.

March 1982. Florence. This is the third time I've come to Florence, and I learn that the Vasari corridor—that airy passageway that links the Palazzo della Signoria to the Palazzo Pitti and passes over the Arno on the second level of the Ponte Vecchio—is stuffed with self-portraits! In the seventeenth century, Cosimo III de Medici had started a collection of self-portraits, carrying off at any price every one that he heard about, and since then it has continued to grow. At the present time there are more than a thousand! *Son già mille tre!* A harem of expressions, a corpus of consciences. What an idea! Deep down, I'm jealous: for several years I've been involved in the same project, in a simpler way, by buying postcards at the exit of museums . . . A well-guarded harem. Closed to the public. Shown only to groups and by appointment. Now, however, on display in a room of the Uffizi are the most recent acquisitions, ninety modern self-portraits, many of which were donated by the artists themselves, principally Italians. By luck, I manage one morning to join up with a tour of the corridor itself, and I pass, alas at a run, between two hedges of self-portraits, "who watch me with familiar eyes." At first I experience a religious feeling, almost terrified, as if, under the guidance of some Virgil, I was visiting one of the circles of the underworld—captive souls, bewitched in their mirror, awaiting we don't know what deliverance. I'm even a little shocked at the commonplace remarks of the guide, who knows his tenants well, points out a colorful detail here, a famous person lost in the crowd there (hey, a Rembrandt). But by the end of several hundred self-portraits, I feel myself overcome by that profane and reductive sense which is both anecdotal and statistical. One nude man, it's an Academy-figure; a hundred, it's a draft board. I find my guide is blasé. I come out of the corridor perplexed, and go to the Boboli Gardens to meditate, as follows.

First of all, the "reading contract" that the collection itself imposes. No more hesitation, the "self" quality is guaranteed. Less surprise, so less pleasure. A fantastic short story by Maupassant, if I discover it in a collection where nothing tells me to expect it, has much more of an effect on me than in his *Contes fantastiques complets* (*Complete Fantastic Tales*). The anthologies always overstate the case. All we have left to do is guess who the painter is or consult the label, which always tells who it is (no anonymous self-portraits).

The collection flattens, deadens, the essential effects of the self-portrait. Impossible for an onlooker to feel ten, a hundred times in a row the kind of "existential" emotion I have described. On the other hand, we very quickly have the feeling of being involved in a competition, at the same time that through the superimposition of images the elementary "rules" of the genre emerge, a rhetoric from which it is impossible to escape, and which grows tiresome. Deceptive crushing, owing to the presentation in series. Because the self-portrait is first of all intended to be seen among other works by the same painter: this is where it breathes, where it plays, where it really means something, through resemblance and difference, through recall and rupture. Uprooted from this natural milieu, it loses a good part of its meaning. Every self-portrait functions a little like this one, which caught my attention: a seventeenth-century painter, specializing in still lifes (flowers in particular), paints in trompe-l'oeil one of his own canvases, punctured in the center, with his own sneering face that appears in the tear. If we don't know what tears the self-portrait, it is less . . . rending. We expect something different from a self-portrait of a portrait artist or landscape painter, from a painter of battles or an abstract painter. Rothko paints immense monochrome canvases; in what color does he see himself? And then the function of the self-portrait must have varied a great deal, both historically, and from one painter to another. Social or familial gesture for some; intimate quest for others. We don't see them in the same way. The litany of self-portraits by Rembrandt, the complacency of Courbet, the "crisis" of Van Gogh become for the onlooker the occasion to play psychologist, to compose little novels, to imagine dramas, to read the passage of Time. But to the obsession of some responds the abstention of others: some painters never painted themselves. The Uffizi could integrate them at little cost into the collection. Some empty frames, for the *invisible* painters. Because the self-portrait is really, in the religious sense, an apparition. The creative spirit is incarnated in one of the figures of its creation. Looks itself in the face, and stares at itself.

But let's have a respite from metaphysics and take a look at statistics. Of the ninety contemporary self-portraits displayed in the Uffizi, eighty-six represent men and four are of women. This is a clear improvement: because in the Vasari corridor, I have no memory of having come across any women (but we went through so quickly). Let's improve the analysis. It would be necessary to know, for each period, the ratio of women painters, to see if the woman painter has more or less of a tendency than the man painter to fall into the trap of the mirror. While waiting, I can classify the genres according to the sex of the model: almost always masculine in the self-portrait; masculine or feminine (fifty/fifty) in the portrait; almost always feminine in the nude. Moreover, the only one of the ninety self-portrait artists to have portrayed (her)self nude is a woman. Many a man has tried, but stopped halfway: Mario Fallani stripped to the waist, in pants, one foot with the shoe on, the other not, the shoe in his hand.

I can continue to count. The young, the old. Alone or in company (very rare). Full face, three-quarter view, in profile, from the back (almost never). Solitary figure, half-length, or full-length. Suggesting that they're in the act of painting themselves (around fifteen of them, one in six). Integrating a reminder of their other paintings (rare). Larger than or less than life size. Etc., etc. Those who have only done one of them, and the repeaters (the exposition doesn't let it be known— except for the two striking masks by the sculptor Giulio Pierucci, metamorphoses of the same face at an eight-year interval).

But I'm no longer very sure of what I'm counting. I'm especially sensitive to the gaps. When the painter does his portrait, he lives a unique experience, so much more "sincere" and "natural" that he chooses the simplest arrangement, that which the situation imposes, the ordinary centering of the portrait. When I see his self-portrait alongside others, that simplicity seems banal to me, commonplace, or, at least endured more than chosen. As a result, I prefer those who have sought a more original effect, who have thought about the onlooker, or reflected on the genre itself, even when the result is visually mediocre. This is the case here: allegorical montage blending with or confronting photo, sketches, and contour lines of the face—or even assembly of medical X-rays (although nothing is stranger, and more invisible, to you than your own skeleton). As for myself, haven't I—who do not know how to paint—long planned on putting together my own "self-portrait" in a collage (which I imagine to be impressive!) of all the snapshots that I have stapled for more than twenty years on so many identification papers? What temporal relief, what a lesson in humility. The main thing is to be the first to have the idea, and undoubtedly I'm getting there too late. Perhaps it is even commonplace already . . .

It's noon, and I leave the Boboli gardens through the Porta Romana.

Chapter 6
The Autobiographical Pact (bis)

There is always an interest in rereading the classics. As I am writing this chapter, I am leafing through *Les Caractères* (*Characters*) by La Bruyère, and I come across, in the chapter on *"ouvrages de l'esprit"* (vol. 2, p. 60), a portrait that I had not noticed until now, and which I have been thinking about:

> *Autopact* is a true scholar: he knows how to consolidate his errors while reviewing them fearlessly. He makes a mistake, then he corrects himself. He makes a mistake in correcting himself, and then he recorrects himself. And he acts on the authority of what this exercise implies of humility in order to be supercilious, next, with all those who have not had the luck to go astray. He gets the better of them by demand and by lucidity. He is the lost sheep of the Gospel. He has demonstrated first of all that all English women are redheads. His talent has given a reddish tint to England, and has allowed this country to be looked at in a new light. Then he made scientific progress by discovering other and multiple colors there. He made the most of it in order to compile a skillful methodological study of the bases of his first error. When all is said and done, English women are like everyone else, but he has become a scholar who is both original and meticulous.

Becoming such a scholar is indeed hard, and La Bruyère's portrait serves as a warning as I embark on a rereading of "Le Pacte autobiographique" (The Autobiographical Pact).[1] But La Bruyère relies, in order to overdraw his character, on a conception of truth (at the level of "reality" and of "common sense") that, to be comfortable, is perhaps unprofitable all the same. Who knows if the round-trip journey of Autopact did not produce something? Has he really returned to the point of departure? Isn't the real diverse and contradictory? I therefore will not allow myself to stop. A study like "The Autobiographical Pact" is of value as hypothesis and as a working tool: it is normal for me to evaluate it or remodel it in light of the work it has allowed me to do, and of the criticisms to which it gave rise.[2] The critical discussions have been invaluable to me; they have helped me to see the imperfections and the limitations of my analyses, and to situate them within the increasingly productive field of study concerned with autobiography. Since 1973, I have reconsidered this problem several times. In 1975, in the final chapter of *Le Pacte autobiographique*, I thought about the different traps, normative and theoretical, that I had not avoided. Then, in *Je est un autre* (*I Is Someone Else*, Paris: Editions du Seuil, 1980), I extended the reflection on identity to include the case of autobiography in the third person and the case of the multiple author, which I had neglected in 1973.

My rereading will deal essentially with problems of method, involving some sensitive points: definition, vocabulary, identity, contract, "style," and autobiographical ideology.

Definition

You might be surprised by the contradiction presented in the beginning of "Pact": first, I promise an empirical and inductive approach (with the reader historically situated, I am going to observe a given field), but then I immediately present a "definition" of dogmatic appearance, with a rather uncertain theoretical status:

> DEFINITION: *Retrospective prose narrative written by a real person concerning his own existence, where the focus is his individual life, in particular the story of his personality.*

Isolated from the text, in italics, this definition looks, in its formulation, like a lexicographical entry, and tends to take on the authority of the dictionary. But where does it come from? In its first part, the definition restates what indeed the majority of dictionaries say ("Life of an individual recounted by himself"), but while adding some frills ("in prose," "a real person") and a long appendix to it that, in fact, correspond to personal choices. So I seem to prescribe as coming from the consensus of speaking subjects the use that I myself am choosing to make of the word. Does it have to do, moreover, with a definition of *word* (as I suggest it does at certain times, on p. 19, for example) or with a definition of *thing* (in which case I would construct a sort of idealized theoretical model of a literary genre)? More with thing, it seems: and the definition dangerously blends theoretical hypothesis and normative assertion.

This critical turn on the definition was prompted less by the objections that could be made to what I was saying than by the approvals, which sometimes threw me into confusion. In my mind the definition was a point of departure from which to set up an analytical deconstruction of the factors that enter into the perception of the genre. But, isolated from its context, cited as an "authority," it could appear sectarian and dogmatic, a derisory Procrustean bed, a falsely magical formula that blocks reflection instead of stimulating it. I no longer recognized myself, but I couldn't deny that this is what I had indeed written and that, moreover, it fit in well with other normative aspects of my text (for example, what I write about identity). My starting point was being transformed into a point of arrival. I was a new Larousse, or a new La Palice.

But . . . I have no regrets. After all, if we rely on this definition, it is because it corresponds to a need. Far from reproaching my readers for having followed my lead, which would be ungrateful, I will take their approval as a sign of relevance. When I hear François Nourissier refer to the analyses of "Le Pacte" to differentiate his strictly autobiographical books (he has only written three of them) from his novels (with which they are often lumped), I tell myself that the definition is useful. The more so since it does not prevent him from then situating his novels in what I have called an "autobiographical space," like imaginary or "prospective" autobiographies.[3]

At first the definition was useful to me, in getting out of an impossible situation, by cutting the Gordian knot. Anyone who goes on about "autobiography" (or about any literary genre whatever) is obliged to confront the problem of the definition, if only in practice, by choosing what to talk about. Like periodization, the generic definition seems to pose a kind of insoluble problem, a sort of vicious circle: impossible to study the object before having defined it, impossible to define it before having studied it. Some stand out by arbitrarily defining a corpus of a hundred autobiographies (May), others by contriving a definition (Lejeune): the illusion is to believe that these two methods are opposed, and to believe that they are "methods." It matters little how we get into the vicious circle. It's all part of the same merry-go-round.

By his gesture, the seeker achieves the construction of an object that was in reality only one of the possible objects to construct. His problem is less to outline limits than to identify a center. Also it is necessary that he keep in mind that with another choice of center the limits would be displaced. He "brings into focus" his perception of the literary field by adjusting it according to a particular organizing element, with the risks that this includes: clearly opposing rather close things (like literary autobiography and certain autobiographical novels), and reuniting relatively different things (as I do by considering equally as autobiographies *Les Mots* by Sartre and *Soixante-deux années de ma vie, récits intimes et commerciaux* (*Sixty-two Years of My Life, Personal and Business Stories*, 1891) by Romain Lhopiteau, Parisian merchant.[4] I would not reproach "The Autobiographical Pact" with having effected such a choice, which is necessary, but with not having resituated it more clearly within the whole of the actual field of publications. I should have started off with an analysis, even a quick one, of contemporary production such as it is reflected and *classified* by the literary press (from *Lire* to *La Quinzaine littéraire* by way of *Le Monde des livres*), a clean-up exercise in hygiene that would have given weight to my initial "relativist" statement. Moreover, when you teach autobiography, experience shows that it is better to begin with the analysis of a corpus rather than to immediately propose a definition.[5]

Once his "chief characteristic" has been chosen, the critic finds himself facing a new dilemma. If he attempts to be clear and precise, he will be inaccurate; if he is accurate, his argument becomes blurred — doubt and shade of meaning blur the broad lines of organization of the real. In order to reconcile accuracy and clarity, I tried to conduct an analytical study that takes into account the (variable) hierarchical organization of different factors and the multiplicity of possible combinations. When, later, I noticed errors or omissions, it seemed to me that I had been mistaken not through excess of analytical formalism, but, on the contrary, for having come to a standstill in the course of this method.

What stopped me is a certain tendency toward "nominalism," and, in a more general way, a dogmatic attitude toward the problem of identity. This is quite obvious when I get to anonymous autobiography. Instead of proceeding with a more exhaustive analysis of the different possible cases (and of the different possible reactions of the readers), I'm stuck. Feeling that I am quite in the wrong, I get out of it by being angry with my readers: "Surely by asserting that it is impossible to write an anonymous autobiography, I am only stating a corollary to my definition, and not "proving" it. Everyone is free to assert that it is possible, but then it will be necessary to start with another definition" (p. 19). There! I decline responsibility, I wash my hands of it . . .

Vocabulary

From the beginning, I've been complaining about the "vagueness that surrounds the vocabulary that is used" (p. 3) in the discussions on autobiography. If the vagueness is a flaw in a scientific discussion, on the other hand, it is an indispensable condition in the proper functioning of the generic vocabulary. It is through their elasticity, their plasticity, their polysemy, that literary terms (like others) promote dialogue and ensure the continuity of language. For example, the current popularity of the expression "life story" in the human sciences is linked not only to the appearance of a new "object" (lives collected on tape), but to the ambiguity of the expression, which allows the new object to be put in touch with past objects (biographies, autobiographies) or with other productions that have appeared in related fields (books, interviews, stories "collected by"). According to the person who uses it, the expression is taken in a narrow or broad sense. And the richness of the "getting in touch" effected in this way is achieved at the expense of misunderstandings.

As for the word "biography," it designates today, depending upon the person who uses it: (1) the story of a person (in general famous) written by someone else (this is the old meaning, and the most common); (2) the story of a person (in general unknown) recounted orally by him/herself to someone else who has created this narrative in order to study it (this is the "biographical method in the social sciences"); (3) the story of a person recounted by him/herself to one or several others who help him through their listening to get his bearings in his life (this is the "biography in training" [*biographie dans la formation*]). There are certainly connections, but also some distance, between a fictionalized biography of Watteau, the taped interview of an old blacksmith, and the biographical work—which can leave no trace—of a person or of a group in self-training.

Consequently, before establishing in what sense I intended to use the word "autobiography," I should have had the prudence to situate it within the range of currently accepted meanings. Quickly, I am going to fill in that gap.

The word "autobiography" was imported from England at the beginning of the nineteenth century and was used with two related but rather different meanings. The first meaning (which I have chosen) is the one that Larousse proposes in 1866: "Life of an individual written by himself." Larousse places autobiography, which is a kind of confession, opposite memoirs, which recount facts with which the narrator might be unacquainted. But, *largo sensu,* "autobiography" can also designate any text in which the author *seems* to express his life or his feelings, whatever the form of the text, whatever the contract proposed by the author. Less known than Larousse, Vapereau explained this meaning quite well in his *Dictionnaire universel des littératures* (*Universal Dictionary of Literature*, 1876):

AUTOBIOGRAPHY . . . literary work, novel, poem, philosophical treatise, etc., whose author intended, secretly or admittedly, to recount his life, to expose his thoughts or to describe his feelings.

Who will determine the intention of the author, if it is secret? The reader, of course. This second meaning of the word reflects, therefore, as much as a new kind of writing, the emergence of a new *way of reading.* Vapereau comments on his definition in terms that must make any adherent of the strict sense shiver:

Autobiography leaves a lot of room to fantasy, and the one who is writing is not at all obliged to be exact about the facts, as in memoirs, or to tell the full and complete truth, as in confessions.

He emphasizes that here we are dealing with a modern genre. The first example given is Rousseau—for *La Nouvelle Héloïse* (*The New Heloise*), of course—

and the most recent are *Les Nuits* (*Nights*) by Musset and some of Mme Sand's novels. Vapereau also includes the *Pensées* (*Thoughts*) of Pascal and the *Discours de la méthode* (*Discourse on Method*).

Today, these two meanings, exact and broad, are still the two poles of the use of the word. The success of the word "autobiography" is undoubtedly linked to the tension between these two poles, to the ambiguity or the indecisiveness that it permits, to the new space of reading and interpretation that it makes possible, to the new strategies of writing that it can designate. And this is even more evident with the *adjective* "autobiographical," which is certainly used as much as the substantive, for it tends to draw on the second meaning rather than the first: autobiographical – poem, novel, story, and so on.

It is completely legitimate to choose the first meaning for the substantive, as I did for the sake of the clarity of my work. But I underestimated the misunderstandings I would cause by taking the risk of calling into question the linguistic competency of others: 'How, according to Lejeune, could such a work not be an autobiography? Absurd!'

But I also ran the risk of hearing someone say: "How, according to Lejeune, could *La Règle du jeu* be an autobiography? Absurd, according to his own definition!"[6] I have indeed used the word "autobiography" to designate broadly any text governed by an autobiographical pact, in which an author proposes to the reader a discourse on the self, but also (and this is the definition found on page 120) a particular realization of that discourse, one in which the question "who am I?" is answered by a *narrative* that tells "how I became who I am." Isn't *La Règle du jeu* more a self-portrait than an autobiography, the thematic and analogical organization prevailing over the narration? Michel Beaujour is right to think that my passion for the writing of Leiris pushed me to append it to the corpus of autobiographies, and that I use in my critical descriptions a more flexible vocabulary than in my theoretical essays. But the majority of autobiographical texts (governed by an autobiographical pact) include, in different proportions and hierarchical organizations, part autobiography (narrative) and part self-portrait (thematic organization). And in *La Règle du jeu* the articulation is inextricable.

Another inadequacy with regard to vocabulary: it is no longer a question of my own terminology, but of the analysis of the terminology used by authors, publishers, and critics to designate and classify texts. Throughout "Le Pacte," I went along as if the label "novel" (in generic subtitles as well as in critical discourse) was synonymous with "fiction," as opposed to "non-fiction," "real reference." Well, "novel" has other fuctions too: it designates literature, literary writing, as opposed to the commonplace quality of the document, to the zero degree of testimony. The two directions of meaning are often linked, but not always. The word "novel" is not therefore more univocal than the word "autobiography." To which is added, in the two cases, phenomena of value: pejorative (novel = mere invention; autobiography = platitude of personal experience untouched by art) or meliorative (novel = pleasure of a well-written and well-managed narrative; autobiography = authenticity and depth of the personal experience). I will take up the study of all this terminology again, no doubt when I comment on the chart on page 16 of "Le Pacte" later on in my conclusion.

Identity

The undeniable normative aspect of "Le Pacte" resides essentially in the cut-and-dried presentation of the problem of identity. Convinced that the locating of identity and of its marks was of major importance in the field that I was exploring (and I am still convinced of it), I tended to fix on an "all or nothing" position, when in reality many intermediary positions are possible: "An identity is, or is not. It is impossible to speak of degrees, and all doubt leads to a negative conclusion" (p. 5). Or further on: "Autobiography does not include degrees: it is all or nothing" (p. 13). When I reread it, I am struck by the contradiction that stands out between this initial first position, absolute and arbitrary, and the analyses as a whole that follow, and that establish, on the contrary, from the chart on page 16 and further on, thanks to the notion of "autobiographical space," the existence of ambiguities and degrees. If I have chosen the title *Je est un autre* in order to regroup the studies written since *Le Pacte*, it is precisely to reintroduce the free play that is inevitably related to identity.

Why have I first adopted such a Jansenist attitude? Undoubtedly because, without saying it, I have always reasoned as if the center of the autobiographical domain was the *confession*. I have evaluated the whole thing by imposing upon it the rules of functioning of one of its parts: confessions must be signed for them to have any value; there can be no compromise with the truth. But such a choice is open to criticism only if the existence of possible degrees is denied; as soon as they are accepted, the point of reference of the confession allows other strategies of writing and reading to be evaluated. The magnetic axis that governs the compass must not be confused with the multiplicity of directions that it can locate. And it must be admitted that there are in reality other axes of organization other than the magnetic axis.

The Contract

The term autobiographical "pact" had fascinated me. It evokes some mythological images, like those "pacts with the devil" where someone dips his pen into his own blood to sell his soul. "Contract" is more prosaic: we are at a notary's office. The analogical use of the two terms is not without danger. If it were only a matter of indicating that someone is living up to his obligations, that he is referring to systems of conventions, fine. But the term "contract" suggests that it is a matter of explicit rules, fixed and recognized in a common agreement by authors and readers: at the notary's office, the two parties sign the same contract, at the same instant. No such thing happens in literature. Valéry said that any judgment establishing a three-party relationship between the producer, the work, and the consumer was illusory, these three parties never existing at the same time in one and the same experience. Undoubtedly autobiography (whether it is literary or not) works precisely to create this "illusion" and functions primarily as an act of communication. In the texts that I have chosen, the contract is not simply one of the conditions of the reading of the text; it is made explicit in the initial part of the text read. In *L'Autobiographie en France* (*Autobiography in France*, 1971), I brought together an anthology of the literary micro-genre that is the preamble of autobiography. Making an agreement with the "narratee" whose image he constructs, the autobiographer incites the real reader to enter into the game and gives the impression that an agreement has been signed by the two parties. But it is evident that the real reader can adopt modes of reading different from the one that is suggested to him, and especially that many published texts in no way include an explicit contract. Well there are, in this domain, no confirmed "lists of obligations," nor any imperative "collective agreements" made between the unions of producers and the associations of consumers. Whence the share that is left to misunderstanding. Yielding to the charm of the prologues of autobiography, I imagined a double process in the form of a singular contract: the agreement and the system of presentation chosen by the author, and the mode of reading chosen by the reader. This takes nothing away from the necessity of describing, as I have started to do, the systems of signs and conventions to which authors and readers refer, but makes it desirable to come up with a sharper description that takes into account the three following points:

1. What I call autobiography can be part of two different systems: a "real" referential system (in which the autobiographical agreement, even if it comes by way of the book and the writing, has the value of act), and a literary system (in which the writing no longer aspires to transparency but is able to mime perfectly, to mobilize the beliefs of the first system). Many of the phenomena of ambiguity or misunderstanding that I will study in regard to the chart on page 16 come from this overlap.

2. As far as the author is concerned, there can be a shifting between the initial intention and that which the reader will finally attribute to him, either because the author misunderstands the effects induced by the mode of presentation that he has chosen, or because between him and the reader there exist other postures: many elements that condition the reading (subtitle, generic classification, publicity, publisher's blurb) may have been chosen by the publisher and already interpreted by the media.

3. Finally, we must admit that different readings of the same text, different interpretations of the same proposed "contract" can coexist. The public is not

homogeneous. Different publishers, diverse collections address audiences who are not sensitive to the same signs, and who do not judge according to the same criteria. In "Le Pacte," I tended to consider myself as the representative of the "average reader," and as a result I established my own reactions while reading as the standard. I did this in order to resolve at little cost the question that I am asking myself now: how do I observe real readings?

"Style"

My entire analysis was part of an obvious fact: "How to distinguish autobiography from the autobiographical novel? We must admit that, if we remain on the level of analysis within the text, there is *no difference*" (*L'Autobiographie en France*, p. 24, quoted in chapter 1 of the present volume, p. 13). Consequently, I concentrated on the elements that, at the edge of the text, made the difference: the proper name and the contract. I came across the same problem again while reflecting on the signs by which we identify a painting as a self-portrait in a museum.[7] And so I left out of the analysis (although I had made them figure in my definition) other elements that, without being adequate, were nonetheless necessary for a text to be perceived as autobiography. I apparently overvalued the contract and underestimated (1) the very contents of the text (a biographical narrative, recapitulating a life), (2) the narrative techniques (in particular the play of voice and focalization), and (3) the style.

A quick word on these last two points. The reader does not perceive in the same way a text that begins by focusing on the experience of a character (for example: "The sky had moved away at least ten meters. I remained seated, not in a hurry. The shock must have broken the stones, my right hand was groping through the debris"[8]) and a text in which a narrator's voice is heard from the beginning ("I was born at the very end of the nineteenth century, the last of eight boys. We lived in the suburbs, in Saint-Maur-des-Fossés"[9]). The use of the first technique is more frequent in novels and in newspaper reporting, the use of the second in autobiography. Of course, it is a question only of dominant characteristics; the uses change, and the autobiographical narrative *stricto sensu* tends to assimilate progressively techniques which have been well broken in in the domain of fiction. The reader comes up against this type of signal well before he is able to develop some idea of the relationship existing between the name of the protagonist and that of the author, for example.

This is equally true for style. I call here "style," for lack of a better term, everything that disturbs the transparency of written language, moves it away from "degree zero" and from the "probable," and makes the work on the words apparent — whether we are dealing with parody, plays on meaning, or versification. By specifying that autobiography was written "in prose," it was this phenomenon that

I was attempting, perhaps awkwardly, to designate. Because who can say where prose ends? And who can say, for every era and for every class of readers, where transparency and probability come to a stop, and where fiction begins? Thus I simply wanted to dismiss whatever might paralyze referential belief, whether by engendering forms of suspicion, or by plunging the reader into the imaginary. Still this is highly disputable material: the paradox of the literary autobiography, its essential double game, is to pretend to be at the same time a truthful discourse and a work of art. It is because he has pondered over this square of the circle and attempted to achieve this balance that Michel Leiris is so exemplary. Consequently, instead of proposing a definition that, curtly, excludes verse, I should have designated as the center of the present system this tension between referential transparency and aesthetic pursuit, and shown, as D. Mansell has done, that on both sides of a point of balance, there existed a continuous gradation of texts going, on one side, toward the banality of the *curriculum vitae*, and on the other, toward pure poetry. At the two extremities of the spectrum, the autobiographical contract, for opposite reasons, is found to lose its credibility.

Poetic Pause

As for verse proper, my attitude was dictated by a simple finding: whereas there exist thousands of autobiographies "in prose," we can count on the fingers of one hand the autobiographies in verse, if we understand by "autobiography" a narrative that recapitulates a life: Wordsworth, always cited for the *Prelude* (whose subtitle is "An Autobiographical Poem"), Hugo with *Les Contemplations*, Aragon with *Le Roman inachevé* (*The Unfinished Novel*). Since then, it is true, I have come across several others, naïve or sophisticated, but the total still does not exceed the number of fingers on two hands. First, a nineteenth-century schoolteacher's account of his life in alexandrine verse. It begins like this:

> Depuis trente ans bientôt j'enseigne la jeunesse.
> Depuis le premier jour, pas un jour de faiblesse,
> Pas un jour de repos dans ce rude métier.
> Mais le voyage est long, étroit est le sentier
> Où je devrai marcher plus de dix ans encore,
> Avant que du repos j'aperçoive l'aurore.

[For almost thirty years I have been teaching young people. Since the first day, not one day of weakness, not one day of rest in this trying occupation. But the journey is long, narrow is the path where I must still walk for more than ten years, before I catch sight of the dawn of rest.]

Already advanced in his career, he succeeded in getting his degree and becoming a high school teacher:

La faculté m'a dit: "C'est bien, et la licence
D'un labeur méritant sera la récompense.
Allez, vous avez fait un calcul excellent,
Et d'un bon professeur vous avez le talent."
Et la grande nouvelle un soir m'est annoncée:
Je passe triomphant de l'école au lycée.
Amis, voilà comment j'ai tracé mon sillon.
De chrysalide un soir, je devins papillon.[10]

[The faculty said to me: "Well done, and the degree will be the reward for a deserving labor. Go, you've done an excellent job, and you have the talent to be a good teacher." And the big news is announced to me one evening: I am going triumphantly from grammar school to high school. Friends, here is how I mapped out my path. From a chrysalis one evening, I became a butterfly.]

How can we not prefer this to the awkward prose found in so many prose autobiographies of the self-educated? For example:

Je suis né tout petit, plus petit que tant d'autres, et ma naissance fût drame, il n'en faut point douter.
Cette année-là, 6 juin, c'était 1904, autour de maman, grande dame si jolie dont la beauté suintait, comme l'odeur d'un parfum, se trouvaient réunis:
Papa, deux demi-soeurs et mon frère Fernand et, du côté de maman, la bien jolie Clotilde et mon frère Marcel; aussi bonne grand-mère et Marie l'inusable la bonne de toujours; Gustave, encore trop jeune, lui, restait dans son lit, bien ronflant à l'écart.
Nous habitions, je crois, 25, avenue Laumière, avenue large et claire, plein coeur du XIXe, encadrée de grands arbres, des platanes feuillus comme pas ailleurs je pense.

[I was born very small, smaller than so many others, and my birth was a dramatic event, there can be no doubt about it.
That year, June 6, it was 1904, around my mother, such a pretty great lady who exuded beauty, like the scent of perfume, were gathered:
Papa, two half-sisters and my brother Fernand and, on mama's side, the very pretty Clotilde and my brother Marcel; also dear grandmother and the everlasting Marie the maid forever; Gustave, still too young, staying in his bed, duly snoring in the background.
We were living, I think, at 25 Laumière Avenue, a broad and bright avenue, right in the heart of the nineteenth arrondissement, bordered by tall trees, leafy plane trees like nowhere else I think.[11]]

But this is flat and awkward only if you imagine that it is prose. It is written, you have noticed, in a rhythm (spoken) of hexasyllable. A story of childhood a hundred pages long follows, written in the same rhythm, acrobatic and bewitching. This candid prowess makes us think less about *Odyssée* (*The Odyssey*) by Victor Bérard, than about Raymond Roussel or the other Raymond, Queneau. In *Chêne et Chien* (*Oak and Dog*), "novel in verse" (1937), Queneau did not disguise his ironic metrics:

> Je naquis au Havre un vingt et un février
> en mil neuf cent et trois.
> Ma mère était mercière et mon père mercier:
> ils trépignaient de joie.
> Inexplicablement je connus l'injustice
> et fus mis un matin
> chez une femme avide et bête, une nourrice,
> qui me tendit son sein.
> De cette outre de lait j'ai de la peine à croire
> que j'en tirais festin
> en pressant de ma lèvre une sorte de poire,
> organe féminin.

[I was born in Le Havre on February 21, 1903. My mother and father were both haberdashers: they were jumping for joy. Inexplicably I came to know injustice and was placed one morning with a greedy and stupid woman, a wet nurse, who offered me her breast. I have trouble believing that I had any feast from this skin of milk by pressing with my lip a kind of pear, the female organ.]

And I think, especially, about the heartrending autobiography by Georges Perros, *Une vie ordinaire* (*An Ordinary Life*), "novel poem" (1967), written entirely in octosyllables.[12] "To eliminate" such texts based on a "definition" would be a rather ridiculous attitude. But the definition allows us to situate these marginal cases in their difference, as much in relation to poetry (use of a clearly autobiographical "I" secured on the proper name of the author, in place of the traditional lyric "I") as in relation to autobiography. After all, the style of Sartre's *Les Mots* is perceived by certain readers to be as "artificial" as Queneau's parodic versification.

Autobiographical Ideology

But I am coming to the main point. By focusing on the contract, not only have I neglected certain elements of generic perception, but I have especially run the risk of seeming a simpleton. Indeed, I have tackled these problems of contract (commitment to telling the "truth," use of proper names, use of the "I," etc.) from an essentially linguistic and formal point of view. My theoretical point of reference has been Benveniste—in the same way that Elizabeth Bruss, in her study comparable to "Le Pacte," relied on Searle. Both of us are grammarians, and we have conducted a kind of "pragmatic" literary study. It is obvious that the problems raised by contract can be analyzed from other disciplines and through other methods: psychology and psychoanalysis, but also sociology and the study of ideology. Well, all these disciplines will adopt vis-à-vis some presuppositions of the autobiographical pact a critical attitude, which sometimes moreover catches up with popular suspicion: what illusion to believe that we can tell the truth, and to believe that each of us has an individual and autonomous existence! How can we think that in autobiography it is the lived life that produces the text, when it is the text that produces the life! My purpose, in "Le Pacte," was not to enter into this debate, but simply to clarify and to describe the positions and beliefs necessary to the functioning of this system. As a result, certain readers, like Ryan and Benrekassa, for whom critical deconstruction is essential, could think that I was taking the effects for the causes.[13] Doesn't the formal quibbling that I practice grant an efficient virtue to what is only a surface phenomenon? Do I not, in dissecting the formal conditions of the effects, forget the other conditions? Where, in "Le Pacte," are the unconscious, the struggle of classes, history talked about? I am myself taken in, and I am a party to the ideology of the genre that I am claiming to analyze. My formalism, exactly like that which I have reproached Todorov for practicing (*Le Pacte*, p. 328; p. 153 of the present volume), is an idealist strategy.

How do I answer this? That my purpose in "Le Pacte" was limited, that subsequently, in *Je est un autre* (1980), I asked myself precisely these questions? You won't believe me. It's better to get on with the confessions: yes, I have been fooled. I believe that we can promise to tell the truth; I believe in the transparency of language, and in the existence of a complete subject who expresses himself through it; I believe that my proper name guarantees my autonomy and my singularity (even though I have crossed several Philippe Lejeunes in my life); I believe that when I say "I," it is I who am speaking: I believe in the Holy Ghost of the first person. And who doesn't believe in it? But of course it also happens that I believe the contrary, or at least claim to believe it. Whence the fascination that *Roland Barthes par Roland Barthes* (*Roland Barthes by Roland Barthes*, 1975) has held for me; it seems to be the anti-*Pact* par excellence and proposes a dizzying game of lucidity around all the presuppositions of autobiographical discourse—so dizzying that it ends up giving the reader the illusion that it is not doing what it nevertheless is doing. "In the field of the subject, there is no referent."[14] To a lesser degree, and more candidly, many autobiographers have outlined analogous strategies. We *indeed know* all this; we are not so dumb, but, once this precaution has been taken, we go on as if we did not know it. Telling the truth about the self, constituting the self as complete subject—it is a fantasy. In spite of the fact that autobiography is impossible, this in no way prevents it from existing. Perhaps, in describing it, I in turn took my desire for reality; but what I had wanted to do, was to describe this desire in its reality, a reality shared by a great number of authors and readers.

Idolatry

I was struck by a sentence by Georges May, at the beginning of his book on autobiography: he congratulates himself for not being "afflicted by some aberrant form of idolatry for this genre of literature" (*L'Autobiographie*, p. 15). I must admit the opposite: the aberrant form that my idolatry has assumed is the desire to write. I chose to work, academically, *on* autobiography, because in a parallel direction I wanted to work *on* my own autobiography. In two words I can try to justify this idolatry which took hold of me fifteen years ago, but which, undoubtedly, took root even earlier than that. I loved the immensity of the field that was opening up before me: I was able, without losing the benefit of earlier works, to change my objective constantly. Nothing about the field is narrow or limited. The study of autobiography causes other disciplines to open up—essentially psychoanalysis and psychology, sociology, history—whence come numerous contacts. It allows the attention to self to be allied with the listening of the other. Around 1972, at the time when I was writing "Le Pacte," I was interested almost exclusively in literary masterpieces; I was studying, for example, the work of Michel Leiris by pursuing a "psychoanalytical" reading—very narcissistic. Today I am involved with some quite different concerns, which I surely could not have foreseen. I became democratized: it is the life of everyone that interests me; no longer the sophisticated texts, but the elementary forms, the most widely known, of autobiographical discourse and writing. I owe it to Sartre for having taken this turn. While studying the film *Sartre par lui-même* (*Sartre by Himself*, 1976) of Alexandre Astruc and Michel Contat, I was struck by the differences between the written and the oral, and by the importance of the media. I especially noticed that, when Sartre was recounting his life orally, he was talking like everyone else.[15] He was truly, as he says at the end of *Les Mots*, "a whole man composed of all men and as good as all of them and no better than any." Why privilege Sartre? Why not turn my attention to "anyone of them"? Every person carries within himself a rough draft, perpetually reshaped, of the story of his life: this is what oral history tries to capture on tape. All around us, there are people, far more than you might think, who put this draft of their life in good order; they write and no one reads what they've written. We can have access to this hidden continent by reading the autobiographies published at the author's expense, for example, in *La Pensée universelle*.[16] Here am I an amateur sociologist. Or even a historian: I set out to take inventory of the entire stock of autobiographies written in France in the nineteenth century.[17] And there I find again the link with my own story, which

I thought I had abandoned when my interest in Leiris ended. With my tape recorder I have explored the history of my parents and my family. And, among these nineteenth-century autobiographers that I am attempting to bring out of oblivion is my own great-grandfather, Xavier-Edouard Lejeune (1845–1918), business clerk, self-taught, author of a wonderful "naïve" autobiography, *Les Etapes de la vie* (*Stages of Life*).[18] This project has given me an opportunity to discover that the unconscious is not deciphered only in dreams and lapses, but in the texture of family history, if only one takes an interest in its secrets. . . . If I recall this entire journey, it is because the image of the formalist definer that "Le Pacte" gives me seems a partial one to me. But it is also to explain the ambiguous situation in which I found myself in order to "formalize."

"Mea Culpa"

As soon as I write, as a matter of fact, I share the desires and illusions of autobiographers, and I am surely not ready to renounce them. I say outloud: "I is someone else," and in a whisper perhaps I add: "but what a shame!" I am therefore inside and outside at the same time, in a situation of overlap that can be a handicap or a resource. Handicap if I act like a supporter: errors of appreciation, a too normative discourse, well-defined formulation on the problems of identity, and so on. Passion comes through under theory. But resource, perhaps, if commitment and lucidity are balanced. In "Le Pacte," a final movement of withdrawal and relativism (p. 28–30 of the present volume) echoes the empiricist proclamation of the beginning (pp. 3–4), surrounding with a varied border the central section illuminated by a cruder light. The same strategy works at the level of the volume as a whole: the final chapter, "Autobiography and Literary History," adds to "Le Pacte" the sharps and flats it was missing, in particular on the problem of the definition (pp. 149–50 of the present volume). Should I not have modified "Le Pacte" itself instead? I preferred to retain a gesture in which "error" and adjustment are balanced. Perhaps the interest that certain readers may have taken in "Le Pacte" was due to a mixture of fervor and analysis that gives the object studied more contrast? It is not up to me to decide, but it will be understood that I prefer this hypothesis to the one suggested by the ridiculous recantations of Autopact. In any case, I have observed a corresponding balance in the criticisms of my work: too formalistic for some, too relativist for others; believing too much in the human person and in the classical subject, or not believing in them enough, and so on.

But . . . one does not escape one's self. Rereading the preceding discussion, I notice that I am only repeating the strategy I had used at the end of "Le Pacte" in order to paralyze all criticism:

> When all is said and done, this study would seem to me, then, to be itself more a document to study (the attempt of a twentieth-century

reader to rationalize and clarify his criteria of reading) rather than a "scientific" text: a document to assign to the file of a scientific history of literary communication (p. 30).

Modest conclusion? Rather strategic reversal: what I seem to lose on one side, I recover on another. I offer myself, to the scholar who criticized me perhaps, as a new object of science. Look at me: autobiography, it is I! As a result, my mistakes become facts to be studied: even if it's on another level, you can't get around what I have written. For want of relevance, I allege a fundamental competence. I am one of the family; it is my native language. I hold such a position in the family that I apply to myself the reasoning that several pages earlier (p. 25) I applied to autobiographers, that of "authenticity": if they make mistakes, distort, and so on, in relation to what we can assume to be reality, this distortion is their very truth! And to those who have a clear perception of things, I refuse the possibility of saying something interesting. "I was wrong—but I was right to be wrong!" Undoubtedly self-criticism, like autobiography, is an impossible undertaking. . . .

And After?

The only excuse for so much complacency is that this little "owner's tour" overflows into a new work. I will indicate here only the point of departure and the directions. It will be based on the chart on page 16.

The chart studies the combined effects of the pact and the use of proper names (relationship of the author's name and the name of the main character). In each square I have marked the effect produced. There are two "blind" squares, corresponding to the cases "excluded by definition." It is undoubtedly I who was blind. First of all because it is obvious that the chart is poorly constructed. For each axis I propose an alternative (fictional/autobiographical, for the pact; different/similar, for the name); I am thinking about the possibility of *neither one nor the other*, but I forget *both at the same time*! I accept indetermination, but I refuse ambiguity. Moreover, this is a common practice. The name of the character can be at the same time similar to the name of the author and different: same initials, different names (Jules Vallès/Jacques Vingtras); same first name, different last names (even if it is only a difference of one letter: Lucien Bodard/Lucien Bonnard), and so on. A book can be presented as a novel, at the level of the subtitle, and as an autobiography at the level of the publisher's blurb. Sixteen squares, then, and not nine. But no matter that the chart is incomplete. The advantage of a chart is that it simplifies, that it dramatizes a problem. It ought to be inspiring. If it were more complicated, it would be more correct, but so confused that it would no longer serve any purpose. This particular chart inspired a novelist (who is also an academic): Serge Doubrovsky. Doubrovsky had published a novel in

1969, *La Dispersion* (*The Dispersion*), of very modern and poetic writing, and undoubtedly of "autobiographical" inspiration—whose hero had no name. In 1973, he was in the process of writing a second novel, along the same lines, when he read "Le Pacte." This is what he has since told me:

> I remember, while reading your study that appeared in *Poétique*, having checked off the passage (that I've just found again): "Can the hero of a novel declared as such have the same name as the author? Nothing would prevent such a thing from existing . . . , but, in practice, no example of such a study comes to mind." I was then right in the middle of writing and that had concerned me, struck me to the core. Even now, I am not sure about the theoretical status of my undertaking, it's not up to me to make such a decision, but I wanted very deeply to fill up that "square," which your analysis left empty, and it is a real desire that suddenly linked your critical text and what I was in the process of writing, if not blindly, at least in semi-obscurity.[19]

That novel was published under the ambiguous title of *Fils* (*Son*, or *Threads*, Editions Galilée, 1977). Through a kind of interior monologue carried on by a writing that draws systematically on signifiers, we follow the protagonist, whose name is Serge Doubrovsky, for an entire day in New York, where he works as a professor. As in *Histoire* (*Story*) by Claude Simon, the day is used to condense the images of a life. I read this beautiful text with enthusiasm. But I noticed afterward that I had read it "badly": I had believed what I shouldn't have believed. This is what occurred to me while listening to Serge Doubrovsky publicly comment on his book. I had been incapable of measuring what made up the fictional part of this book, which he presents as an "autofiction."

From this misunderstanding, I began to reflect on the problems of proper name and fiction. I was aided in this by Serge Doubrovsky himself who, in the manner of Ricardou, has since 1977 commented freely on his own novel and on its theoretical status.[20] The problem posed by Doubrovsky is both general and quite current: these last years, many "novels" have been published in which the protagonist was given the author's name. To cite only a few of them: *Le Têtard* (*The Tadpole*) by Jacques Lanzmann (1976), *L'Infini chez soi* (*Infinity at Home*) by Dominique Rolin (1980), *Joue-nous España* (*Play Us España*), "memoir novel" by Jocelyne François (1980). From "to lie truly" ["*mentir vrai*"] to "autofiction," the literary autobiographical novel has come closer to autobiography, to the point of casting more doubt than ever before on the boundary between the two areas.[21] That uncertainty is especially stimulating for theoretical reflection.[22] Under what conditions can the proper name of an author be perceived by a reader as "fictitious" or ambiguous? How, in these texts, are the referential use of language—for which the categories of truth (opposed to the lie) and reality (opposed to fiction) remain relevant—and the practice of literary writing for which the categories are blurred – articulated? I will try to reconsider, from the perspective of a completely grammatical study of "pragmatics," the broad questions that have been so widely debated.[23]

Appendix

1. Parallel Studies

1974 Elizabeth W. Bruss, "L'Autobiographie considérée comme acte littéraire," *Poétique* 17, pp. 14–26; further elaborated in *Autobiographical Acts: The Changing Situation of a Literary Genre* (Baltimore: Johns Hopkins University Press, 1976).

1975 John R. Searle, "The Logical Status of Fictional Discourse," *New Literary History* 6 (Winter), pp. 319–32.

1976 Darrel Mansell, "Unsettling the Colonel's Hash: 'Fact' in Autobiography," *Modern Language Quarterly* 37, pp. 115–32; reprinted in *The American Autobiography : A Collection of Critical Essays*, ed. Albert E. Stone, (New York: Prentice Hall, 1981), pp. 61–79.

2. Critical Discussions

1975 *Revue d'histoire littéraire de la France*, Nov.–Dec., an issue devoted to autobiography. P. Lejeune, "Autobiographie et histoire littéraire," followed by a discussion with G. Gusdorf (pp. 931–33) and with Y. Coirault (p. 936); G. Gusdorf, "De l'autobiographie initiatique à l'autobiographie genre littéraire," especially pp. 959–64 and the discussion, pp. 995–96.

1977 Michel Beaujour, "Autobiographie et autoportrait," *Poétique* 32, pp. 442–58 (see also *Miroirs d'encre*, Paris: Editions du Seuil, 1979).

Christophe Miething, review in *Archiv für das Studium des Neueren Sprachen und Literaturen*, pp. 232–36.

1979 Gérard Genette, *Introduction à l'architexte* (Paris: Editions du Seuil) pp. 75 and 84.

Lawrence D. Kritzman, "Autobiography: Readers and Texts," *Dispositio* 4, pp. 117–21.

Paul de Man, "Autobiography as De–facement," *Modern Language Notes* 94, pp. 919–30.

Georges May, *L'Autobiographie*, Paris: P.U.F.

1980 Michael Ryan, "Self–Evidence," *Diacritics* 10 (Summer), pp. 2–16 (He subjects two texts – the article of the American Declaration of Independence which states that all men are created equal and the text of the "Le Pacte" – to a double analysis: a logical deconstruction inspired by Derrida and a Marxist interpretation).

1981 Georges Benrekassa, "Le dit du moi: du roman personnel à l'autobiographie; *René/Werther, Poésie et Vérité/Mémoires d'Outre Tombe*," in *Les Sujets de l'écriture*, ed. Jean Decottignies (Lille: Presses de l'Université de Lille) pp. 85–140 (especially pp. 85–90).

Joshua Wilner, "Autobiography and Addiction: The Case of De Quincey," *Genre* 14 (Winter), pp. 493–503 (on the basis of the *Confessions of an English Opium Eater*, published anonymously, the essay reveals the presuppositions and limitations of what the "Le Pacte" proposes regarding the proper name as a marker of self-reference).

II. Autobiography, History, and Contemporary Civilization

Chapter 7
Autobiography and Literary History

To take a modern and contemporary genre as an object of study is to place oneself in an ambiguous situation, which is both a resource and a limitation. The choice of object is not innocent: insofar as genres are social institutions, to isolate a genre in order to constitute it as an object of knowledge can be a way of collaborating with the institution as much as doing scientific work.

Literary genres are not beings in themselves: they constitute, in each era, a sort of implicit code through which, and thanks to which, works of the past and recent works can be received and classified by readers. It is in relation to the models, to the "horizons of expectation," to an entire variable geography, that literary texts are *produced* then *received*, that they satisfy this expectation or that they transgress it and force it to renew itself.[1] Like other social institutions, the system of genres is governed by a force of inertia (that tends to ensure a continuity facilitating communication) and by a force of change (a literature being alive only insofar as it transforms the expectations of readers). The system of genres is linked to other institutions: the educational system, which plays a part in maintaining permanence by making problematics function that are no longer current; the critical response of newspapers and magazines, in which current expectations are expressed spontaneously; and the publishing industry, which exploits and eventually changes these expectations through the game of "series."

The academic study of genres, as scientific as it might be, is involved, in its own way, in the institution: it often plays a part in constructing or in consolidating what it claims to analyze or describe. It rationalizes or systematizes, in order to ground in law and in dignity the genre studied. We see it currently in the case of critical literature on genres like the comic strip,[2] science fiction, and the detective novel, where the phenomenon is more visible, because, instead of bringing into question the interior limits of literature, it displays the very fluctuations of the boundaries of literature. Memoirs and autobiography have had a status outside literature as well, before being more or less integrated into it. Critical studies of genre play a part in its change of status and in its "promotion."

Linked to the genre as institution, critical literature on autobiography is subject at the same time, insofar as genre is historical, to the conditions of any "historical operation," to use the language of Michel de Certeau.[3] History is not written in a timeless place, but in a present, and it is when we forget about it that the present is most noticeable. With some perspective, the historical text produced in this way becomes itself a dated document, which reflects the effort of an era to structure its universe. I was struck by this while reading a nineteenth-century study on the genre of memoirs, *Les Mémoires et l'Histoire en France* (*Memoirs and History in France*, 1863) by Charles Caboche.[4] A century later, the errors of method and their presuppositions become rather evident, but I was surprised when I realized that these presuppositions were analogous to those on which the greater part of the criticism on autobiography rests. It is therefore possible for us to commit the same kind of errors and to be, on this point, disciples of Caboche. I will try to show this through some examples.

Everything really happens as if the institutional function of critical literature on genres made it difficult to conceive of history. The breakdown of the object, the search for invariants, the normative and theoretical desire, not counting the affective fixation on the object studied, are the reason that everything originating in history — relativity and variability — is relegated to the background, and imagined in an off-centered perspective. In this, moreover, it encounters general problems of today's literary history, which continues, under different forms (the belief in the existence of "facts" on the practical side, or of "types" on the theoretical side), to work as if there existed a timeless place where absolute knowledge would be possible, and as if history were a surface phenomenon unfolding on a permanent foundation. This chapter will therefore give me an opportunity to reflect upon what literary history should be, understood in the strict sense, that is to say, as the study of the evolution of literature as system.[5]

The objective of this chapter is therefore twofold: to show how genre as institution functions, by analyzing the presuppositions of critical literature; and to reflect on the paths that open onto a new literary history.

The Illusions of Perspective

The desire for permanence that is at the heart of the idea of "genre" can lead to two optical illusions, apparently contradictory, which are in fact variations of one single error.

The first is *the illusion of eternity*. Autobiography has always existed, even though in varying degrees and under diverse forms. One is therefore going to be able to write its history from antiquity up to our day, to trace its evolution, its progress, its detours, up to and including its modern accomplishments. To those who declare that autobiography is an essentially modern genre, a thousand examples will be found to the contrary. Certainly, there is a problem here of vocabulary, but when it is examined more closely, we see that it hides a more basic problem.[6]

This illusion is very natural: it corresponds to the most spontaneous historical operation, which makes us constantly redistribute the elements of the past depending upon our present categories. The anachronism consists here of taking a characteristic that is relevant today in our system of defining genres (discourse in the first person associated with some form of personal commitment) and believing that this characteristic has always had the same kind of relevance, that is to say, that the system of opposition is inherent in the characteristic, whereas it is purely historical and dated. This would amount to confusing, in J. Tynianov's terminology, form and function.[7]

The anachronistic attitude is acceptable when we are in the register of interpretation; our dialogue with the past would hardly be possible without the swarming of distortions that the gap between the code of emission and the code of reception causes. Consequently, it happens quite often that works change "genre" while passing through, in the course of history, different systems of expectation: a secondary characteristic of the work is obviously allotted the main function. With autobiography, the mistake is so much more tempting that, in our system, the use of discourse in the first person in agreement with the autobiographical pact has as its function to create the illusion of person-to-person communication. From the single fact that he addresses himself directly to the readers, and that *we* are now his readers, the autobiographer of two centuries ago can give us the impression that he has abolished time. Insofar as he expressed himself in a code not too different from our own, the mistake is not serious. This transformation of reading must itself become the *object* of a historical study, but it could not be its *foundation*.

Such a thing is particularly obvious when we imagine civilizations quite distant from ours, like those of antiquity and of the Middle Ages. This is the main objection that can be made to Georg Misch's monumental attempt, whatever the interest of his inquiry.[8] To decide that autobiography (very vaguely defined as the fact of recounting one's life) is an essential and profound vocation of humanity, one of its most noble tasks, and to follow the progressive awakening of the human consciousness from the biographies of the pharaohs to J.-J. Rousseau is an ideological and mythological endeavor without great historical relevance, even though it does inevitably come across a number of real historical problems. Is it legitimate to study "autobiography" in the Middle Ages, and to regroup in that way texts that had no connections between them at the time, like the *Vie* (*Life*) by Guibert de Nogent, which inscribes itself in the Augustinian tradition of confessions, and the *Histoire de mes malheurs* (*Story of My Misfortunes*) by Abélard, who is an extraordinary case, but atypical? In his analyses on medieval poetics, Paul Zumthor has shown that none of the conditions of modern autobiography existed then (absence of the notion of author; absence of autoreferential literary use of the first person). The apparent exceptions are due to the retrospective illusion of modern readers mistaken about the codes of the age.[9]

The problem is pretty much the same in the history of art. Do we imagine that we can write a treatise "on still life" by assuming that it is an eternal vocation of painting, and by placing on the same level with the systematic production of the Dutch in the seventeenth century, stylized motifs of a decorative and symbolic function found on ancient pottery? Or, to make a comparison that brings us closer to our subject, is not the illusion analogous to the one that has moved some modern art critics to pay systematic attention to the *self-portrait*,[10] constructing vast corpora in which are juxtaposed all the known self-portraits since the Middle Ages, in an instructive way certainly, but also debatable insofar as this collection of self-portraits is not related to the history of the social function of the portrait, nor situated differentially in relation to portraits and to other works of the painters in question? Or, to come back this time to the literary domain, could a history of the "letter" as literary genre display something other than the permanent variability of the system of genres and the boundaries of what we presently call literature? There is no eternal essence of the letter, but the fluctuating and contingent existence of a certain mode of written communication, which, combined with other characteristics, has been able to fill different functions in different systems.

Studies of the genealogical type that isolate a currently relevant element in order to follow its trail by going back into history have, then, an illusory quality, exactly like historical studies of etymology and semantics that focus on an isolated word. It is the evolution of the system of language in its totality that can be the object of history. If an inquiry, starting with a particular trait, does not end up surpassing it and integrating it into the general history of the system, but tends to solidify it and eternalize it, it has a mythological function. In our particular case, the inquiry must contribute to the feeling of permanence necessary to the "genre" and give it its patent of nobility. Moreover, the very idea of becoming a specialist on a literary genre often implies a kind of affective fixation, similar to what is found among regional and local historians. Charles Caboche, writing the history of memoirs, talks about authors he is studying by humorously calling them "my clients;"[11] he therefore sees his role as that of an advocate. This tendency toward partiality and blindness to everything that is not the studied corpus is the stumbling block of all particular histories; and since the definition of the object is based on the presupposition of its permanence, it is very difficult for the study to become really historical.

But the redistribution of the past according to modern criteria and the belief in permanence, not of genres, but of the elements that make them up, can be productive attitudes from the moment that they are well controlled.

As a matter of fact, literary genres are themselves the product of a redistribution of formal traits in part already existing in the earlier system, even if they used to have different functions in it. On condition of grasping this evolution of the systems, the investigation of origins and of continuity allows us to focus on the elements of the game from which new genres are constructed, and the manner in which the horizons of expectation have been progressively transformed. Thus, in the French domain, it is difficult to understand autobiography as it was written by Rousseau without situating it in relation to the tradition of religious confessions, or without seeing how, since the middle of the seventeenth century, a game of exchanges between memoirs and the novel had little by little transformed the narrative in the first person. This type of study must be carried out in a precise manner, without our attempting to show that a particular aspect is "already" part of autobiography, or, in the opposite sense, without our wanting to prove that autobiography "is only" the secularization of the centuries-old genre of religious confessions. Marc Fumaroli, in his study "Les Mémoires du XVIIᵉ siècle au carrefour des genres en prose" ("The Memoirs of the Seventeenth Century at the Crossroads of Prose Genres"),[12] analyzed in quite a relevant way the circulation of different models: the grafting of the Augustinian model around 1660, the borrowing by the novel of methods from memoirs, used in a different system. On this last point, we have an exact study by Philip Stewart, who indexed the methods used at the beginning of the eighteenth century by the novel in memoir form, but without situating them in a general study of exchanges between the two domains.[13] Often, as a matter of fact, the division of the studies of literary history between genre specialists ends up making us lose sight of the system as a whole; and it is difficult to reunite studies done from "regional" perspectives.

There exists a second illusion of perspective: that of the *birth* of genre, after which the new genre, born all of a sudden, would last in accordance with its essence. Here is a very tempting form of illusion, particularly in the French domain, where Rousseau established a sort of model that has obsessed autobiographers for a long time. It is comforting for the critic to find an "origin" that allows him to clearly separate a "before" (which he will call protohistory, as Wayne Shumaker has done,[14] or prehistory, as I have done) from an "after," in a messianic perspective: "Finally Rousseau came . . . " Insofar as the origin is at the same time a model, it disqualifies the past and closes off the future. We are thus led to underestimate the factors of continuity with the past and to overestimate the coherence of the modern development of the genre; we treat the two centuries that separate us from Rousseau as a vast synchrony. In a way, we will be tempted to think that the first autobiographers achieved the archetype of the genre,[15] or that the latter, since, has only fallen into ruins.[16] This attitude, too, leads us to sidestep reflection of a historical nature. But it is not devoid of relevance, and there are two reasons for this.

First, it reflects perfectly the presuppositions that make the functioning of genres possible. For the readers of one era, there is "genre" only where there exist, on the one hand, canonical texts that function as archetypes, that realize in an almost ideal manner what is believed to be the essence of the genre, and, on the other hand, the presumption of a continuity of writing, the production of a certain number of texts that, without conforming to the model, are in keeping with the same problematic, as so many variations and departures.

Next, it is true that the texts making up the corpus of a genre such as it functions in a given age have engendered one another and can, from a certain point of view, be seen as the transformation of one and the same text. With autobiography, this is particulary evident: to the methods that seem to be dictated by the situation of the autobiographer are added those that are in fact imposed by convention and the prior reading of other autobiographies.

This attitude is therefore less illusory than the one that consists of believing in the eternity of the genre and of seeking its remote origins. Here, as a matter of fact, we are looking for the *invariant* in a domain where it has historically existed and where it has functioned as relevant element; and the definitions that are given are clearly presented as useful only in a determined period. But history is not made up only of invariants, and the invariants themselves are only convenient approximations (like the "periods" in the domain of chronological breakdown). The illusion consists of seeing only the invariant and of transforming the real relative autonomy of the corpus into an absolute mythical independence. Criticism of the genre often gives in to this temptation and in this way fulfills its institutional function.

I will give two examples of this, chosen with a movement back in time or space that allows lucidity.

When Charles Caboche imagines the history of memoirs, he sees them strictly as a fixed and closed corpus. Fixed: from the Crusades up to Guizot, the genre knew no other evolution than that of the history it reflects; the infinite variety of tones and stories refers to the permanence of a spontaneity, itself constant and fixed, which forms the essence of the genre.[17] Closed: Caboche is blind to what is not memoirs. His is a total "regionalism." If he traditionally opposes memoirs and history, as has been done since the seventeenth century, he seems to have no idea, in 1863, of the exchanges that could be produced between memoirs and novel, nor of the upheavals that could intervene in literary geography over two centuries. The development of the chronicle of private life and the appearance of autobiography escape him: at the beginning of his book, he eliminates purely and simply all the narratives that do not have as their object the life of the nation; he perceives the narratives by the gentlemen of Port-Royal, the *Mémoires* of Marmontel, and the *Confidences* of Lamartine strictly on the same level, as a minor parasitical phenomenon, which would have always existed in the same way on the fringe of the noble branch of memoirs.[18] This blindness before the contemporary mutation ought to serve as a warning for us: who knows if the present theoreticians of autobiography, absorbed with consolidating the past, do not commit some comparable error?

Two quite remarkable studies have appeared recently in the United States: by Francis R. Hart, "Notes for an Anatomy of Modern Autobiography," and by William L. Howarth, "Some Principles of Autobiography."[19] These two authors attack — I will show later in this chapter — the normative function of the criticism of genre. So it is all the more surprising that they themselves remain faithful to the "regionalist" and "timeless" perspective and that, writing in a journal used to found a new literary history, they take such a scant account of history.[20] Hart and Howarth speculate on a fixed corpus of autobiographies: Hart, from Rousseau to our day; Howarth, since Saint Augustine. They move about here without difficulty as in a homogenous milieu, without raising the problem of definition. The implicitly constructed corpus is equally closed: if autobiographies are compared between themselves, they are scarcely seen in the framework of historical ensembles where they have really functioned (other "genres," other texts produced by the same authors).

Normative Function

Genre is based upon presuppositions of permanence and autonomy. It therefore implies belief in a kind of identity, which can be produced only by a series of distinctions and precepts that are intended both to isolate the genre from other productions and to hierarchize and center the domain enclosed in this way. Any public tends to classify what it receives and to receive it through the classification of everything that it has received before. This job of classification, of standardization, is done at first in an empirical manner: Hans Robert Jauss has suggested it be designated by the expression "horizon of expectation," a horizon against which any new production appears, fulfilling the expectation faithfully, falling short of it, or forcing it to change.[21] The expression "horizon" is excellent: its hazy distance represents the way in which all prior experiences of reading tend to dissolve into a sort of model landscape; and we know that in its literal sense, a horizon is a relative phenomenon of perspective that changes when the observer moves (here, in time). Far from leading to an idealistic typology, the concept of horizon of expectation becomes a fine tool for contemplating historical evolution, as I will soon demonstrate. This horizon of expectation can remain implicit, and it is moving. But the tendency of the vast majority of the public (and the critics) in all ages has been to want, if I might say, to *fix* the horizon, to stabilize it. The novelties and the redistributions that we accommodate are always the last, after which we close. The theories of genres are part of this system of inertia that is necessary to the continuity of literature (and, by this very fact, to its subsequent change).

We live with the idea that the criticism of genres was normative in ancient times (from the time of poetics), but that since the start of the modern era, it has become descriptive and has more or less skillfully made its way toward the scientific, from the biologism of Brunetière to present poetic theories. It is undoubtedly an illusion: on the one hand, we inevitably come to know the ancient normative texts through the caricatural usage that the scholastic apparatus has made of them; on the other hand, only norms that are not our own can seem like norms to us; we inevitably take ours to be the laws of nature (laws of nature that are today linguistic and psychological). The normative work is necessary and permanent, even if it is exercised according to changing modalities in which we do not recognize it right away. Journalistic criticism, like academic criticism, takes part in the normalization. Any novelty that breaks an old expectation provides at the same time its own horizon, whose codification it initiates. And critical discourse, as soon as it succeeds in identifying this horizon, hastens to solidify it and to construct it in concrete, in laws, types, and essences.

Only certain kinds of criticism can adopt a descriptive posture: criticism that is concerned with genres belonging to past and foreign literatures, or criticism that deals with genres in which custom and use as consumer products impose a nonevolving list of specifications. In these cases the normative function no longer needs to be practiced, or rather is practiced by another method. But for current and modern genres, the normative function must be exercised. It is very instructive to leaf through an anthology of critical texts on the novel written within the last hundred years;[22] the critics consolidate *a posteriori* the authors' discourses, all in search of definitions and essences whose function is to project into the absolute and to ground in law that which with some perspective we easily identify as particular and dated aesthetics. T. Todorov has shown how this normative temptation was presented in the works of theoreticians like Lubbock and Bakhtin.[23]

An analogous phenomenon has been occurring in front of our eyes for ten years with the "new novel," which has brought with it its theoretical and normative decor. And it is a matter of course, in this perspective, that current theories on the outdated nature of the division of genres, in particular those advocating the abolition of the boundaries between novel and poetry and the promotion of the concepts of writing and of text, are part of a redistribution of the horizons of expectation, and, whatever their "theoretical" foundations, exercise a normative function indispensable to modern literature.

For the different genres of personal literature, things happen in the same way.

Charles Caboche's discourse on memoirs was prompted by the memorialists. He puts in order, collects, and dilutes what was said by the memorialists that he judges typical; he confesses to owing a great deal to Mme de Motteville.[24] Part of the critical literature on autobiography has done the same kind of work on Rousseau and his successors. In passing from authors to critics, discourse takes on a more normative aspect.

The normative behavior of the critic will most often be concealed under the appearances of a "descriptive" and objective behavior; he is going to do his best to give a *definition* of the genre, as if a historical phenomenon ought to be "defined," and not simply described at first. In order to define, the critic is going to be led not only to say what the genre is, but what it *must* be in order to be what it is. To have to be and to be become confused, and the description becomes normative. The critic begins to determine what is the essence, or the model of the genre:

> From among all the memoirs and writers of memoirs studied carefully, a kind of model has stood out, which is made up of the original qualities of all the others; and under this model, which it would be fanciful to claim to come across somewhere, have remained all the particular examples that the inexhaustible French genius was able to offer and will offer again in the future, every time that it will want to relate episodes of our history.[25]

The inductive step, releasing the common elements in a "corpus," is confused with the deductive step, since the corpus itself has been built upon the definition. The operation is circular: it corresponds to a rationalization of the horizon of expectation, to a change of language (from empiricism to theoretical language) rather than to a change of method. The ambiguity of the word "model," like that of the word "rules," facilitates and masks the circularity. In this way Caboche is going to elaborate his model of memoirs which is simultaneously descriptive (it makes the different levels of opposition function with the genre of the story) and normative (all the characteristics are specified in "qualities"; and it is a particular aesthetic of the genre that is imposed, through successive restrictions, around three adjectives: memoirs must be "personal," "individual," and "simple").[26] This attitude should not be scorned as illusory, for it is instructive on the "horizons of expectation" of the genre, and it can often entail an effort of description that, in another methodological context, could be continued in a fruitful way. It must only be controlled and surpassed.

I proceeded in this manner in *L'Autobiographie en France*: I wanted to give a definition of autobiography and to establish a coherent "corpus." Faced with such a blurred and many-sided domain, it was tempting to decide that a certain type of narrative was consistent with the essence of the genre. I followed the lead of Roy Pascal in his fundamental work *Design and Truth in Autobiography*,[27] identifying autobiography with a particular type of autobiography, that in which the individual focuses on the genesis of his personality. Once having settled on the choice of model, I built the "corpus" through a system of exclusions. We will judge either as failures or aberrant cases, or as elements outside the corpus, everything that is inconsistent with the model. The genre becomes a sort of "club" of which the critic makes himself the guardian, selecting with the help of exclusions a relatively pure "race." If the criteria are too precise, we run the risk of schematizing the "horizons of expectation," of being blind to related phenomena and to historical evolution.

The index that I had made up according to these criteria also suffers from a distortion of a different kind. Among the criteria of selection, there is one that acts even without the knowledge of the collector. This is what Escarpit calls "the first law of Lehman,"[28] which states: "In the historical vision that a human group has of literature, the residue of contemporary production tends to be equal in importance to the residue of the past." It is certainly probable that this fault is alleviated by the existence of a real increase, over two centuries, of the number of "autobiographies" published each year. But such a quantitative study could only be done by starting with systematic lists, and not with a course in which works are selected according to "norms of the genre" and the sorting of value to which any past production is subjected.

The normative function can be exercised slyly through the illusion of an objective definition; it can also be confessed frankly in attempts that are made in order to establish an "art of autobiography," whether it is on a pragmatic or theoretical level.

Richard G. Lillard drew up an amusing list of "qualities to cultivate" and "defects to avoid," in the very pedagogical perspective of hints addressed to students of autobiography.[29] The latter quite often have no experience in literary composition and naïvely believe that their "competence" on the subject will suffice. *"Do It Yourself"*: Lillard gives them hints that he bases on the analysis of papers handed in by earlier classes, as in the reports published by examination judges. These hints are presented according to an average model of the autobiographical narrative, and they emphasize the minimum requirements of relevance and coherence necessary to ensure communication with the reader. It is in this same pragmatic and pedagogical perspective that we must locate the recent manual by two American professors, R. J. Porter and H. R. Wolf,[30] who try to train their students in the reading, but also in the *writing*, of autobiography: they suggest some true autobiographical "practical exercises" to the students, which ought to make them aware of the minimum requirements of the genre such as it is understood today.

On the level of aesthetic theory, B. J. Mandel has tried more ambitiously to define in the absolute an "art of autobiography."[31] The guiding principle is apparently flexible and liberal: it is the adaptation of the means to the ends aimed at by the autobiographer. But, since the ends can be numerous and difficult to establish, since the gamut of means is equally very vast, since the demand for unity and relevance is in reality arbitrary, Mandel's findings are uncertain and translate in absolute terms some particular aesthetic choices. For example, according to these criteria, Stendhal's autobiography is judged a failure because of its *disorder*. It is one possible value judgment. Others are equally possible. All are interesting as documents to add to the history file, but none of them could serve as a basis for writing history.

In a recent article in *New Literary History*, Francis Hart conducted a systematic analysis of this normative attitude and of the excessive simplifications that it entails.[32] I will give a general outline of the article. Hart begins by focusing on the rigidity and arbitrariness of the choices that the critics (G. Gusdorf and R. Pascal, on the one hand, W. Shumaker and B. J. Mandel, on the other) make on the three problems of "truth," technique, and autobiographical intentions. Then he proceeds a little like Maupassant does when, in his preface to *Pierre et Jean* (*Peter and John*), he gathers an impressive list of European "novels" to show that it is arbitrary to present a particular aesthetic as the law of the genre. Hart has chosen some forty modern autobiographical texts since Rousseau in order to show for each of the points the great variety of solutions and attitudes adopted by the autobiographers. His study, which is presented like an "anatomy," is based on an excellent dissociative method (to distinguish some problems too often confused, to dissociate factors and categories); our only regret is that this method is applied to just a few autobiographies (regionalist illusion of the closed corpus). It emphasizes that there surely does not exist one unique model of autobiography: in a way, it would tend rather to suggest that each autobiography has its own standard, founded on an original combination of solutions to the problems common to all of them. Indeed, this internal multiplicity is based on a global unity of the field that is accepted by Hart as fact and never questioned. The problem of limits, boundaries, connections, and oppositions with the rest of the system of genres hardly appears. Everything happens as if Hart had not followed through to the end of his dissociative method, and as if the illusion linked to the criticism of genre could be demystified on one point, only by giving into it on another, from the moment when we have agreed to be situated within the framework of the genre.

The difficulties that one has in trying to break away from a simplifying typology are well illustrated in an article by William L. Howarth, published in 1974 in the same journal.[33] Continuing Hart's investigations, Howarth tried to look at how elements disssociated in this way could be rejoined, by supposing that the distinctive traits must in spite of everything be brought together in a regular way in secondary types. These regroupings led him to identify three types of autobiographies: oratorical (under the patronage of Saint Augustine), dramatic (under that of Cellini), poetic or problematic (under that of Rousseau). These terms refer to the analyses of Frye, by whom Howarth is greatly inspired. The demonstration is brilliant, but sometimes arbitrary by dint of coherence: it reintroduces, it is true by reducing it, and, therefore, by putting it into perspective, the normative and archetypal attitude. The dissociative flexibility is counterbalanced by a desire for classification at all cost. Do all works fall into these categories? Can't a work be part of several categories at one time? Couldn't a fourth category exist? And couldn't the categories be divided according to different and historically variable criteria? Not one of these questions is asked.

The analyses of Hart and Howarth are, then, in relation to the criticism of the genre, in an ambiguous position: on the one hand, they are part of the mythology of the genre, since they never go beyond the implicitly defined corpus and neglect historicity; on the other, they challenge this mythology by refusing value judgments, by reestablishing a plurality of models, and by practicing a dissociative analysis of the factors that would be quite fruitful if pursued further. It is undoubtedly, as Howarth's example shows, because they are stopped along the way by another form of illusion related to the literature on genres: the theoretical illusion.

The Domain of Theory

Genre criticism has as its function to consolidate the genre studied by establishing its permanence and its autonomy, and by rationalizing its normative system. I have spoken until now only about "regionalist" attempts made on the level of particular genres. But it is clear that this active participation in the system of genres can also be situated on a higher level, on the level of the overall system of genres. A. Thibaudet said: "A theory of genres must remain the highest ambition of Criticism with a capital 'C'."[34] This ambition still seems to be shared by the critics. The most impressive endeavor in this direction is Northrop Frye's *Anatomy of Criticism*.[35] The objection that I have made to "regionalism" applies in this case, but it is likely to be replaced by still more serious objections, insofar as such endeavors end up refusing to conceive of history, and plunge whoever gets involved in it into a theoretical impasse. At the basis of these endeavors is an error concerning the domain in which theoretical reflection can be practiced.

To elaborate a "theory of genres" is to try to formulate a synthesis in the absolute by making use of concepts that make sense only in the historical field. In this way we could only end up with ingenious constructions, with a complicated syncretism founded on anachronism. "Genres" are complex historical phenomena that exist only in the system. To rely on Aristotle to construct a "theory of genres" is to postulate the existence of a structure immanent to literature, and to make of history a simple surface phenomenon, which could be reduced to variations or combinations of fundamental archetypes that would not change. This antihistorical idealism projects into the heavens the "types" of ideas of which historical genres would be the incarnations. In order to grasp the methodological error, we can compare the problem with the one posed in linguistics. Establishing a "theory of genres" (which is not really a theory, but a classifying system) is a little like trying to *re-create* out of historical languages an immanent universal language, of which they would be the various incarnations, and which could be in reality only a kind of Esperanto, an artificial synthetic language (in which we would nonetheless recognize the predominance of the inventor's language). What could be said of a semantician who would try to construct a "universal vocabulary," instead of trying to establish the laws of functioning of semantic systems? Who would stick to contents, instead of studying *operations*?

Todorov has criticized Frye's practice and its arbitrary nature by showing that it is scarcely consistent with the principles of method, interesting for the most part, that he had set down at the beginning of his work.[36] But he is not sure that certain "poetic" approaches are not based on idealistic and platonic postulates equivalent to those of Frye. In a historical perspective, it is the category of "types" that ought to be questioned. Following other authors, Todorov proposes to distinguish "historical genres" from "theoretical genres," which he suggests be called "types" in order to avoid confusion. But if confusion exists, it is not the fault of vocabulary, which is only the sign of it, and changing the word changes nothing about the thing: the type remains no less an idealized projection of the genre, a reassuring phantasm analogous to those that serve as the foundation of the institution of genres such as we all live it in practice by supposing that oppositions of fact are the consequence of oppositions of essence. The distinction between theoretical genres and historical genres makes us think about the distinction between the soul and the body, which one is hard-pressed to have communicate once they have been separated. The joining is difficult. It is therefore necessary to redivide the theoretical genres into "elementary genres" and "complex genres," and to imagine that "historical genres form a part of complex theoretical genres."[37] These distinctions seem to have the prime function of saving the idealist category of the type placed in question by the evidence of variability and historical complexity.

Actually, at the level of theory, we do not see why it would be necessary to imagine fundamental categories whose system of oppositions would reflect, *most simply*, the system of oppositions that makes up real genres; nor why these systems should have fixed hierarchized forms, descending by degrees and divisions from the ideal to the real. We do not even see why there should be a classification of types. At the level of abstraction where theory is situated, we could find:

1. Only elementary categories, dissociated through analysis, and situated in multiple domains, without any hierarchization *a priori*, insofar as the relevance and the hierarchy of oppositions that ground the different historical "systems of genres" (that is to say, the horizons of expectation) are eminently variable and also completely legitimate. The domains to which these categories belong should be thought of as an indefinite number, with regard to the most diverse aspects of

the mode of communication, of the internal structures, and of the contents of the works. Analytical reflection in all these areas could not run into essences, but simply into the laws of functioning on the level analyzed.[38] No analytical category, by itself, is in a position to account for the system of real works, and by deciding *a priori* on the articulation of these categories, we could only construct mock-ups that would be irrelevant and useless. Theories of "types" are based most often on the choice of a privileged domain upon which the others depend, and on categories in very reduced numbers. The list of "typologies" catalogued by Todorov reveals this common flaw.[39] But this flaw is not due to the clumsiness of critics confusing genres and types; it is inherent in the false notion of type.

2. Only types of operations, resulting from the analysis of the functioning of the real system of genres: how different traits are hierarchized in the genres, and how the genres of an era are opposed between them (synchronic study); how genres are constituted and modified—diachronic study that makes sense only insofar as it does not take an isolated genre into consideration, but a part or the whole of the system, in order to analyze the differentiations, the cross-breedings, the borrowing or the apparition of new traits, their redistribution in new sets that are otherwise hierarchized, and so on. The "typological" theories are incapable not only of explaining, but even of describing historical variability, and they perceive real genres only as degradations or mixtures of some rare pure essences, which they have distilled by letting nine-tenths of the historical data evaporate.

The job of the theory is not, therefore, to construct a classification of genres, but to discover the laws of functioning of the historical systems of genres. I have apparently strayed from autobiography in order to establish this proposition, which might seem obvious, but which is often misunderstood in practice. I will now make use of the particular case of autobiography in order to show, through two contrasting examples, the dangers of theoretical idealism and the possible resources of a relativist analysis.

To illustrate theoretical idealism, I have chosen to examine what Frye says about autobiography in *Anatomy of Criticism*, both because his work has a great influence in English-speaking countries, and because it is exemplary. Frye wants both to construct a coherent "theory of genres" and to account for the entire empirical real; he therefore no longer avoids the difficulty, as do other typologists who choose in the real whatever suits them. But Frye's empiricism does not go as far as starting from the real: he only tries to make the real, after the fact, enter into an *a priori* conceptual framework. His analysis is based on Platonic concepts (p. 243), on Aristotelian concepts (pp. 243–44), and on the divisions of classical rhetoric (p. 245). The real will be deduced from the summit of the pyramid of essences. The point of departure of his theory is the trinitarian division of the ancients between the epic, the dramatic, and the lyric. Frye observes that this division rests on the original mode of presentation of the work (conditions of communication between the author and the public). This remark is outwardly quite accurate. But two criticisms come immediately to mind. To decide that this factor is always determining is to prejudge the complexity of the facts and to sink into a botanical system of classification that will prevent us from conceiving of the system of genres as a variable system with multiple factors, and whose hierarchy can change. On the other hand, if this is the way it is, the role of the theoretical critic would be to reflect on all the possible variations of the situation of communication, and this in an analytical (without imagining that a given situation is a kind of whole or unimpaired essence) and inductive manner, starting from the analysis of the real. Among the variables would figure a certain number of historical facts (both technical and sociological). Instead of devoting himself to this work, Frye chooses four complex situations that, from the single fact that they have had a historical predominance, he is going to treat as simple essences upon which all the rest should depend. The four fundamental genres would be: the *epos* (speech addressed to an audience), *fiction* (prose genre in which an isolated reader is addressed through the intermediary of the book), the *drama* (where the author is hidden), and the *lyric* (where the public takes part in the discourse that the poet addresses elsewhere). In the analysis that follows, Frye tends to confuse a distinctive trait of a situation of communication and certain genres in which it has had a dominant position. This creates endless difficulties, from which he could extricate himself only through complicated quibblings and arbitrary generalizations. The example I will use will have to do with autobiography. Frye subdivides each of his genres into particular forms. For what he calls "fiction," there would exist four particular forms (no more, no less), which would be the "novel," the "confession," the "anatomy" or satire, and the "romance." These four forms would be intermingled in their turn in order to produce real works. Let's look at autobiography (pp. 307–8):

> Autobiography is another form which merges with the novel by a series of insensible gradations. Most autobiographies are inspired by a creative, and therefore fictional, impulse to select only those events and experiences in the writer's life that go to build up an integrated pattern. This pattern may be something larger than himself with which he has come to identify himself, or simply the coherence of his character and attitudes. We may call this very important form of prose fiction the confession form, following St. Augustine, who appears to have invented it, and Rousseau, who established a modern type of it. The earlier tradition gave *Religio Medici*, *Grace Abounding*, and Newman's *Apologia* to English literature, besides the related but subtly different type of confession such as it was practiced by the mystics.

Are we dealing here with the theoretical definition of a form? The form is not exactly defined here, except in a plan, which, moreover, has no universality ("the majority"); and although this vague definition scarcely gives it shape, this form is given the name of a real historical genre, whose forms are quite varied, and which includes many other distinctive traits. Afterward, we could never know to which of the distinctive traits of the genre the use of the word "confession" refers: does it have to do with the autobiographical pact, with the discourse of the narrator, with the retrospective narrative in the first person, with the use of an internal focalization, with the choice of contents (story of private life or inner life), or with an attitude (construction of a structured model)? When, in whatever work, Frye recognizes one of these traits, he concludes that this work is a *blend* of "confession" and of something else. We will thus learn that the essay such as Montaigne practices it is a "reduced form" of the confession; that by blending the confession with the novel, we obtain the imaginary autobiography, the *Kunstler-roman* and other related types; that it is not necessary that the subject of the "confession" be the author himself; that the "stream of consciousness" technique allows the grounding of the confession and the novel, and so on. Here again, the confusion of vocabulary reveals a confusion of method. The word "confession" cannot be used sometimes for one of these traits, sometimes for another, so as to make the autobiographical genre appear like a simple essence that could enter into different combinations, whereas it is itself only one combination among many others. This confusion prevents the analysis from going to the level where it would be effective, that is to say, to the level of traits.

Frye's method is irritating and fascinating: irritating because it ends up in an unusable system of classification and is built on a sort of logic that belongs less to the domain of scientific thought than to that of "untamed thought" [*la pensée sauvage*]; fascinating because the error has a grain of truth in it—Frye has the very accurate idea of an empirical combination, but which he applies from falsely abstract categories, with mechanical rules of combination (on the order of the cocktail), and without imagining that the historical evolution of the system of genres could be grasped from such a combination.

Opposing Frye's study, and putting the combinative method back on its feet as it were, is Elizabeth W. Bruss's "Autobiographie considérée comme acte littéraire."[40] Bruss agrees on many points with my study on "the autobiographical pact," but she presents on the theoretical level some more general and, it seems to me, very fruitful propositions. Her originality lies in having articulated the principles of the Russian Formalists on literary evolution, with the modern theories of the linguistics of the illocutionary act. Bruss thus succeeds in situating within the development of the whole of literature what could be the study of the development of a genre.

Following Tynianov, Bruss recalls the distinction between forms and functions (the forms being capable of different functions, and the functions appearing in different forms), concluding that there exists no fixed correlation between forms and functions, but a historically variable combinatory system. In the case of autobiography, she shows that the generic function (that is, the autobiographical pact) is a variable that is theoretically independent from the formal aspects to which it is often practically associated. It is this systematic method of dissociation of factors that allows the contemplation of variability. Since her study is easily accessible, I will not summarize it here. Bruss establishes the different orders of "variabilities" that can affect a genre, then shows this variability through a series of examples taken from history, thus putting into motion methods of study that could answer the questions that I was asking in the first part of this chapter.

Extending her analysis, Bruss tries to analyze in a sharper way "the distinctive functional traits of autobiography as we know it." She turns to the methods of analysis that Searle uses for illocutionary acts (the promise, the request, the hint, the warning, and so on).[41] She clearly shows that the autobiographical pact is itself not a simple essence, but a complex act, subject to an analysis which, isolating and hierarchizing all the conditions of the act, allows us, at this level as well, to understand historical variability. Thus she finds there a linguistic model of description that corresponds exactly to the problems posed on a more general level by Tynianov:

Searle suggests seven different dimensions which, although they overlap, are likely to enter into the definition of an illocutionary act, and we can anticipate that any genre will be defined and redefined in one of these ways. The domain of what we have called the "center" of the autobiographical act (identity of the author/narrator/protagonist element and the assumption of the verifiable quality of the subject treated by the text) most often escapes change. In fact, these rules form the illocutionary "center" only because it is proven that they are not subject to change. Nevertheless, while these central points seem absolute, there exist some marginal or peripheral elements in each genre (and in the entire system of literary genres as well) which are indistinct, zones in which the distinctions are unnecessary and in which several types of literary activity are mixed. It is in these poorly defined zones and in relation to these unnecessary criteria that change appears.

H. R. Jauss[42] remarked that a theory of genres always bore the mark of the situation in which it was born. My own theories or those of Bruss on the autobiographical act or pact naturally tend to overestimate the problem of the "reading contract," for me, and of "the illocutionary act," for Bruss, and to place in second position the other aspects of the text, because these other aspects do not have a primary function here. But autobiography could not really be studied if the dissociative analysis did not grapple both with the problem of the forms of narrative and with the problem of *contents*.[43]

The contrasting examples of Frye and Bruss show clearly what the true site of theoretical study is: no longer a syncretic typology, but an analysis systematically dissociating the factors and giving as its objective to establish laws of functioning. This analytical method, destined to allow us to think of literature as a system in its historical evolution, has until now been defined more than applied. The way was opened by Tynianov, and it seems that in order to progress, his propositions must be reworked in diverse directions: recourse to new linguistic models (illocutionary acts, theories of communication); widenings of perspectives like the one Jauss produced with the notion of horizon of expectation; extension of reflection to arts other than literature, with the problem of genres, of horizons of expectation and of variability also coming up, even if it is in somewhat different terms, in painting and in music. This method will lead not to the hasty elaboration of syntheses, but to thorough and analytical studies; the latter could profitably utilize the empirical work and the observations accumulated by traditional literary history, in order to establish, little by little, models of the functioning of literature as a system.

Research Projects

I wanted to show here the temptations to which criticism of genre is exposed, how much these temptations themselves reveal about genre as institution, and how we should proceed in order to carry out a more really historical reflection. For me, it was a matter of taking stock before starting new inquiries.

The two projects that I am thinking about doing are based on a common method: on the one hand, to start no longer with literary texts or their writing, but with their *reception*; on the other hand, not to take as the point of departure an isolated genre, but a much broader domain whose limits could be questioned again in the course of the inquiry. They both assume as vast a collection of information as possible, so as not to prejudge too much the objects studied; but they should result, beyond a simple inventory, in a definite contribution to the theoretical study of the functioning of genres such as I have presented it here.

The first project would consist in studying the makeup of "personal literature" in France in the nineteenth century. This implies a partial redistribution of literary geography, in relation to the breakdown adopted by traditional bibliographies that follow outlines of schools or of periods, or classical divisions by genres (novel, poetry, theory, history, criticism, and so on). But this redistribution must not be carried out by adopting a retrospective schematization that is done according to our current categories, or by adding monographs on particular genres, as is the case at the present time where the field is divided up again only by specialized studies on the personal novel, the private journal, and the autobiography.[44] The field will have to be defined starting with concepts drawn from the era being studied. That is why I have chosen the term "personal literature," according to the article-pamphlet by Ferdinand Brunetière, "La Littérature personnelle" ("Personal Literature," 1888), the end result of a polemic that was developing since the 1850s, and which has continued, under different forms it is true, up to the present day.[45]

The study should start with the *critical discourse* on the works, such as it evolves in journals and magazines, that is to say, in critical reception. It would analyze the contents of the discourses on personal literature and all the attitudes of "autobiographical" reading. Through such a study, the program defined by H. R. Jauss to trace the history of genres would be realized: to study "the temporal process of the establishment and continual modification of a horizon of expectation"[46] but by extending it, beyond a genre, to an entire sector of literature that would thus be redesigned. In this way we could regroup the texts that have been read with the same perspective (principally novels, autobiographies, private journals, correspondence, memoirs) and neutralize the effect of the "first law of Lehman" by restoring the corpus of texts that were actually read and discussed at the time.

Valéry already said that it was not the author, but the *reader* "whose formation and fluctuations would constitute the true subject of the history of literature."[47] Naturally this reading can only be observed indirectly, in critical discourse, with the expectations that it manifests, the classifications that it uses, and the value judgments that it issues. Critical readings have hitherto been studied solely through partial diachronic outlines that brought to light the changes in interpretation of the works of the past: either the transformation of the reading of *a* text or of *an* author through time,[48] or the readings of different works of the past done by *a* critic at a given moment.[49] What is suggested here is different, and complementary: it is the synchronic study of one of the systems of reading of a given era.

This synchrony would naturally be presented in the form of a series of synchronic outlines: from 1830 to 1850, from 1850 to 1880, the system of expectations was transformed. Extended to the whole of the modern era, such a study of the "continual transformation of the horizons of expectation" would inevitably confirm a number of other phenomena: the discourse of universal subjectivity and of intimacy such as it has been practiced in France since the beginning of the nineteenth century (lyric poetry and personal novel [*roman intime*]); the critical approach of the "man and the work" which invades critical and journalistic discourse after 1850, transforming the reception of works from the past and the expectations about recent works; the passion of sincerity from the end of the nineteenth century to the 1930s; the development of journalistic standards and "personalizing" strategies of publishers; but also the metamorphoses of the historical and documentary curiosity of the general public (extension of "eyewitness" and documentary literature well beyond the domain of history and politics *stricto sensu*).

These perspectives lead me to touch upon a second project, which would consist of studying the present structure of our horizons of expectation. Since 1972, starting with the bibliographical announcements published by *Le Monde des livres*, *La Quinzaine littéraire*, and the *Bulletin du livre*, I have made up a file of all the books published in France that are based, closely or loosely, on some form of autobiographical pact: memoirs, autobiographies, childhood memories, private journals, correspondence, "actual documents" ["*documents vécus*"], testimonies, conversations, essays, pamphlets, and also, if we believe their bibliographical classifications, some novels and history books. Vast as it may be, this inventory is still limited, since we must not lose sight of other horizons of expectation in relation to which this inventory is situated both by oppositions and by divisions: the domain of fiction, and that of information and scientific discourse. To the inventory itself must be added the study of the critical discourse created by these books.

In putting together such an irregular corpus, my intention is not to consolidate or to invent a "genre," but to proceed with an analytical study of the factors of classification (pact, form, and contents), and to dissociate them systematically in order to see how they are combined and hierarchized. Quite obviously, given the multiplicity of features, one and the same text is likely to be perceived as belonging to different genres, and the partial corpora that we are tempted to assemble have hazy outlines and overlap. These phenomena are difficult to analyze from the "substantialist" views of genres; on the other hand, they are clarified if the distinctive features are analyzed and we see that they are hierarchized according to *dominant* variables.

The autobiographical pact, which served as an index in choosing the texts, should not itself be considered as a whole—this would be a return to the imaginary—but dissociated in its different components (identity, resemblance) and articulated in favor of these dissociations with, on the one hand, the forms of the referential pact, and, on the other, with those of the fictional pact. The autobiographical pact does not have the same function in all texts: in certain cases, it is in the *dominant* position, and the text is built around it; in other cases, it corresponds to a secondary specification in relation to a different expectation (expectation of information on a subject, for example). On the other hand, the dissociation of identity and resemblance produces intermediate or mixed forms of pact, "phantasmatic" or indirect pacts, voluntarily practiced by authors, encouraged by publishers (because they combine two motivations for reading) and received with favor by the critics who find there the justification for a preferred "topos."[50]

The analysis of the pact must also take into consideration a series of other factors linked to the context of production and publication of texts:
   —prior notoriety (or the absence of notoriety) of the author, and the domain in which it takes place: the expectation and the mode of reading depend on it;
   —the mode of production of the published text, a problem that has been coming up for several years with the intensive development of "oral" autobiography, which could modify the conditions of communication and the forms of the text;[51]

—the "collective agreements" reached between authors and readers through the intermediary of the publishers, whose game of *series* determines both the production and the reading of texts.[52]

I touch briefly here only on the distinctions and dissociations necessary to the analysis of the pact; the same method should be used for the problems of form and contents.

The analytical geography of our horizons of expectation constituted in this way should allow us to grasp the movement of history better: on the theoretical level, by showing that we are dealing with a complex and unstable system, where the possibilities of mutations are numerous, whatever the invariants that are maintained over a long period; on the practical level, by proving, if necessary, that the expectations of a reader of 1974 are not the same as those of a reader of 1874, and have only a remote connection with those of the reader of 1774, a truism that is forgotten when the corpus of modern autobiographies is treated like a vast synchrony spanning two centuries.

In truth, it is not even certain that these expectations have not been substantially modified in the course of the last twenty years: the study done on the years 1972–74 should undoubtedly be based on parallel surveys done for example on the years 1952–54. It is very striking that the main body of critical literature on the autobiographical genre has been written in these last twenty years, starting with the fundamental study by Georges Gusdorf (1956). And undoubtedly we are presently in the process of witnessing or participating more or less in a process of *canonization* of autobiography.

Literary History and History

One final question remains to be asked: that of the relationship of literary history, such as I have presented it here, and of history in general. In our particular case, we can believe that this comes down to asking ourselves what relationship exists between the autobiographical phenomenon and the modern occidental civilization in which it developed. Asked in this way, the question can only be answered with brief responses, which will especially reflect current ideological debates and oppositions.

Everyone is pretty much in agreement on one point: there exists a correlation between the development of autobiographical literature and the rise of a new dominant class, the middle-class, in the same way that the literary genre of memoirs has been intimately linked to the evolution of the feudal system. Through autobiographical literature appears the conception of the person and the individualism characteristic of our societies; we would find nothing similar in ancient societies, or in so-called primitive societies, or even in other societies contemporaneous with our own, like the Chinese Communist society, where the individual is, as a matter of fact, prevented from looking at his personal life like private property that is capable of having exchange value.

Once this brief correlation has been established, the ideological debates and the uncertainty of method begin. Most of the critics who devote themselves to the autobiographical genres take part in the ideology of our society and adopt an attitude favorable to the autobiographical phenomenon, in which they can take a personal interest. This is true for G. Misch, who tries to trace the remote origins of this birth of the human person, and for me when I state, keeping an admiring distance, that autobiography is "one of the most fascinating aspects of one of the great myths of modern occidental civilization, the myth of the *self*."[53] In the opposing camp are the condemnations of Marxist critics who, already being outside the bounds of this civilization, are no longer sensitive to the singing of individualist sirens nor to the discreet charm of literature: "Biography and autobiography are indeed in the bourgeois ideology of the general forms of representation, constructing the image of man coupled with that of society," states Renée Balibar in his study on the academic models of the narrative of childhood.[54] The attitudes of glorification or of rejection give information more on the position of their authors than on the phenomenon studied.

What remains is to understand how a historical study might view this correlation. Do we not risk ending up with simplified, or even simplistic, views when we try to establish direct relations between "autobiography," taken as a whole, and the "bourgeoisie," conceived as a coherent and stable being? Obviously the bourgeoisie was not in the same situation, either in different countries, or in different phases of its development; its ideology has evolved and includes numerous contradictions. On the other hand, the ideological phenomena have a relative independence in relation to economic and social conditions.

But perhaps the problem has been badly stated. First of all, it is no doubt impossible to establish a relationship between a particular genre and society by disregarding the literary system taken in its entirety; it is on the level of this system that a reflection on its conditions of possibility and on its social function can be developed. On the other hand, literature should not be thought of as an autonomous whole, which we would study in itself and which we would try to link after the fact to other social series and to society as a whole; its independence is only relative, and it is primarily a social system itself.

It is also important to study the functioning of the literary system, including, as Etienne Balibar and Pierre Macherey propose, its scholastic and linguistic determinations, and its ideological effects.[55] Undoubtedly the study of the horizons of expectation is in this perspective the center of gravity of literary history, because it integrates all the analyses of form and content, but does so by avoiding the traps of timeless idealism, and because, without being overly sociological, it allows us to display the social dimension of the literary phenomenon.[56]

Chapter 8
Autobiography and Social History in the Nineteenth Century

Is autobiography a "bourgeois" genre?

It is tempting to make such an assertion, but it is undoubtedly as risky as it is tempting. The question presupposes a sort of independent existence of literary forms and social classes: the double trap of formalism and sociologism. The simplified correlations that it comes to establish are likely to have scarcely more basis than those of astrology. And why not ask ourselves first about the more obvious correlations, with the history of education, with that of the media? Furthermore, the question is based on a certain ignorance: the "autobiography" that we will tend to talk about will be the one that has survived, in general the one by writers, which is perhaps after all only one particular case.

To escape these traps, and this ignorance, I have conducted a survey whose first results are presented in the form of an inventory (see the appendix to this chapter).[1] Recorded here are all the autobiographies by businessmen, manufacturers, and financiers of the nineteenth century whose trail I could recover. Other sections of this inventory will later bring together autobiographies written in the nineteenth century, classified according to the author's field of experience: farming lives, lives of workers and craftsmen, administrative lives, lives of teachers, lives of artists, religious lives, political lives, military lives, and so on.

The idea for this survey came to me while seeing historians of proletarian literature complain about the rarity of autobiographical texts written by workers in the nineteenth century.[2] But aren't autobiographies by employers even rarer than those written by workers? Must we, in a sort of naïve sociologism, hope that the autobiographical archives of an era will be like a little Noah's ark where each social species would have come to deposit something to reproduce? Does this genre of "lack" have some significance? Does it always have the same significance? We are of course amazed when we discover that there exists no autobiography by a servant in the nineteenth century, whereas the servants, numbering one million, represented one-fourteenth of the active population of France.[3] Practically no autobiography in peasant society either, which represented even more than one-half of the French population.

In the case of rural society, we can show the naïveté of our surprise, and the limits of this type of research by social class or by economic sector. The absence of peasant autobiography was foreseeable; traditional rural society constituted by definition an "antiautobiographical" cultural space: insularity, cyclical time, orality, community life. But this rural society was shaken by the French Revolution and the wars of the Empire, then by the migration to the cities, which began to accelerate around the middle of the century. Let's hypothesize that autobiography appears at the point where that traditional civilization cracks, but it does so under the most diverse forms. It is first of all linked to *social mobility*: rural society (idealized or not) is the backdrop of numerous narratives of childhood by workers or people of the middle-class who came directly from the country. It is also linked to different forms of *deviance*: criminal peasants, like Pierre Rivière; physically handicapped, like Xavier Thiriat, and all the small peasant men and women, shepherds and shepherdesses who had apparitions or died in a state of grace.[4] But it is perhaps linked as well, as a number of family record books show, to the *management of a business*.[5] It is not only industry and business that have their self-made men; the first important peasant autobiography to see the light of day, that of Henri Norre, *Comment j'ai vaincu la misère* (*How I Overcame Poverty*), is not at all a moving ethnographic document (as Guillaumin's *La Vie d'un simple* [*The Life of a Simple Man*] is on the level of fiction), but an exemplary narrative pointing out the road to success to other peasants.[6] These examples, given rapidly, show the complexity of the problems, the variety of the texts: the autobiographical act can have very different functions, which must not be artificially combined.

It seemed to me that the first job to be done was to put together a serious and accurate investigation of autobiographical production in the nineteenth century, without prejudging conclusions that might be drawn from it. I have given this work the form of an annotated inventory. To set up such an inventory is a job that is both serious and tricky, and questionable in its very conception.

In order to locate those autobiographical texts that are, with the exceptions of the first, practically unknown, I went through the list at the Bibliothèque Nationale of all the works corresponding to the call number LN 27. Under this call number are brought together the "individual biographies," that is to say, all the texts, regardless of their extent or form, that have to do with the life of a real individual. There are all sorts: biographies, pamphlets, reviews, obituaries, memories "of," letters, etc. – and, in the middle, lost among the rest, the autobiographical texts, which represent one to two percent of the whole. From the point of view of this *Catalogue de l'histoire de France* (*Catalog of the History of France*), it is of secondary importance whether the text dealing with an individual was written by that individual or by someone else. Moreover, this mixture has the great advantage of replacing the autobiographical text in its natural milieu, minor and rare excrescence of the statistically dominant discourse which is that of biography. It is still like looking for a needle in a haystack. There are more than 90,000 works cataloged under this call number. I actually went through 63,000 entries. And I am presenting to you 23 industrial or commercial life stories. The yield is low: but that's the price of any historical work.

And then, how to choose? Such an inventory is inevitably precariously balanced between the expectations of literary history and those of social history. People who are interested in literature will be disappointed to see that I take no account of the "quality" of the book: everything is jumbled together. I will answer them by saying that I am offering them the possibility of knowing the civilization of the nineteenth century in the way that its participants saw it. But what is too much for some is not enough for others: for the specialists of social history, autobiography is only one document among many others that they will be sorry that I have excluded. It is because my project is different from theirs: I look at these autobiographical texts not as *documents* containing information about the author (information that could, if necessary, be obtained elsewhere), but as *social facts* in themselves, in their reality as texts.

I thought about starting this inventory with the lives of craftsmen and workers. I began with employers, following a twofold discovery. Once, while moving, I came across the autobiography (manuscript) of one of my great-grandfathers – born in 1845, draper's assistant under the Second Empire, fur salesman under the Third Republic, died 1918 – who recounts his business career in detail. Autobiography and social history came together here for me, in another way. Marguerite Yourcenar and Jean Delay have recently shown what benefit there is for all of us in the reconstruction of our family history: knowing as much as possible about where we come from. All the more so if one of your ancestors offers you his/her collaboration in this way. Here, furthermore, the practice of autobiographical writing was like the symbolic realization of a social promotion mediocrely achieved by the interested party, but well fulfilled in the next generation by his sons.

While going through the call number Ln 27, I noticed that my great-grandfather was not alone: a certain number of small employers or great industrialists rewarded themselves the luxury of having their autobiography printed for the edification of their entourage. People like César Birotteau or Octave Mouret, but for real, and their texts were sleeping in the Bibliothèque Nationale. It is this small corpus that I am going to analyze now. All of these texts are autobiographies in the strict sense, the author looking at the whole of his life. The field of professional activity corresponds approximately to the categories presented by Théodore Zeldin in chapters 3 to 7 of volume 1 of *France, 1848–1945*: "Notaries," "The Rich," "Industrialists," "Bankers," and "The Ambitions of Ordinary Men."[7]

I. Social and Historical Situation of the Corpus

Is this corpus sociologically representative — and of what?

I have had, throughout this analysis, the feeling that you may have while leafing through its findings: the feeling of chance. The chronological order accentuates that impression: a butcher, a spinner from the North, a sucker. It sounds like Prévert. Furthermore, we would expect to find autobiographies of famous people, as in the United States, where you can read the life of Ford or of Carnegie — of great bankers, of captains of industry, of great inventors, and so on.[8] They are all absent from the roll call, or nearly. It would be impossible to reconstruct a significant chart of "leaders of enterprise," or to think that we are reading the Life of Illustrious Men. It is by chance that so-and-so wrote; by chance that his text reaches us. The coherence, I will show later, is located on another level, namely that of a discourse.

Some characteristics: the writers are all men; two are Protestant; half of them come from rural or artisanal backgrounds, and it is precisely they who occupy the most mediocre positions; those who have been most successful practically all come from a bourgeois milieu. But it is difficult to extrapolate on so few cases. In this disparity, however, we can manage some regroupings. Texts 1 to 4 were addressed to the public by great "entrepreneurs" of the Revolution and Empire eras. Starting with text number 5, we are dealing with a rather different type of narrative, written essentially for a private audience; it is to them that I will pay particular attention. Among the authors are a majority of representatives of the traditional occupations: craftsmen-businessmen (manufacturer of musical instruments, butcher, jeweler, carpenter-contractor), businessmen (grocer, tailor, two specialists in the dry goods business), and two provincial notaries. Small fry. But we also find people of the grander scale, likely representatives of the industrial movement of the nineteenth century: an "iron master" (Charrière), a founder of a spinning mill (Faucher), a railroad builder (Veysseyre), an engineer specialist in mechanical constructions (Lalance), a very great wholesale dealer (Roy).

The social history of employers is like that of the workers: it tends to privilege certain types of men. Among workers, militants. Among employers, those who have succeeded, and especially those who have succeeded in some types of new, more modern activities. My autobiographical lottery, as nonrepresentative as it is, has this slight advantage of counteracting the epic tendency that social history can have when it is no longer strictly statistical. It shows the weight of the traditional forms of enterprise and career. It emphasizes (and this thanks to a subgenre, the autobiography of the persecuted) the existence and the forms of failure. The success of an enterprise is undoubtedly based on the exploitation of workers, but also on the crushing of competitors. For every builder of an empire, there are dozens of bankruptcies.

I have often thought about *César Birotteau* while reading these texts (in particular the one by Romain Lhopiteau, who indeed rhymes with him, in every sense of the word). Balzac does a wonderful job of showing the articulation of success and failure, and especially the conflict of two types of economic mentalities: the prudent and virtuous ethic (even if it is a bit hypocritical) of the European commercial bourgeoisie, and a more dynamic and less scrupulous spirit of enterprise, even if it is concealed in an analogous moral discourse.[9] *César Birotteau*: above all, the pleasure of reading was the same, and maybe even greater, by the mere fact that the texts I was unearthing were authentic. Not only was I discovering them, but I was taking them by surprise, because most of these discourses were not intended for me. I had the impression that I was becoming their author, through the retrospective, and at times ironic, foolishly condescending glance that I was casting on them. Many of these texts can seem naïve. All of them are filled with concrete detail. They would undoubtedly have been uninteresting for the contemporary public, because of their banality and their too private side; with the passing of a hundred years, they have taken on a great deal of flavor. Some very average people, clinging to their life. I detested some of them, especially Joray, particularly when he tells how he had to kick his pregnant daughter out of his home: he asks the reader to feel sorry for *him*. I liked others, for example, the virtuous Alphonse Fouquet—maybe because one of my great-grandfathers was a craftsman-jeweler. Others made me laugh, like the unhappy Lhopiteau and Delhaye, the epicurean notary. All this to say that if this inquiry contributes only some scattered illustrations to social history, it can be instrumental in giving some ideas to contemporary publishers. At the present time, for the autobiographical texts of the nineteenth century, there are two publishing opportunities to aim for: the Maspero space (the proletarian and the militant) and the Foucault space (the "parallel lives" of dropouts: parricides, hermaphrodites or erotomaniacs). I propose a new space, at the center of the target (if I may dare say), that of honest people: *Actes et Mémoires de la Bourgeoisie* (*Acts and Memoirs of the Bourgeoisie*).

The title of this future collection leads me to my purpose. Others besides myself have already had this idea—it was exactly one hundred years ago, in the 1880s. Frightened by the political instability born of the French Revolution, and especially by the social conflict that was brewing, some of Le Play's disciples tried to find a remedy (indirect!) for the social problem in certain practices of autobiographical writing. Their reasoning was the following: "Everything is going badly. Why? Because the traditional family is falling apart (the family as social and economic cell, heritage and enterprise). To check this decline, let us restore the old practice of keeping the family record book." This was perhaps to confuse the effects and the causes. But it led these historians to publish, beginning in 1869, texts that had hitherto been totally unknown: family record books, accounting books, journals, memoirs of private life, dating from the sixteenth, seventeenth and eighteenth centuries, and related essentially to forms of bourgeois life (even if all the authors were not from the middle-class; but the nature of a dominant cultural form is precisely to permeate the other social groups). Furthermore, Charles de Ribbe has compiled a synthesis of all these documents in order to draw up a *model* that he suggests his contemporaries imitate: *Le Livre de famille* (*The Family Book,* 1879) is a sort of manual or practical guide for the familial autobiography.

This corresponded actually to a need. The proof of it is the existence of the autobigraphies recorded here, in which I would tend less to see a specifically modern and new phenomenon than a continuation of this organic activity of the traditional bourgeois world. By "organic," I mean the fact that it was largely and spontaneously practiced, and had no need of a published model. In France, we are fascinated by Rousseau's *Confessions,* to the point of seeing in them a sort of archetype of the modern autobiography. But these texts would no doubt exist just as well without Rousseau. One single author quotes him, in order to reject him (Morieux). Instead of Rousseau, moreover, we would think about the *Autobiography* of Benjamin Franklin (bedside book of the notary Chabert). But well before Franklin, there were written in France, amid the many family record books, narratives in certain respects similar to those that I am gathering here: for example, the *Mémoires* of Jean Maillefer, middle-class merchant from Reims (1611–84), who combined the genres of autobiography, self-portrait in the style of Montaigne, moral notices [*avis moraux*] and the family record book. But this model of the bourgeois autobiography in the classical era remained unpublished until 1890 and has been barely read after that. They didn't need him to do the same thing.

The same, or nearly. The family record book is a collective work (passed on from father to son) in the form of a journal, centered on the heritage and the business of the family. The lives gathered here are individual retrospective narratives, focusing on a career: from now on, the model is the biography. The family record book is linked more to an economic and ideological activity of maintenance; the career story, to a conquest. The family record book is always a manuscript. Here we are dealing with printed matter. But what type of printed matter and to whom is it addressed?

II. The Circulation of the Text

Almost all the texts, from number 5 on, are part of an ambiguous category, which I will call *private publication*.

All societies have undoubtedly practiced the genre of exemplary narrative, but the "example" does not circulate in the same way with regard to eras and classes. We have gone, in the course of the history of humanity, from the lived example to the spoken example, from the spoken example to the written example (heard, then read) – and from there to the printed example, and today the audiovisual. At the same time the field of distribution of the exemplary model was expanding. At the time of the family record book, the single copy of the manuscript allows the familial history to be submitted to later generations; it was a process of conservation (in time) rather than distribution (in space). The bourgeois autobiographers of the nineteenth century are no longer content with the manuscript; they write a retrospective narrative of the past intended for an immediate audience, for very small groups (familial or professional) to which they belong. They have themselves completely printed alive.

The people of the nineteenth century (not just these autobiographers) were obsessed with printing. Reading the texts collected under the call number Ln 27 (or at least their titles, often colorful) shows that for a mere trifle, they brought a few pages to the printer's, at their own expense of course, if only to later distribute the brochure or booklet themselves. Thanks to the fact that copyrighting was necessary by law, we have acccess to an immense and monotonous production of texts, printed certainly, but which were never commercialized, and which are related to outstanding moments of the social life of very small groups: anniversaries and jubilees, accession to high office or promotion, eulogy, funeral notices or orations, for the laudatory texts; and trials, lampoons, and diverse attacks, on the other hand. Circulation was limited, suited to the size of the audience concerned, which did not often go beyond the circle of family and friends. Sixty copies were printed of Eugène Charrière's autobiography, "a very limited number of signed and numbered copies" of Paul Amiel's. There even existed another formula, intermediate between manuscript and printing, the *autography* (lithographic reproduction of writing) which was used for a certain number of autobiographies (but there are no examples of them in this corpus). All these procedures allowed the number of copies to increase and made it possible for the text to achieve the dignity and weight of a book, while remaining within a very restricted social circle. No doubt it is necessary to differentiate: texts having an apologetic function are aimed in general at a more extensive public than uniquely exemplary texts – someone wants to reestablish his good name in the eyes of his clients or in local opinion. But this never goes very far, and the author remains the only distributor of his text.

What we keep seeing in the titles of this series is the obsession with the familial audience: "To my dear children and grandchildren." Of course, since the world began, parents have imparted their experience to their children. But perhaps they do so in a more emphatic way when they have the feeling that they are the founders of a dynasty, and they are transmitting, along with their experience, their business. Because marriage is, in these circles, essentially a commercial transaction, the relationship with children hides an economic transfer. The tender grandfather who tells of his difficult beginnings and sets down the laws of success is addressing his successors. Nature provides you with heirs, but a successor must be trained. In the story that is told, we see an individual confront society; but his story is given as an example to his family, within the framework of the family. Individualism, no doubt, but subject to *familialism*. This trait is accentuated especially in commercial or industrial families, but it is of course a general trait of bourgeois civilization: the spirit of the clan or tribe (which makes it appropriate to engage in aristocratic procedures like genealogy), the accumulation of written archives (and, a little later, photographic), and the investment in children. The "private" publication of exemplary autobiographies must therefore be put back among the characteristic traits of the modern bourgeois family such as historians like Philippe Ariès have analyzed it.

This system of confidential publication raises a series of questions. First, that of the "literary" competence of the author. There is no control, no censorship of the text: the printer prints what he is given. Paying is enough. Thus the somewhat jumbled appearance of this corpus. Not that a kind of first "natural" state of autobiographical discourse, beyond all literary ambition, is expressed here, such as would take place orally in the family circle. Instead we see people of a very unequal cultural formation face the job of putting a book together (rather short books, you will have noticed). Three of them (Gourmont, Hamot, Amiel) come off badly according to our criteria, no doubt. They get tangled up in chronology, or in discursive coherence. It is the first time they are writing; they get by as best they can. Of course we smile while reading them. But their blunders point out the laws and difficulties of the genre. The education narratives are in general well put together. The career narratives are trickier: what must one assume is known, to what degree of detail must one go? Some (like Charrière, Lhopiteau) do not hesitate to draw up calculated balance sheets, almost year by year, and quite obviously most of them rely on the rereading of their own financial archives or the account books of their business. Some narratives end suddenly at the precise moment when we would like to know what happens next (Faucheur, Lalance, very quick on the end of their career). But others manage to balance information and demonstration in their story, and find satisfying solutions. The notary Delhaye, whose life is rather devoid of events, constructs it in the form of the essay and self-portrait. Lhopiteau, very organized, divides it into periods, bases it on accounts, illustrates it with photos, supplements it with a genealogy, and gives a nice, stifling picture of petit bourgeois family life. The two most well-controlled stories: of the unassuming type, the one by Fouquet; of the ambitious type, the one by Roy—we almost want to compare his great peroration on the nineteenth century to the epilogue of *Mémoires d'Outre-Tombe* (*Memoirs from Beyond the Grave*). This prize list, quick and subjective, is meant only to suggest the problems encountered and the variety of the solutions.

On the other hand, the limited distribution of these texts makes it impossible to attribute to them any influence whatsoever on the evolution of French society. Moreover, no market existed for books of this type unless they dealt with nationally known figures. Autobiographies of criminals, great actors, and edifying lives could be sold to the general public (and eventually created or fabricated), but not autobiographies of merchants. And in the literary sector (in fiction), the merchant and manufacturer were seen more as social types (sometimes caricatured) than as epic models.

These texts must therefore be considered not as causes, but as signs. We should not be misled by their small number and their meager distribution; what appears here in autobiographical form is an omnipresent discourse on the social life of the nineteenth century. There exist without a doubt in the private archives of bourgeois families many other texts of this type, still unpublished. I have placed in this inventory the story by my great-grandfather, although he was a very modest man, to set an example for everyone: do as I have, and divulge, publish, or bequeath to a public library the autobiographical writings of your ancestors. To that should undoubtedly be added numerous correspondences.[10] And especially an enormous heap of texts which we are not too sure whether to characterize as biographical or autobiographical. Every employer was prompted a certain number of times in his life to write a story about his career: either on the occasion of an anniversary of his business (the business is itself a large family, the employees bring their wishes to "their dear boss," who answers with a speech, recounts his beginnings, gives his example),[11] or in support of a request of an authority (file for the Legion of Honor, etc.), or at the request of a compiler of biographies (because it is always the interested party who furnishes the "elements" of the notice). It is following a request of this type that Fouquet had the idea of doing more, and of writing a detailed narrative of his "industrial life." Biographical dictionaries of commerce and industry can be looked at as collections of "autobiographical" notices written or transcribed in the third person, in which the interested party presents to its best advantage the path of his success.[12]

What is the specific character of the autobiographical text? First of all, its length: it is not just a summary molded into a stereotyped form, but a detailed and concrete narrative that inevitably expresses a personality and provides the possibility of formulating judgments other than the ones suggested. Whatever the length, the autobiographer exposes himself and takes some risks. Next, and especially, one notes the complexity and possible diversity of discourses. The review is always very flattering to the individual and is never problematic for the social system. Even when it performs the same function, it is the task of autobiography to justify and make a case for praise. And it happens that it has other functions.

No one has ever asked a bankrupt or a failure for the "details" of an account. But no one can prevent them from writing their autobiography.

III. The Consistencies Of Discourse

Defining these consistencies is quite easy. Titles, dedications, prologues, and, throughout the narrative, persistent commentaries show that we are dealing with a pedagogical literature. Literature, certainly, at degree zero: no one prides himself on his ability to write. Nor on enriching or turning aside a known model in order to make an impression with new meanings. This is, moreover, the nature of all the texts recorded in my inventory, whatever the profession of the author. Literary autobiography is an exception.

Accordingly, the classifications that I am going to suggest belong more to the domain of elementary rhetoric. The literary effect−I was aware that it was my reading that caused it. I was the perverse narrator of "naïve" stories, by the simple fact that I was reading them *in a series*, and that I was organizing a counterpoint with other narratives that these bourgeois people could not know (for example, the autobiographies of workers)−*that they lived on by ignoring*. The blindnesses, the contradictions, the presence of an unspoken−I was the one who was imagining them. I made myself the unanimist novelist, who thinks he can, through the articulation of witnesses, see the real in its complexity, and who reconstructs by the montage of univocal texts a problematic whole.

I have differentiated three attitudes: *exemplary, apologetic, critical.* One or two texts escape this framework; I will come back to them later in the chapter. All the others are centered on the problem of success. Is it success that creates value, or value that leads to success? Are they compatible or incompatible? This is the same problem found at the heart of romantic literature, at the heart of the Balzacian novel of apprenticeship in particular. Everyone wants to get out of a scrape, dreams of fortune. Those who succeed find that all is right with the world. The others have more complicated attitudes: is it the world that is going wrong, or them? They are going to flounder in this trap; and some will resolve to fight the system that rejected them; so, between the exemplary autobiography of the employer who has succeeded and the militant autobiography of the employee is found a continuous range of intermediate and sometimes ambiguous texts.

The exemplary texts are the most numerous here. They function as a reciprocal insurance system between the "exemplary" individual (who proves by his example the truth of the official dominant discourse on the balance of value and success) and this discourse itself (which allows the exemplary individual to think that he is completely and individually responsible for his success). This double action of exemplary discourse has some risks, if we put too much emphasis on one of the poles (general preaching or self-satisfaction); but in general our authors come off well. We are very close to the structure of the didactic novel—to those didactic novels that recount positive exemplary apprenticeships[13]—with one difference: the hero does not start off from a negative ideological position, but a neutral or indeterminate one, in order to reveal himself little by little, in action, endowed with those qualities that, in a well-built society, success always comes to reward. The narrative is all the more exemplary because the hero, neutral, starts off from a negative material position (poverty, humble origin, absence of education or support): there is no other help beyond the qualities that are unique to him. It is the ideology of the *self-made man* that we find in Laffitte, Richard-Lenoir, Courmont, Fouquet, and Veysseyre, and in many other authors to a lesser degree. Even when they confess to having had the benefit of help, in particular in the form of education and example that they themselves have received—and also in more materialistic forms—they place the emphasis finally on their individual merit and inevitably ignore the circumstances that made their success possible and the price that it cost others. The discourse of equality masks the circumstances in which the hierarchy is constructed. Individualism and selection are related; and it is, moreover, because they have the feeling not of having "succeeded" in a banal manner, but of having escaped failure and catastrophe, of having *survived* in situations where so many others failed, that they are so proud of their success and so willing to believe both in their own value and in that of the system.

The catalog of virtues that leads to success varies from one book to another. On the whole, they focus on practical abilities (ingenuity, talent for some type of activity, inventiveness) and moral virtues (thrift, foresight, honesty of course, prudence), and especially will, courage, and *work*. The great law is that of work. They all wore themselves out on the job. From story to story, we find time and again the same motto that is learned in childhood and which guides their whole life. I let Narcisse Faucheur speak for himself:

> I learned to read and write in a little school like all the boys my age. Upon leaving that school, I was put into the care of an old Benedictine, a very good teacher, but excessively severe. Father *Chirac*, that was his name, had a habit of saying constantly:
>
> > *Labor improbus omnia vincit*
>
> a sentence he translated in this way:
>
> > Persistent work conquers all.
>
> He also said: I prefer to teach a hardworking ass than someone who is lazy and does not have the intelligence to understand that work is the basis not only of a good education, but also the basis of all successes in life; this work is rational and it is accompanied by a spirit of order,

perseverance and the firm resolution to accomplish by honest means everything one has resolved to do.

These precepts of Father Chirac have remained deeply etched in my mind, I realized that they were true, and I found myself, quite young, in the absolute necessity of putting them into practice; because, barely at the end of adolescence, I had to fight against so many obstacles, disappointments, disillusions, mistakes, hardships, toils and perils, that I don't know what I would have become if the maxims of Father Chirac had not been so deeply etched in my mind.[14]

Would the world go wrong? These narratives in no way conceal injustice, violence, disloyalty, the backdrop of apprenticeship. But all is right with the world: work triumphs over all, and our heroes never have the feeling of having failed at justice or engaged in violence themselves. They confess sometimes to having made mistakes (most often through lack of prudence, they have been the victims of dishonest associates). But their conscience is completely clear. Again, Narcisse Faucheur:

Everything succeeds according to my desires; in a short time I built up in St.-Amand a workshop of more than three hundred embroideresses, in the home of the Dutordoir ladies. The first pieces that I put on sale brought me a far more significant profit because the cost of the workmanship was very low. It was at the time when business was at its best that I got married, so I had a wedding dress made for my intended out of embroidered tulle; your mother still has it and keeps it like a relic.[15]

Conclusion (that embroideresses would be interested in thinking about): With courage, energy, and thrift, a forgotten quality today, an intelligent man can always create an honest position for himself.[16]

And if he doesn't succeed? If he doesn't succeed and continues to believe in the dominant discourse, he will write an *apologetic* autobiography.

Apologetic texts are as varied as exemplary narratives are alike, to the point where we might think that we are leaving sociology for pathology. After the beautiful people who are satisfied with having succeeded, we have the persecuted, the failures, the unfortunate guys. As we know (since Rousseau!), the persecuted have an irresistible propensity for autobiography. Their position is complex, because they recognize the legitimacy of the dominant ideology, by which they feel condemned, and before which they are going to make their appeal. A mistake has been made. Or else it isn't their fault; but as a result, if it is the fault of the system, the system cracks. As for the mistake (Colette-Quenouille, Courmont), it is sufficient to plead the case, to show off one's success, prove one's virtues, explain one's failures, attempt to win back local public opinion. If there is no mistake, if someone really has failed, or gone bankrupt, he becomes involved in a pathetic and potentially problematic discourse, since he is going to establish that you can be honest, hardworking, etc., and fail. Whose fault is it? Narcisse Faucheur had been very explicit: "an *intelligent* man." This adjective says a lot. But no autobiographer admits to being stupid: at most he made a mistake on this or that occasion. Joray, for example, by getting married: his family life was a hell. Part of his failures came from that; the foundation of small and average businesses is, indeed, a united couple. Lhopiteau, on the contrary, was happily married twice (his wives were hard workers), but twice widowed, and undoubtedly not astute enough to follow the fluctuations of the market. This leads to bankruptcy, which is the greatest tragedy of the nineteenth century, the inevitable reverse side of all those displayed successes: an undeserved dishonor, unbearable sometimes, which leads to suicide or to autobiography. A small businessman from lower Normandy, Pierre Ameline, renounces suicide only for one reason: he did not have enough money to buy the paper that he would use to write the autobiography that would exonerate him. He survived, therefore, and later wrote that autobiography.[17]

Why did someone go bankrupt? He was the victim of dishonest people. His credit was cut off. The market changed. But he was honest and hardworking. And like César Birotteau, he settles his accounts. And into the bargain, he writes his autobiography in order to vindicate himself, but respectfully, without attacking the system. The model of the genre is Romain Lhopiteau's narrative, which combines in the same narrative, vis-à-vis two different addressees, exemplary discourse and apologetic discourse.

A less good soul, or someone more convinced of his own worth, could on the contrary combine apologetic discourse with critical discourse, and switch to the counterattack, by aiming this time at a broader public. Morieux, who pleads innocent and reveals different swindling techniques, does this naïvely. And Constant Lepage, who dresses himself up with a proletarian title, and who is undoubtedly more a déclassé and a "persecuted man," does it eagerly. No matter. What is interesting is that he has given himself as a task, pedagogically, to prove by his example that all the prevailing discourse on success was false. It is an exemplary narrative in reverse, a would-be demystifier: six hundred pages of Lost Illusion or of Sentimental Education (but it looks more like Arnoux than Frédéric), so as to conclude in favor of the necessity of socialism.

To continue the analysis of this field of discourse, we would have to get away from the corpus collected here. I would simply like to point out the existence of a large intermediate zone between the exemplary narrative of employers and the militant narrative of workers. Thus Prosper Delafutry, worker, then peasant, then schoolteacher, asserts at the same time that society is unjust (when he thinks about his experience as a worker), and that it is just (since it gives everyone a chance: he was able to become a schoolteacher).[18] His socialism is consequently very moderate and reformist. He is not far from being of the same opinion as Narcisse Faucheur.

One last word on the people who write, not to prove, teach, or vindicate themselves, but to remember or to write. The tailor Amiel writes his life story "without pretention and for his personal pleasure." As for Xavier-Edouard Lejeune, he writes out of his inclination for writing: compensates for his probable failure in his business career by making himself the ethnographer of his colleagues. He is twenty-three years old, and he judges the world. Here is how he situates himself, clearly and proudly:

> I was in no way gifted with the true qualities of the merchant, audacity, absence of moral prejudice, what they call relative or conventional honesty, the *flair* for business, that sense that makes of the crudest and most ignorant of men the most accomplished businessman.
>
> I was too intellectual to succeed in that career; I found myself going astray and condemned to leading an uninteresting life going from one firm to another with no hope of definite success. The only knowledge that I had acquired was the observation of the customs, the characteristics, the facts and gestures of all the personalities of the human comedy evolving around me. And so I took up my position from a philosophical and social rather than a commercial point of view, according to my temperament.
>
> The result of this frame of mind is that I wandered through some twenty firms, until the age of twenty, without being able to settle in any of them.
>
> It is the story of these peregrinations that I am going to tell as briefly as possible.[19]

I am going to conclude as briefly as possible at the end of my own peregrinations. As a matter of fact, this is not the end, but barely the beginning of an undertaking that could turn out to be a long one. This preliminary work brings to the surface the danger that lies in putting together such a corpus: the breakdown seems to transform a characteristic distinct among others (the autobiographical pact and discourse) into a characteristic that we will tend to think is dominant. And we will associate the texts chosen in this way with others in which this characteristic will not have the same function at all. No doubt this situation will become still clearer when the inventory is expanded to include other social categories and other types of texts. But right now, it appears very difficult to link autobiography and social history without first putting autobiography back into the vaster systems of discourse: on the one hand, biography, the most fundamental genre (and the least studied); on the other hand, the system of discourses on social success. It is dangerous to bury ourselves in the contemplation of an imaginary object and to believe in an essence of autobiography. We must be open to a multidisciplinary approach, and to see in this inventory simply one instrument among others with which to study the social history of discourses.

Appendix

Inventory of Autobiographies Written in France in the Nineteenth Century
Section 1, Commercial, Industrial, and Financial Lives

1. 1747. Caire-Morand:

Autobiography of Caire-Morand, or Historical Memoir of the Rock-Crystal Factory Established in 1778 in Briançon under the Auspices of the Government, published by Paul Guillaume, archivist of the Hautes-Alpes, Gap (Jouglard Printing-House, 1883) 32 pages (BN. 8. Ln27 57657).

Goldsmith-lapidary, founder of this factory. Autobiographical memoir (story of a vocation and a business) addressed in the year X to the Prefect of the Hautes-Alpes to argue in favor of this factory ruined by the Revolution. Text remained unpublished until 1883.

2. 1756. Jean-Antoine Chaptal:

"Personal Memoirs Written by Himself," in *Mes Souvenirs sur Napoléon (My Memories about Napoleon)*, by the Cte Chaptal, published by his great-grandson the Vte An. (Chaptal, Paris, Plon, 1893) 412 pages (BN. 8. Lb44 1488).

Chaptal's autobiographical text, at the front of the *Memories* on Napoleon, covers the period 1756–1804 (pp. 9–102). Chaptal's industrial activity is recalled rather quickly in the midst of the other aspects of his life: education, intellectual career (studies in medicine, then in chemistry), organization of the production of saltpeter and gunpowder under the Revolution, and especially his work as a reformer from 1800 to 1804 as Minister of the Interior.

3. 1765. Richard-Lenoir:

Memoirs of Mr. Richard-Lenoir, Former Wholesale Merchant, Manufacturer and Leader of the 8th Legion of the National Guard of Paris, Including Curious Details on the History of the Cotton Industry (Paris, Delaunay Bookstore, 1837) 424 pages (BN. 8. Ln27 17378).

These memoirs, published during the lifetime of Richard-Lenoir – died in 1839 – were undoubtedly written by Herbinot de Mauchamps, who signs the Preface ("To Commerce," pp. 1–8). Only volume I, which goes up to 1814, was published.

Success story. Started with nothing, son of Calvados farmers, at first the assistant to a cotton fabric merchant in Rouen, then a waiter in a bar in Paris, Richard sets himself up in his own fabric business right before the Revolution. His business prospers quickly. He takes on another merchant, Lenoir Dufresne, as a partner and comes up with the idea of introducing the spinning of cotton in France to compete with the English. Started with boldness, supported by Napoleon, his business takes on great dimensions. In 1812, he employs a work force numbering 15,000. In 1814 he is ruined by the return of English products to the market.

4. 1767. Jacques Laffitte:

Memoirs of Laffitte (1767–1844), published by Paul Douchon (Paris, Firmin-Didot, 1932) 347 pages (BN. 8. Ln27 64370).

Laffitte was very popular both as a politician and as the image of the *self-made man*. See the anecdote (false) of the pin that he is supposed to have picked up in the courtyard of the banker Perregaux. He says himself: "From the simple apprentice carpenter that I was, I succeeded in founding a new dynasty." At the age of seventy-seven, he recounts the story of his success at the bank, then his role in political life from the Empire to the July Monarchy, then his second banking career (founding of the General Commerce and Industry Bank). Memoirs written primarily for his family, but also of course for the public, in the framework of a posthumous publication.

5. 1770. J. D. Holtzappfel:

Memoirs of J. D. Holtzappfel, maker of musical instruments, certified by the Emperor, Strasbourg, Publisher G. Silbermann, n.d. (1837), 97 pages (BN. 8. Ln27 9851).

Son of a lathe worker from Strasbourg. Protestant. Works at first with his father. Leaves in 1791 for Switzerland, then settles in Lyon as a weaving loom turner. Tries to establish himself as a manufacturer of looms. Failure. Goes to Paris around 1798, decides to set up his own business. Recounts the difficult beginnings of his manufacture of musical instruments. Marries, around 1799, the daughter of a piano maker. Unfinished narrative, which ends in 1799 at the end of the first part.

The story, intended for his children, should "serve as their guide and teach them that, if one day I leave them my fortune, although I never came into any inheritance, it is no less a legitimately acquired fortune. They will have no reproach to fear from anyone, because what I possess is not the fruit of a game of chance; intrigue and trickery have nothing to do with it; it is not a fortune amassed in a revolution; nor does it come from speculations done at the expense of others either; I have never abused the confidence of anyone. What I have is absolutely only the fruit of work, economizing, order."

6. 1786?. Colette-Quenouille:

Summary of My Life, or That of the Man Who Is Called a Schemer, Who Succeeds at Nothing, THEY SAY, and This, Out of Jealousy, and in Order to Prevent Him from Bringing to a Successful Conclusion the Building of the Railroad from Dieppe to Rouen, which He Undertook at Risks and Perils to Himself, Before Any Company Became Involved, and When Some People from Dieppe Only Laughed at His Studies and His Approaches to This Subject (Dieppe, Publisher Emile Delavoye, 1844) 4 pages (BN. 8. Ln27 4548).

Rather brief narrative, characteristic of the "persecuted" category. Born in the country. Gets into business at the age of sixteen. Wholesale grocer and promoter of different enterprises, in construction, in navigation (equips a steamboat) and the railroads (originator of a layout for a railway line between Dieppe and Rouen).

7. 1794. Narcisse Faucheur:

My Story. To My Dear Children and Grandchildren (Lille, Publisher L. Danel, 1886) 396 pages (BN. 8. Ln27 36834).

Autobiography of a founder of a spinning mill for flax. His motto: *Labor Improbus Omnia Vincit* [Hard work conquers all]. Comes from a bourgeois family in Clermont ruined by the Revolution. Although admitted to the Ecole Polytechnique, he cannot continue his studies for lack of money. Account begins in 1812. The largest part of the book (pp. 45–315) recounts his military life from February 1812 to August 1814. In 1814, he begins a business career in textile. Shop assistant, then traveling salesman for different firms; he ends up starting a business firm himself in Lille (lace, then linen). To supply his business, he starts a spinning mill for flax. Then he gives up his business to devote himself to the mill (story of his commercial and industrial career until 1852, pp. 320–83). This story, written between 1865 and 1869, was published after his death (1875) by his son and successor.

8. 1805. Eugene Charrière, Associate Director of Allevard blast furnaces and Allevard forges:
   Story of My Industrial Career, Told to My Grandchildren (Grenoble, Publisher Maisonville and Son, 1878) 96 pages (sixty copies printed) (BN. Res. 8. Ln27 30793).

Son of a grain wholesaler from Valence, supplier of grain to the army. Works first with his father, who goes bankrupt in 1827. Therefore has to manage all alone. Starts as an employee in charge of the ledger and correspondence in a large business firm in Lyon. Then takes care of matters in dispute in Grenoble, which leads him to direct, on behalf of a bank, the Allevard blast furnaces and forges. From 1833 to 1878, for forty-five years, directed this enterprise and made it prosper, first on behalf of the bank, then on behalf of a joint-stock company that he himself founded in 1842. Exciting story of an industrial success, in a world ruled by competition and technical innovation.

9. 1805. Lucien Delhaye:
   Mes confidences (*My Secrets*), followed by *Family Advice Given by a Father to His Children* (Valenciennes, Publisher G. Giard and A. Seulin, 1876) 77 pages (BN. 8. Ln27 29460).

Happy and quiet life of a notary. Born into the lower middle class. His studies allowed him to "climb a few rungs of the social ladder": he becomes a clerk in the office of a notary; he marries the man's daughter and assumes the responsibility for his business. After a calm and prosperous career, he cedes in his turn his responsibility to his son-in-law and retires to enjoy his pension. In 1867, he writes "under my arbor" or "in my meadow" a narrative of his life; here he enumerates the seven causes of his happiness, sketches his self-portrait, and gives his children some advice full of prudence: "Man is only really happy in the midst of a mediocre fortune. Save only to have it for you and yours and don't go beyond that."

10. 1808. Courmont:
   The Life of an Old Man from Douai Offered to His Children, Grandchildren and Great-grandchildren (Douai, Publisher L. Dechristé, 1881) 46 pages (BN. 8. Ln27 32710).

Born of a carpenter father. Himself a carpenter, then a building contractor. After a brief narrative about his education (pp. 3–6), he piles up all the evidence of his abilities and his virtues (letters received, affidavits, newspaper articles, etc.), most often in regard to the buildings that he constructed and decorated. "I recall all this, my children, to make you see how much I have worked with my head and with my hands . . . ; quite often it was said that I had been lucky: it's a very handy word for the uninformed and those who lack energy; I let them talk: with nothing, they do nothing, that's another useful word for the incompetent; the less polite have said with an angry look that I was an upstart; I answered them, to avenge myself, that I would have liked someone to say as much to them, and I would have been quite certain that they would not have been angry."

11. 1814. A. Hamot:
   The Life of a Worker. Work Containing a Notice about the Author's Place of Birth, His Autobiography, the Treatment of a Hernia and Some Other Complaints, Some Advice and Some Useful Tips, Followed by Authentic Anecdotes, by A. Hamot, inventor of the truss in movable pieces. Patented S.G.D.G., on sale at the author's home. . . , (Asnières, 1891) 107 pages (BN. 8. Ln27 40388).

As precise as it is, this title omits essential information: we are dealing with the autobiography of a *pork butcher*. Son of farmers from Seine-et-Oise, he goes to Paris to do his apprenticeship in a pork butcher's shop. Sets up his own business in 1839. A difficult start. Once his fortune is made, in 1863 he sells his business, invests in the building trade, enjoys his profits, and devotes himself to the passion of invention (treatment of chilblains, fireplace draughts, preserving of gherkins, etc.). In 1870, during the siege, returns to the pork butcher shop (blood sausage, then sausage made from horse meat).

"At the risk of wounding his well-known modesty, we can affirm that this courageous pioneer, this man of means, by his persevering energy succeeded in making a real fortune. It is necessary to add that we are happy to state that contrary to many others, who succeeded less honorably perhaps, he was able to remain simple, affable, obliging" (Preface).

12. 1815. J. Lefebvre:
   My Biography, Nantes, Publisher V. Forest and E. Grimaud, n.d. (1876), 15 pages (BN. 8. Ln27 29272).

Born in Caen to a mother who is a worker. From twelve to twenty years of age works as a sculptor-carpenter (sculpts the tops of armoires). A neighbor teaches him singing; he then makes a career as a light tenor. Director of the Theater of Amiens from 1847 to 1848. Employed in the charity offices in Paris from 1848 to 1851. In 1851, he directs the Theater of Reims, and goes bankrupt—30,000 francs in debt, which he pays off during the next twenty years. Starts over again in a career as a clerk, in insurance companies. In 1864, he is converted. From 1866, starts successively two insurance companies, one founded on the principle of decentralization (*The Alliance of Departments*, 1866), the other inaugurating a system of free insurance (*The West*, 1871). His goal: "To allow the working class the benefit of fire and life insurance."

13. 1823. Gustave-Emmanuel Roy, merchant:
   Mémories (1823–1906) (Nancy, Publisher Berger-Levrault, 1906) 341 pages (BN. 8. Ln27 52919).

This is the model of the autobiography of the conquering middle class. G. Roy, heir of a family of Protestant merchants, does his apprenticeship in the family business, in which he then becomes a partner: wholesale woolen business, then cotton fabrics. The narrative follows in parallel the chronicle of his personal and family life, and the story of an exceptional professional success, due especially to daring and lucky speculations on fabrics at the time of the coup in 1851 and at the time of the Commune. In 1860, he participates as an expert in the elaboration of the treaty of free trade with England and accumulates from then on all sorts of offices, in particular the presidency of the Chamber of Commerce (high point of his career). Business booming, he buys in 1866 an estate of Bordeaux wines.

This narrative is intended for his children and his grandchildren. A final chapter, entitled "The Nineteenth Century," associates the personal triumph of Gustave Roy with the progress of civilization in general in the nineteenth century.

14. 1825. Constant Lepage:
Sixty Years in the Life of a Proletarian, by X. Epagel (Paris, Léon Vanier Bookstore, 1900) 703 pages (BN. 8. Ln27 53878).

Autobiography of a déclassé and a failure. Exactly the opposite of the preceding case. Son of a bourgeois (his father was a founder in Le Havre). Does his apprenticeship as an adjuster mechanic, his sights set on becoming the boss in his turn. But his whole life will only be a series of failures. He will be successively a factory manager, civil engineer, clerk, manager of a lumberyard, then draftsman-engraver, then artist painter (specializing in the representation of industrial installations), then retoucher of negatives and photographs, and he will end his life as a drawing teacher. While young, he has a falling out with his father. Then he is persecuted by his stepmother and more or less betrayed by all of his employers, partners, and competitors. Jack-of-all-trades, failure, and finally "socialist." What is interesting about this somewhat delirious and garrulous, but very lively, story is that it systematically reverses the habitual discourse of middle-class success (see, for example, the appendix of part 1, pp. 153–56, commenting on *Enrichissez-vous* [*Enrich Yourself*] by Guizot).

Strange mode of presentation: the narrative by Constant Lepage is supposed to have been "collected" by a young friend, Paul Mélée, and published by X. Egapel. In fact one suspects that Lepage played the three roles.

15. 1826? Joray:
Memoir. A Life of Labor (Paris, Publisher Charles Schaeber, n.d., 1902) 51 pages (BN. 8. Ln27 49140).

Son of a blacksmith worker from the Vosges. Thanks to his metallurgic abilties, he goes to Paris, invents a procedure for silvering and galvanizing wires. Hired by a German manufacturer to install a wire mill (1855–60). Having returned to Paris, he sets up his own business and starts a tool factory for the weaving of velvet. Ruined by the War of Secession. Finds in 1866 a silent partner and rapidly makes his fortune again in metallurgic manufacturing. The sequel to the narrative is a double settling of accounts: his wife and his sons betrayed him. And when he retired, first his successor robbed him, then dragged him into court. Apologetic text ("A Life of Labor") in reply to this double betrayal.

16. 1828. Alphonse Fouquet:
Story of My Business Life (Paris, Publisher Michels and Son, 1899) 72 pages
(BN. 8. Ln27 46644).

Autobiography of a jeweler. Son of ruined small business merchants from Alençon, he is apprenticed to a jeweler at the age of eleven. After starting with nothing, by means of work and talent (he finds he has great abilities for modeling and the design of jewels) Alphonse Fouquet is at the age of seventy at the head of a flourishing jewelry business. Clear and detailed narrative of a success that is both artistic and commercial. Fundamentally optimistic and elevating; it is the model of the exemplary autobiography. This narrative, written at the request of his children and his friends, ends with a hymn to work: "Work! . . . Everything is there. It has been for me a source of satisfaction and relative prosperity. Through it I came out of the lowly conditions where destiny put me; through it I have acquired a knowledge that made me esteemed and looked up to; through it I broke away from the help of other people."

Alphonse Fouquet also spent his life writing verses, which he himself published at the age of eight-two: *Prosaic Verses*, 1910–12, 3 volumes.

17. 1828. Romain Lhopiteau
Sixty-two Years of My Life. Personal and Business Stories, followed by *Genealogical Chart of the Lhopiteau Family, August 1, 1890* (Paris, Publisher Michels and Son, 1891) xiii–383 pages (BN. 8. Ln27 40383).

Autobiography of a businessman. Son of farmers from Beauce. Sent to boarding school in Chartres: likes mathematics, land surveying, and business. Serves his apprenticeship with a drapery merchant in Chartres. Clerk in Chartres, then in Paris (1847) in different firms. In 1852, he goes to London where he learns English and ends up managing the "ready-to-wear" department of a dry goods store. Sets himself up in business in Paris in 1854 and marries. Balzacian narrative, calculated and impassioned, of a career in the dry goods business under the Second Empire. His wife dies. Start of financial difficulties. Remarries. Goes bankrupt. Story of a failure. His second wife sets up a lace store with his help. He speculates in potatoes during the siege of Paris, then becomes a commercial traveler (he sells Bordeaux wines in England). His second wife dies in 1876. Calculated and detailed balance sheets of all that the death of his two wives cost him. At sixty-two, he is a widower, his two daughters have married well, and he has just about what he needs to live.

This ample narrative has a double function, made explicit in two different prefaces: *exemplary*, addressed to his children (a lesson of courage, to show "what work, perseverance and the most unshakable will in the face of adversity and in the face of situations bristling with difficulties and traps can do"); *apologetic*, addressed to relatives who threw stones at him when he went bankrupt.

Genealogical tree. Six family photos.

18. 1829. F. M. Chabert:
Autobiographical Secrets, Metz, Typography and Lithography by Nouvian, 1867, 116 pages (BN. 8. Ln27 22837).

Son of a surgeon-medical officer. Studies in high school, then law in Paris. Returns to the city of his birth to be trained as a notary, the most beautiful occupation in the world. But at the time that he is setting up his own notary business, he chooses to withdraw to a rural town in order to establish it as a *model town*. Alas, his undertaking clashed with a general feeling of ill will, and he is persecuted. This delirious and fuzzy narrative is especially interesting for the list of virtues that the author attributes to himself; as bedside reading he chose the autobiography of Benjamin Franklin and follows his precepts to achieve moral perfection.

19. 1830. Auguste Lalance:
My Memories. 1803–1914. (Paris, Nancy, Berger-Levrault Editors, 1914) 77 pages (BN. 8. Ln27 58911).

Son of a technical director of the mines of Ronchamp (Loire), who had married the niece of André Koechlin, founder of the Mechanical Constructions of Alsace. Serves his apprenticeship in this enterprise while studying mathematics and works there later as engineer in charge of installation of machines (which allows him to travel throughout Europe). In 1855 he sets up an export office of Engish machines. In 1868 he starts a mechanical construction business in Mulhouse. Remains in Mulhouse after the German annexation. Persecuted by Bismarck because of his pro-French positions. Settles in Paris in 1889, where he sets up an electric company (electrifies the district around the Place Clichy).

Exemplary narrative: the key to his success is to have looked primarily for quality in a product, regardless of the cost, and to have sought to lower the price only afterward (while maintaining the quality).

At the same time, political memoirs of the Alsacian resistance.

20. 1834. J. Veysseyre, the elder:
My Sixty Years. 1894. (Nice, Publisher "Petit Niçois." 1894) 77 pages (BN. 8. Ln27 45753).

Son of a farmer, he is first a notary clerk, an office boy for an attorney, then apprentice accountant in a hardware store. Thinks about setting himself up in the hardware business, but finally becomes an accountant in a public works firm that builds railroads. So successful that he becomes director of operations, then ends up starting his own business as a public works contractor, and makes a fortune in building structures and railroads. Exemplary narrative dedicated to his grandchildren: "It will be enough for me to see one day that you have become loyal, industrious, honest and affectionate men, to be consoled of my sorrows, rewarded for my work."

21. 1844. Paul Amiel:
Mémories 1844–1911. (Angoulême, Working-class Publisher, 1914) 94 pages (BN. 8. Ln27 58914).

Tailor. Born in Toulouse; his father was a tailor. First a bookkeeper in Bordeaux at the age of eleven. Then apprenticeship in Paris with a jeweler. His parents take him out of apprenticeship and place him as a clerk with a manufacturer of vesicant linen and stockings for varicose veins. Works next as a clerk in different clothing stores, then with a tailor, whom he will succeed in 1872 (after having in 1868–1869 organized one of the first employees' unions, for the purpose of getting Sundays off). After 1872, the narrative piles up rather incoherently the remarkable events of a well-ordered life (swindlings of which he is the victim, death of his son, family quarrels, list of vacation trips he made, etc.). Conclusion: "I end these memories here, written unpretentiously and for my personal pleasure during the month of March 1913." At the beginning, he had cautioned: "This work has not been placed in the bookstore; only a very limited number of signed and numbered copies were run off."

22. 1845. Xavier-Edouard Lejeune:
Calicot, edited and introduced by Michel and Philippe Lejeune, Arthaud-Montalba, series "Archives privées," Paris, 1984, 367 pages.

Descended from family of peasants and craftsmen from Laon. Natural son of a Parisian dressmaker. Spends childhood with his grandparents in Laon. His mother takes him back to Paris with her in 1855. Attends the elementary school. It is love at first sight while reading Le Génie du Christianisme (The Spirit of Christianity), and he begins at the age of fifteen a long career as an autodidact and scribbler. But he has to live: he is apprenticed as a draper's assistant in different dry goods stores. Poor success, because of his independent and dreamy spirit. Writes his autobiography from the age of fifteen. At eighteen (1863) focuses on the first two parts of Stages of Life, which recount his childhood, his arrival in Paris, and the beginnings of his career in business. Careful and detailed narrative which aspires to being a kind on monograph on Parisian business seen from the inside. The third part, unfinished, covers the period 1863–68 (written around 1868). The continuation of this career is recalled in a narrative in the form of letters that covers the period 1870–71 (Correspondence. Volume I. Letters of the Siege and the Commune, 1870–1871, manuscript, 240 pages), then in a brief retrospective text written in 1913 (Thirty Years in the Felix Jungmann Company, 1882–1912, manuscript, 26 pages) at the time that he was awarded the medal for old workers. In 1872, actually, he gets into the furrier business and directs the commercial services of the Jungmann company from 1882 to 1912 – without starting his own business, because of his lack of ambition.

He has also left four volumes of stories about vacation trips and numerous poems from which he himself made the selections for the work entitled Les Traces du Passé (Traces of the Past) (1917, manuscript). He died in 1918.

23. 1847. Henri Morieux:
Autobiography. Memoirs of a Sucker (Lille, Publisher-Bookseller Camille Robbe, 1903) 137 pages (BN. 8. Ln27 51936).

Son of poor laborers. Messenger for the Northern railroads from twelve to fifteen years of age, then farm worker until the age of nineteen, then schoolteacher. But he scarcely talks about his career as a schoolteacher. Analyzes his career as a speculator for the education of his children and for the public's as well. By detailing all the times that he was a victim of swindling and dishonesty, he shows how his moral qualities led to his ruin.

Chapter 9
The Autobiography of Those Who Do Not Write

Who Is the Author?

"A life has only one author," declared the publisher François Maspero peremptorily, in the course of a polemic that brought him into conflict with Annie Mignard, writer of an "autobiography" (*La Mémoire d'Hélène*, *The Memory of Helen* by Hélène Elek) whose signature she asked to share.[1] For him, of course, the author was the one who had *lived* this life which was sufficiently unhappy or exemplary for it to be presented to the public, and who had taken responsibility for narrating it in front of the tape-recorder; the rest is technical work, more or less well done, which confers no privilege. Maspero therefore compares the role of the writer with that of a translator.[2] Annie Mignard, on the other hand, brought to light the initiative she had had in leading the questioning and in organizing the responses in the form of a narrative, a job which brought her closer to the role, and to the responsibility, of the *biographer*. Beyond the personal quarrel that divided them, the publisher and his "ghostwriter" extended their reflection to the entire field of "collaborative" literature and ended up finding themselves practically in agreement in condemning as a paternalistic imposture the present vogue of the "taped" autobiography of common people.

The reader is disturbed by this final encounter: more troubled still in noticing that he was successively convinced by the argumentation of the two adversaries, each one presenting, as is normal in a polemical joust, the aspects of the debate that strengthen his/her position. But beyond these skillful maneuvers, there remains a complicated problem, and the idea that this complication comes perhaps from a double confusion:

—use of a notion that is precisely the cause of the problem, that of author, around which the two polemicists tear each other apart without explaining the basis of the notion;

—confusion in the same argument of types of production that are only apparently similar (the productions of "ghostwriters" and the taped autobiography of common people).

I will set aside for the moment this second problem, in order to try to sort out the first on its own ground, that of "autobiographical collaborations." It is not only a question of a "scandal," where it would be necessary to judge, or to come to a decision, by condemning the exploitation of some people by others, or by demanding control of the method of manufacturing products offered to the consumer.[3]

My idea is that if somebody yells "scandal," it is because these productions compete with books really written by the people who sign them. And they compete with them only because they are based on the same methods and perform the same function. They suddenly get the people who write to see their own practice as in a distorting mirror: or rather the other side of their practice, its unthinkable side.

It is not the inauthenticity of these books that people condemn, but the fact that they let the cat out of the bag. They cast suspicion, no doubt legitimately so, on the rest of the literature. On a certain number of points, autobiography by people who do not write throws light on autobiography written by those who do: the imitation reveals the secrets of fabrication and functioning of the "natural" product.

Twisting the Contract

Secret collaboration is not a novelty. It has been practiced for a long time, first in a perspective of *secretaryship* (famous men, politicians in general, using literary people to elaborate or improve their texts, sometimes their memoirs), then, at the beginning of the nineteenth century, of *subcontracting* (organized this time by publishers or best-selling authors). Some words have appeared to designate these new roles: the collaborators were "hacks" or "cleaners," then "ghostwriters."[4] The collaboration was never admitted and was only the object of disapproving or derisive rumors. On the other hand, it was a question of exchanges of services between people who, to different degrees, were all capable of writing; and in the practiced genres (discourse, novel, theater, and so on), the name of the author did not have the same function as in the autobiographical genre. This type of collaboration is still practiced today, still unacknowledged, still giving rise periodically to rumors.

Closer to our problem seems to be the phenomenon of apocryphal memoirs, such as was developed during the Restoration. After the fall of the Empire, the public was ravenous for memoirs on the *ancien régime*, which publishers tried to exploit by fabricating false memoirs signed by people who lived in that other century or by anonymous writers. Between the authentic memoirs and the historical novel developed an intermediary genre, whose "poetics" has been analyzed by the critics of the *Globe*.[5] We should retain this judgment, which, at the cost of some transposition, is still relevent today:

> People complain about the apocryphal memoirs that are now flooding literature. Those who in good faith believed that these memoirs were written by the people indicated in the title as the authors were angry at having been deceived and cried out at the lie. Indignant at having been taken in, they have avenged their self-esteem on the books themselves, and have found nothing but wretchedness in these works that they devoured with eagerness when they thought they were true memoirs.
>
> We acknowledge that the greatest part of the originality of confessions disappears when we know that they are not the work of the penitent. But that these books cannot instruct and entertain at the same time, this is what we think is unacceptable. They can even have a distinguished literary merit.[6]

The transposition to be accomplished is due to the fact that the apocryphal memoirs were entirely false, written without the collaboration or consent of their alleged authors, who had been dead for a long time or who were fictitious. It was a question, then, of deceptions. And the deception, even if it momentarily gives the people who let themselves be taken in by it a guilty conscience, is in spite of everything a kind of homage that the lie renders to the truth. The author of the deception imitates in its totality the autobiographical process, and, while cheating in effect on the level of the contract, he respects the effect of unity inherent in the genre.

The interest in autobiographical texts results from the belief in a discourse coming directly from the interested party, reflecting at the same time his vision of the world and his manner of expressing himself. Even when the reader becomes aware of the existence of a *writing*, this work, coming from the "author" himself, takes nothing away from the authenticity of the message, even adds some value to it. The device of the autobiographical contract results in facilitating a confusion between the author, the narrator, and the "model" and in neutralizing the perception of the writing, in rendering it transparent. This fusion takes place in the autobiographical signature, at the level of the name on the title page of the book.

Unlike the apocryphal autobiography, the autobiography composed in collaboration such as it is practiced today in a more or less acknowledged manner, introduces a flaw into this system. It calls to mind that the "true" is itself an artifact and that the "author" is a result of the contract. The *division of labor* between two people (at least) reveals the multiplicity of authorities implied in the work of autobiographical writing, as in all writing. Far from imitating the unity of the authentic autobiography, it emphasizes its indirect and calculated character. A person is always *several* people when he is writing, even all alone, even his own life. And it is not a question here of intimate debates of a divided "I," but of the articulation of the phases of a work of writing that assumes different attitudes, and that links the one who is writing both to the field of texts already written and to the request that he chooses to satisfy. By relatively isolating the roles, the collaborative autobiography calls into question again the belief in a unity that underlies, in the autobiographical genre, the notion of author and that of person. We can divide the work in this way only because it is in fact always divided in this way, even when the people who are writing fail to recognize this, because they assume the different roles themselves. Anyone who decides to write his life story acts as if he were his own ghostwriter.

Writing

Insofar as writing is a solitary practice, it is difficult to observe and scarcely needs to explain its operations. Whence the atmosphere of mystery that surrounds it, and the archaeological care that is put into reconstituting the different phases of the production of texts, by piously reassembling the traces that remain of it or by going to question writers in order to know how they work.[7] Writing in collaboration suggests the possibility of a kind of spectral analysis of the production of the text, of the different authorities and phases of the work. In the particular case of autobiography, the exercise of memory and the exercise of writing are ensured by different people, in the midst of a process of dialogue that is likely to leave oral and written traces. Undoubtedly this is wishful thinking: the ghostwriters are not sentimentally attached to their sources; the models accord value only to the finished written product; and the publishers have no interest in possible judgments of the nature and the breadth of the work accomplished. Nevertheless, the possibility of such an observation device remains; the practice of scientific investigators, who try to recover a memory of before writing, proceeds in this direction. We are free to turn this observation device around, in order to grasp what writing is without memory.

Certainly, the two people who collaborate do not exactly coincide with such a division of roles: the model always has more or less an idea of what he wants to pass on to the reader, and the writer contributes to the exercise of memory. But ideally, we could summarize the distribution of work in the following way:

The function of the model is to tell what he knows, to answer questions; he is momentarily relieved of responsibility. By the mere fact that the other listens, notes, questions, and must later take on the composition of the text, the model is reduced to the state of *source*. Being free from the restraints related to written communication, he can let his memory take over.

The writer, on the contrary, is entrusted with all the duties of structuring, of control, of communication with the outside. It was perhaps *The Memory of Helen*, but it is Annie's writing. Condensing, summarizing, eliminating the inferior parts, choosing the lines of relevance, establishing an order, a progression. But also choosing a mode of enunciation, a tone, a certain type of relationship with the reader, elaborating the authority who says "I," or who seems to write it. The work necessary to achieve the final product is sometimes defined in a sort of "list of specifications," as in this letter, cited by Jean-Marc Théolleyre, in which a publisher specifies to a recalcitrant ghostwriter what "the elaboration and composition of a book of memories" consists of:

> What this means, and this according to numerous precedents, is the questioning of the author, most often with the help of a tape recorder, on the different elements that might serve as a basis for the composition of the work in question, the ordering of these elements, the shaping of the author's narrative (by suppressing the turns of spoken language, but by respecting to the fullest the style of the author, so that the reader has a feeling for his personality), along with a certain process of selection so that the work is as interesting as possible and the character of the author comes off in a sympathetic light; his questioning, afterward, on the lacunae that appear, for example to set the scene and to recreate the atmosphere of what he lived.[8]

What this text defines with a cynical precision is a certain form of narrative that is in reality independent of the model and his memory. Certainly we ask that the writer remain faithful to the tone of the model in his oral performances, but it is especially a question of adapting what the model has said to the laws of the genre and to the demand of the public to which it is directed, by having recourse to narrative and descriptive methods that might be quite different from his own. In so doing, the interviewer-writer does not impose his point of view or his personal style; he opens himself rather to a double exercise of pastiche, effecting a coming-and-going between this nebula or this rough draft that is the image of life floating in the memory and spoken word of the model, and the narrative forms that are currently on the market. He takes upon himself, then, both the demand of the public and the supply of the model to that demand, as we ourselves would do if we had to write our life story.

So this writing, which negotiates between the model's supply and the public's demand, is not really Annie's, that is to say, it is not the writing of an identifiable and personal "other," but a kind of floating writing, an autobiographical form with no subject to ground it, but which, on the contrary, grounds in its role as subject the one who is responsible for it or the one to whom the responsibility is given.

Whence the uncertain position of the person who is playing this role. The ghostwriter must first intervene and can only do so in the midst of an interpersonal relationship of dialogue; but he must next erase his intervention and take over the relationship with the reader *as if he were the model*. No doubt he will often accept this change in role with relative indifference, anticipated from the beginning from what he sees only as an alimentary work. But if he grants some value to his writing, he will live through this difficult position in the form of frustration and humiliation, of *deprivation*; or else in the lyrical form of enthusiasm, of *possession*. This depends not only on the types of institutional and personal relationships that exist between the model and the writer, but also on the genres that are taken as point of reference.

Annie Mignard aspires to the status of biographer and emphasizes that, even if she would try to be as faithful as possible to the image that the model wants to give of herself, it remains that it is she who is constructing that image, and she claims the right to show her personal opinion. An understandable claim, but contrary to the rule of the game. The writer should contribute only insofar as this can appear to be coming from the model. The expression of a plurality of points of view (that of the model on his life, and that of someone else on the model) defines immediately *another* type of texts (with *another* type of reading contract). In diverse forms (which are basically varieties of testimony) we are dealing with intermediate texts between autobiography and biography. A person's life can appear through someone else's narrative. Better: the spoken word or the writing of the model can be collected and put together by a third party. Thus, to take three examples that are quite different from one another: in the *Life of Samuel Johnson* by Boswell, in *Goethe's Conversations with Eckermann*, or in *Cahiers de la Petite Dame* (*Notebooks of the Little Lady*) about Gide. The modern developments of interviewing techniques, while leaving room for rewriting and editing, make the person asking the questions and the one who is being questioned intervene in an explicit way in the final text, and have opened the possibility for new intermediate solutions: we are coming closer to biography if the intervention is critical and creative, or rather to autobiography if it tries simply to relay the model by discreetly effacing itself. The public really likes these acknowledged positions of compromise, with which radio and television have familiarized them; they can in this way consume the object of their desire (the *life* of a famous person) in a presentation that is, in a way, stereographic, and both auto- and heterobiographical.

The writer of a collaborative autobiography is, during the first phase of his work, in that interpersonal position of listening and questioning. But then he must renounce the corresponding personal role. The only place that he can imagine himself occupying therefore, if he wants to give dignity to his work, is that of the novelist. Instead of playing on distance, he must count on identification. Steeped in the spoken word of the model, imbued with his story, he is going to try to imagine himself as the model in order to be able to write in his place. Some writers state that it is necessary to "put some imagination and your own guts too into it if you want the character to really live, if you do not want to betray his expressions, his heart and sometimes his soul," and come out of the test exhausted like Pythias. Of course, the operation of possession is reciprocal: the writer allows himself to be possessed by the model, but at the same time he possesses the model himself in traditional narrative and rhetorical forms. He finds himself, like Flaubert facing Madame Bovary, in a sort of state of lyrical depersonalization. Thus Max Gallo presents to the reader the work that he did on the spoken word and the character of Martin Gray:

> I had to cut down: at each step this life was a story. I remembered only the essential; I recombined, compared, set the scenes, attempted to recreate the atmosphere. I used my words. And I also utilized all of the impressions that life has left in me. Because little by little I settled down into Martin's life, little by little I stuck to that skin that was not my own. The expression is wornout, no matter: I was that other person, the kid from the ghetto and the fugitive from Treblinka and Zambrow, the immigrant discovering the United States, the man stabbed in the heart.[9]

This job of writing is a literary creation like any other. The relative disrepute that surrounds the genre is due equally to the obviousness of commercial speculations, to the monotony of the journalistic techniques used, and to the mediocrity of the majority of texts produced. In the event that the writer has talent and an understanding is reached between him and his model, books of great quality can be born: and so readers will ask themselves fewer questions about authenticity, and will not sulk over their pleasure. They will simply recognize a new genre here, realizing an original coupling of the novel and autobiography, a variety of the "real novel" that biography wants to be.[10]

Nevertheless, it happens sometimes that this division of roles is abruptly called off by a permutation in the course of work, and that in this way the autobiographical situation is reestablished. It is sufficient that the model, after having played the role of source in the first phase of the work by answering the investigator's questions on tape, takes his place in the second phase of the work so that he himself can draw up a narrative from the transcription of his conversations, becoming in this way the ghostwriter of his ghostwriter, that is to say, a full-fledged autobiographer.[11]

This is what Christiane Rochefort has done, constructing her own very original self-portrait in the place of the answers that she had given to her "investigator," and mockingly including at the end of her book, like residue, the list of questions that had been put to her.[12]

This is what Simone Signoret has done, much more classically, by writing down her answers in *La Nostalgie n'est plus ce qu'elle était* (*Nostalgia Is Not What It Used To Be*, 1977). And it is for not believing it that Anne Gaillard was dragged into court.[13] This example shows two things admirably: an unfolding, then a folding up, of the postures at play in the autobiographical work; and the uncertainty that surrounds the problem of the definition of the author, with the suspicions and susceptibilities that this uncertainty engenders.

The Signature

Collaboration blurs in a disturbing way the question of responsibility, and even damages the notion of identity. The model and the writer both tend to believe that they are the principal, if not the only, "author" of the text. The more the elaboration of the text is pursued (and the text "successful"), the more the feeling of exclusive responsibility of each of the parties develops. The model ends up acting as if he had written the life (quite frequently the case), the writer ends up believing that he lived it (less frequently the case) or at least by looking at the model as his creature. The plays of illusion engendered by this mode of work are therefore not reserved for readers, who would be fooled by them: the model and the writer can, themselves, be seized with vertigo, or with optical illusion. And it is true that the "life" in question belongs to both of them—but perhaps also, for the same reason, belongs neither to one nor to the other: would not the literary and social form of the life story, which preexisted their undertaking, be the "author" to both of them?

We are never really the cause of our life, but we can have the illusion of becoming its author by writing it, providing that we forget that we are no more the cause of the writing than of our life. The autobiographical form gives each person the opportunity to believe that he is a complete and responsible subject. But it suffices to be two people within the same "I" for doubt to arise, and for the perspectives to be inverted. We are perhaps, as complete subjects, only characters in a novel without an author. The autobiographical form is undoubtedly not the instrument of expression of a subject that preexists it, nor even a "role," but rather that which determines the very existence of "subjects."[14]

To tell the truth, collaboration engenders such metaphysical doubts only for the reader who really wants to reflect on them: these reflections, suggested by a particular case, make him quickly question all autobiographical writing, even the "authentic" variety. For the parties involved, either this sharing of identity meets with sympathy, or else it sets off conflicts, which, if they are serious, are brought to bear not on the metaphysical level, but on juridical ground.

The point is that behind these problems of identity are hidden problems of power relations (at the same time as money problems), and constraints that come from rules characteristic of different circuits of communication.

The author of a text is most often the one who wrote it, but the fact of writing is not sufficient to be declared an author. One is not an author in the absolute.

It is a relative and conventional thing: one becomes an author only when one takes, or finds oneself attributed, the responsibility for the emission of a message (emission that *implies* its production) in a given circuit of communication.[15] The determination of the author depends as much on the laws of this circuit as on the materiality of facts. The question is complicated by the fact that the notion of author refers as much to the idea of *initiative* as to that of *production*, and that the production can itself be shared (equally or in a hierarchical way) among several people.[16] Finally the status of author has different aspects, which can be dissociated and possibly also shared: the juridical responsibility, the moral and intellectual right, literary ownership (with the financial rights related to it), and the signature, which, at the same time that it refers to the juridical problem, is part of a *textual* device (cover, title, preface, etc.) through which the reading contract is established. Everything, then, is not as simple as the formula used by Annie Mignard—indignant at seeing that "one writes, the other signs"—would have us think.

This system itself has nothing of the absolute. The mention of the author has concealed, throughout the centuries, some very different practices, and that undoubtedly is linked to the evolution of the media. At the time when texts were recopied by hand and when reading was done aloud, the notion of author did not have the same meaning as it does today.[17] And new media, like the cinema (and television), have led to bending it or shattering it. François Maspero is shocked at the idea that a title like *Histoire de ma vie* (*Story of My Life*) can be published under the signature of two people, "Hélène Elek and Annie Mignard." He speaks ironically: "Briefly, this 'my life' henceforth had two possessors." Quite obviously, it is the "story" that has two people responsible for it, and the device of the title appears burlesque. But that simply shows that there is room to change the generic formulas for the printed book. In the cinema, the author of the screenplay and the director of the film are generally not the same person, and both figure in the credits. For example: *La Mémoire d'Hélène* (*The Memory of Helen*), from a screenplay by Hélène Elek, directed by Annie Mignard. Certainly, here, everything is complicated by the fact that the author of the screenplay is at the same time the subject of the narrative, and that this identity is one of the elements that motivates us to buy the product. On the other hand, the division of labor does not correspond completely to what is implied in the cinema by the screenwriter/director distinction.

We could therefore not continue the parallel with the cinema without artificiality, at least on this level. But behind a film, there is a producer, behind a book, a publisher, who has a strategic function in the marketing of cultural goods.[18] With the autobiography written in collaboration, the publisher (or his series editor) is not a mere cog in the machinery; he often takes the initiative and has an appreciable responsibiity for the existence and very form of the book. He is the one who conducts the market research, determines the areas of publicity to be exploited, puts in touch and joins, through a contract and a list of specifications, the owner of the deposit of memory to be exploited (a deposit whose value is derived either from the intrinsic value of the vein, or from its location near the main routes of fame) and the professional writer. The model and the ghostwriter are capable of acceding to the status of author (and can then fight about it) only by this professional's intervention. In fact, in certain sectors some real *workshops* are in operation, where we can say that in a way the models are interchangeable and the ghostwriters as well, and where the real author is the contractor who follows public demand and does whatever he has to to satisfy it. Unless, when all is said and done, the real author is the public itself, whose desire and obliging credulity (which asks only that some form of deception be included) give all these books the weight (the *authority*) that they would perhaps otherwise lack.

It is instructive to expand the notion of responsibility and that of production; but in doing so, of course, we are going completely against the mythology of the author which is necessary for the system to function. Not only is the system of the author a formal condition, it is in a certain way the fundamental message that the autobiographical genre conveys. What the public consumes is the personal form of a discourse assumed by a real person, responsible for his writing as he is for his life. We consume the full-fledged "subject," which we want to believe is true. This important requirement is naturally going to come into conflict with the attempts at "honesty" which, taking the desire for truth literally, would shatter the model's illusion of plenitude and responsibility. The public finds itself in an ambiguous situation, a situation of bad faith, always ready both to suspect the authenticity of a text and to yell "scandal" (but even here the public portrays itself in its own eyes as an amateur demanding authenticity, and recognizing this quality in all the other texts that it consumes blindly), and at the same time always prepared to lend itself to the games of illusion and not see through the transparent veils that cover the production of the text, the essential being to enjoy it.

Thus the mediation of the "ghostwriter" will either be hidden, or, if it is admitted, it will be blurred or changed.[19] The ghostwriter gets bad press; the victim of a system that exploits him, he is at the same time the fall guy, like the prostitute. It is true that the ghostwriter's employer, like the pimp, is also seen in a bad light. This atmosphere of distrust has developed since the beginning of the nineteenth century, that is, since the role of the author has become highly personalized (since we have become used to consuming the person). The book by Quérard, *Les Supercheries littéraires dévoilées* (*Literary Frauds Unmasked*), republished and enlarged throughout the nineteenth century, shows well the development of the practice of collaboration or of imposture, and of the susceptibility of critics. Today we see in the ghostwriter less a "public writer," an advocate or an actor for the cause of others, than a sort of junkman or make-up man, a specialist of autobiographical "ready-to-wear" or of "made-to-order."

If the public knew what the "author" (that is to say, the model) really produced, wouldn't he be tempted to revolt? Would he accept reveling in coloring? Actually the answer is not obvious. First of all because all writing is coloring. And then it seems that it is more the act of concealment of the collaboration, than the collaboration itself, which engenders rumors, scandals, inquiries. Finally, it is quite possible that the public is not homogeneous; it is especially the "intellectual" public, the people who write or feel themselves capable of writing, who are touchy on this point. The general public, to whom many of these productions are addressed, admits more easily that one brings oneself to get help with the writing when one is not "in the profession."[20]

Consequently, collaboration today is often mentioned in the credits, in modest forms it is true, with understatements that deceive only those who allow themselves to be deceived. The writer generally does not accede to the signature of the book; he is mentioned in the background, in a role as intimate secretary: "story taken down by . . . " The formula suggests dictation or confidences taken down with a pious fidelity. If we squarely confess the work of writing and composition, the writer at the same time must assume, in a preface, the status of biographer or novelist. And it is desirable, then, that he have something to recommend him to the public. Max Gallo was himself a writer of some notoriety: his preface brings to Martin Gray's book a literary guarantee. It allows us to push away the phantom of the ghostwriter ("Thus this book was not written with the applied indifference of the professional") and to give the reader the example to follow, that of identification ("I was that other person").

But whether it is concealed, half-admitted, or openly displayed, collaboration in any case rarely leads the writer to accede to the strategic place reserved for the "author": the signature. The facts don't matter. It is the logic of the reading contract that is at issue. We will be convinced of it by comparing the genre that we just described with the genre, *apparently* closely related, of the taped autobiography of common people.

Investigations on "ghostwriters," indeed, are only aimed at bookstore ventures where one attempts to exploit the interest in uncommon lives (heroic, exemplary, strange, etc.) or the curiosity that any well-known person inspires.[21] In the two cases, from the moment when one chooses to have the model tell his life story in a book (instead of being glorified in a biography), the model must take over the writing: the status as author is part of this *value* that the reader admires. The illustrious, or exemplary, person must be a full and complete subject. If God is, by definition, perfect, he must possess to their highest degree all possible attributes, including existence. Likewise, as soon as he discloses his life in a book, the hero must be in control of the writing, or at least what represents it symbolically, the *signature*. Whether that writing is embodied by the intermediary of the pen of someone else is of little importance, since the reader has faith. "Read, because this is my life." What is important is the real presence of the body of Christ in the host. Of course, there is always a baker, too, who has a hand in it.

These comparisons, which are not meant to be disrespectful, tend only to emphasize that a phenomenon that permeates our entire cultural field appears in this area of publishing: the *charismatic strength*, the belief in the existence of the hero with whom the crowd wants to come into contact in order to attain some value. "Know the well-known people better!" advised the short-lived periodical *Saga* which attempted in 1978 to exploit this theme. It is in the framework of an ethnology of these magical practices, to which the modern media have given an enormous power, that we can understand in the final analysis the problems of publishing debated here. The autobiographical signature has become one of the attributes of the hero.[22] He is in a way "author *honoris causa*," according to a system of which the French Academy [*L'Académie française*] has sometimes set the example.

In the taped autobiography of the common people, the techniques of work and the division of roles are apparently the same, but the power connections and the imperatives of the reading contract are exactly reversed. What one tries to capture in writing is the voice, the autobiographical discourse *of those who do not write*: old workers on retirement, peasants, craftsmen, immigrant workers, and so on. Their story takes its value, in the eyes of the reader, from the fact that they belong (that they *are perceived* as belonging) to a culture other than his own, a culture defined by the exclusion of writing. The bookstore exploits an *ethnological* type of curiosity, which involves a reversal in the setup. The admission of collaboration was a last resource in the case of the ghostwriters; it becomes here an essential piece of the system: it is a matter of guaranteeing that the model has written *nothing!* — at the risk of also guaranteeing that what has been written is a faithful image of what he said (but that's another story). The writer, who has often taken the initiative to create a story which otherwise would remain concealed in silence, appears like a mediator between two worlds, almost like an explorer. He must flaunt his presence and assume the status of full-fledged author, with the social prestige and the financial advantages that this entails.[23] The name of the model appears principally on the title page, and if the writer does not take credit for the whole signature himself, but shares it, it is out of scruple or generosity on his part (whereas in the other system, it is generosity on the part of the model to share the signature with his "ghostwriter"). The power connections are inverted: for a star, a hero, or an explorer, who has a life at his disposal to write, there are dozens of ghostwriters in the job market; for an amateur "ethnobiographer" who wants to capture a life, there are hundreds of thousands of possible models, and the model chosen should consider himself happy to attain a notoriety for which he was in no way destined. All merit in his story is a merit added by the writing, or rather by the new network of communication into which the mediator introduces him: the unhappy person would understand it if he then takes it into his head to write himself. His credit would collapse. He is in fact the creature of his ethnographer.

The signature system of a book changes therefore according to whether the model is hero or antihero, according to whether he belongs or does not belong, on a symbolic level, to the world of writing. In *Au nom de tous les miens* (*In the Name of All My Own*), Martin Gray is the author who signs, whereas it is Max Gallo who wrote the book (which makes the title strange, Max Gallo writing in the name of Martin Gray, who speaks in the name of all his own). In *Gaston Lucas, serrurier, chronique de l'anti-héros* (*Gaston Lucas, Locksmith, Chronicle of an Antihero*, Plon, 1976), Adélaïde Blasquez writes and signs the book; Gaston Lucas is no longer the author but the subject of the book: the antihero is at the same time an antiauthor, whose "chronicle" has been captured. Well, in the two cases, the writer has furnished the same type of work, even if it is in a different perspective (heroic gesture or populist listening).

I have chosen here a case in which the opposition is clear-cut, striking. We could find, of course, some counterexamples and, especially, many intermediate situations.[24] And the system that I am describing has nothing of the eternal about it; it is simply the system current in France at the present time. But this opposition manifests the essential point: a *life* (that is, a written and published story of a life) is always the product of a transaction between different postures, and the determination of the "author," in the case of an acknowledged collaboration, depends above all on the type of effect that the book has to produce. It is not a metaphysical question to be solved in the absolute; it is an ideological problem, linked to reading contracts, to the possible positions of identification with "persons," and to relations of class. Martin Gray is the owner of his life. That of Gaston Lucas acquires the unity and the dignity of ownership only in Adélaïde Blasquez's listening.

The polemic opened up by Annie Mignard is very enlightening because she has put herself in a very delicate position and has led François Maspero to reason as she did at the same time in the two systems. She also brings to light the connections of violence and exploitation in which writing is at stake, and the power that she represents: "ghostwriters" stripped of their work and their authority, "models" excluded from writing and appropriated by those who possess it. In writing, as elsewhere, "authority" is always on the side of the one who has the power.

Annie Mignard recommends therefore that the power be given to the people by giving them writing. According to her, publishers should turn directly toward the "common people" and offer them "writing contracts." "The people, for their part, are perfectly capable of writing without expecting someone to come and grill them on tape." No doubt. But write *for whom*? For the people who read. Annie Mignard's generous proposition remains locked in spite of everything in the vicious circle imposed by the market of cultural goods. She seems to ignore the relative failure of "proletarian literature," and its reasons. It is this vicious circle that I am going to explore now, by resituating in recent history the confrontation between popular writing and populist writing, the latter always having finally the advantage, as shown by the current success of the autobiography by those who do not write.

Life Story and Social Classes

We turn our attention today to "popular memory"; we piously gather traces of it, reconstructing our story. But as soon as we go back more than sixty years, we practically have to give up trying to find written expressions of that memory, at least in the form of the autobiographical life story. The value that is placed on the memoirs of Perdiguier, of Nadaud, of Benoit, of Dumay, is due to the rarity of such accounts.[25] It is moreover a matter of militant craftsmen or workers: in the country even fewer autobiographies would be found. The one by Pierre Rivière has only come into our reach thanks to a crime, by which this young peasant intended, while avenging his father, to win fame and "rise above his state"; its publication in 1836 went unnoticed by his contemporaries.[26] The success of Emile Guillaumin's story, *La Vie d'un simple* (1904), is due to the fact that the public, after sixty years of rustic novels, believed it was hearing for the first time the voice of a true peasant.[27]

Why this "silence"? Because they did not know either how to read or how to write, and they transmitted their memories orally? It would be naïve to think so. Education became widespread throughout the nineteenth century. But those who knew how to read and write used their education for other ends, in other forms; why, or for whom, would they have written the story of their life? Behind this problem of literacy and acculturation is hidden another: that of the network of communication of the printed work, and of the function of the texts and discourse that are exchanged through its channel. This network is in the hands of the ruling classes and serves to promote their values and their ideology. Their autobiographical narratives, quite obviously, are not written only to "pass on memory" (which is done through word and example in all classes). They are the place where a collective identity is elaborated, reproduced, and transformed, the *patterns of life* appropriate to the ruling classes. This identity is imposed upon all those who belong to or are assimilated into these classes, and it rejects the others as insignificant.

Undoubtedly it is useful, in order to convince ourselves of it, to spend a little time on the nineteenth century. We are too far removed from the period of the memorialists and the *ancien régime*; and our own era is quite possibly somewhat opaque to us. In order to appreciate the anachronism that the fact of looking for peasant or working-class autobiographies in the nineteenth century implies, it suffices to open a voluminous, austere, but fascinating book, the *Catalogue de l'histoire de France* (*Catalog of the History of France*), established in the nineteenth century by what is today the Bibliothèque Nationale. The section on individual biographies presents in alphabetical order all the referential texts written (and printed) that have to do with individuals.[28] Leafing through it, one has the impression of hearing in a way the *ground noise* of this society. There are, of course, all the biographies, the accounts, memoirs and souvenirs, the correspondence published concerning famous people, those who came into contact with the government, took part in wars, or *succeeded* in some area of social life, arts, or letters. Behind the texts about these people of "national" dimension is a much greater mass of printed texts (and printed undoubtedly in a very limited number of copies) about people of more local dimension, but which indicate the basic rites of the sociability of the ruling classes.[29] There are academic commendations, biographical notices about scholars, funeral orations, pious biographies ordered or written by survivors, sometimes judicial speeches, but also at times autobiographical texts. Less prestigious, but more numerous and significant, these commemorative texts concern the most varied social types: doctors, religious, engineers or scholars, artists or men of letters, manufacturers, merchants, landlords, prominent local people. We always remain within the sphere of those who have succeeded, whose life has acquired some social value.[30] They have become owners of their life, are able to arrange it in career or in destiny, and make of it the place for passing on social values. Of course, all the individuals in these categories do not accede to the printed life, but it is only they who have access to it, and they all recognize one another.

On the other hand, individuals in other groups (peasants, artisans, city laborers, clerks, etc.) have practically no chance that their life will be told in writing (by themselves or by someone else) and be printed. The discourse on their life remains contained within the memory of their group (village, trade-guild) and rarely goes beyond this circle. Enclosed in one and the same milieu, their life does not have the type of individuality needed to arouse interest, and which is often linked to social mobility and success. Insofar as individual form is concerned, it has, in the eyes of the people who are likely to produce and use the printed work, no value. Consequently, is it not in the chapter of individual lives that we have to look for signs of the "personal life" of peasants and laborers? Or else only in the stories written by people who have emerged from these milieus, and whose labor or rural experience is relegated to a story about childhood or youth—but then they are no longer writing as peasant or laborer.

The personal life of the controlled classes, in fact, is not in their hands. As Pierre Bourdieu suggests, "the controlled classes do not speak, they are spoken."[31] Their personal life is *studied* from above, from an economic and political point of view, in investigations which, in that era, did not become part of the life story. It is *imagined* in the journalistic and fictional discourse of the dominant classes, and it nourishes both their dreams (especially the peasants') and their nightmares (especially the laborers').[32] From the moment when the peasant and working-class milieus accede to the practice of writing (and in particular to the life story), they will do so with images of themselves that have already been formed, that they find along their way. On the other hand, the fact of taking in his hands his own life story (and eventually trying to publish it) will be more or less voluntarily an act of social ascension and of assimilation into the dominant culture, even if it is within the framework of a militant struggle destined to arouse class consciousness. We enter here into a complex set of contradictions, linked to relationships of power and to the laws of the networks of communication of the printed work.

Working-class speech of the nineteenth century did not take the form of the individual life story. The first militants had no need of it when they addressed their peers or when they responded to middle-class discourse.[33] It was not a question of creating a *memory*, but first of all a class consciousness, based on the analysis of the present. The stories by Nadaud show it well; their work was a job of literacy, of education, of association; their discourse, an ideological discourse of struggle. The recalled written text, centered on an individual life, does not correspond to a need, and this all the less because the life story can take on a demobilizing aspect owing to the fact that it is retrospective and plunges you into a past world. Certainly the individual written account could be employed, in internal use, to make the different divisions, isolated and separated, of the controlled classes communicate among themselves; but this communication was realized differently, through the trade-guild and then the first working-class associations. It could have had an external usage, aimed toward the general "reading" public; but we find nothing in France that resembles the stories of fugitive slaves in the United States, instigated (and sometimes written) by Northern abolitionist whites intended for the white public.[34]

Thus there exists no "popular" autobiography from the nineteenth century, because there existed neither a public nor a means of distribution for it. The texts that are unearthed today either have remained unpublished until the twentieth century, or else have known only an insignificant distribution. Exceptions are rare. Among them, we come across autodidactic texts, like the gripping *Mémoires* by Norbert Truquin, which have really only been read since their reissue in 1977.[35] The relative success of the narratives by Perdiguier and Nadaud is due to the historical aspect of their portrayal of the trade-guild or the life of the working class under the July Monarchy, to their great ideological moderation—and to the local reputation of Nadaud, a militant, but also a "self-made man" from the Creuse.

The only literary genre that appears and is developed in the second half of the nineteenth century is the autobiography of militants, who lived in 1848 or 1871, and who write not only for other militants, but also for the general public. Only the practice of action, political and trade union commitment, allow a working-class life to have an identity, that is to say, a structure and a value, which makes it reach the mode of distribution of the printed biography. The life story becomes, then, the place where class consciousness can be formed, and it is used for the inculcation of more or less revolutionary models and values.[36] On the other hand, in the eyes of the dominant class, these stories acquire value through the participation of their authors in struggles that are part of history: they enter into the category of political memoirs and accounts. But the effect of the militant autobiography is thwarted by the tightness of the channels of distribution to what would be its virtual public, people of controlled classes who do not read, or who read, but read the literature of the ruling class.

The historian who explores this domain must be very prudent. Looking at the culture of the controlled classes from the narrow perspective of the life story, I have chosen a criterion that perhaps has no relevance. But no doubt we see more easily the prejudices of others: those of Michel Ragon, in his *Histoire de la littérature prolétarienne en France* (*History of Proletarian Literature in France*),[37] struck me. Disciple of Henri Poulaille, Michel Ragon endeavors, for more than thirty years, to compose a history of proletarian literature, by writing manifestos, anthologies, and this *Histoire*. It is a matter of endowing with a past (a tradition and a kind of legitimacy) a contemporary movement of expression. Thus in one history (which is in fact more of a catalog) will be brought together some series of facts belonging to different groups, providing that they refer (but by the most diverse means) both to the idea of literature and to the idea of the people. What Ragon studies is in a way the intersection of two groups: on the one hand, all forms of the culture of the people; on the other, all forms of representation of the people in written literature. To study only the common part of these two groups is to devote oneself to collecting facts that are few in number and heteroclite, a vacillating fringe without a structure of its own. However, this history is founded entirely on criteria of value: Ragon declares that he wants to sift out of literature written by the common people "that which can show the authentic face of the people, their evolution, their aspirations, their complaints and their joys."[38] This leads him to eliminate writers who come from the ranks of the people and who do not give a correct image of them, but also to amalgamate into proletarian literature writers already distanced from their popular origins but who do talk about the people correctly. Discussions on the *pedigree* of proletarian writers indeed show these ambiguities.[39] The *Histoire* by Ragon is no less valuable as a source of information and is interesting as *historical fact* — because the contradictions with which he himself as historian grapples are precisely those that proletarian writers run into.

The principal contradiction is that of the network of communication: "proletarian writers do not reach the working class."[40] Or if they reach it, it is by mediation of the ruling class. A peasant like Emile Guillaumin does not directly write down his peasant experience for other peasants; he writes from romantic literature that has been assimilated into the communal school, and for the Parisian publication network, which alone is able to legitimize and distribute it. Within these limits (which are also conditions of possibility), he transforms the image of the peasant sufficiently so that the Parisian public has the impression of authentic peasant speech, and in order to reach other people like him all over France. And if he succeeds in doing so, it is because he meets a *demand* of the ruling classes (the same demand which the rural novel satisfied for a half-century). In this system, the risk is great of either not finding a response or of finding it only at the price of appropriation (expected or endured).

This is the problem in which proletarian literature has been involved since the beginning of the century. If we exempt the accounts by militants, most of the "popular" writers of the nineteenth century and the beginning of the twentieth were especially involved in writing poetry or fiction (of autobiographical inspiration). It is only after 1918 that accounts and autobiographies written by autodidacts began to appear to any relatively plentiful degree. In the last part of his book, Michel Ragon gives quite a complete census of those texts that have been published.[41] Between the two wars, militant writers tried to organize this sparse and diffuse literature, and to ensure that it would have a new type of distribution, by creating magazines (*Nouvel Age* [*New Age*]), meeting places (the museum in the evening), or even a publishing house, in order to get around the traditional network. Although this effort was fruitful, Michel Ragon reaches a disillusioned conclusion:

> The network of publishing houses is not made to reach a popular audience. The publisher does not find the reader, and the reader does not find the book. Where would you get most of the works I talk about in this *Histoire de la littérature prolétarienne*, except in several specialized bookstores. Many of these books were published by companies that have gone out of business (Valois, Rieder) and turned to pulp; others were published at the author's expense.[42]

Undoubtedly this problem of communication within the working class can be illustrated by bringing together two accounts by miners, each in his own way a writer. Louis Lengrand, born in 1921, suffering from a bad case of silicosis, beneficiary of an early retirement, gives an account of his reading practices, while responding to Maria Craipeau:

> It's not that I read so much. I read the union newspapers, everything that concerns the miners. But if Pompidou caught a slight flu, that doesn't interest me at all. I don't really like to read, but if I like a book, I'll read it straight through to the end. During all those years of mining, I never read anything, I didn't even have the time to read the newspaper. At the sanatorium, I read—what do you want me to do? I read *Le Comte de Monte-Cristo* (*The Count of Monte-Cristo*), I remember by heart the ten volumes that I read. Sometimes, at one o'clock in the

morning the nurse came, she told me "You have to go to sleep," I answered "Yes, yes, I'm only going to finish the book." I liked that. I also read *La Porteuse de pain* [*The Bread-carrier*], that I saw at the movies and on television . . .
  We've had television now for fifteen years. As for me, I like war films and westerns. Films by Jean Gabin too. Films about love, they bore me. I go up to bed. My wife watches them. She sometimes watches plays too. My wife, she doesn't read books. She reads the serials in *Nord-Matin*.[43]

Louis Lengrand has only been reading since his illness and his retirement, which pushed him at the same time to bear witness. In the preceding generation, the proletarian writer Constant Malva (1903–69), also a miner, wrote while working, and he evaluated in an expressive way the impact of his writing:

We do what we can. And I think that all the same we, proletarian writers, have our usefulness. Workers cannot always digest the often heavy and complicated texts of the great revolutionary theoreticians. As for us, we have that advantage of charming them while educating them. This is also working for the revolution by showing detail by detail the miserable situation of certain laborers, both men and women, to other laborers, also both men and women. I know they don't get carried away after reading our works like they do after hearing an impassioned speaker, but they nonetheless come to realize what they are. Then, writing allows us to come together, to recognize ourselves. We say: there, in Paris, or elsewhere, I have brothers, real brothers. And that consoles us for the weakness, for the apathy of our other brothers.[44]

At the same time that he is showing the alienating life of the miners, Malva himself comes up against this alienation, which makes of him a person set apart in the mine, and a writer without a public.[45] Did Louis Lengrand ever read Constant Malva? About the only chance for the written account of a worker or of a peasant to be reported (and valued) is in the ruling class, either in the committed intellectual milieus or among the general public.
  We might think that the more or less important ability to manage written language and narrative techniques would constitute an additional handicap. The practice of publishing at the author's expense allows us to appreciate this difficulty, by giving us narratives to read that through their awkwardness are barely publishable, even if historians find them interesting.[46] And in the opposite direction, the fact of assimilating too well the techniques of "lived" narrative and of current novel writing can so integrate the narrator-worker into the dominant culture that he loses in the specific quality of his class.[47] But such judgments, clearly, are contradictory and reflect only the prejudices, the "populist" expectations, of the literate public. Many people of the ruling classes also write very

poorly, or too well. It suffices to read a certain number of "proletarian" books in order to discern in them the same proportion of "success" as in "nonproletarian" literature. Let's cite, at the two extremes of the genre, the admirable *Cahiers autobiographiques* (*Autobiographical Notebooks*) by Dominique Lagru,[48] self-educated worker become "naïve" painter, then autobiographer in his old age, and *Travaux* (*Works*) by Georges Navel,[49] a masterpiece nurtured over a long period. If such voices were stifled, it is not due to lack of talent, but lack of audience.

Undoubtedly it would be necessary to distinguish two aspects of this literature of testimony: books relating ordinary lives by autodidacts, who really are witnesses, and whose narratives may possibly not be firmly constructed on the ideological level (and which as a result can be read as documents by historians or as populist literature by the general public); and the accounts of committed militants, who write in order to propose an analysis as much as an account, and in order to justify their action. These latter texts have had more chance to be published than the others, because they had a potential public, limited but real, in the apparatus of political and union organizations. And today they are readily regrouped (in series, anthologies) because they serve to trace concretely the history of the workers' movement.[50]

To Write or to be Written?

The relative failure of autodidactic accounts written since 1900 contrasts with the success that accounts transcribed (or rewritten) of peasants and artisans are experiencing at the present time. This is because for a dozen years in France popular speech has been recovered by the official network. Today, to perform the function of inquiry, or build a fantasy, one can get the collaboration of the model, and launch into discourse *about* him by letting him speak and by seeming to quote one of *his* speeches. The analysis or the evocation of the life of the controlled classes is accomplished through the harnessing of an autobiographical speech that one creates and behind which one is sheltered. The strategy of recorded discourse outwardly neutralizes the opposition between the one who is entitled to speak and the one who is not.

This reversal of situation is due in part, but only in part, to the development of recording methods. Before 1948, American sociologists and historians used stenography to take down people's life stories. Needless to say, technical invention has caused tremendous expansion in this type of collection. The two principal stages were the commercialization of the first reel tape recorders in 1948 (but this heavy and costly equipment was looked upon as a kind of professional material rather than an ordinary instrument of work), and later, after 1963, the appearance of cassette recorders, of reduced size and price, and very simple handling, which has made taping a banal procedure that anyone can pick up. In a parallel direction, listening to radio and watching television have gotten the public used to this type of apparently direct contact and have created a new form of verisimilitude. The collecting of life stories has developed simultaneously in two areas, that of the human sciences, and that of publishing and journalism. In the human sciences, it is a rather recent development, in France at least. The French Society of Ethnology organized in May 1978 a meeting to promote cooperation and to coordinate efforts among the specialists in different disciplines that, for four or five years, had been using the systematic collection of oral documents (history, sociology, social psychology, geography, political science, linguistics).[51] Not that this method was new. Collecting oral documents (including life stories) has been for a long time one of the basic techniques of ethnography: we will be sure of it by reading the stories in the series "Terre humaine" ("Human Earth").[52] And this method had been applied not only to societies without writing, but also to the controlled classes of our own societies. The idea had first come to American sociologists, at the beginning of the century, in large cities like Chicago where the settling of still poorly assimilated immigrants, cut off from their culture of origin, but not integrated into American life, created grave problems of order and security. To understand and curb delinquency and crime, it was useful to grasp from *within* the logic of such regrettable behavior. Whence the project to create, first through writing, personal documents, which could be cross-checked between them, but also with exterior sources of information. The first important work realized according to this method was the one by Thomas and Znaniecki, *Polish Peasant* (1918–20), which gave rise to numerous similar inquiries between 1920 and 1940 in Chicago. It is in the tradition of the Chicago school that we must place the works of Oscar Lewis, whose translation in French (1963, *Les Enfants de Sanchez* [*The Children of Sanchez*]) awakened public taste for human documents that were as fascinating as fictional works, and the interest of French sociologists for a method of inquiry that had hardly been used until then.[53]

After ethnology and sociology, history took it upon itself to turn to the life story. In the beginning, the motivation was different: it was a matter of using modern methods of recording to capture the memory of historical figures before they disappeared. What was being constructed then was a new type of *archives*, for instant analysis of course, but especially for historians of the future. The idea originated in the United States, where it was carried out from 1948 on. American oral history underwent a tremendous development that is difficult to imagine in France. Innumerable institutions (universities, research centers, local organizations, clubs) have collection programs and list magnetic, transcribed, indexed, and cataloged tapes, which have been placed at the disposition of possible users.[54] Contrary to what is going on in France today, oral American history is not socially oriented toward the speech of the controlled classes but is interested in all the participants of history and especially the leaders. On the other hand, the idea of *archive* is predominant: there is a complete dissociation of those who collect the life stories and those who, eventually, will use them.

In France, historians realized much later the urgency that there was in fixing memory by recording speech. The oral history that is now in its early stages[55] shows preferential interest in the controlled classes and in the forms of life and culture that are in the process of disappearing. It systematically links collecting and research: it is the same team that creates life stories, according to the study that it wants to make, and exploits them. This practice can certainly be more productive than simple record keeping. It also results in the circumstance that these documents will remain unpublished for some time.

But the public did not wait. Journalists and writers knew how to take advantage of this new type of reporting, in which the reporter stays in the background in order to let those who are never heard speak. In the wake of *Les Enfants de Sanchez* (*The Children of Sanchez*), some ethnological documents appeared on the workers who had immigrated to France, *Un noir a quitté le fleuve* (*A Black Has Left the River*, Editeurs francais réunis, 1968), by Annie Lauran, and especially *Grenadou, paysan français* (*Grenadou, French Peasant*, Editions du Seuil, 1966), by Alain Prévost, who realized the ethnographic scenario acted out sixty years earlier by Emile Guillaumin with *La Vie d'un simple* (*The Life of a Simple Man*).[56] Some attempts followed, for the most part the work of isolated sociologists, pioneers in this area: Juliette Minces, *Un ouvrier parle* (*A Worker Speaks*, Editions du Seuil, 1969); Jacques Caroux-Destray, *La Vie d'une famille ouvrière* (*The Life of a Working-Class Family*, Editions du Seuil, 1971), and *Un couple ouvrier traditionnel* (*A Traditional Working-class Couple*, Editions Anthropos, 1974); and Maurice Catani, *Journal de Mohamed* (*Mohamed's Journal*, Stock, 1973). Starting in 1974 there appeared in the bookstores a wave of stories collected by journalists or writers: *Louis Lengrand, mineur du Nord* (*Louis Lengrand, Miner from the North*, Editions du Seuil, 1974), by Louis Lengrand and Maria Craipeau; *Mémé Santerre, une vie* (*Grandma Santerre, a Life*, Editions du Jour, 1975), by Serge Grafteaux; *Gaston Lucas, serrurier* (*Gaston Lucas, Locksmith*, Plon, 1976), by Adélaïde Blasquez; *Marthe, les mains pleines de terre* (*Martha, Her Hands Full of Earth*, Belfond, 1977), by Jean-Claude Loiseau; *La Mémoire du village* (*Memory of the Village*, Stock, 1977), by Léonce Chaleil; *l'Escarbille, histoire d'Eugène Saulnier, ouvrier verrier* (*The Cinder, Story of Eugene Saulnier, Glassmaker*, Presses de la Renaissance, 1978), by Michel Chabot, to cite only a few. The market is overrun with these accounts, of very uneven quality. The publishers are prompt in exploiting this new demand of the public by creating series, like "La Mémoire du peuple" ("The Memory of the People," published by Jean-Pierre Delarge), "La Vie des hommes" ("The Life of Man," Stock), and "La France des profondeurs" ("The France of the Depths," Presses de la Renaissance).

Speech Before Writing

The common desire, present as much in scientific investigations as in bookstore publications, is to see, and to make seen, what is hidden from sight, to grasp what cannot be grasped, to constitute as the object of knowledge a kind of absolute *other*. This hidden treasure is defined negatively: it is what is *on the other side of writing*. Ethnographers who explore civilizations where writing does not exist do not have this problem: their whole job is to neutralize their intervention in order to observe what would happen or would be said if they were not there. Our investigators also have this job to do, of course. But, living in a society of writing, which is *their* society, they must first rebuild an ethnological domain, by considering systematically as a screen, an alteration, or a deformation any account that was assumed by the person involved in a written text. It is on the other side of this crust of writing that real speech, authentic memory, these layers or these deposits that the investigator wants to reach, would lie.

Certainly I am defining here an extreme attitude in which few researchers will recognize themselves. Quite obviously they take into account written documents that already exist. And what they avoid in writing (ideology, stereotype, role), they will inevitably come up against also in speech, and even in memory; and they will be forced to take these forms, which are not only deformation, into account. But the important thing is that they grasp the "natural" way that each person has of looking at his own life, before this life story is taken over by the person concerned in a fight or any form of social exchange and goes beyond the network of communication that is appropriate to him. This investigation of the "life story in the budding state" inevitably engenders the same type of paradox that, in psychological literature, the investigation of a mythical "sincerity" does. In a way, what we try to capture exists only in the potential state and could never take the form of speech without the intervention of the investigator. This is what is different about the ethnographic investigation, which esssentially gathers stories that are already in current use within the community being studied.

The method of inquiry (oral questioning of people who have been chosen, who have agreed to speak, but who are not familiar with the process) defines, then, a new field of study, where different objects could be constructed, according to the scientific plan of the investigator. It also defines, in the case of writers or journalists, a new type of object for consumption (paradoxically written), the picked-up or surprised speech of someone who does not write. In the two cases, it is a kind of *underside* of the autobiographical text that is produced: what would come to light is the truly lived memory, the spontaneous word, everything that writing uses but transforms, and finally hides. From this comes, in the methodological reflections of certain researchers, a systematic omission of narratives already written (considered by definition as beyond the field of study) or a sort of suspicion in regard to the writing of the model. I will give several examples of this.

Sélim Abou, in the extensive preface of *Immigrés dans l'autre Amérique* (*Immigrants in the Other America*),[57] tries to situate the originality of this new genre that is the life story collected on tape. He starts by constructing a parallel between the realistic novel and what he calls the "autobiographical document." At no time in the remainder of his very rich analysis of the application of his theory does he think about establishing another parallel, equally obvious, with the autobiographical text that his models would have possibly been capable of producing themselves. Daniel Bertaux, in *Histoires de vies, ou récits de pratiques?* (*Stories of Lives, or Narratives of Practices?*),[58] makes no comparison between these life stories that sociologists and historians create and the autobiographical stories published by the concerned parties themselves since the beginning of the century. Everything happens as if these written, assumed, and published stories were impure, irregular materials produced under unverifiable conditions and thus unusable for sociological analysis—and this all the more because in writing them, the authors had in some way already used and interpreted their memory. They had done so in such an excellent fashion that in order to reuse these stories, it would be necessary to undo the job of writing, by analyzing this writing itself, the purpose of the book, the models used, the structures and techniques—that is to say, to produce a piece of work that would shed light on the text as text but that would not illuminate more accurately the underlying experience in the perspective in which the researcher wants to analyze it. Thus the necessity of short-circuiting writing in order to reach a given of which the researcher is going to become the author.

Because he is really the author of it in every sense of the term, and sometimes, moreover, he is only that. He had the initiative; the collected narrative accomplishes his plan, and not that of the model; he is in control of the work; and he is ultimately its signer and its guarantor with regard to the new network of communication (scientific or literary) into which he introduces it. And, as Daniel Bertaux observes, it often seems that he has exhausted all his powers to construct, sometimes by quite literary means, this new given, and that once the object of study has been constructed, he is as unequipped to analyze it as he would have been when faced with the stories already published. He chose a situation untarnished by any writing in order to observe a memory and spontaneous speech, and ultimately his job was to take on all by himself what writing implies, by trying to make it the most transparent work possible. Here, at least, is one of the impasses of this type of method: an impasse from the scientific point of view, of course, because from the literary point of view, this gave rise to some admirable documents, like *Les Enfants de Sanchez* (*The Children of Sanchez*), which allows the reading public to become acquainted with "the culture of the poor."

Suspicion of writing is revealed as vigorously with those who do not put this paradoxical return to writing into action. Collecting life stories in the worker's milieu, the historian or ethnologist investigator will tend to distrust stories of militants, union or political, whose accounts will be the best controlled and the most coherent, because the struggle has given structure and meaning to their lives, and also of course because they have acquired a "theoretical" language to describe their experiences. The investigator will be afraid to let himself be confined within this type of language, which he knows already, which he perceives as stereotyped, and which he suspects of not being representative of the "lived experience" and the attitudes of the masses he wants to study. He will therefore attempt to extend his investigation to the silent majority and to make this silence speak, by letting, in the first stages of the conversation, the stereotypes be expressed and then by getting the real speech to express itself, through a more confiding relationship; and he will tend to find this speech all the more authentic in that it does not manage to express itself, seeing in the moments of silence or of superabundant and confused discourse moments when the synthesis of a "shattered" memory takes place. He might even want to go back *on the other side of speech*, toward gestures, the framework of life, familiar objects, there where memory becomes a way of being, a silent, rooted, unformulated, unconscious practice; and he will try to capture it this time on video tape.[59] On this level, the plans of the "Oral Archives of France" or of the Ecomuseum of Creusot tend to complete the work of the Museum of Popular Arts and Traditions. If we use the speech of the model, it is less to *give* it to him than to *take* it from him. There is the ambiguity of any ethnological attempt: the act that fixes and preserves the memory of an "oral" society, at the same time alienates it, recovers it, and reifies it. We question the model so that he surrenders his memory as it is, and not so that he himself makes something of it. And if, as happens sometimes, the investigation arouses in him an autobiographical vocation, and if he buys a notebook to write his own life story, the investigator will have the feeling of being in his turn short-circuited, and will be irritated or moved by this effort of the model to take his life in hand again.[60]

Indeed, this careful study of a "lived experience" before writing (film exposed but not developed, which the investigator is going "to reveal" and "to print" through his investigation) is not practiced indiscriminately just anywhere in the social field. The investigator is always a person of writing, belonging (whatever his political opinions might be) to the ruling classes and linked to an institution (publishing, newspaper, university, museum); he investigates on behalf of the general reading public or the "scientific community." And he is going to investigate where writing does not exist, where people are incapable of formulating their life story, or else where a speech perceived as ancient persists. In order to *undo* writing, it is necessary to go in the opposite direction of the work of social hierarchization and in the opposite direction of history. To find again in our own society the scenes of a prehistory, or of a repressed or oppressed speech. In the ruling classes, the terrain of the "lived experience" has been plowed in every sense by writing (the novel, account, psychoanalysis), so that there hardly exists any unsatisfied desire capable of giving value to what could be obtained through a taped investigation, whose crude result would seem an unpolished rough draft and whose elaborated result would be lost in the mass of journalistic investigations, and literary and scientifiic works that have already been published. Accordingly, the desire to study memory in its natural state, or to capture spontaneous autobiographical discourse, is always linked and subordinate to other desires, and to other *gaps*. *Nostalgia* compels us to collect all the vestiges of a disappearing civilization; it is the principal motivation of the "Oral Archives of France," which, in wanting to fix the image of "the France we have just left," is devoted exclusively to collecting the autobiographies of workers, artisans, peasants (rightly since that is where the direct knowledge of experienced attitudes is weakest, and that is the most important part of the population). And *curiosity* urges us to explore an unknown civilization in the very midst of our society, the working-class culture that is its repressed side, and which often does not "know" itself.

Every experience is thus collected in an ethnological perspective and is constituted as an object in the gaze, the listening or discourse of a subject who assumes responsibility for it according to his own identity, his own interest. The "personal" discourse of the people being questioned, to whom the investigation apparently offers the chance to become the organizers of their own lives, becomes in fact the field of study or the product of consumption (of delight) for someone else, the person who has the power to write and to read. At the same time that it is a form of rescue or help, intervention is an act of violation or voyeurism, a form of abuse of power. These words will undoubtedly seem too strong, and in fact, almost all investigators and writers do their best, as much through genuine scruple as practical necessity, to tone down as much as possible what might be shocking or condescending in the investigative process, to blur the relationship of domination that grounds their procedure. And for their part, the models chosen believe they are of greater value because of this listening, which sometimes surprises them ("my life is not interesting"), but which most often arouses in them an unsatisfied desire of theirs to speak. But quite obviously the process of investigation is not reversible, the exchange is one way, without reciprocity. Pure memory or authentic collected speech is thus found to have two "subjects" who support it: he who, fleetingly, at the time of the questioning, remembers and speaks, and he who listens, constructs the memory, and integrates it into the universe of writing. This duality and this hierarchization are magnificently expressed in the title that *Les Nouvelles littéraires* recently gave to a study on this problem: "Our Popular Memory."[61] The "our" tends to efface in a sort of national union (which covers in fact only the reading public) the relationship of class that is, in spite of everything, evoked by the word "popular." But who, when all is said and done, remembers? The people or "us"? By definition, popular memory existed before the investigation.

Furthermore, is this memory really the model's? Yes, in its content and its form, no doubt; but not in the form of its form, if I can put it this way. From the moment when it is fixed in writing, this natural memory appears passive. The act of writing assumed by another person brings to light the absence of initiative and of a plan, the fact that this act of memory is not a creative act, that it is of no use to the one who remembers, even if it arouses nostalgia and vague desires. The realization, the processes of analysis and of knowledge are the doing of the investigator (who can *compare* several stories, refer to other data, locate the alienation and the defense mechanisms in the alienation, etc.), and not of the model, who is left unchanged by the investigation. Ethnological listening does not have the function of intervention that psychoanalytical listening has.[62] Moreover, the collecting of life stories has to do by definition with a more or less remote past; it always addresses people retired from active life; it encircles a memory cut off from the action and from the present. It serves less to reactivate the mechanisms of transmissions of a tradition within the same milieu, than to divert it and annex it in favor of listening in another milieu. It is part of a vast collective transference of memory.

The addressee of the book or text taken from the conversation is not the social group to which the model belongs. This is obvious for the *Journal de Mohamed* (*Diary of Mohamed*) and for *Ahmed*, both illiterate, and incapable of imagining the effect that their transcribed speech would produce.[63] The parents of Jacques Destray have never, it seems, read their son's book.[64] Madame Grenadou was hostile at first to the project of doing a book ("Who could be interested in all these things?"), and once the book was written, she refused to leaf through it ("I know our life by heart").[65] These are two extreme cases. Mémé Santerre and Gaston Lucas received letters from readers born into the same milieu as they, but whose social destiny had no doubt been different—and television counts for as much in all this as the book. No doubt Louis Lengrand's book was read in the North, Emilie Carles's in the Briançon region; but it is a secondary effect of *repetition*, and these books could never have been published only for the local public.[66]

The Ethnological Gap

For some time, movements (analogous to what proletarian literature was in the 1930s) have tried to suppress this ethnological gap and to make those concerned take charge of their own memory. These attempts are often based at the same time on the rebirth and the conservation of local and provincial traditions. In 1977, the Ecomuseum of Creusot organized a symposium on the "collective working-class memory" whose explicit aim was to break this rift and to bring "the concerned parties," that is, the historian and the worker, face-to-face. Could a dialogue be started? Could historians be brought out of the ghetto of writing and ethnological listening and workers put in a position to take responsibility for the construction of their memory? The symposium was, it seems, stormy. It was a question of trying to break down the logic that maintains that, as soon as the working-class memory *is written*, it ceases to belong to the working class and circulates only among limited circles of militants or intellectuals (and, for all that, without reaching the general public). It is in this contradiction that "proletarian literature" between the two world wars was trapped, and this is what explains, as Michel Ragon himself confesses, his failure. More recently the study of the history of the workers' movement, started by Jean Maitron and supported by the magazine *Le Mouvement social*, came up against the same difficulty: "a workers' history without the workers"![67]

The working class is undoubtedly divided between two stances: on the one hand, forms of evasion, alienation, or promotion flashed by the ruling class through the mass media, and, on the other, forms of militant action and discourse. As a result, it is much less likely to consume its own memory, such as it is reflected by ethnologists, in the form of writing.

This gap appears, then, in conflicts, when a group claims to regain its memory; or else when it is *interiorized* by an individual, who finds himself belonging to two worlds at the same time.

It might be a matter of a pleasant internalization, when writing is placed at the service of a civilization in the process of being obliterated. This is exemplified by Pierre-Jakez Hélias, who in *Le Cheval d'orgueil* (*The Horse of Pride*, 1975) reconstructed, according to his memories but also according to those of his mother and other people, the Breton world of his childhood. Written first in Breton, this auto-ethnology was intended to circulate within the milieu studied and to help maintain its identity. The enormous success of the French version published in the ethnological collection *Terre humaine* (*Human Earth*) caused him to play another role at the same time; he provided the general public in the cities with a substitute memory and tradition, and they were happy to have rediscovered their roots in this way.

The internalization can also be tragic and can reveal the explosion of an identity. One of the most gripping collections of life stories of the working class is the one composed by a worker's son become student in sociology, who took as his model his own family: *La Vie d'une famille ouvrière* (*Life of a Working-Class Family*), by Jacques Destray. He plays the different roles. His preface, which addresses the intellectual, academic public, reveals that he belongs to the world of writing and theory; it shows him at the same time freed from the alienation of his family and his class, which he is going to try to analyze, but also relatively cut off from it and anxious not to rejoin, by becoming an intellectual, the side of the people who are oppressing the working class. In the main part of the book are heard, in alternating song, the voice of his parents, captured through the listening of the son-investigator, but also the voice of the son himself, captured using the same method (but by whom?). The listening of popular memory is thus integrated into an authentically autobiographical act; it is the same subject who is split between speech and writing, and who tries to create a liberating work.[68]

Such cases are relatively rare in this type of ethnological literature; they bring about a form of return to the traditional autobiographical situation, in which it is the subject who is his own informer, who takes the initiative, and whose plan in writing is to *construct* his identity.

These two examples can also be used to separate types of attempts that I have confused a bit too much until now, those of the scientists for whom the collection of life stories is a means, and those of the writers or journalists for whom it is an end. The confusion stems from the fact that the two attempts can result in publications that look alike. Books by ethnologists or sociologists end up playing for the general reading public the role of "authentic documents" that are as exciting as psychological and populist novels, the most striking example being *Les Enfants de Sanchez*; this is Zola reexamined and corrected by Faulkner. In the opposite direction an "unauthorized" investigation done by a writer can take on new life after having received a sort of "scientific" investiture, as is the case with *Grenadou, paysan français* (*Grenadou, French Peasant*), republished with the preface written by a historian. At the level of publication, there is thus a kind of overlapping and reversibility of project.

But scientific listening and the listening of the reading public (which determines the large circulations and guides the strategy of publishers) are different. On the side of the public, memory is very selective, and the listening of "France des profondeurs" ("The France of the Depths") surely privileges what corresponds to a desire. This memory has gaps, indifferences, amnesias; and in the opposite direction, obsessions. Attached to the past, folkloric, utopian, it has the function of restoring roots and of preaching an old wisdom of endurance, optimism, or resignation to the middle classes of the cities.[69] The world of peasants and craftsmen will thus be privileged (because it corresponds to the near or remote origins of many, and to the desire to return to the "country" or to nature that the increase in second residences also reveals).[70] We are plunged back into the past not to better understand the present, but to forget it. Success will thus come to *Mémé Santerre*, *Grenadou*, *Gaston Lucas*: their memory will be heard. Or else we will want to see, in *Pierrot et Aline* (*Pierrot and Aline*), the slow social rise of a family of little people, whose instructive story we follow through three generations. On the other hand, the mythological desire invested in the worker or in the immigrant laborer is much weaker; it is instead replaced by a fear that engenders a certain deafness or amnesia. The lengthy title of a book published in 1973 says it well: *Ahmed, une vie d'algérien, est-ce que ça fait un livre que les gens vont lire?* (*Ahmed, The Life of an Algerian, Is This a Book People Are Going to Read?*) Some people, perhaps, militants, social workers. But *the* people, the general public, it's less certain. People will prefer to read *Léonard, maçon de la Creuse* (*Leonard, Bricklayer from la Creuse*), which nevertheless also represents the life of immigrant workers of the time; but this was precisely *in the past*, in another world, where people no longer feel a responsibility, a world that has the charm of history, of folklore, of roots. And in the accounts of today the ear of the general public is opened more readily to the story of basic people, to ordinary lives, than to stories about committed militants who are sure of what they are doing. The person who is asked to remember in front of the tape recorder does not realize that listening to his memory answers to a strategy other than his own participation in the act of memory.

Can this ethnological gap be abolished? A certain number of researchers and militants hope so. The only possible way to get beyond the current contradiction seems to consist in having the groups being studied internalize the attention that the messengers of the ruling classes are focusing on them, in order to allow them to reappropriate and use for their own ends the means of knowledge and the instruments of analysis. Such a reversal of situation is in part imaginary, because if the model becomes his own observer, he perpetuates the system of observation (and the values that it presupposes) and continues to define himself as model. The real reversal would consist in transforming the former investigator into model and in observing him from another point of view—this would be a revolution. Perhaps the second reversal is at the end of the first, but it does not depend solely on ethnographical practices.

On a theoretical, prospective level, this is the objective, set by Benoît Verhaegen, of what he calls "instant history," the investigator struggling to share his knowledge with his model and to submit to criticism the result of his work, so that the division is abolished to the advantage of the political practice of the model:

> Education, whatever its form, should allow the masses to attain a new level of expression that results in their mastery of the essential tools of scientific knowledge; second, as to the publication of research, the results (provisional and open to criticism) of the first step of knowledge should be directed first to the historical subject rather than to the learned community. Instead of an elitist system of publication geared toward the top (learned authorities) or laterally (colleagues and the intelligentsia), the broadest and most accesssible diffusion possible is necessary, without financial or intellectual barriers, within the ensemble of historical participants who are concerned with the study so they can criticize it and pursue it according to their action and their historical projects.[71]

Utopia or alibi? The project remains ambiguous, insofar as the investigator keeps the initiative and remains owner of the knowledge; but we have here the whole problem of the relationship of the intellectual with the masses.

On a more practical and modest level, this can mean taking over their own "instant history" by local groups and by workers' organizations. Exemplary in this regard is the strategy perfected by the Ecomuseum of Creusot, in collaboration with the I.N.A., in order to neutralize the ethnological relationship. The essential choice was to abandon *writing* and to produce audiovisual life stories, by turning not to cinema but to video techniques. Certainly, these costly techniques, relatively awkward, are not yet popular, individually manageable means of expression.[72] But the advantages are enormous. Information recorded in this way is incomparably richer than that of life stories recorded on tape and retranscribed. On an ethnographical and historical level, this is quite obviously the solution of the future (all the more because nothing prevents us from also making more manageable transcriptions from these documents if we want). But especially the fact that we don't have to go through writing and printing allows us to establish immediately a communication and a collaboration with the model, and to make of the recording a means of dialogue within its milieu. The language universally understood today in France is the televisual image. With the video tape recorder, the life story can be played anywhere on a television set and can serve as the point of departure for lively meetings and local discussions. A "mirror effect" is produced, which stimulates discourse, memory, and eventually the critical awareness of the audience. The Creusot team has produced six life stories of working-class people in this way, one about a former Communist deputy of Creusot, and one about a woman who did charity work and was involved in relieving misery, thus setting in motion a "polyphonic" vision of the life of the region.[73] It is too early to tell what the concrete result of this attempt will be on the local level. But the documents already produced are very rich indeed. The apparatus that has been set up should not be looked upon as an alibi that ethnologist would set up for themselves to assuage their guilty conscience, but rather as the search for a compromise, for a lesser evil, for a moderate ethnographical situation. Time will tell whether this work of emancipation and distanciation will have contributed to changing the game of social relationships, of which the work itself is the product.

Chapter 10
Teaching People to Write Their Life Story

Is it possible to teach people to write their life story? When, and why, does one teach autobiography? The idea of a survey on this theme came to me while noticing that American bibliographies regularly mentioned the publication of scholarly manuals of autobiography and practical guides intended for the general public: *How to Write Your Personal History.* I had never seen books of this genre in France. Was it an American speciality? In a certain way, yes. This will be seen by looking at the chart in this chapter which presents the results of the bibliographical survey I did in 1981–82. The only significant production takes place in the United States. It seems that books of this type are not published in Italy, in Germany, or in Spain. In England, only one such volume exists. And for France, the number of titles should not be deceiving: the only guide that deserves this name is the one by André Conquet (no. 23), clear and brief, effective, and relating more, as its title indicates, to "family memories" rather than to personal history.[1]

Most of these books are the result of a pedagogical practice. But some practices do exist that do not lead to the publication of guides; in order to complete my survey, I have tried to spot them in the most diverse fields (therapy, publishing, local activity, and so on). Perhaps, before revealing the results, I should situate the ambiguous attitude I had as investigator. I was both curious and distrustful.

Curious, because I was myself searching for new outlets for my own autobiographical expression. Certainly, I was convinced that a renewal could come only from discovery, in my readings, of a form of writing that I would want to appropriate for myself (as I had attempted to do with that of Leiris); or, in my life, of an encounter or an event that would shed new light on the past. I have therefore not taken these manuals at face value, as would a prospective user looking for hints; needless to say, though, they have often made me dream, have spurred me on, have filled me with great longing. But I had another reason to be curious: perhaps such publications were responding to questions that I was posing as a teacher. Was it normal for me to teach autobiography (and, what's more, "autobiography today") without suggesting that the students practice this type of writing themselves? If I tried, how would I go about it? What were the risks? And then in my investigations of oral history, I happened to meet people who were "on the verge of autobiography," as one is on the verge of tears, but who hesitated to venture in. I wondered whether I should encourage them? Jumping immediately to a conclusion, I will state what I have drawn from my own experiences. The important thing is not the rhetoric and the art of writing, but the request for someone to listen, the search for the addressee, the relationship that is created, and which renders all the rest possible.

But I was distrustful, no doubt because I was saturated with autobiographical ideology. Simply stated, my reaction was as follows: "If I write my life story, I do so in order to construct my identity in a personal language or to pass on a particular experience. Well, from the opening pages the author of the manual seems to already know the context of my uniqueness, and he knows the means that will allow me to communicate it. Here I am brought back to generality: my uniqueness is . . . a standard production. On the whole, these books are simply manuals of morals and treatises of elementary rhetoric, situated and dated. Opening them is like going into a ready-to-wear store, submitting to a sort of "Body-graph." My life is written there in advance . . . " Undoubtedly there was also another reaction, French and elitist: "Writing cannot be taught."

My plan here will be simply to classify my questions, and to shed a little light on this undoubtedly motley field where I have brought together everything that had something to do with the apprenticeship of autobiography. Some books are entitled, classically: *How to Write Your Autobiography*. But before the question of *how* comes that of *why*.

UNITED STATES

General Hints
1. Richard G. Lillard. *American Life in Autobiography, a Descriptive Guide*. Stanford, CA.: Stanford University Press, 1956. 140 pages. (On pp. 6–13, the author discusses flaws to avoid, qualities to cultivate.)

In Education
2. Don M. Wolfe. "Autobiography: The Gold of Writing Power." *English Journal* 7 (1971), pp. 937–46.

3. Roger J. Porter and H. R. Wolf. *The Voice Within. Reading and Writing Autobiography*. New York: Alfred Knopf, 1973. xiii+304 pages.
4. Robert Lyons. *Autobiography: A Reader for Writers*. Oxford: Oxford University Press, 1977. xi+404 pages.
5. Madeleine Grumet. "Autobiography and Reconceptualization." *Impact*, New York State Association for Supervision and Curriculum, 14 (Spring 1979).
6. Marilyn Smith. "Teaching Autobiography to Senior Adults." *College English* 44 (November 1982), pp. 692–99.

For the General Public (Autobiography and Family History)
7. J. Malan Heslop and Dell Van Orden. *How to Write Your Personal History*. Salt Lake City: Salt Lake City Bookcraft, 1976. viii+56 pages.
8. Patricia Ann Case. *How to Write Your Autobiography. Preserving Your Family Heritage*. Santa Barbara, CA.: Woodbridge Press, 1977. 112 pages.
9. Janice T. Dixon and Dora D. Flack. *Preserving Your Past. A Painless Guide to Writing Your Autobiography and Family History*. New York: Doubleday, 1977. 334 pages.
10. Katie Funk Wiebe, *Good Times with Old Times. How to Write Your Memoirs*. Scottdale, PA.: Herald Press, 1979. 176 pages.
11. Lois Daniel. *How to Write Your Own Life Story. A Step by Step Guide for the Non-Professional Writer*. Chicago: Chicago Review Press, 1980. 172 pages.
12. Ruth Kanin. *Write the Story of Your Life*. New York: Dutton, 1981. 219 pages.
13. Wilson Ketterer. *How to Write and Sell a Book of Your Intimate Thoughts and Personal Adventures*. Albuquerque, NM.: American Classical College Press, 1980. 44 pages.

The Personal Journal
14. Ira Progoff. *At a Journal Workshop. The Basic Text and Guide for Using the Intensive Journal*. New York: Dialogue House Library, 1975. 320 pages.
15. Christina Baldwin. *One to One. Self-Understanding through Journal Writing*. New York: Evans, 1977. 186 pages.
16. George F. Simons. *Keeping Your Personal Journal*. New York: Paulist Press, 1978. 144 pages.

GREAT BRITAIN
17. Peter Abbs, *Autobiography in Education. An Introduction to the Subjective Discipline of Autobiography and Its Central Place in the Education of Teachers*. London: Heinemann Educational Books, 1974. 182 pages.

FRANCE
Guides To Learn How To Write:
18. André Conquet. *Comment écrire pour être lu . . . et compris* (*How to Write to be Read . . . and Understood*). Le Centurion, 1966. 64 pages. (3rd ed., 1977).
19. Jean Guénot. *Ecrire. Guide pratique de l'écrivain, avec des exercices* (*Writing. The Writer's Practical Guide, with Exercises*). Published by Jean Guénot, 85 rue des Tenneroles, 92210 Saint-Cloud, 1977. 517 pages.

In Education
20. Paul Le Bohec. "Les biographies dans la formation" ("Biographies in Education"). *Le CREU*, Journal of the Center for Research and University Exchanges (ICEM, Freinet Movement), 3 (April–June 1977), pp. 20–26.

Personal Journal
21. Claude Bonnafont. *Ecrire son journal intime* (*Writing Your Personal Journal*). Edition Retz, 1982. 199 pages.

Autobiography and Family History Manuals
22. Charles de Ribbe. *Le Livre de famille* (*The Family Book*). Tours: Mame, 1879. 283 pages. (Elaborates, from the model of "family record books," a family history guide).
23. André Conquet. *Comment rediger ses souvenirs de famille* (*How to Write Your Family Memories*). Le Centurion, "Mieux vivre après 50 ans" series, 1978. 120 pages.

Universities for Senior Citizens
24. "Education permanente au delà de 60 ans" ("Continuing Education after 60 Years of Age"). *Gérontologie et société* 13 June–July 1980, 192 pages.

Why

These books should be considered within the more general context of supply and demand, in an overall arrangement of which my inventory gives only a small picture, since, inevitably, it concerns only the printed work, and supply is read here more than demand.

On the side of *supply*, we can ask ourselves where the people come from who offer their services to apprentice autobiographers. What type of authority or competence do they allege? What services do they offer to provide, and for what purpose?

Here are five possible situations:

1. *Writing professionals*, who sell a certain know-how. This is the case of a recently founded business, S.O.S. Manuscripts, to which people who want to write their life story, or who have already written it but want to improve their text, can apply.[2] Their situation is studied; an estimate is done for them, for the job of composing or of reworking in which they are included. "The majority write to recount their professional or love life, their experience of war, of travel, of illness, of faith. For my part I have the impression of playing the role of confessor, obstetrician, psychotherapist," says Michel Dansel, founder of the firm. To tell the truth, they substitute themselves for the "clients" rather than teach them something: let's say they help them. They come here looking for a personalized listening, as much as for technical advice – something that a manual could scarcely offer them. As for the people of S.O.S. Manuscripts, they earn a living, and have the impression, which is justified, of responding to a new social demand.

Other forms of services can be proposed to student autobiographers, but they do not involve a writing apprenticeship. First, the materials of "blank books," bound in leather, intended for those who write and save on those pages, among other things, an "intimate journal, memories of vacation and travel, professional career, sentimental adventures, history of your family, birth, marriage, death," and so on.[3] Then the proposal to compose and to print several dozen copies of your autobiography, based on taped conversations: this is the original idea, quite well adapted to a familial or friendly distribution, of "J'étais une fois" ("I Was Once Upon a Time").[4] Finally the proposal, which is deceiving, to "publish" at your expense 3,000 copies of the autobiographical (or other) text that you have already written.[5] There is, therefore, an entire autobiography market.

2. *Professionals in education* who teach in the mother tongue (that is to say, professors). It is here that the difference between France and the United States is the greatest.[6] In France, the exercise of writing is traditionally considered elementary, reserved for the young classes. When we grow up, we write essays; it's more serious. On the other hand, the academic universe and real life are, in the minds of students and teachers, rather clearly separated. Whence the surprise or the skepticism of the French teacher when he opens the instruction manuals of autobiography intended for students, which seem to correspond to a real pedagogical practice (nos. 3 and 4). These two manuals offer a methodological progression in learning, give models drawn from the best classical and contemporary authors, and suggest "exercises." The objective that is determined, for example, by Lyons (no. 4), is to teach students to write and to compose. Autobiography seems to him a good area in which to learn, because the student already knows the subject to be treated (!) and can therefore apply all his effort to the writing and the composition. The book by Porter and Wolfe (no. 3) is less utilitarian in its design and is better focused on the important existential problems that au-

tobiography reflects. The problem is to know if this supply responds to a demand, and what type of commitment the teacher makes in his relationships with students. This type of teaching undoubtedly is convincing only if the teacher has already done or knows how to do what he claims to teach — which leads us to the following case — or if he has laid out a coherent plan of "group dynamics" and training — which leads us to the fourth case.

3. *Missionary aficionados.* By this I mean all those who, feeling very comfortable about writing their autobiography or about keeping a journal, have come up with the idea of teaching it to others (this is true of the group nos. 7 to 16). Often the book itself is the result of a real pedagogical practice (seminars, courses, workshops) and prolongs a sort of "crusade" which is as much moral as it is literary. The book by Ira Progoff is used as a beginnning text by the hundreds of "journal workshops" organized each year under his direction. In the autobiography manuals, the author risks his own skin in giving his own texts as examples: the book by Katie Funk Wiebe, for example, is both a guide *and* an autobiography.

4. *Training professionals* for whom the autobiography (written or oral) of the trainee is this time not an end but a *means.* Their purpose is not to teach people to write their life story, but quite simply to live, by becoming aware of their past. In the background, and at the historical origin of this movement, there is of course psychoanalysis, insofar as it systematically encourages the patient's recollection and sees in the expression and the reevaluation of the past one of the means to the "cure." No. 17 (to train future teachers, to make them write the story of their own education), and especially no. 20, belong to this category. Paul Le Bohec, who was first a Freinetist schoolteacher, next perfected, while working in IUT and within the scope of continuing education, an original exercise that he calls "co-biography." The exercise begins with a comparison, done orally, in a group, of each person's biography, which then leads to a written exercise that can take different forms: classical, like the solitary writing of an autobiography; or less classical, like the following joint exercise that Le Bohec suggests. In a notebook, the "biographer" writes his story on the right-hand pages, and Le Bohec writes questions, remarks, bits of personal narrative, beginnings of interpretation on the left-hand page; these interventions, through a system of references, are used by the "biographer" as a new point of departure for his writing on the pages to the right, which Le Bohec in his turn will comment on again, and so on. The notebook goes back and forth, the two writings being linked by numerous gears. We are far removed from all literature: the knowledge upon which the teacher relies is of the psychological and sociological order, and the texts that are written are only accounts and the residue of a transformation exercise of the self. They have their full meaning only for those individuals who have lived through this exercise (they are like words exchanged in analysis).[7]

5. Finally, the *catalysts*, those whose only offer is that of listening or of reading, and who, without giving advice and without intervening, trigger in others

a desire to write and make them act on it. This is often an involuntary process: in surveys of oral history, it happens that the person being questioned, whose memory is set in motion by the questions and who was aware of the interest that his answers aroused, decides to go through with writing the story of his life himself; he buys a notebook and begins to write. This is the same kind of result that Jacques Ozouf unintentionally induced by launching a survey in which he sent questionnaires to 20,000 retired schoolteachers. Besides the completed questionnaires, he received 300 autobiographical texts. This result can be obtained deliberately, as was the case in Poland between the two wars with the *autobiography competitions* set up by sociologists and by the newspapers which published the best of them. With this last case, we return to a much more general fact of civilization: the call to witness and to individual expression (interviews, surveys, accounts of cases, etc.) that the means of collective communication continuously sets in motion.

But there can be more active "catalysts": as in the case of Ken Worpole, who created in Hackney, a working-class district of London, a self-managed "autobiographical workshop," where he gives courses and advice on writing. Participants interview one another before going on to a composition, which is, of course, individual, but under "collective" control (public reading, critiques, and so on). These texts produced in a militant atmosphere are like the collective autobiography of the working class of this district.[8]

When we look more closely at what is going on in the United States, we notice that training is supplied essentially by three institutions: the university; different "psychologies" of Jungian, Gestaltian, or other inspiration (nos. 14 to 16); and different churches (Mennonite, no. 10; Catholic, no. 16; Mormon, no. 7). Maybe Salt Lake City is today the capital of autobiography as it is of genealogy. In any case, the little Mormon guide, direct and simple, is very well done. When we look at it even more closely, we see that psychological inspiration and religious inspiration overlap. It is still a matter of teaching a kind of psychosynthesis that results in the balance of the personality: Build your Self! Reach the *Elan Vital!* In France, neither the university nor the church has launched such a crusade. And if the new "psys" encourage the discovery and expression of the self within a group, they have not, it seems, elaborated individual or collective methods that make use of writing.

And the *demand*? It is more difficult to define. I don't know the number of copies printed and the sales figures of the different American books that I mention. We know what goes on in firms like S.O.S. Manuscripts only by what their managers say. No statistical survey has ever been done on the practices of personal writing: who keeps a personal journal? who wanted to write his life story, but didn't dare, or didn't know how to? Who writes poems? Whereas in the domain of sexuality, numerous statistical surveys have given us information, in recent years, on the practices and opinions of men and women of all ages and the social conditions, writing practices and desires for writing practices remain unknown. We have a rough idea about this hidden layer of writing through the efforts of those who aspire to publication: the volume of manuscripts refused by publishers, the solution (illusory) found in publication at the author's expense, for example, by La Pensée Universelle. But beyond this, there are all those people who write for themselves or for the people around them, as well as all those who would like to write and who are waiting for someone or something to help them.

The American books cater to people who are tempted to write but who do not dare. The addressee of the manual is already assumed to be convinced of the advantage of personal writing; if not, he would not have bought the book, of course. It is, therefore, not a question of carrying out conversions in the crowd—which is all the same rather sizable—of people who are not stirred up by the desire to write their life story (although some authors are not far from suggesting that it is normal to write, thus abnormal not to do so). The obstacle faced by the questioner (real or potential) can be of two different types. The first type is related to the writing itself and is linked undoubtedly to social class and education ("I don't know how to spell," "I could never write a book," say those who have an inkling, after spelling, of other difficulties, or who put writing and publication together). But as a matter of fact such obstacles are found in all milieus and often screen another type of obstacle, a more basic one, of communication, or of an obstacle before life itself. The essential need is therefore that of listening, and of a structuring and reassuring relationship.

Needs also differ according to age. At twenty, we may not want to go in for imitations of the autobiographies of prestigious septuagenarians. Adolescent writing par excellence is the personal journal (which we start to write all alone because we need to and because we have read the *Diary* of Anne Frank), or else the poem or fiction. The manuals that deal with the personal journal (nos. 14 to 16) are not at all meant for adolescents, but for adults going through periods of crisis who need to take stock of the situation and regain their self-control. As for autobiography, it is more an activity of maturity or of what we call today senior citizens. Books nos. 7 to 10 and no. 23 are written for people who have at least reached the age of fifty, or the age of retirement, and who are thinking about passing on their experience to their grandchildren. We might think that the ideal situation for a pedagogy of autobiography would be the clubs for retirees and the universities for senior citizens. As far as I have been able to ascertain, such is not the case. None of the universities for senior citizens that have been created in France in the last few years (no. 24) has set up a workshop for writing autobiography. No doubt there are several reasons for this: senior citizens come to the university to be young again, to have once again a future before them, and not to be reenclosed in their past and confronted with death. And then, for them to have the courage to turn their attention to their life and take stock of it, they have to be sure that the image they make of themselves will be given new value—that there is something to gain here. Finally the possible addressee (young people) is not here: one is among older people. But there is nothing ineluctable here, and some American books (no. 10) are based on the experience of teaching senior citizens, primarily women.

One might think that the demand for books on autobiography has existed for a long time, although the development of education, social mobility, and the lengthening of the life span have no doubt contributed to the rise in demand. Supply is recent and is part of a vast movement of civilization, similar to the development of psychology, the appearance of oral history, and the diffusion by the media of documentary accounts of the "lived experience," which tend to attract the individual's attention to himself. Indeed, the objective of these books is not to transform their readers into published writers; they teach essentially the private experience of writing, each person writing for the small circle in which he lives, or for his heirs, or for himself. This supply encourages the transformation of the autobiography into a mass phenomenon; to be more exact, it democratizes the autobiography. It is tempting, even if it is only an approximation, to compare the development of modern autobiography with the construction of the middle-class "subject." Autobiography is a human right. Become the owner of your life! Everyone is invited to become the owner of the individual property of one's life, to build a house of writing on one's little plot of existence. Milan Kundera, in *Le Livre du rire et de l'oubli* (*The Book of Laughter and Forgetting*, 1978), foresees the day when everyone will write and no one will read anymore. Let's resist this catastrophic prophecy. The current autobiographical crusade no doubt reveals something that already existed in innumerable other forms, namely, the mechanisms of reproduction and control of individuals, which every society is in need of.

I thought I distinguished, among these different books, three strategies vis-à-vis individuals. I am going to present a general outline of them, calling them: *status quo*, *deconstruction*, and *stabilization*.

1. *The status quo*. The strategy of books written for the elderly (nos. 7 through 13) is conformity and flattery. The addressee in no way intends to call his life into question, but to increase its value by expressing it. Accordingly, these books emphasize the methods of work, the procedures of presentations of the text, the art of writing. For what we can assume to be the basis of the problem (life), they adopt a gentle and reassuring attitude. First postulate: "you are the best-known authority on yourself" (Heslop, no. 7, p. viii). This postulate is debatable (and surprising for people who believe in God?). Its main purpose is to make the beginner confident: he is guaranteed not to expose himself to any unpleasant surprises while delving into his past. Of course, it is also sometimes said that autobiography allows us to reevaluate the past, to better understand it, etc.—but it is not directly related to any of the recommended practices. Second postulate: "your life has value, and other people are interested in knowing about it." Historic value (family

traditions, events, and milieus) and moral value are included. It is always as- sumed that life, of course, is full of highs and lows, of crises and evolutions; but all the same, it is on the whole a positive itinerary of apprenticeship that leads to the wisdom and the present faith of the candidate autobiographer. No manual considers the hypothesis in which the candidate would instead be disgusted with his life or would have unpleasant things to say about himself or would like to write a text with a polemical aim. Of course, in this case, he wouldn't have bought the guide. But as a result, to the people who read them without looking for advice, these guides seem to suggest a rather self-righteous model. Your life is a treasure that we are going to help you develop.

2. *Deconstruction*. Represented by only one book here (Le Bohec, no. 20), deconstruction is based on the opposite postulates: "you do not know your life," and "there is something that is not going right in your life." This is the fundamen- tal attitude of the majority of "psys," and it is intended for younger people looking for a solution to their difficulties. The work therefore goes through an interper- sonal relationship (dual or collective), most often oral, and the text produced, if there is one, is only a by-product. Le Bohec emphasizes that the important thing is not only the listening, but the passing through generalization, which allows the illusion of having lived through something unique to dissipate, and makes us es- cape the guilt: we are less responsible than we imagined. Of course these decon- structions are always done in view of a reconstruction, of a resurrection of a more viable individual. They are based on a more or less explicit ethic, which can give the work of the trainee the quality that letters of spiritual guidance had in the past.

3. *Stabilization*. What I call *stabilization*, for lack of a better word, is the strategy of the personal journal found in the American guides (nos. 14 through 16). It is a combination of the two preceding attitudes. Apparently it is a matter of helping people to "deconstruct" themselves, to free themselves through all sorts of exercises (fictitious dialogues, and so on). But this movement is contradicted by the perpetual fetishization of writing (appropriate to the genre of the journal) and the fixation on the self that it encourages, and especially the imposition of a moral of balance and wisdom that perhaps has as its function to subjugate the individual by making him believe that he has become his own master. Such is the impression, a rather nauseating one, that Simons's book (no. 16) had on me.

Why schematize and caricature like this? On the whole, these books have the great advantage of presenting openly, candidly, and explicitly that which under- lies all practices of autobiographical writing, even the most sophisticated and the most subtle. I suppose that a Marxist analyst who would like to study the construc- tion of the "subject" in autobiographical ideology would save himself a good deal of work by skipping the real autobiographies and using these guides as objects of study. And my polemical reaction is explained no doubt by the discomfort I felt in recognizing *myself* in a distorting and magnifying mirror.

How

The question of *"how"* remains. It has two aspects: that of the *medium* of apprenticeship, and that of the *means* used (among which I will distinguish the *models* and the *tracks*).

1. *The medium.* Is the book wellsuited to guide an apprenticeship? The question arises for all apprenticeships: can we learn the game of chess, or the art of loving, in a book? Certainly here, as it is a matter of learning to write, the book is perhaps more indicated. But in autobiography, as in the other two cases cited, the book can hardly take the place of the relationship with the other, which is essential to the process. No doubt it is necessary to distinguish two possible functions of the manual: the function of incitement, and the function of apprenticeship itself. To incite, the book must be short, direct, and simple (this is the great virtue of nos. 7 and 23). Or, if it is long, it must try to be persuasive through a constant chatter that puts the candidate autobiographer at ease by familiarizing him with some fundamental ideas (no. 14). Personally, I rather tend to be discouraged by the manuals that try to be complete, that look at all the problems in detail: the guide seems to me longer than the text that it will perhaps allow me to write. The two academic manuals (nos. 3 and 4), very well put together, are overwhelming at first sight (and, moreover, intimidating by the prestigious models that they suggest). I admit to having found a more appetizing quality in less sophisticated and more disorganized books, which you can leaf through like a guide. The problem is that the book can adapt its supply to the demand of the reader only at the beginning: afterward, its counsel is less relevant, and the apprentice autobiographer will need advice adapted to *his* text. In fact some of these manuals work better as *teachers' manuals*, intended to train teachers, than as books directly adapted to the needs of the trainees. They are the reflection of real pedagogical experiences, which they systematize in order to diffuse them through the book, while knowing very well that we cannot capsulize a lived pedagogical relationship. This inevitable disjunction is perhaps also responsible for some of my reactions: a piece of advice, or an exercise, can seem simplistic or make us smile when we read it, without putting it to the test. But what if the advice or exercise *works*? And don't we smile because we are afraid of trying? Who would think of judging a cookbook in and of itself, without tasting the dishes that it allows you to make? I might find the book by Ira Progoff (no. 14) garrulous; nonetheless the private journal workshops that he organizes from one end of the United States to the other obviously work successfully. What can I say about his book if I have not seen and experienced what's going on here?

To the book, then, should be added, in one form or another, an interpersonal relationship. It alone can structure and support the *time* necessary for an apprenticeship of this type. How much time is necessary to write one's life story? Not everyone is quite as fast as a professional writer, as an Yves Navarre who was able, in six short months, to complete the 700 pages of his *Biographie* (*Biography*, 1981). Many of the amateur attempts at autobiography go no further than the preface written one courageous day (or on a day of misery), no further than preparatory notes. No doubt you decide to do it the day when you suddenly understand *for whom* you ought to write. A manual, as warm and encouraging as it may be, rarely offers the relationship that allows you to start working and the compulsion that helps you continue. This is because you must have time to understand, to go back over what you've written; and eventually you must have the support of a discipline or a rhythm that comes from outside—the practical help of someone, at the right moment, helping you to cross over the threshold or to evaluate what you are doing.

This relationship can take different forms. In any case, it implies consent and excludes authority (whence the difficulty of imagining such apprenticeships in the French system of teaching). It especially implies a feeling of security: it is necessary to have confidence in the teacher, to be certain that you won't be attacked by the other members of the group, to be free to keep quiet, to keep your texts for yourself, in a word, to preserve your privacy. The atmosphere that prevails in different apprentice groups, in the United States as well as in France (Progoff's workshops, the training by Abbs, Le Bohec's "co-biography" groups), is therefore as far removed as possible from the psychodramas that "group dynamics" sometimes encourages. It is irenic and liberal.

The benefit provided by the relationship varies enormously from one system to the other. The purpose of Progoff's workshops is especially to wrench people out of their daily routine, to set aside a time for their organized and controlled personal meditation, more than to put them in touch with one another or to offer them a form of diagnosis on their cases. On the contrary, Le Bohec banks on reciprocal listening, the sharing of experiences, and the understanding of cases, in order to allow each person to compare and better understand what has made him what he is.

People want to write to fill an emptiness, to restore a lost relationship. The groups involved in learning to write autobiography ponder over two points at the same time in order to carry out this function of "supplement": writing and the group. In a group the presence of a real, unforeseeable "other," more difficult to manipulate than the phantom addressed by autobiographers, can produce some unexpected effects, some upheavals that solitary self-analysis and writing rarely produce, and, in time, can make it less necessary . . . to write.

2. The *model*. How to learn to *write* an autobiography? The question, of course, does not arise for "therapists" or for teachers of private journal writing. The journal must obey the rules of presentation that make the rereading by the interested party easy, but it has neither to fascinate nor to inform the reader; it doesn't have to follow any rule of composition. The private journal writer is even sometimes warned against the temptation to *overwrite*, which is harmful to sin-

cerity. The question is only asked, then, for academic manuals and actual autobiographical guides.

At the beginning of his work, the apprentice autobiographer has a certain feeling of competence: the story that he is going to write already exists, at least potentially, in his mind. The practice of oral history in recent years confirms the existence, in each one of us, of stories that are already formed, and sometimes even "broken in" by numerous oral repetitions. But they equally reveal that the narrator is always surprised, and also rather disappointed, when he has the transcription of what he said before his eyes, which was interesting and alive when he was saying it and which is on paper no more than a stammering. Written communication obeys other laws, which it is necessary to learn. Therefore the manuals teach these elementary laws, the tricks of the trade, which professional writers use when they have to write, from tapes, the autobiography of an important person. Writers know how to catch the reader's eye; to tell an anecdote in an interesting way, and make it mean something; to clarify what the oral story generally leaves implicit, in particular through descriptions and portraits; especially, to be always specific, precise, and concrete; to give the narrative as a whole a progression and a rhythm; to find the tone appropriate to the reader one has in mind, and so on. On this level, it is impossible to teach something other then a perfectly conventional "art"; the invention of new forms or of a personal style can intervene only after the basic techniques have been acquired. One learns to write the same way one learns to draw, and having an apple at home cannot make someone a Cézanne — contrary to the illusion of the apprentice autobiographer who thinks or says: "My life? It's a novel!"

The manuals of family history are meant for people whom one assumes have never "written" before; they stick therefore to basic hints of composition. The least ambitious, but perhaps the most effective, is André Conquet (no. 23), who makes eight suggestions while quickly commenting on them: (1) the reader prefers short sentences; (2) call a spade a spade; (3) preferably stay away from colloquialisms; (4) cut down on useless words; (5) active verbs, please; (6) write the way you speak; (7) use words that create an image; (8) boredom once was born of sameness. He adds some advice on punctuation. Some American manuals give expanded courses on writing and composition, with examples. University manuals aim higher and offer more sophisticated exercises based on the study of selections from major authors, systematically patterning the writing after the *reading*.

The first sentence of Rousseau's *Confessions* — "I have resolved on an enterprise which has no precedent, and which, once complete, will have no imitator." — might seem quite risky today. One writes for having read, and even the form that one's life takes, before all writing, in his memory carries the imprint of his readings. The problem that these manuals of autobiography pose (like all manuals that use selected passages) is knowing if the revelations that one has

while reading can be programmed and gauged in this way. I like to read an autobiography *in its entirety* if only to then look more closely at how it is written. I like
to approach it without too many intermediaries. The advantage of selections, certainly, is to show quickly the extreme variety of possible solutions. But the
teacher's guide freezes the choices. In the field, the teacher can encourage a complete reading of the texts he likes, whether they be classics or current books, and
he can make suggestions suited to the tastes and problems of the student. The essential thing is to organize encounters with texts. Must these texts necessarily be
autobiographies? I'm not sure. The richness of the autobiographical genre is due
to the fact that, following the example of the fictional genre, it can be nourished
by everything: poetry, theoretical reflection – and the novel itself. The great
authors that we suggest that students imitate never started by writing their autobiography; they always had, outside of the experience of life itself, that of other
forms of writing. Why not do as they did? It's useless to get ahead of schedule.
A workshop or writing exercises whose objective is not autobiography are perhaps more effective than teaching that strictly follows the standard practices of
the autobiographical genre. We learn the resources of writing better in a space
of chance and freedom, when we are not trapped by the obligation to tell the
"truth". This at least is what I have learned from my own personal experience:
I came to autobiographical writing only after I had written for my own pleasure –
it didn't matter what. Let's simply say that there are several possible paths, and
that the straight line is not always the shortest route. The important thing is to
learn to write. Autobiography will come afterward, or won't come – what does it
matter?

3. *The tracks*. It is exacting to learn to "write," even if it is indispensable. This
is the boring side of the enterprise. It always comes last: no manual suggests that
writing can be a means of *discovery*; it is always treated as a means of *exposition*
of material already found in other ways. Is it left to poets to explore their past
by following the thread of words? But everyone is a poet, and I was able to measure, by suggesting them to groups, the virtue of exercises inspired by Michel
Leiris's game, *Glossaire: j'y serre mes gloses* (*Glossary: My Remarks in Brief*).[9]
And everyone can invent variations on them. Several years ago, I was making
mistakes in reading, in the street (posters, inscriptions, etc.). Once I realized my
mistake, I tried to write texts that, through networks of associations, connected
the erroneous reading with the correct reading. This game, inspired by psychoanalysis as much as poetry, raised large chunks of memories and obsessions
every time. Above a kind of slot machine hung on the wall of a clinic, in the waiting room, I read, with astonishment, the following words: MANGEUR DE CHAIR HU-
MAINE [EATER OF HUMAN FLESH]. It takes me only a half-second to restore the "correct" version: CHANGEUR DE MONNAIE [MONEY CHANGER]. But a good hour to explore,
pen in hand, what stands out in this sudden crack in language. Of course what
comes next is to find out how to communicate this to others, how to fascinate.

No doubt it was tips like this that I was hoping to find in reading these manuals. Their morals and their rhetoric bored me or irritated me, but I have often been stimulated or inspired by the tracks they nevertheless provide. Memory is a labyrinth, and so is language; autobiography seemed to me to be a variety of track games [*jeu de pistes*], for which one can set up rules for oneself, invent channels. For example, can one can use fox and geese to explore one's political itinerary? This is what two "geese," Geneviève Mouillaud and Anne Roche, did in a relentless game that allowed them to write their autobiography together (*La Cause des oies* [*The Cause of the Geese*], 1978). Certainly, in creating new forms, we risk breaking off communication. But, on the contrary, by facilitating communication through the use of conventional techniques, we risk losing what we had to offer others that was perhaps new.

The most fascinating part of the manuals is generally found toward the beginning: you are told how to define your life, how to contain it and index it. To begin to write your autobiography is to invert the relationship that you ordinarily have with your life. It is to become again, imaginarily, the master. My life is an island that I am going to dominate with a look, and whose map I am going to draw. "Take a full page of your journal and with colored pens or pencils draw a map of your soul country. Perhaps you conceive of yourself as a continent, a peninsula or an island, as a small or large nation surrounded by others. Shape your coastline or boundaries and then as you draw them, name the mountains and valleys, the lakes, rivers, jungles, deserts, cities, etc." There is a "Map of Love" [Carte du Tendre] or "Mysterious Island" side to autobiography. It gives rise to the diagrams, symbolic or chronological, to be constructed, with thresholds and periods, in one or several columns. And then dossiers to open in order to classify the materials (this is the stationery aspect or "first day of school": index cards, notebooks, files, colored pencils). And then questionnaires intended to make sure you don't forget anything. This looks a little like the "interviewing guides" that ethnologists and historians complete at the beginning of a survey of oral history; or like an administrative file, a *Curriculum Vitae*, or a police investigation. Naturally, personal profiles outlined in this way are very conventional. A person was born; he had a family, childhood memories, initiations; he went to school, served time in the military, had an occupation, got married, had children, had a "career," then retired. No question of being single, homosexual, or unemployed. The most spectacular manual in this regard is the one by Patricia A. Case (no. 8), which obviously is intended especially for mothers and grandmothers. To write your autobiography, according to her, all you have to do is answer, using one sheet of paper per answer, a questionnaire of around 400 questions grouped into ten chapters: Early Childhood, School Days, Teenage Years, Becoming a Young Adult, Starting a Family, Raising a Family, Earning a Living, Retirement, Creativity, Highlights and Special Thoughts. You can skip certain questions and develop certain answers. When you've finished, you bind the sheets of paper and give the whole thing to your children or grandchildren.

But nothing prevents you from making up your own questions, outlining other tracks, moving around. What is most interesting are the beginning incentives, everything that uproots you from the opaque evidence of the present. Certainly, the track opened in this way could be only a kind of narcissistic "owner's tour," which will have brought about no change and no enrichment, save that one will feel more at ease within himself. There will be a chance to produce something only if it is based on a relationship with another person or on a theoretical reflection that allows us to relocate the causes and the effects. Still it is necessary to have made the start. Here, then, are some exercises recommended by one or the other, in rather different frameworks it is true. Describe the room you are in; there are inevitably cherished objects around you (photos, family furniture, etc.). Why are they there? why do you keep them? who gave them to you? (Conquet, no. 23). Describe the house where you grew up and make a detailed sketch of it (Wiebe, no. 10). Introduce yourself from the viewpoint of some of the people you are close to or acquainted with (Simons, no. 16). One can also write his/her death notice (as Stendhal did)—and much more. But the question that seems the best to me, and which Paul Le Bohec suggests (no. 20), is the following: Could you talk to me about your given name and your first name? what do they remind you of? Experience shows that it is an inexhaustible question, and an absolutely central one. Dear reader, it's up to you to answer it. What is your name?

Epilogue

Throughout the course of this essay,[1] I have presented the progress of my reading, and I have not hidden the character of the interpreter. I wanted to show *how* I was reading, leaving my reader free to read differently. I did not keep myself from playing with words, from following my ideas and my humor, so that in the presence of the interpreter whose role I was assuming, a reader could ask himself not only how he was reading, but *why*. I am now going to try to answer this question, or rather to give some elements of an answer: hoping that each person will in turn ask himself the question: Why do we read autobiographies?

A first answer comes to mind: to get to know other people. An unexpected opportunity to know from within, behind the scenes, experiences that are different from my own. That is what I felt while reading the *Vie* (*Life*) of Saint Teresa of Avila, *Les Mots* by Sartre, or the autobiography of the Chinese "well-read pauper" Chen Fou. I found here the means to enter into a spiritual or intellectual universe that was foreign to my own, and better than the experience I could have had by reading *Le Château intérieur* (*The Interior Castle*) or *La Critique de la raison dialectique* (*The Critique of Dialectical Reason*). But, especially when it is a question of contemporaries, reading could not be reduced to the satisfaction of a curiosity that does not involve us, and which could be satisfied otherwise. It is inevitably experienced as an act of communication, in which we have a role to play.

This "communication" is no doubt an illusion, and I believe, as Valéry did, that any proposition that establishes a three-term relationship between the author, the text, and the reader is an empty proposition, these three terms never being brought together in any real experience. It is the nature of autobiography to create this illusion. Insofar as it postulates the possibility of direct communication, the autobiographical text is therefore the scene of a misunderstanding. Consequently, analysis must distinguish between two different experiences: the one that is written in the text in the form of a relationship between the narrator and his implicit or explicit narratee; and the one that is experienced in the reading by the real reader, who himself comes to the text with a certain demand, and who must situate himself in relationship to the narratee of the text.

As the reader, I can first of all imagine that I am the one for whom the demand of the narrator is intended, and I put myself conscientiously in the place assigned to the narratee. I will get a comforting feeling of existence and necessity from it, since this other person, as rich, pathetic, or exceptional as his life is, suffers nonetheless from that fundamental poverty of needing to tell it to someone in order for it to exist in his own eyes. He needs me: it is in my expression that he looks for proof of existence, certificate of worth, response of love.

But it is rare that I really coincide with the narratee; in truth, such a thing is practically impossible. I remain myself, with my own story and my own demand. Certainly, I play the game, and I put myself in imagination in that place where discourse must be received; but I do not give up my own for this. The effect that the reading has on me depends upon the extent of that inescapable gap, upon that disjunction. As soon as I no longer sufficiently meet the demand expressed in the text, I take this demand obliquely as a theatrical performance and sense in the narrator the existence of a lack, which after all appears at the same time within me, since I no longer find in the text that complete something that I was undoubtedly looking for there, nor anything to respond to.

I come back to the case of Leiris: everything happens as if he had written his autobiography by erasing the narratee as much as possible, and by making it difficult to identify the reader with this evanescent "narratee." As if he had anticipated and voluntarily created a gap that is produced in general *in spite of* the narrator. This clever strategy must be taken not as an impossible renunciation of the demand of love, but as an act that is diverted in order to achieve his ends, a maneuver to approach the reader obliquely in his turn. Actually, the reader feels an uneasiness of which he unburdens himself by denigrating the work (dry, twisted) or the author (sly character, masochist); his uneasiness is due to the fact that he is cheated, as a reader, of his habitual pleasures: the pleasure of being taken for someone else, the pleasure at the same time of not being fooled. Certainly, upon reflection, he will find the flaw in the system and reintegrate Leiris's attitude into the norm, as I have just tried to do. But first he will have had the feeling of dislocation. The erasing of the narratee results in the text sounding at the very first like empty speech, quite unusual behavior in autobiography. The dumbfounded reader, not seeing whom the author has a grudge against, can neither respond to his demand nor let it get lost; and he is referred back to his own demand.

Most readers will live through this in a bad mood, as I did at first, finding the problematic of the "bull's horn" more ridiculous than pathetic; it is true that I saw a demand stick up there, which I was happy not to satisfy, since after all, I was the one being asked to play the role of this bull's horn. I was also in a bad mood when I expected a story to come to an end, and searched for a rule to its discovery. As long as I was acting like the classical reader who asks that someone speak to him, and that someone reveal something solid (a meaning) to him, as long as I experienced my relationship with the text as a mythical communication where complete values would be exchanged, without loss, I was disappointed and did not manage to read much.

Everything changed as soon as I stopped wanting to be the impossible addressee, when I abandoned the attitude of communication, and I read the text like those poems where an "I" without referent and without context belongs to whoever wants to take it. So the person of Leiris became indifferent to me; he stopped irritating me (and even, in a way, interesting me), when I stopped taking seriously the discourses through which he was hiding his method, bulls' horns and rules of the game. While beginning to read the text a little more closely, I seemed to hear all sorts of things that were new to me. Perhaps it was necessary for me to imagine that I heard them, in order not to see that I was saying them. But very quickly I began to carry out my reading in two parts, not trying to avoid projection and identification, but to utilize them at best by avoiding their traps as much as possible. It became a deciphering of images and fantasies, often overwhelming because of their repetitions, which the euphoria of writing succeeded in balancing. This exploration of fantasies, as hypothetical as it was, made me aware of the manner in which Leiris was going about it (in which we could therefore go about it) in order to stay closest to the truth while avoiding what is irreversible. I took care not to mix up my story with Leiris's, but I had no qualms about taking writing lessons from him. For the first time, it seemed to me that I was seeing how a person could talk about himself. As an epilogue to this book, and because it seems to me that such analyses are not unimportant for a general reflection on autobiographical writing, I present two texts, composed in the course of writing this volume, in which I have tried to sum up what Leiris taught me and the meaning and function of my attempts at interpretation.

I

What fascinates me about Leiris is the way in which he talks about the self.

For a long time, I had been tempted to decipher my own life story. But the genre of autobiography seemed out of reach to me. I thought that this was due to the insignificance of my story. I know today that it isn't my story that's insignificant; it's the autobiographical genre that has become antiquated. The usual techniques of this genre are inadequate to the object that it claims to have in view. And I am often confused by the naïveté and the simplicity of mind that takes hold of people who are nevertheless intellectually gifted, and who have acquired a reputation in literary, psychological, or philosophical areas, when they take it into their head to talk about their own life. Not only does critical sense vanish, and they no longer estimate very well what might interest other people (a reproach, moreover, that many readers must make against Leiris); but it especially surprises me that they themselves might be interested in what they are relating, and recognize themselves in it.

Most autobiographers use a narrative model that has only a remote relationship with what they are living, at least we hope so for them: we have the impression that they are filling out a questionnaire sent by a punctilious administration, in short, a *Curriculum Vitae*, to pick up the title given by Jean-Claude Hémery to the caricature, very animated, that he had done of the autobiographical narrative. They are born; we can't escape a family tree (paternal, maternal branches, and so forth); then one or more "first memories"; next they go dutifully to school; they make the first discovery of everything they should, while drawing a spicy, compassionate, or incisive picture of the family milieu; the crisis of adolescence comes along; and so on. From time to time, they question themselves vaguely on the order of their narrative or allude to their current problems. In a word, they use the narrative model of the biography, while filling it with everything they think is most personal or intimate to them, without realizing that it is the form that determines the content. Whatever they could really have that is personal becomes, in this system, anybody's; and that is why, moreover, when Mr. Anybody reads them, communication is established so easily.

I will not compare myself to Valéry, claiming not to be able to write the sentence on the Marquise. But between "The Marquise went out at five o'clock" and "I was born on August 13, 1938," I scarcely see any difference. One is as arbitrary as the other. And I would feel pretty stupid writing a similar sentence that is only a double lie, even if the date is "historically" exact. First of all because it is a cliché; next because, in fact, this story of birth has only come to me third hand, and because I am not at all sure that it concerns me. I admire all these people who believe they are born, who seem to know what it is to be born, and who do not ask themselves more questions than this. We have the impression while reading their autobiographies, that their birth is like a piece of property that they would own in the country, or like a diploma. This grounds their entire narrative on an irrefutable beginning, a kind of cornerstone like the ones used in unveilings. Would it only be for this, the model of the biography seems to me unusable for autobiography. I was not born. I am writing today, and my birth is everywhere. My birth will become a historic event only when I'm dead. We cannot write "I was born the . . . ," any more than "I died the . . . " Not that autobiography should give up narrative; but it must put it back in its place, and not allow it to decide, by means of a cliché, an undecidable question, the question of origin. What I like in Leiris is that he changed the terms of the problem and placed autobiography on its true ground. Tritely, this would come down to saying that the "past" exists only in the present; and that the present exists only in writing. This is not falling back into the personal journal, but rather finding oneself in a situation analogous to that of the analysand who knows that the moment when he speaks is the center of his story, in the sense that everything is repeated here. Naturally, writing is not speaking; a blank piece of paper is not a couch. But the work is done here on language and by language. So personal a search naturally disconcerts the traditional reader who no longer finds what he's looking for: a coherent and completely ordered story, the picturesque evocation of milieus and people. Disconcerted, he formulates his criticism by making use of traditional reproaches: sexual exhibitionism for *L'Age d'homme* (*Manhood*); verbal decay for *La Règle du jeu* (*The Rule of the Game*). Leiris will inevitably remain an author for a *happy few*, precisely because of the level on which his search is situated. The ordinary consumers of autobiography will always see in him an aberrant exception, whereas he is perhaps the only autobiographer of the twentieth century to have practiced the real rule of the game, that is to say, to have tried to invent a form. Besides him and Sartre, I see no one else.

When faced with studies like Leiris's, it is often said in a contemptuous tone: "He's contemplating his navel." As if the navel was an area without interest! It is the original scar. But this accusation means: "He is not looking at me and wants me to look at him." Maybe I was also tormented by the navel, but the interest that Leiris has in his has never bothered me. No doubt this is also due to the exigency with which Leiris carried out his search. In *L'Afrique fantôme* (*Phantom Africa*), he says, in regard to the minute detail of his journal that is both ethnological and intimate: "It is by pushing the particular to the limit that we attain the general, and through the maximum of subjectivity that we border on objectivity." This recaptures the anthropological aim that autobiography had had, in its beginnings, with Rousseau. There again, Leiris is, with Sartre, one of the rare autobiographers to recover the profound meaning of the genre.

For me, what was important at first was that Leiris showed me that an autobiography could be written by abandoning the biographical model, without for all that falling into the personal journal or the thematic essay. The traditional biographical narrative had intimidated me for a long time, a little like a concern reserved for grown-ups: it was so dominated, so clear, things connected so well, the perspectives on other people had such insight, portraits were so alive! Within me, it was a jumble of old stories that I had more or less gone over and over again in my mind, and which, once written in the narrative form, rang false; outside of me, other people and the world disappeared into comomonplaces as soon as I tried to pierce through the fog. Wherever I had passed, I had seen nothing, and the little that I had seen, I was incapable of recounting in the way novelists do. My story was neither biography nor novel; it had been composed in the crumbling repetition of the personal journal, and since it had abandoned the journal, it was looking for another language.

My reading of Leiris was my apprenticeship of this language. *Leiris: s'y lire* (*Leiris: Read Oneself Here*). I experienced the truthfulness of plays on words; the patience to no longer blurt out the least thing, as futile as it seemed, without having extracted the most meaning from it; the gliding of associations; the flaws, the resistances of my own writing, stubbornness in retying the threads left hanging throughout a millimetric progression; apprehension, sometimes, in the face of what remained to be written. I experienced the kind of vertigo brought on by the decision to write, preferably, what hurts you, and also, preferably, what you wouldn't want anyone else to read, with the vertigo that this engenders – but which is offset, once the decision has been made, by the sensation of being at the center of oneself, and the certainty, suddenly, that whatever you say, you're hot. It is an overwhelming demand, offset secretly no doubt by the intuition that in risking something in writing, you risk nothing. And that all this writing is in place of a spoken word that you will never say.

Unbalanced people are often accused of choosing to study psychology or psychiatry. In order to cure themselves, it is ironically argued. Antipsychiatrists would say, on the contrary, that it is cowardice, and for want of having the courage or the talent to be crazy, that they choose what brings them the closest to their "illness" and change their nostalgia into scientific interest. Perhaps this would also be true for some "professors of literature": did I not become one because of my inclination to write, and to stay, despite my difficulties in writing, as close as possible to the lost paradise? We read for want of writing; we write our reading; we plead the case of others, and our own throughout, always hoping that someone will exclaim, as in *Cyrano de Bergerac*: "How you read this letter!".

This indicates the interest I have in Leiris, but also the limits of my attempt at reading. If I put down *L'Age d'homme* after the third chapter, it is not only out of a feeling that he has already said everything, but also because of the conviction that to really understand what Leiris is saying, I would be better off turning my attention to myself.

II

"Reading Oneself" (*s'y lire*) is one of the most contentious operations: what does this other story, implicit in my text and in reality guiding my step matter to my reader? It would interest him only if my work, after a period of confusion, was used to separate these two carbon copies, to detach from the surface this layer of phantasms and obsessions that is my own – "layer" that is not a "pattern" applied to the text arbitrarily and *a priori*, but which is only built upon Leiris's text. Barthes talks about the "text-tutor," around which his own text begins to proliferate like a vine, or like one of those soft and flexible but exuberant plants that needs the vertical and sterile support of a pole stuck in the ground. Can the "text-pupil" free himself without crumbling? The *pupilles* [wards] were for me, once upon a time, ambiguous things in which extreme neglect and the tenderest love were united: "war orphans" [*pupilles de la nation*], kinds of administrative children, bags of marbles in a gray cloth bag, doomed to black overalls and the school desk, the *nation* appearing to me less like a supreme mother than a scrap heap, barracks, or vacant land, a school where we lined up out front so our rations of milk could be distributed to us; to which is opposed the pupil of the eyes [*la pupille des yeux*], sparkling and precious, which used to be called by a softer and more somber name (as if this was what appeared in the opening of the pupil), the "apple" [*prunelle*] of my eye, a thing so precious that this was what we were compared to ("to care for one's children like the apple of his eye," to swear on one's children's lives), but the pupil was still someone neglected. The word had some suspicious aspects: I never knew how to pronounce it; do you say "pupEEL" (as in the *pile* [pier— pronounced pEEL] of a bridge) or "puPEE" (as in *fille* [daughter— pronounced fEE])? Even today I avoid using it or I muddle the end confusedly, as if I were going to suddenly be naked and idiotic in the middle of a gathering of properly dressed people. Similarly, I have to think twice about not mixing up the prodigal son with the child prodigy. They are both extraordinary types of children whom adults make a lot of fuss over and whose story is told to little boys to give them something to think about, either to put them on guard against emancipation, or to flaunt the possibility of going from their childhood to the status of an adult in miniature; whether this is because they ran away from home or through genius, these children attain the age of manhood more quickly than some others, in the midst of reproachful or amazed looks. The *gue* of *prodigue* [prodigal] is severe and difficult, whereas the *prodige* [prodigy] glides gently; but the meanings of the two words are equally obscure to me. In any case, they signified states of exception or exclusion that blur the normal order of things in a disturbing manner, like the existence of adopted children (Isabelle and Jean, who, I was astounded to learn, were not their parents' children, and furthermore, were not really brother and sister—around them, throughout my childhood, hung an uneasy and erotic atmosphere, an odor of incest) or like the existence of war orphans. Even when we are dealing with girls, prodigal sons and child prodigies all have the status of boys; pupils, on the other hand, can only be girls, from the very fact that they are neglected. They depend on their *tuteur* [guardian], a strict man like a firm corset, the protector being a kind of professional of authority (like the inspector, the director—the schoolteacher), inflexible and suspicious (especially if he is a "surrogate"). Emancipation is something confused, both administrative and erotic; it's like being engaged to life. I believed I was emancipating myself here, or I have at least established the relationship of the critic and the text in terms of a filial relationship. The writer Leiris is of the same generation as my father; he has the same first name, and in library card catalogs their names follow one another very closely. Leiris has published works of ethnography that are as technical and serious as my father's works on the epigraphy of ancient languages, and I could, continuing this false parallel (weaving it and spinning it against all probability in the manner of Leiris), discern in them a common taste for the things of language, for the deciphering and practice of plays on words. Text-tutor, pretext – or text-father? Surrogate-father: a father chosen in such a way that I can identify with him, recognize in his texts, carried to the adult state and transformed by an extraordinary work of expression, my own problems as a child that arise from the opposition to the real father. The only name I could come up with for Leiris that would better describe my relationship with him is "father-prodigy," offering a way out to a frantic desire for identification that is reconcilable with the projection, since he is at the same time a "prodigal father," one of those runaway adults who spend their time going back to their childhood home, a home that I have not left, any more than he has.

Reading oneself [*s'y lire*] or being closely connected [*s'y lier*] like ivy with its tendrils? I have acted not like a reader [*lecteur*], but like a reading person [*liseur*]. The reader is stiff and professional; he is the colleague of "the author," to whom he is often joined by language, and by whom he is challenged. He is the agent of the reading. An abstract notion, like those "vectors" by which are designated what we called, as children, "lines." In "reader" [*lecteur*], nothing remains of the softness of the verb to read [*lire*]; as reading person [*liseur*], I read for my own pleasure. I do readings [*lisures*]. And even parareadings [*paralisures*]; or analyses [*analises*]; I mark out the path [*je balise*]; I explore the edges [*les lisières*]; I use and I abuse. Like a parasite. No doubt I needed a certain dose of naïveté to throw myself into an undertaking like this. Or at least there would be naïveté or abuse only if I had believed for an instant in any truth whatever to tell about Leiris. Well, it was a question neither of truth nor of Leiris; it was a matter of starting to read, perhaps for the first time – with that excitement found in all deciphering, but also with that slow takeover of a language which ought to allow you, finally, to write it. Insofar as it was in the final analysis that strategy of writing that I in my turn should have been able to produce, the question of error became unimportant. I was hoping, by presenting my own reader with the story of this journey through Leiris's text, accompanied by his progressive self-criticism, to reunite progressively, no longer some secret kept by Leiris, but the experience of the secret and of the lost object that is his writing. I have since read the *Fragments d'une grande confession* (*Fragments of a Great Confession*) by Theodor Reik, with interest and disappointment; interest in the "research journal" aspect that the deciphering of Goethe's autobiography takes (in, it is true, minute detail and experiment by trial and error that is tolerated less well than in the narratives of Freudian analysis), but especially in the fact that the analysis turns in on itself. But Reik spent twenty years bringing about this reversal, which is more interesting than the initial analysis, and this reversal is made in the form of a narrative of his adult life, without reference to childhood. In my experience of reading Proust and Leiris, it is, on the contrary, at the very instant that the literary text presents itself as double text, since I *re*cognized [re*connaissais*] here another text that in reality I did not know [*connaissais*] before. And the work of deciphering is coupled with a work of apprenticeship, with a language that for the first time allowed me to write a story without narrative. I put my mind to appropriating a *savoir-faire* as much as to deciphering. The anguish or the veritgo of deciphering was balanced by the joy and the security of this instantaneous reciphering that is writing: this balance that I experienced in writing my reading is no doubt the very one that is the law (and not the rule) of Leiris's movement.

In doing this, in any case, I produced a text that could be read only by a reader of goodwill, sufficiently knowledgeable to accept the ambiguous game that I was proposing between critical discourse and autobiography. A doubly disappointing text, since it played for some time the game of "psychocritical" deciphering, but ended up recognizing it was just a game, the echo of a personal autobiographical inquiry whose existence we were allowed to suspect without any precise details being divulged. This uncertainty was not calculated; I had to write this narrative inquiry because at that time it was the only way for me to carry on an honest critical discourse and express that part of me that could not be said more directly. It is a scrupulous honesty and timid confession that dedicate this text to a life as discreet as mine. But still today, I wonder what else can be written about Leiris or let's say rather from Leiris. The very reason for my work was to discover why I had to write about Leiris: this is what allowed me to rise above the obvious difficulties of this type of endeavor.

July 1971–December 1973

Notes

Notes

Unless otherwise indicated, translations of foreign language quotations are my own. When the cited passage is taken from a published English-language translation (which occurs most frequently in chapter 4), page numbers of both the original and English editions are cited in the text, with the reference to the original edition listed first. — TRANS.

Foreword

1. In *Autobiography: Essays Theoretical and Critical*, ed. James Olney (Princeton: Princeton University Press, 1980), p. xi

2. Paul de Man, "Autobiography as De-facement," *MLN* 94 (1979), p. 920; Avrom Fleishman, *Figures of Autobiography: The Language of Self-Writing in Victorian and Modern England* (Berkeley: University of California Press, 1983), p. 36. For a more extended discussion of de Man's essay, see Paul John Eakin, *Fictions in Autobiography: Studies in the Art of Self-Invention* (Princeton: Princeton University Press, 1985), pp. 185–87; for additional commentary on Fleishman's *Figures*, see Paul John Eakin's review, *Notre Dame English Journal* 14 (1981), pp. 71–76.

3. Linda H. Peterson, *Victorian Autobiography: The Tradition of Self-Interpretation* (New Haven: Yale University Press, 1986).

4. "Discours du récit," in *Figures, essais III* (Paris: Editions du Seuil, 1972), pp. 67–273; translated in English as *Narrative Discourse*, trans. Jane E. Lewin (Ithaca: Cornell University Press, 1980).

5. See Richard G. Lillard, *American Life in Autobiography: A Descriptive Guide* (Stanford: Stanford University Press, 1956); Louis Kaplan et. al, *A Bibliography of American Autobiographies* (Madison: University of Wisconsin Press, 1961); William Matthews, *British Autobiographies: An Annotated Bibliography of British Autobiographies Published or Written before 1951* (Berkeley: University of California Press, 1955); Roy Pascal, *Design and Truth in Autobiography* (Cambridge: Harvard University Press, 1960); and Wayne Shumaker, *English Autobiography: Its Emergence, Materials, and Forms* (Berkeley: University of California Press, 1954).

6. Philippe Lejeune, *L'Autobiographie en France* (Paris: Armand Colin, 1971), p. 5. Further references are given in the text.

7. For the distinction between factual and fictional modes of discourse, see also John R. Searle, "The Logical Status of Fictional Discourse," *New Literary History* 6 (1975), pp. 319–32; Darrel Mansell, "Unsettling the Colonel's Hash: 'Fact' in Autobiography," *Modern Language Quarterly* 37 (1976), pp. 115–32; and de Man, "Autobiography as De-facement," pp. 920–21.

8. As Lejeune rightly states, only the author can establish his or her narrative as an autobiography; efforts by critics to do so after the fact, as, for example, William Spengemann's decision that *The Scarlet Letter* is Hawthorne's autobiography, are misguided and unpersuasive. See Spengemann, *The Forms of Autobiography: Episodes in the History of a Literary Genre* (New Haven: Yale University Press, 1980), pp. 132–65.

9. Philippe Lejeune, "Autobiographie, roman et nom propre," in *Moi aussi* (Paris: Editions du Seuil, 1986), pp. 37–72. Further references to this and other essays collected in *Moi aussi* are given in the text, preceded by *Moi*. References to "The Autobiographical Pact (bis)" and other essays included in the present volume (*On Autobiography*) are given in the text, preceded by *OA*.

10. See, e.g., James Olney, *Metaphors of Self: The Meaning of Autobiography* (Princeton: Princeton University Press, 1972), p. 35; and Mandel, "Full of Life Now," in *Autobiography: Essays Theoretical and Critical*, pp. 49–72. Anyone who has worked on autobiography has encountered a reader who assumes, commonsensically, that it is the business of autobiographical criticism to validate the factual authenticity of the resemblance between the central figure of an autobiographical account and the historical, biographical model on which it is presumably based. Norman Holland's research on the reception of nonfiction prose suggests that readers instinctively do adopt a reality-testing posture of this kind in dealing with texts that they take to be based on fact. See "Prose and Minds: A Psychoanalytic Approach to Non-Fiction," in *The Art of Victorian Prose*, ed. George Levine and William Madden (New York: Oxford University Press, 1968), pp. 314–37.

11. The central importance Lejeune gives to the act of naming in the history of the self is confirmed both by theorists of human development like Susanne Langer and David Bleich and by autobiographical accounts as well—I am thinking in particular of the deaf-mute Helen Keller's celebrated experience in the well-house in which self and language entered her consciousness simultaneously. See Langer, *Philosophy in a New Key*, 2nd ed. (1951; rpt. New York), p. 126; and Bleich, *Subjective Criticism* (Baltimore: Johns Hopkins University Press, 1978), p. 61.

12. See *Fictions in Autobiography*, pp. 194–98, 209–16.

13. De Man, "Autobiography as De-facement," pp. 920–21. De Man takes Lejeune to task (pp. 922–23) for his "stubborn" appeal to the "transcendental authority" of the reader, whose responsibility it becomes to judge the "*authenticity*" of the author's signature. Lejeune's position is rather different from de Man's characterization of it here, as I shall suggest in the rest of my discussion of "The Autobiographical Pact."

14. Paul de Man, "The Resistance to Theory," in *The Resistance to Theory*, ed. Wlad Godzich (Minneapolis: University of Minnesota Press, 1986), pp. 11, 10, 11.

15. Bruss draws on the speech act theory of J. L. Austin and J. R. Searle in an effort to formulate the "rules" or criteria that must "be satisfied by the text and the surrounding context of any work which is to 'count as' autobiography" for the reader. See *Autobiographical Acts: The Changing Situation of a Literary Genre* (Baltimore: Johns Hopkins University Press, 1976), p. 10. For a comparative evaluation of the approach of Bruss and Lejeune to the problem of generic definition, see Lawrence D. Kritzman, "Autobiography: Readers and Texts," *Dispositio* 4 (1979), pp. 117–21.

16. Michel Beaujour, "Autobiographie et autoportrait," *Poétique* 32 (1977), pp. 442–58.

17. Philippe Lejeune, *Lire Leiris: Autobiographie et langage* (Paris: Klincksieck, 1975), p. 16. Further references are given in the text.

18. Similarly inspired by the example of Leiris, John Sturrock called in his manifesto of 1977 for "a new model autobiographer" who would free the genre from the stultifying conservatism of biogra-

phy and the mindless linearity of chronological order. See "The New Model Autobiographer," *New Literary History* 9 (1977), pp. 51–63.

19. See "L'Autobiographie à compte d'auteur" (1983), in *Moi aussi*, pp. 292–309.

20. See Paul Ricoeur, "Narrative Time," *Critical Inquiry* 7 (1980), pp. 169–90; Avrom Fleishman, *Figures of Autobiography*, pp. 475–78; and Janet Varner Gunn, "Autobiography and the Narrative Experience of Temporality as Depth," *Soundings* 60 (1977), pp. 194–209.

21. See Holland, "Prose and Minds"; and Hans Robert Jauss, "Literary History as a Challenge to Literary Theory," *New Literary History* 2 (1970–71), pp. 7–37.

22. See Fleishman, *Figures of Autobiography*, pp. 15–19. When Fleishman observes that "the most stable conventions we can hope to find in autobiographies are the rhetorical traces of a literary tradition, by which writers play the role of desiring to have their work read in that generic context" (p. 18), it seems to me that willy-nilly something on the order of Lejeune's pact is the best we can do. The alternative, as illustrated in Fleishman's own work, is finally unsatisfactory. Like de Man, Michael Sprinker, and others, Fleishman concludes that because of the essential undecidability of autobiography, because of its readiness to collapse into fiction for lack of a stable basis in reference, generic definition is a hopeless task, and he proceeds in his massive book on Victorian and modern autobiography to treat autobiographical novels for the purposes of analysis as virtually indistinguishable from autobiographies.

23. See Bruss, *Autobiographical Acts*; Gusdorf, "Conditions and Limits of Autobiography," in *Autobiography: Essays Theoretical and Critical*, pp. 24–48; and Weintraub, "Autobiography and Historical Consciousness," *Critical Inquiry* 1 (1975), pp. 821–48.

24. Michael Ryan, "Self-Evidence," *Diacritics* 10 (1980), p. 13.

25. Philippe Lejeune, "Ça s'est fait comme ça," *Poétique* 35 (1978), pp. 269–304. See also "Sartre et l'autobiographie parlée" (1979), in *Je est un autre* (Paris: Editions du Seuil, 1980), pp. 161–202. Further references to essays collected in *Je* are given in the text, preceded by *Je*.

26. See also Roland Barthes, "An Introduction to the Structural Analysis of Narrative," *New Literary History* 6 (1974–75), p. 261.

27. Pierre Bourdieu, "La Production de la croyance, contribution à une économie des biens symboliques," *Actes de la Recherche en Sciences Sociales* 13 (1977), pp. 3–44.

28. Jean Starobinski, "The Style of Autobiography," in *Autobiography: Essays Theoretical and Critical*, p. 75.

29. For other studies of collaborative autobiography, see Albert E. Stone, "Two Recreate One: The Act of Collaboration in Recent Black Autobiography—Ossie Guffy, Nate Shaw, Malcolm X," in *Autobiographical Occasions and Original Acts: Versions of American Identity from Henry Adams to Nate Shaw* (Philadelphia: University of Philadelphia Press, 1982), pp. 231–64; William L. Andrews, *To Tell a Free Story: The First Century of Afro-American Autobiography, 1760–1865* (Urbana: University of Illinois Press, 1986); and Paul John Eakin, "Malcolm X and the Limits of Autobiography," in *Autobiography: Essays Theoretical and Critical*, pp. 181–93.

30. Wilhelm Dilthey, *Selected Writings of Wilhelm Dilthey*, trans. and introd. H. P. Rickman (Cambridge: Cambridge University Press, 1976); and Georg Misch, *A History of Autobiography in Antiquity*, trans. E. W. Dickes, 2 vols. (Cambridge: Harvard University Press, 1951).

31. James M. Cox, "Recovering Literature's Lost Ground Through Autobiography," in *Autobiography: Essays Theoretical and Critical*, p. 124.

32. "Les Instituteurs du XIXe siècle racontent leur vie," *Histoire de l'Education* 25 (1985), pp. 53–104; "Crime et testament: Les Autobiographies de criminels au XIXe siècle," *Cahiers de Sémiotique Textuelle* 8–9 (1986), pp. 73–98; and "Autobiographie et homosexualité en France au XIXe siècle," *Romantisme* 56 (1987), pp. 79–100.

33. In Xavier-Edouard Lejeune, *Calicot*, ed. Michel and Philippe Lejeune (Paris: Montalba, 1984), p. 10.

34. See note 32 above.

35. In *Cahiers de sémiotique textuelle* 3 (1984), pp. 3–69.

36. See Philippe Lejeune, "L'Autobiographie à compte d'auteur" (1983), in *Moi aussi*, pp. 292–309; and "Apprendre aux gens à écrire leur vie" (1982; translated in English in the present volume as "Teaching People to Write Their Life Story").

37. Fleishman, *Figures of Autobiography*, pp. 471, 478.

38. Of the scholars and critics with whom I discussed Lejeune's work in Paris in 1985, only the late Claude Abastado seemed to appreciate the significance of his research into the life stories of ordinary people. Abastado noted that Lejeune began with an orientation toward the classics, especially Rousseau, whom he elevated to exemplary status in *L'Autobiographie en France*. Abastado was struck by the fact that Lejeune had been able to accept the radical evolution of the form of autobiography, an acceptance he saw dramatized in the contrast between *Le Pacte autobiographique*, a closed and classical performance, and *Je est un autre*, a wide-ranging book that deals with texts that have nothing to do with Rousseau.

39. In conversation with the author in Paris, May 1985.

40. Jonathan Loesberg, "Autobiography as Genre, Act of Consciousness, Text," *Prose Studies* 4 (1981), pp. 169–85.

41. See, e.g., Lejeune's recent commentary on François Nourissier in the form of a diary of reading notes, "Friselis: Chronique de lecture," *Romance Studies* (Wales) 9 (1986), pp. 7–19; translated in English in the same volume as "Making Ripples: A Reader's Chronicle," pp. 21–34.

42. Jean-Michel Olivier, "Lire Lejeune," *Diagraphe* 22–23 (1980), pp. 45–64; Claude Mauriac, "Michel Leiris en manuel," *Le Figaro*, 22 November 1975, p. 15.

43. Pascal, *Design and Truth in Autobiography*, pp. vii, viii.

44. For a similar view, see Sturrock, "The New Model Autobiographer." The sprawling, inchoate mass of Mark Twain's autobiography stands as a monument to the ultimate failure of this conception of autobiography to yield a satisfactory solution to the problem of form.

45. The title of Lejeune's early essay on Proust, "Ecriture et sexualité," could serve as a capsule formula for the drift of a great deal of his criticism of autobiography. *Europe* 502–3 (1971), pp. 113–43.

46. Olivier, "Lire Lejeune," p. 49.

47. See "Ecriture et sexualité;" "Le Dangereux supplément, lecture d'un aveu de Rousseau," *Annales* 4 (1974) , pp. 1009–22; "La Punition des enfants, lecture d'un aveu de Rousseau," *Le Pacte autobiographique* (Paris: Editions du Seuil, 1975), pp. 49–85; "Ça s'est fait comme ça"; and "Postscriptum à *Lire Leiris*."

48. The importance of this model for Lejeune is reflected in his evident disappointment at discovering that Serge Doubrovsky's account of his analysis in *Fils* is mostly a fiction. See "Autobiographie, roman et nom propre," in *Moi*, pp. 66–68. For additional commentary on Lejeune and psychoanalysis, in particular his interest in Lacan, see Olivier, "Lire Lejeune," pp. 58–59. Lejeune himself is careful to disclaim any authoritative mastery of Lacanian theory (*Moi*, p. 170).

49. Lejeune had said as much in conclusion to his study of the dynamics of confession in Rousseau: "I am left with the feeling that confession in autobiography is an impossibility, because of the absence of an addressee and because of the mediation of writing." *Le Pacte autobiographique*, p. 84.

Chapter 1. The Autobiographical Pact

1. Philippe Lejeune, *L'Autobiographie en France* (Paris: A. Colin, 1971).

2. Gérard Genette, *Figures, essais III. Discours du récit* (Paris: Editions du Seuil, 1972). English translation: *Narrative Discourse: An Essay in Method*, trans. Jane E. Lewin (Ithaca, N.Y.: Cornell University Press, 1980).

3. Claude Roy, *Nous, Essai d'autobiographie* (Paris: Gallimard, 1972), pp. 33–39.

4. For example, Rousseau, *Confessions*, Book 4: "Poor Jean-Jacques, in this cruel moment you

scarcely hoped that one day . . . "; see also Claude Roy, in *Moi je* (Paris: Gallimard, 1970), p. 473, supposedly talking to the person he was: "Believe me, my child, you shouldn't. . . . You shouldn't have." On this page, Claude Roy, opposing the narrator (actual) to the protagonist (past), uses the second and third person at the same time in order to talk about the latter.

5. Emile Benveniste, *Problèmes de linguistique générale* (Paris: Gallimard, 1966), section 5, "L'Homme dans la Langue." English translation: *Problems in General Linguistics*, trans. Mary Elisabeth Meek, "Man and Language." Miami Linguistics Series No. 8 (Coral Gables, Fla.: University of Miami Press, 1971).

6. On the linguistic aspects of the problem of the proper name and the way it contributes, in enunciation, to the reference, see Oswald Ducrot and Tzvetan Todorov, *Dictionnaire encyclopédique des sciences du langage* (Paris: Editions du Seuil, 1972), pp. 321–22.

7. The problem of reference in *written* enunciation, where the transmitter and the addressee no longer have a common situation (and may not even know each other), is only rarely raised by linguists, and then considered to be something that it would be necessary to study—but which one doesn't study (see Benveniste, "L'Appareil formel de l'énonciation," *Langages 17* [March 1970], p. 18).

8. Cases of fraud or the problems of the identity of the author (anonymity, pseudonymity) can be studied, starting with some classic works by J.-M. Quérard, *Les Supercheries littéraires dévoilées* (1847), or by A. Barbier, *Dictionnaire des ouvrages anonymes*, 3rd edition (1872). See an amusing inventory of recent frauds in *Gulliver* 1 (November 1972).

9. Raymond Abellio, *Ma dernière mémoire, I, Un faubourg de Toulouse, 1907-1927* (Paris: Gallimard, 1971), pp. 82–83.

10. Bertrand Poirot-Delpech, in *Le Monde* of October 13, 1972.

11. "She recovered her speech, she said: 'My' or 'My dear,' followed one or the other by my Christian name, which, by giving the narrator the same first name as the author of this book, made: 'My Marcel,' 'My dear Marcel.' " *A la recherche du temps perdu* (Paris: Gallimard, Bibliothèque de la Pléiade, 1954), vol. 3, p. 75. English translation: *Remembrance of Things Past*, 2 vols., trans. C. K. Scott Moncrieff and Frederick A. Blossom (New York: Random House, 1944). The occurrence on page 157 is only a repetition.

12. Michel Leiris, *L'Age d'homme* (Paris: Gallimard, 1973), p. 174.

13. Despite appearances, this is not the case with the *Vie de Henry Brulard* by Stendhal. This text poses some very delicate problems owing to the fact that it is unfinished, and not prepared for immediate publication. Consequently, it is difficult to decide if Henry Brulard is a pseudonym for the author or just the name of a character, since the text never took the form of a manuscript meant for publication: the humorous titles were conceived, not for *publication*, but for "MM. de la Police"—in case of surprise; the subtitle *Roman imité du Vicaire de Wakefield* has the same function of burlesque fraud. The fact that it concerns a veritable autobiography, provisionally "camouflaged," appears obviously in the reading of the text itself. The name Brulard appears only three times in the text (*Oeuvres intimes*, Paris: Bibliothèque de la Pléiade, 1955, pp. 6, 42, and 250): two of these three occasions show the camouflage: p. 6, Brulard is imposed over the name Beyle; p. 250, the "seven letters" of Brulard were at first *five*; and in this whole enjoyable passage, Bernard is to Brulard as Brulard is to Beyle. The rest of the time, the family name is represented by "B." (which can be applied impartially to Beyle or to Brulard) but also quite simply by Beyle, whoever signs the autobiography (pp. 60, 76, 376) or by "S." (Stendhal) (p. 247), which amounts to the same thing.

14. These anonymous *Mémoires* are, in their second edition (1843), prefaced by A. Aumétayer. This preface carries the ambiguity to its peak.

15. See Jean Starobinski, "Stendhal pseudonyme," in *L'Oeil vivant* (Paris: Gallimard, 1961).

16. François Nourissier, *Un petit bourgeois* (Paris: Gallimard, 1969), pp. 81–84.

17. Jacques Madaule, *L'Interlocuteur* (Paris: Gallimard, 1972), pp. 34–35.

18. Interview granted to *Le Monde*, May 14, 1971.

19. André Gide, *Si le grain ne meurt* (Paris: Gallimard, 1972), p. 278. English translation: *If It Die: An Autobiography*, trans. Dorothy Bussy (New York: Random House, 1957).

20. François Mauriac, *Commencements d'une vie*, in *Ecrits intimes* (Geneva and Paris: La Palatine, 1953), p. 14.

21. Albert Thibaudet, *Gustave Flaubert* (Paris: Gallimard, 1935), pp. 87-88.

22. See "Gide et l'espace autobiographique," *Le Pacte autobiographique* (Paris: Editions du Seuil, 1975), pp. 165-96.

23. Jean-Paul Sartre, "Autoportrait à soixante-dix ans," *Situations* (Paris: Gallimard, 1976), vol. 10, p. 145 (interview with Michel Contat in 1975). English translation: "Self-Portrait at Seventy," in *Sartre in the Seventies*, trans. Paul Auster and Lydia Davis (London: André Deutsch, 1978).

24. On this problem, see chapter 7 of the present volume, "Autobiography and Literary History."

25. See Jacques Rustin, "Mensonge et vérité dans le roman francais du XVIIIᵉ siècle," *Revue d'histoire littéraire de la France* (January-February 1969).

Chapter 2. Autobiography in the Third Person

1. This study is a sequel to what I have written about autobiography "in the third person" in "The Autobiographical Pact" (1975). See chapter 1 of the present volume, pp. 5-8. I will use the same terminology here, and for the poetic of narrative, I will refer to the vocabulary proposed by Gérard Genette in "Discours du récit," *Figures, essais III* (Paris: Editions du Seuil, 1972). English translation: *Narrative Discourse*, trans. Jane E. Lewin (Ithaca, N.Y.: Cornell University Press, 1980). I use "autobiography" here in the broad sense of the word, whether it has to do with a retrospective narrative or a journal. On the use of the personal pronouns in the private journal, see Béatrice Didier, *Le Journal intime* (Paris: P.U.F., 1976), pp. 147-58.

2. Michel Leiris, *Frêle Bruit* (Paris: Gallimard, 1976), p. 287.

3. Emile Benveniste, *Problèmes de linguistique générale* (Paris: Gallimard, 1966), p. 252. English translation: *Problems in General Linguistics*, trans. Mary Elisabeth Meek, Miami Linguistic Series No. 8 (Coral Gables, Fla: University of Miami Press, 1971), p. 218.

4. Autobiographical discourse "in the second person" is a more current figure than autobiographical discourse "in the third person." This figure can sometimes even be lexicalized, as happens in the south of France, where monologues are carried on in the second person in order to lecture or to encourage oneself. It is equally common, in the short run, in examinations of conscience or judgments: one prepares one's own trial; one speaks to oneself as if one were one's superego. See, for example, the Afterword of *La Difficulté d'être* (1974) by Jean Cocteau, the intimate meditations to which Régis Debray surrendered himself in prison, *Journal d'un petit bourgeois entre deux feux et quatre murs* (1976), or the journal of Pavese.

Autobiography in the second person is not a "genre," but simply a figure that can be used in a most varied manner, depending on whether one uses the "*tu*" [you-familiar] — examination of conscience — or the "*vous*" [you-polite] — which mimics the social discourse of indictment or of academic address; depending on the extension given to the figure, and the type of relationships that it maintains with the other sections of the text; depending on whether the "I" who says "tu" [you] remains implicit or emerges textually by manifesting a split or by starting a dialogue in several voices, and so on.

Jorge Semprun, with *L'Autobiographie de Federico Sanchez* (Paris: Editions du Seuil, 1978), gave a dazzling demonstration of the possibilities of this figure of enunciation in autobiography, by multiplying to the point of parody the shiftings and the skiddings that prevent the "*tu*" from becoming as massive as a traditional "I," and maintaining until the end the gap and the tension.

5. Possible listener or reader who can also indeed be . . . me.

6. See, for example, in the next chapter, the analysis of effects that Vallès draws from an apparently singular "I."

7. Daniel Guérin, *Autobiographie de jeunesse* (Paris: Pierre Belfond, 1972), p. 233.

8. Max Frisch devoted several pages of his journal to exploring this question of the function of the "I" and of the "he" in autobiography (*Journal, 1966-1971*, Paris: Gallimard, 1976, pp. 299-302): we see him hesitate here between the temptation of the simplifying diagnosis and the analysis of complex and varied textual situations where these "I" and "he" appear.

The series of personal pronouns "I, you, he" presents a sort of permanent temptation for the "savage" (mythological) thought which lies dormant in each of us: classification grid or diagram of opposition which we make use of to signify (while seeming to justify) the most varied classifications and oppositions. We find this mythology of personal pronouns in poetic texts, as is natural (see Michel Leiris, *Aurora*, Paris: Gallimard, 1977, pp. 39-40), but also in theoretical texts (Tzvetan Todorov, *Introduction à la littérature fantastique*, Paris: Editions du Seuil, pp. 163-64; English translation: *The Fantastic: A Structural Approach to a Literary Genre*, trans. Richard Howard, Cleveland: Case Western University Press, 1973) and in some essays (*Roland Barthes par Roland Barthes*, Paris: Editions du Seuil, 1975, pp. 170-71; Engish translation: *Roland Barthes by Roland Barthes*, trans. Richard Howard, New York: Hill and Wang, 1977) pp. 168-69.

9. André Gide, *Journal, 1889-1939* (Paris: Gallimard, Bibliothèque de la Pléiade, 1948), pp. 628-29 (journal from August 1917) and pp. 718-19. See also the three fragments of self-portraits attributed this time to fictitious narrators, "Edouard" and "I" (pp. 775-80). English translation: *The Journal of André Gide, 1889-1949*, trans. Justin O'Brien. (New York: Vintage Books, 1956).

10. Roland Barthes, "Introduction à l'analyse structurale des récits," *Communications* 8 (1966), p. 20. English translation: "An Introduction to the Structural Analysis of Narrative," *New Literary History* 6 (1974-75), p. 262; on the inverted transposition, see, for example, Emile Benveniste, *Problems in General Linguistics*, pp. 228-30.

11. Michel Leiris, *Frêle Bruit*. Fourth volume of the autobiographical series *La Règle du jeu*, *Frêle Bruit* includes in its last part a series of fragments "in the third person" interspersed between classical autobiographical fragments (pp. 287-88, 304, 307, 320-21, 380-81). We could compare in particular two related fragments on the same theme, pp. 304 and 305.

12. Barthes, *Roland Barthes par Roland Barthes*.English translation: *Roland Barthes by Roland Barthes*, trans. Richard Howard (New York: Hill and Wang, 1977).

13. Ibid, pp. 114-15, 148, 167.

14. André Gide, *Journal*, pp. 628-29. English translation: *The Journals of André Gide*, ed. Justin O'Brien, 2 vols. (New York: Vintage Books, 1956), vol. 1, pp. 272-74.

15. Claude Roy, *Somme toute* (Paris: Gallimard, 1976), pp. 9-12.

16. André Gide, *Journals*, p. 273.

17. Roland Barthes, *Roland Barthes*, p. 65.

18. Michel Leiris, *Frêle Bruit*, p. 380.

19. Authors are often asked for data that can be used in their bibliographical notice. They can respond: (1) in the form of a written text "in the first person," which is a sort of classical autobiographical sketch (e.g., the "autobiography" that Mallarmé drew up at Verlaine's request); (2) in the form of a text written "in the third person," where they themselves assume the perspective and the style of a biographer. In the latter case, the problem is that we may not know whether the notice is published anonymously or whether it is the work of the person involved (e.g., the long biography that Saint-Jean Perse composed himself for the edition of his *Oeuvres* in the Bibliothèque de la Pléiade, 1972).

Some authors write their notice "in the third person" while combining the traditional presentation with some stylistic effects and some value judgments that can only come from themselves. This mixture, if it is badly proportioned or badly controlled, produces some strange effects (thus the naïveté in the pride of André Suarès in *Ignorées du destinataire*, Paris: Gallimard, 1955, pp. 137-39). If it is well proportioned, it seems like a humorous game that makes an accomplice of the reader: thus in Stendhal, who was writing biographical, or even obituary, notices for his own pleasure, about himself (see *Oeuvres*, Paris: Gallimard, Bibliothèque de la Pléiade, 1955, pp. 1487-90, 1490-92, and 1495-1500), and in Alain ("Autobiographie," *La Table ronde* [May 1955], pp. 77-82).

20. We can think, however, about *Mes fils* (1874) by Victor Hugo.

21. Stendhal, *Oeuvres intimes* (Paris: Gallimard, Bibliothèque de la Pléiade, 1955), p. 1045 (note of 1819 in the margin of his 1811 journal).

22. Jean-Paul Sartre, *Les mots* (1964; Folio edition, Paris: Gallimard, 1972), p. 201. English translation: *The Words*, trans. Bernard Frechtman (New York: George Braziller, 1964), pp. 239-40.

23. Claude Roy, *Nous* (Paris: Gallimard, 1972), pp. 33-39.

24. Gide, *Journals*, vol. 2, p. 362.

25. The series "Ecrivains de toujours" offered at the beginning some volumes entitled *Untel par lui-même, images et textes présentés par X (So-and-So by Himself, Pictures and Texts Presented by X)*. Then the presentation changed: X was more clearly given as the author of the book, whose title was *Untel par lui-même*. In a third stage, *par lui-même* was abandoned. When Barthes put himself in the place of X to make a Barthes in the series (in which he had already written a Michelet), the title became: *Roland Barthes par Roland Barthes*, with a typographical game such that the name seems to be framed by itself and we can no longer tell whether "par Roland Barthes" is an indication of the author or whether it is part of the title.

What we are concerned with, then, is a return to the autobiographical situation within the framework of a "biographical" series which itself claimed in the beginning to reconstruct the self-portrait of the author. We must not confuse this situation with that—much more widely known but more simple situation—of series which from the very first require that authors talk about themselves and their works. Thus the series "Les Auteurs juges de leurs oeuvres" ("Authors as Judges of their Works"), published by Wesmael-Charlier, where André Maurois published in 1959 *Portrait d'un ami qui s'appelait moi (Portrait of a Friend Named Me)*, a self-portrait where only the title is detached. Or the series "Les Sentiers de la creation" ("The Paths of Creation"), by Skira.

26. On the play on personal pronouns, Barthes explains himself in *Roland Barthes*, p. 168, and in an interview in *Magazine Littéraire* 97 (February 1975), p. 32. On the theoretical problems posed by the self-portrait, see in particular, in *Roland Barthes*, "La Coincidence" ("The Coincidence"), pp. 55-56; "Le Second Degré et les autres" ("The Second Degree and the Others"), pp. 66-67; "L'Imaginaire" ('The Image System'), pp. 105-6; "Le Livre du Moi" ("The Book of the Self"), pp. 119-20; "La Recession" ("Recession"), pp. 152-53.

27. *La Quinzaine Littéraire* 205 (1-15 March 1975).

28. See "Individu et série" ("Individual and Series"), *Je est un autre* (Paris: Editions du Seuil, 1980) pp. 307-12.

29. Arlette and Robert Bréchon, *Les Noces d'Or* (Paris: Albin Michel, 1974). Anne and Nicolas, the heroes of this epistolary novel, are a married couple, like the authors of the book. Everything leads us to believe that the book is very largely autobiographical, but strictly speaking, it is not an autobiography.

30. Maria Van Rysselberghe, called "La Petite Dame," wrote for more than thirty years what she called *Notes pour l'histoire authentique d'André Gide (Notes for the Authentic Story of André Gide)*. These notes were published under the title *Les Cahiers de la Petite Dame (Notebooks of the Little Lady)*, (Cahiers André Gide, 4-7, Paris: Gallimard, 1973-77).

31. *The Autobiography of Alice B. Toklas* (1933) is a sort of exemplary case. It combines two symmetrical paradoxes: at once "autobiography in the third person," concerning Gertrude Stein, and "biography in the first person," concerning Alice Toklas. The case is all the more exemplary because today we can compare this text with the "potential" texts that it combines: subsequently Gertrude Stein continued her narrative in the form of a classic autobiography in the first person, *Everybody's Autobiography* (1938), and Alice B. Toklas ended up writing her own memoirs once and for all, *What Is Remembered* (1963).

32. Jean-Jacques Gautier, *Cher Untel* (Paris: Plon, 1974).

33. Jean-Jacques Rousseau, *Oeuvres complètes* (Paris: Gallimard, Bibliothèque de la Pléiade, 1958), vol. 1, pp. 657–992. See Michel Foucault's introduction to the edition of the *Dialogues* in the "Bibliothèque de Cluny" (Paris: A. Colin, 1962).

34. *Oeuvres complètes*, vol. 1, p. 663.

35. On the autobiographical games of Torres Villarroel, see the study by Guy Mercadier, "Diego de Torres Villarroel (1694–1770): une autobiographie permanente," *Revue de l'Institut de Sociologie* 1-2 (1982), pp. 127–41.

36. In "Le Peigne cassé" ("The Broken Comb"), *Poétique* 25 (1976), pp. 1–30, I tried to show how the plays of voice and focalization were utilized in the *Confessions* in order to create a pathetic "fake" analogous in its function to the system of fictitious characters in the *Dialogues*.

37. *Oeuvres complètes*, vol. 1., pp. 776–875.

38. Ibid., pp. 837–42.

39. Paul Valéry, *Cahiers* (Paris: Gallimard, Bibliothèque de la Pléiade, 1973), vol. 1, section "Language," pp. 379–476. The passage cited as the epigraph for this study is found on p. 440.

Chapter 3. The Ironic Narrative of Childhood: Vallès

1. Vallès has not written any narrative of childhood that is strictly autobiographical; he has furnished successively three versions of his childhood in novel form: in 1861, the "Lettre de Junius" ("Letter from Junius"); in 1869, *Le Testament d'un blagueur* (*Testament of a Joker*); in 1879, *L'Enfant* (*The Child*). The first two texts can be found in the recent edition of the *Oeuvres* (*Works*) of Vallès by Roger Bellet (Paris: Gallimard, Bibliothèque de la Pléiade, 1975, vol. 1). The text of *L'Enfant* will be quoted according to the Garnier-Flammarion edition, 1968.

2. In a broader version of this study (published in the Proceedings of the *Jules Vallès Colloquium* [1975], Presses de l'Université de Lyon, 1976, pp. 51–74), I presented the "autobiographical" project of Vallès and the problem of the pact. Here I will deal only with the narrative voice. On the techniques of Vallès, see Jacques Dubois, *Romanciers français de l'instantané au XIXe siècle* (Brussels, 1963), and M. Jutrin, "Le Sens du monologue intérieur dans *L'Enfant* de Jules Vallès," *Revue des Langues Vivantes* 5 (1972), pp. 467–76.

3. "Autodiegetic" narrative according to Gérard Genette's terminology, which I will use in this study ("Discours du récit," in *Figures, essais III* [Paris: Editions du Seuil, 1972]; English translation: *Narrative Discourse*, trans. Jane E. Lewin, [Ithaca, N.Y.: Cornell University Press, 1980]).

4. The incipit of *Sans Famille* (*Without Family*) (1878), "I am a foundling," is extremely clever. On the one hand, it is a "paralepsis," that is, a lie by omission, for if the hero Rémi was indeed a foundling, the narrator must know very well that he is Rémi Milligan, a lost child, found, then *found again*, but he must hide from the reader the rest of his story, for fear of destroying the suspense of his "family novel." On the other hand, this nonsituated affirmation can give the reader the illusion that it is a child who is the narrator of the book.

5. On the different functions of the narrator, see Genette, *Figures, essais III*, pp. 261–63. On the functions of the narrator in autobiographical discourse, see my description in *L'Autobigraphie en France* (Paris: A. Colin, 1971), pp. 73–80.

6. See, for example, the manner in which Vallès uses the narrative present in his report on mines (*Oeuvres*, Bibliothèque de la Pléiade, vol. 1, pp. 907–16).

7. *L'Enfant*, chap. 1, pp. 46–47. The originality and effectiveness of this "dissolve" can be measured by seeing how A. Daudet has treated an analogous scene (debate of conscience of a child) in *Le Petit Chose* (Paris: Nelson, 1950), chap. 3, pp. 35–36.

8. As Jean Peytard has shown ("Oral et scriptural: deux ordres de situations et de descriptions linguistiques," *Langue Française* 6 [1970]), the problem of the "levels of language' (child or adult registers, familiar or literary, etc.) must not be confused with that of the written or oral realization of utterances. On the one hand, Vallès blends different "levels of language." On the other hand, he

presents his written narration in a form that suggests its oral realization. He blends the traditional presentation by means of paragraphs that form a whole, with a more broken up and airy disposition that evokes rhythm, silences, ellipses, and repetitions of speech. There is a sort of Vallèsian "verse," corresponding to an oral scansion, to the breath and the effects of a spoken narration. This ambiguous character of the rhythm of the narration contributes to the uncertainty of the origin of the enunciation.

9. *L'Enfant*, chap. 8, p. 101.

10. On the indirect free style, see Marguerite Lips, *Le Style indirect libre* (Paris: Payot, 1926), and the actual state of the question prepared by Gérard Strauch in "De quelques interprétations récentes du style indirect libre," *Recherches Anglaises et Américaines 8* (1974), pp. 40-73.

11. In the *direct free style*, no introductory verb or sign (quotation marks, dash) distinguishes the repeated discourse from the discourse that repeats it. On the direct free style, and the manner in which it completes the system of direct and indirect "styles," see Derek Bickerton, "Modes of Interior Monologue: A Formal Definition," *Modern Language Quarterly* (1967), p. 233, and Gérard Strauch, "De quelques interprétations récentes du style indirect libre."

12. *L'Enfant*, chap. 7, p. 94.

13. On this problem, see the clarification by Gérard Genette in *Figures, essais III*, p. 194.

14. With Vallès, the "monologue" or the "private journal" of the protagonist always remains an integral part of the narration of the first narrator, even if it is a rather imperceptible link. But it would be sufficient to give autonomy to this discourse and to this narration of the child in order to obtain another type of narrative, of which Vallès is indirectly the precursor: the novel of childhood whose narration is deemed to be given by the child himself. Hence two solutions are possible: the writing of a journal involving a "simultaneous" narration (e.g., Colette, *Claudine à l'école*, 1900; and in the framework of literature for children, Colette Vivier, *La Maison des Petits Bonheurs*, 1939), or the emission of a retrospective narration, done at a precise (e.g., Emile Ajar, *La Vie devant soi*, 1975) or an undetermined moment (e.g., Christiane Rochefort, *Les Petits Enfants du siècle*, 1961). Even in these cases the duplicity of the enunciation remains patent, and none of these texts can be read like a journal that is kept or a narrative done by a child or an adolescent. In terms of context, that presence of the adult who pulls the strings is displaced: he is no longer a retrospective narrator included in the text, but the author. The fictional pact prevents us from believing in the simplicity of the enunciation. And this all the more as the stylistic marks of another speaker are visible: many pathetic or ironic effects are produced unknown to the candid protagonist whose discourse is made up by one adult for other adults. The matter is less emphasized in fictional "journals" that attempt to comply with the laws of verisimilitude on children's language and of private writing; it is highly visible in retrospective narrations where the author can make up a voice by violently blending the adult register and the child's register, literary language and popular language, as is the case with Christiane Rochefort and Emile Ajar.

15. *L'Enfant*, chap. 20, p. 242. In *Le Testament d'un blagueur*, some very complicated effects are produced within the framework of this second narration. Not only can the child relate what has happened to him "recently," but at the end of the work, the hero-become-adolescent casts a global glance at his entire past and then behaves like an autobiographer in a long sequence in historical tenses (literary past [*passé simple*]/imperfect), in the midst of which he uses, out of concern for contrast or variety, . . . the narrative present! (*Oeuvres*, Bibliothèque de la Pléiade, vol. 1, pp. 1128-31).

16. This technique will be used in an especially coherent way in *Le Bachelier* and in *L'Insurgé*, where the narration often *seems* to be taken over by the protagonist himself soon after the events. But it is a question there of a *figure*, of an "as if," this taking charge being mimed by an irretrievable narrator in the story (he never takes into account the knowledge that he ought to have of the sequel to the story or of the way in which he is situated in this sequel), but a narrator that is textually necessary to imagine. The text of *L'Insurgé*, in particular, is strained between the perspective of the protagonist contemporaneous with the events, who often seems to be telling the story, and that of the narrator who is writing after the Commune and in light of his defeat.

17. *L'Enfant*, chap. 5, p. 77.

18. In terms of theory, we can ask ourselves if such an interference is accidental, as Charles Bally maintained ("Antiphrase et style indirect libre," in *A Grammatical Miscellany Offered to Otto Jesperson* [London: Allen and Unwin, 1930], pp. 331-40), or if on the contrary it is not consubstantial with the use of the "mention." See the study by Dan Sperber and Deirdre Wilson, "Les Ironies comme mentions," *Poétique* 36 (November 1978), pp. 399-412.

19. In *Poil de Carotte* (1894), Jules Renard offered a different solution to the problem of the ironic triangular enunciation. The use of the narrative "in the third person" in the present results in the reader asking himself fewer questions about the degree of conscience or the attitude of the child since he is apparently not responsible for the enunciation.

20. Thus the ironic demonstration of "Mes humanités" (chap. 20, pp. 241-43), whose mechanism makes us think about the one used by Pascal in *Les Provinciales*.

21. Thus the scenes of "good manners" that make us think of Molière: the meal with Mr. Laurier (chap. 16, pp. 180-82) and the reverence (chap. 18, p. 223).

22. *Correspondance avec Hector Malot*, Editeurs Français Réunis, 1968. From this point of view, we can also compare *Le Bachelier*(1881) with *Souvenirs d'un étudiant pauvre* (1884), an autobiographical text that covers the same period as the beginning of *Le Bachelier*. When he reappears in *Souvenirs*, the classical autobiographical narrator makes the essential aspects of the ironic effects and the verve of *Le Bachelier* disappear, replacing them with a very conventional discourse.

23. On Célinian narration, see Danielle Racelle-Latin, "Lisibilité et idéologie," *Littérature* 12 (1973).

Chapter 4. The Order of Narrative in Sartre's *Les Mots*

1. See Maurice Halbwachs, *Les Cadres sociaux de la mémoire* (1925) (Paris: P.U.F., 1952).

2. The lectures of Maurois, published under the title *Aspects de la biographie* (Paris: Grasset, 1930), are the testimony of a biographer on his own ideas, rather than a true study of the genre. Even in English, literary criticism on the genre is slight, contrary to what one might think, given the vogue of biography in England. See the panorama of studies on the genre proposed recently by Paul Murray Kendall, *The Art of Biography* (New York: Norton, 1965), p. xiv. Sartre is undoubtedly the first to have based the technique of biography on the conception of an original method (see *Questions de méthode* [1960], Paris: Gallimard, 1967). This makes all the more surprising the methodological naïveté of Francis Jeanson in his biography of Sartre (*Sartre dans sa vie*, Paris: Editions du Seuil, 1974). Postscript (1987). The lacuna that I noticed in 1975 has since been filled by a book by Daniel Madelénat, *La Biographie (Biography)* (Paris: P.U.F., 1984).

3. See Simone de Beauvoir, *La Force des choses* (Paris: Gallimard, 1963), vol. 1, pp. 382-84. English translation: *Force of Circumstance*, trans. Richard Howard (London: André Deutsch, Weidenfeld and Nocolson, 1965), pp. 359-61.

4. G. Genette in "Discours du récit" (*Figures, essais III*, Paris: Editions du Seuil, 1972; English translation: *Narrative Discourse*, trans. Jane E. Lewin, Ithaca, N.Y.: Cornell University Press, 1980), analyzing the case of "subsequent narrating" (pp. 232-34; 220-23)—which is the case of all autobiographies—indicates that if sometimes the date of the narration appears, the narration never has duration. This is true of almost all fictional narratives, but not for most autobiographies. Very often the duration of narration is indicated just by *two* dates placed at the end of the narrative (see the end of *Un petit bourgeois*, by Nourissier; of *L'Age d'homme*, by Leiris, etc.); often this duration is dramatically represented in the narration itself. For *Les Mots*, written from 1954 to 1963, this duration manifests itself involuntarily in the text through incoherences of chronology, on which Sartre has explained himself in his interview in *Le Monde* of April 18, 1964.

5. On this point, see André Vial, *Chateaubriand et le temps perdu* (Paris: Editions 10/18, 1971).

6. For the analysis of different "ruptures" of chronological order, see Genette, "Discours du récit," pp. 77–121; "Narrative Discourse," pp. 33–85.

7. Simone de Beauvoir, *Tout compte fait* (Paris: Gallimard, 1972), "Prologue," (English translation: *All Said and Done*, trans. Patrick O'Brien, New York: Putnam, 1974), takes up again the analysis of the disadvantages of chronological order already outlined in *La Force des choses* (see above, note 3). As a matter of fact, *Tout compte fait* will seem to readers less well written than previous volumes; choosing thematic order, which in reality is not an order, but an addition, Simone de Beauvoir does not avoid chronological order because of this.

8. Mikhail Zochtchenko, *Avant le lever du soleil* (Paris: Gallimard, 1971). This technique of the total inversion of the chronological order is also mentioned by Claude Roy in *Nous, essai d'autobigraphie* (Paris: Gallimard, 1972), p. 338. Claude Roy sees here only a harebrained hypothesis, which after all would finally change nothing in the order of life such as the narrative reflects it.

9. See "Michel Leiris, autobiographie et poésie," in *Le Pacte autobiographique* (Paris: Editions du Seuil, 1975), pp. 245–307.

Postscript (1987). Undoubtedly it would be necessary today to add to Sartre and Leiris Claude Mauriac, for the montage he attempted to put together of his journal in the nine volumes of *Le Temps Immobile* (Paris: Grasset, 1974–1986) and in *L'Eternité parfois* (Paris: Belfond, 1977).

10. Jean-Paul Sartre, "Plaidoyer pour les intellectuels," in *Situations* (Paris: Gallimard, 1972), vol. 8, pp. 401–4. English translation: "A Plea for Intellectuals," in *Between Existentialism and Marxism* (London: New Left Books, 1974), 274–76. Autobiography is presented both as a necessary moment in a dialectical study and as a necessary hygiene to eradicate the attitudes acquired during childhood.

11. On the different aspects of Sartre's project in *Les Mots*, and on the problems of parody, see the study by Jacques Lecarme, "*Les Mots* de Sartre: un cas limite de l'autobiographie?" *Revue d'Histoire Littéraire de la France* 6 (1975), pp. 1047–61.

12. All the references in *Les Mots* refer to the edition that appeared in the Folio collection, Gallimard, 1972; English translation: *The Words*, trans. Bernard Frechtman (New York: George Braziller, 1964).

13. Sartre, "The Itinerary of a Thought," in *Between Existentialism and Marxism*, p. 63, and "Self-Portrait at Seventy," in *Sartre in the Seventies*, trans Paul Auster and Lydia Davis (London: André Deutsch, 1978), pp. 14–15. On the problem of the sequel to *Les Mots*, see my study "Sartre et l'autobiographie parlée," in *Je est un autre* (Paris: Editions du Seuil, 1980), pp. 161–202.

14. See *Situations* (Paris: Gallimard, 1964), vol. 4, pp. 130–88. (English translation: *Situations*, trans. Benita Eisler [New York: George Braziller, 1964], pp. 113–73.) Sartre talks about his adolescence in an interview with Francis Jeanson in June of 1973 (see *Sartre dans sa vie*, pp. 289–95), and in certain passages from his conversations with Gavi and Victor, where he stresses the role played by his stepfather as authority figure (*On a raison de se révolter*, Paris: Gallimard, 1974, pp. 171–72).

15. See *Les Mots*: "When I was thirty, friends were surprised: 'One would think you didn't have parents. Or a childhood' " (pp. 200; 239).

16. *On a raison de se révolter.*

17. *Questions de méthode* (1960; Paris: Gallimard, 1967), pp. 81–93; English translation: *Search for a Method* trans. Hazel E. Barnes (New York, Alfred A. Knopf, 1963). *Les Mots* is an exemplary illustration of the "mediation" of the family; we know that Sartre sees a second mediation, in the adult, this time, by belonging to *groups*: we imagine that this would have been the basis of the sequel to *Les Mots*, if Sartre had written it.

18. Simone de Beauvoir, *Le Deuxième Sexe* (1949; Paris: Gallimard, 1970), vol. 1, p. 285; English translation: *The Second Sex* trans. and ed. by H. M. Parshley (New York: Knopf, 1964), p. 267.

19. Thus, for the family comedy, the two paragraphs on pp. 36, 39–40.

20. See "liberated" from his father, pp. 19–20; 19–21; and the coddled child, pp. 30; 32.

21. *Qu'est-ce que la littérature?* (1947; Paris: Gallimard, 1970); English translation: *What is*

Literature? It is interesting to compare the two texts; but in order to do so, it is necessary to take into account both the difference in date, and especially the difference in perspective, of a general historical analysis, and of an autobiographical narrative. Thus the developments on *reading* are made from rather different points of view in *Les Mots* (pp. 37–61; 40–69) and in *Qu'est-ce que la littérature?* (pp. 55 ff.). On the other hand, the analysis of the myth of the writer in *Les Mots* refers rather faithfully to the one in *Qu'est-ce que la littérature?* (pp. 136–79;); we see, moreover, that the figure of the Writer-Hero corresponds in the child to the mythology of the romantic generation of 1830. The whole mythology of the avenger, of the scapegoat, etc., such as it is watered down and degraded until 1914, from Alexander Dumas to Zévaco, dates from 1830 (see above the excellent restatement by Jean Tortel in the *Encyclopédie de la Pléiade, Histoire des littératures*, 1958, vol. 3, pp. 1579–1603). The Writer-Martyr, such as Sartre describes him, dates from the following half-generation, that of Baudelaire and Flaubert; the analysis of *Les Mots*, pp. 150–74; 177–207 is open to comparison with that of the writer without a public who invents the mystique of literature and the idea of fame, in *Qu'est-ce que la littérature?*, pp. 154ff., and in the tableau that Sartre provides, on pp. 206–10, pp. 247–49, and pp. 254–55, of the literary climate in which his generation had its beginnings.

22. On p. 140 (p. 165), Sartre had ironically placed his narrative under the patronage of Chateaubriand.

23. See *Les Mots*, pp. 61–2, 115, 122, 174–75; *The Words*, pp. 69–71, 134, 143, 207–9.

24. We also find confirmation of this in the interview granted to Francis Jeanson in 1973 (*Sartre dans sa vie*, pp. 289–95).

25. If the remarriage of the mother is mentioned, the figure of the stepfather is never positively recalled in *Les Mots*. It is necessary to refer to other texts to find his portrait, or rather his execution: in the biography of Nizan (*Situations*, vol. 4, pp. 160–61; *Situations*, trans. Benita Eisler [New York: George Braziller, 1965], pp. 145–46), and in *On a raison de se révolter*, pp. 171–72.

26. This is also the situation of a character in *Le Sursis* (1945), Philippe, whose mother was remarried to a general.

27. On the resemblance between Nizan and Sartre in the eyes of others, and on their squint, see *Situations*, pp. 126–27.

28. The very story of the writing of *Les Mots* still remains obscure, despite the direct testimony of Sartre (interview in *Le Monde*, April 18, 1964), the allusions that can be found in *Les Mandarins* (1954; Paris: Gallimard, 1968, vol. 1, pp. 60–63, and p. 323; the autobiography of Robert Dubreuilh, unfinished and never published, so as not to give weapons to his enemies), and the narrative by Simone de Beauvoir in *Tout compte fait* (pp. 54–5, 107) (*All Said and Done* [pp. 44, 92–93]).

29. See the interview granted to *L'Idiot International* in September 1970, reprinted in *Situations* (Paris: Gallimard, 1972), vol. 8, pp. 456–76.

30. *L'Imaginaire* (Paris: Gallimard, 1970), p. 263; English translation: *Psychology of the Imagination* (New York: Philosophical Library, 1948), p. 195.

31. *Baudelaire* (Paris: Gallimard, 1947), pp. 214–15; English translation: *Baudelaire*, trans. Martin Turnell (New York: New Directions Books, 1950), p. 185.

32. See Genette, *Figures, essais II* (Paris: Editions du Seuil, 1969), p. 97. Genette's analyses on function and motivation echo Valéry's and Sartre's remarks on the deception of all narratives, composed implicitly starting from their conclusion (see Valéry, *Oeuvres*, Bibliothèque de la Pléiade, 1960, vol. 2, pp. 776–77; Sartre, *La Nausée*, Paris: Gallimard, 1961, pp. 60–63 [English trnslation: *Nausea*, trans. Lloyd Alexander (New York: New Directions, 1964), pp. 38–40]): even in *Les Mots*, the narrator stigmatizes the retrospective illusion such as it is practiced by biographers on the "lives" of men who have become famous, and the perverse application that the child makes of these narratives in his own case (pp. 168–73; 199–206). But isn't this illusion at work in *Les Mots* also? Sartre responds: "This error of perspective does not disturb us because we recognize it; we have the means

of correcting it" (pp. 169; 201) – presumably by showing the shifting between the imagined future and the future as it was realized.

33. Claude Burgelin, "Lire *L'Idiot de la famille?" Littérature* 6 (May 1972), p. 115.

34. For a restatement of Sartre's attitude toward psychoanalysis, see James Arnold and Jean-Pierre Piriou, *Genèse et critique d'une autobiographie: 'Les Mots' de Jean-Paul Sartre*, Archives des Lettres Modernes (Paris: Minard, 1973).

35. One is tempted to superimpose these two narratives, not only because of the numerous elements that Sartre has borrowed from his own childhood in order to utilize them in the fiction of *L'Enfance d'un chef*, but also to show the analogies in the descriptive and explanatory system of the origin and manifestations of the neurosis. From the point of view that interests me here, it is also necessary to see the difference between the two: in a work of fiction, the writer is no longer hindered by chronology; nothing prevents him from composing the story starting from the analysis, very classically. Whence the strictly linear and very simple development of the narrative. The narrative follows the order of a story that is composed by starting from the order of the analysis. A real life does not lend itself to such treatment so easily.

36. The density is produced by a very rich work of *writing*: cultural allusions, pastiches, plays on the indirect free style, subtly violent mixtures of hyperliterary style and oral bluntness. On these problems, see the study by Jacques Lecarme cited in note 11.

This ironic style becomes inevitably blurred when Sartre orally recounts his life instead of writing it, for example, in his interviews (see the narrative of his adolescence prepared at the request of Francis Jeanson, in *Sartre dans sa vie*). He himself explains at length this gap and this stylistic inequality between the *written* and the *oral* in an interview with Michel Contat in 1975 (*Situations*, Paris: Gallimard, 1976, vol. 10, pp. 136–38; English translation: "Self-Portrait at Seventy," in *Sartre in the Seventies*, pp. 5–6).

37. With the exception, it is true, of *L'Enfance d'un chef*.

38. *L'Etre et le Néant* (Paris: Gallimard, 1943), pp. 150ff. English translation: *Being and Nothingness*, trans. Hazel Barnes (New York: Washington Square Press, 1966), pp. 159ff. For the autobiographical perspective, see the entire sequence on "Mon Passé" (pp. 577–85; 637–47), in which Sartre shows how we spend our time redefining the meaning and the order of our past in light of our present project: "Furthermore, this decision with respect to the value, the order, and the nature of our past is simply the *historical choice* in general" (p. 581; 642).

39. But he was thinking already about the problem of biography. See the study by Victor Brombert, "Sartre et la biographie impossible," *CAIEF* 19 (1967), pp. 155–66.

40. Simone de Beauvoir, *Tout compte fait*, pp. 9–10; (English translation: *All Said and Done*, trans. Patrick O'Brian (New York: Putnam, 1974), prologue.

41. "But Sartre always tried to see me as part of my own scheme of things, to understand me in the light of my own set of values and attitudes." Simone de Beauvoir, *Memoirs of a Dutiful Daughter*, trans. James Kirkup (Harmondsworth, England and Baltimore, Md., 1963), pp. 340ff.

42. *L'Idiot de la famille* (Paris: Gallimard, 1971), vol. 1, p. 56; English translation: *The Family Idiot*, trans. Carol Cosman, (Chicago: University of Chicago Press, 1981), vol. 1, p. 46.

43. What is, in reality, the result of a free choice is made to appear in the retrospective narrative as necessary and determined: nowhere do any other possibilities appear that the choice would have eliminated – because freedom is not choice, but invention. Only the imagined outcome is imaginable. That is why reverie on the possible considers not other possible reactions to the situation, but other possible situations; reverie not on freedom, but on chance. Thus in *Les Mots*, pp. 76; 87, the reverie on a rich father ("Had he left me property, my childhood would have been changed. I would not be writing, since I would be someone else"), or pp. 134; 158, on a grandfather encouraging genius ("If Charles had flung his arms wide open and cried out from afar: 'Here comes the new Hugo, here's a budding Shakespeare!', I would now be an industrial draughtsman or a teacher of literature.") Any reverie on chance makes apparent, *a contrario*, the necessary character of the choice made by free-

dom. See, for example, the procedure used by Simone de Beauvoir in *Tout compte fait*, pp. 11-40; 1-30.

44. "A life develops in spirals; it passes again and again by the same points but at different levels of integration and complexity," in *Search for a Method*, trans. Hazel E. Barnes (New York: Alfred A. Knopf, 1963), p. 106.

45. *Saint Genet comédien et martyr* (Paris: Gallimard, 1952), pp. 9; 9-10.

46. Genette, *Figures, essais III*, p. 75. English translation: *Narrative Discourse: An Essay in Method*, trans. Jane E. Lewin (Ithaca, N.Y.: Cornell University Press, 1980), p. 30.

47. See *Les Mots*, pp. 208-9; 248-50; *Situations*, vol. 9, pp. 32-33.

48. Postscript (1987). This study was written in 1973 and published in 1975. Since 1975, before and especially after Sartre's death in 1980, the corpus of autobiographical productions of Sartre has grown considerably. The most important events have been the release of the film by Alexandre Astruc and Michel Contat *Sartre par lui-même* (1976), the publications by Simone de Beauvoir in 1981 of *Entretiens* (*Conversations*) that she had with Sartre in 1974 (following *La Cérémonie des adieux*) and in 1983 of *Lettres au Castor et à quelques autres*, but especially the publication in 1983 by Arlette Elkaïm-Sartre of *Carnets de la drôle de Guerre*, which testify to the autobiographical work done by Sartre in 1939-40 at the very moment when he was preparing *L'Etre et le Néant*.

I have tried to analyze the development of this corpus in a series of studies: "Ça s'est fait comme ça" (*Poétique* 35 [September 1978], pp. 269-304) on the film *Sartre par lui-même*; "Sartre et l'autobiographie parlée" (*Je est un autre*, 1980, pp. 161-202); and "Les Enfances de Sartre," in *Moi aussi*, (Paris: Editions du Seuil, 1986), pp. 117-63.

Chapter 6. The Autobiographical Pact (bis)

1. "Le Pacte autobiographique" ("The Autobiographical Pact") was written in 1972 and published in *Poétique* 14 in 1973. It was reprinted, almost without modification, in 1975 at the beginning of the volume with the same title, *Le Pacte autobiographique* (Paris: Editions du Seuil). Quotations and references will refer to the translation in Chapter 1 of this volume.

2. In the appendix I refer to three American studies comparable to "Le Pacte" and to some critical discussions of the "Le Pacte" that reflect upon different aspects of my study.

3. In Jérôme Garcin's television program *Boîte aux lettres*, devoted to autobiography (FR3, May 29, 1983). The three books governed by an autobiographical contract are *Un petit bourgeois* (1963), *Lettre à mon chien* (1975), and *Le Musée de l'homme* (1979).

4. The narrative of Lhopiteau is one of the autobiographies of merchants that I have presented in "Autobiography and Social History in the Nineteenth Century" (see chapter 8 of the present volume).

5. See "Par où commencer?" ("Where To Start?"), *Moi aussi* (Paris: Editions du Seuil, 1986), pp. 224-45, in which I presented two ways of approaching the study of autobiography at the university.

6. This is the objection made by Michel Beaujour in "Autobiographie et autoportrait." *Poétique* 32 (November 1977).

7. See "Regarder un autoportrait," translated as "Looking at the Self-Portrait" (chapter 5 of the present volume).

8. Beginning of *L'Astragale* (1965) by Albertine Sarrazin.

9. Beginning of *Mes Ecoles* (1977) by Edouard Bled.

10. F. Vasseur, *Le Poème de travail, Souvenirs d'un instituteur* (Paris: Librairie du *Petit Journal*, 1873), p. 1 and pp. 93-94.

11. Robert Baratte, *Au creux de mon enfance* (Paris: La Pensée Universelle, 1981), pp. 19-20.

12. Raymond Queneau and Georges Perros have both, moreover, also written prose narratives of their childhood. For Queneau, it is a matter of a biographical note focused on the story of his fam-

ily, written, it seems, after the Second World War, thus subsequent to *Chêne et Chien* (see *Raymond Queneau plus intime*, exhibition at the Bibliothèque Nationale, Paris: Gallimard, 1978, p. 14). For Perros, it is a matter of an actual initial version, in prose, of what became *Une vie ordinaire (Notes d'enfance)* (Paris: Quimper, Calligrammes, 1979). These two pairs of texts constitute types of "Rosetta Stones" that could allow some reflection on the effect produced by versification.

13. Undoubtedly, it is ineluctable that generic criticism be the object of a deconstruction. I tried to show, in *Le Pacte autobiographique* (pp. 311 ff.; pp. 141 ff. of the present volume), that discourses on the autobiographical genre are themselves *part* of this genre; as clear as we might be, we always end up sharing the illusions we claim to analyze. Accordingly, the process of deconstruction can take as its object almost any discourse on autobiography, as shown by the subtle study of Jonathan Loesberg, "Autobiography as Genre, Act of Consciousness, Text," *Prose Studies* (September 1981). Loesberg reviews all the essays contained in the collection by James Olney (*Autobiography: Essays Theoretical and Critical*, Princeton, N.J.: Princeton University Press, 1980), in order to show that they are all weakened by posing from the author's point of view problems that can exist only from the reader's point of view. Despite my statements at the beginning of "Le Pacte" ("I begin from the position of the reader: it is not a question of starting from within the mind of the author, which indeed poses a problem, nor is it one of establishing the canons of a literary genre," p. 4), I suppose I would have fallen under the blow of the same criticisms.

14. Parody was the only way I found to tear myself away from this fascination (See "Le Roland Barthes sans peine," *Moi aussi*, Paris: Editions du Seuil, 1986, pp. 103-16).

15. See "Ça s'est fait comme ça,' *Poétique* 35 (September 1978), pp. 269-304.

16. See "L'autobiographie à compte d'auteur," *Moi aussi* (Paris: Editions du Seuil, 1986), pp. 292-309 (and also "Women and Autobiography at Author's Expense," *New York Literary Forum*, "The Female Autograph," 1984, no. 12-13, pp. 247-60).

17. I have completed up to now four sections of this index: autobiographies of merchants and manufacturers (see chapter 8 of the present volume); the autobiographies of schoolteachers (see "Les instituteurs du XIXe siècle racontent leur vie," *Histoire de l'éducation* 25 (January 1985), pp. 53-104; the autobiographies of criminals (see "Crime et testament: Les autobiographies de criminels au XIXe siècle," *Cahiers de sémiotique textuelle*, 8-9 [1986], pp. 73-98); and the autobiographies of homosexuals (see "Autobiographie et homosexualité en France au XIXe siècle," *Romantisme* 56 [1987], pp. 79-100).

18. See Xavier-Edouard Lejeune, *Calicot*, edited and introduced by Michel and Philippe Lejeune (Paris, Arthaud-Montalba, "Archives privées," 1984).

19. Letter from Serge Doubrovsky, October 17, 1977.

20. For example, in "L'Initiative aux maux," *Cahiers Confrontation* 1 (Spring 1979), pp. 95-113, and "Autobiographie/Vérité/Psychanalyse," *L'Esprit createur* (Fall 1980), pp. 87-90.

21. As Jacques Lecarme and Bruno Vercier clearly show in their panorama of recent evolutions, *La Littérature en France depuis 1968* (Paris: Bordas, 1982); see "Indécidables et autofictions," pp. 150-55.

22. See, for example, Albert Stone's study of this phenomenon in contemporary American literature, "Factual Fictions," *Autobiographical Occasions and Original Acts* (Philadelphia: University of Pennsylvania Press, 1982), chap. 8, pp. 265-324.

23. This study was finally published under the title "Autobiographie, roman et nom propre," *Moi aussi* (Paris: Editions du Seuil, 1986), pp. 37-72.

Chapter 7. Autobiography and Literary History

1. On these problems, see the studies of Hans Robert Jauss, through whose perspective the present critical study has developed: "Littérature médiévale et théorie des genres," *Poétique* 1 (1970), and "Literary History as a Challenge to Literary Theory," *New Literary History* 2 (Autumn 1971).

2. For a study of the manner in which academic criticism contributes, at the same time as other factors, to the canonization of a genre, see Luc Boltanski, "La Constitution du champ de la bande dessinée," *Actes de la Recherche en Sciences Sociales* 1 (January 1975).

3. Michel de Certeau, "L'Opération historique," in *Faire de l'histoire*, under the direction of . Le Goff and P. Nora (Paris: Gallimard, 1974), vol. 1, pp. 3-41.

4. Charles Caboche, *Les Mémoires et l'Histoire en France*, 2 vols. (Paris: Charpentier, 1863). The first volume includes an "Introduction" (pp. 1-101) that elaborates a theory of the genre.

5. On this strict definition of literary history, see G. Genette, "Poétique et l'histoire," *Figures, essais III* (Paris: Editions du Seuil, 1973; English translation: *Narrative Discourse: An Essay in Method*, trans. Jane E. Lewin [Ithaca, N.Y.: Cornell University Press, 1980], pp. 13-20), and T. Todorov, "Histoire de la littérature," in the *Dictionnaire encyclopédique des sciences du langage* by O. Ducrot and T. Todorov (Paris: Editions du Seuil, 1972), pp. 188-92.

6. Todorov is right to emphasize that the genres should not be confused with the names of genres (*Dictionnaire*, p. 193), and that a study on the life of the names of the genres is dependent upon semantic history (ibid., p. 189). But, even if it can not be substituted for "literary history," such a study must inevitably be integrated into it, insofar as it is in no way immaterial to know the evolution of one of the elements of the communication code between authors and readers. Furthermore, the methodological problems of an eventual "semantic history," which barely exists at the present time, are parallel to those of the new literary history whose principles were laid down by Tynianov.

7. J. Tynianov, "De l'évolution littéraire," in *Théorie de la littérature* (Paris: Editions du Seuil, 1965), pp. 120-37.

8. G. Misch, *A History of Autobiography in Antiquity*, 2 vols. (London, 1950); this is a translation of the beginning of *Geschichte der Autobiographie*, 8 vols. (Frankfurt, 1949-69). Misch states that in writing this history, he wanted to carry out the project conceived around 1790 by Herder and Goethe: to assemble a corpus of all the autobiographical texts written in all times and in all countries, in order to show the progressive liberation of the human person. Academic criticism and literary history are clearly presented here as participating (belatedly) in the work that literature does to invent a past and a tradition for itself.

9. Paul Zumthor, *Essai de poétique médiévale* (Paris: Editions du Seuil, 1972), pp. 68-69 and pp. 172-74; and "Autobiographie au Moyen Age?" *Langue, Texte, Enigme* (Paris: Editions du Seuil, 1974). See also the study by Evelyn B. Vitz, "Type et individu dans 'l'autobiographie' médiévale," *Poétique* 24 (1975).

10. See, for example, M. Masciotta, *Portraits d'artistes par eux-mêmes, XIV-XXe siècle* (Milan: Electra Editrice, 1955); Ernst Benkart, *Das Selbstbildnis vom 15. bim zum 18. Jahrhundert* (Berlin, 1927), and Ludwig Goldscheider, *Fünfhundert Selbstporträts* (Vienna, 1936). See also the beautiful book by Pascal Bonafoux, *Les Peintres et l'autoportrait* (Skira, 1984). In French, the term "autoportrait" was created at the beginning of the twentieth century.

11. Caboche, *Mémoires*, vol. 1, p. xv.

12. Article published in *XVIIe siècle* 94-95 (1972), at the beginning of an issue dedicated to "Mémoires et création littéraire."

13. Philip Stewart, *Imitation and Illusion in the French Memoirs-Novels, 1700-1750, the Art of Make-Believe* (New Haven and London: Yale University Press, 1969).

14. Wayne Shumaker, *English Autobiography, Its Emergence, Materials, and Form* (Berkeley: University of California Press, 1954).

15. Philippe Lejeune, *L'Autobiographie en France* (Paris: A. Colin, 1971), pp. 65-66.

16. Roy Pascal, *Design and Truth in Autobiography* (Cambridge, Mass: Harvard University Press, 1960), pp. 160-61.

17. "From this condition of minds unique to our country, is born a genre of literature that has been the expression of that condition from the beginning. We understand easily that such a genre is original; it has been in existence for more than six centuries. Since this genre is most often what the chances

of the accidents that are to be told make it and the equally capricious chance of the kind of man who confides his feelings or his memories to it, the genre changes tone, accent, I'll say almost language, from book to book" (Caboche, *Mémoires*, vol. 1, p. xiii). Insofar as Caboche claims that memoirs are not a traditional literary genre, the fixity resides not in obedience to the "rules of a known theory, to satisfy the taste of a public formed by models" (vol. 1, pp. 7-8), but in a *constant* mobility.

18. Caboche, *Mémoires*, vol. 1, pp. i-vii.

19. Francis R. Hart, "Notes for an Anatomy of Modern Autobiography," *New Literary History* 1 (Spring 1970), pp. 485-510; William L. Howarth, "Some Principles of Autobiography," *New Literary History* 5, (Winter 1974), pp. 363-81.

20. William L. Howarth notes only that in the last of the three types of autobiographies that he distinguishes (poetic or problematic autobiography), all the authors are modern; and he also notes that many are Americans. This would be the place to point out another type of behavior in genre criticism, linked to its participation in the institution: chauvinism. It is well known that autobiography is a British genre (*passim*); that the French have a gift for autobiography (*L'Autobiographie en France*, p. 5); and that autobiography is an especially American genre (Sayre, *The Examined Self*, Princeton, N.J.: Princeton University Press, 1964, pp. 38-42; James M. Cox, "Autobiography and America," in *Aspects of Narrative*, ed. J. Miller, New York: Columbia University Press, 1971, pp. 143-72; etc.); it is surely also a very German genre and typically Russian. There are undoubtedly some national specificities, which critics interpret too quickly in terms of preeminence or of exclusivity, both out of national pride, and out of relative ignorance of other literatures.

21. See above, note 1.

22. See, for example, the anthology prepared by Michel Raimond in *Le Roman depuis la révolution* (Paris: A. Colin, 1967), and the chapter devoted to "La Définition du roman," in *La Crise du roman, des lendemains du naturalisme aux années vingt* (Paris: Corti, 1967), pp. 138-58.

23. T. Todorov, *Poétique* (Paris: Editions du Seuil, 1973), pp. 99-101.

24. Caboche, *Mémoires*, vol. 1, p. xviii.

25. Ibid., p. xix. My own discourse echoes this one, for example, in *L'Autobiographie en France*, p. 13.

26. Caboche, *Mémoires*, pp. 10-24.

27. Roy Pascal, *Design and Truth in Autobiography* (Cambridge, Mass.: Harvard University Press, 1960), chap. 1, "What Is an Autobiography?"

28. Robert Escarpit, *Le Littéraire et le Social* (Paris: Flammarion, 1970), p. 151.

29. Richard G. Lillard, *American Life in Autobiography, a Descriptive Guide* (Stanford, Calif.: Stanford University Press, 1956), pp. 6-13. For the author, the ten capital sins of autobiography would be: stereotyped writing, abuse of anecdotes, detailed (and improbable) reconstruction of scenes and dialogues, insertion of undigested diary entries, ancestral and family catalogs at the beginning of the book, overly detailed travel narratives, memories of youth that have no relevance, name dropping, too hasty narratives, camouflage of the truth. And the six cardinal virtues would be: sadness, recognition of one's errors and failures; affective communication with the reader from the beginning; original details and characteristics of the era or the personality; coherent point of view, exploited for a new insight; personal frame of reference in the story; sense of progression or change. Each point is illustrated with examples.

30. Roger J. Porter and H. R. Wolf, *The Voice Within, Reading and Writing Autobiography* (New York: Knopf, 1973).

31. Barrett John Mandel, "The Autobiographer's Art," *The Journal of Aesthetics and Art Criticism* 26 (1968-69), pp. 215-26.

32. Francis R. Hart, "Notes for an Anatomy of Modern Autobiography," *New Literary History* 1 (1970), pp. 485-511.

33. William L. Howarth, "Some Principles of Autobiography," *New Literary History* 5 (1974), pp. 363-81.

34. Cited by J. Pommier, "L'Idée de genre," *Publications de l'Ecole normale supérieure*, "Section des lettres" (1945), vol. 2, p. 77.

35. Northrop Frye, *Anatomy of Criticism* (Princeton, N.J.: Princeton University Press, 1957).

36. T. Todorov, *Introduction à la littérature fantastique* (Paris: Editions du Seuil, 1970), chap. 1, "Les Genres Littéraires."

37. Ibid., p. 20.

38. These reflections confirm those of Dan Ben-Amos in "Catégories analytiques et genres populaires," *Poétique* 19 (1974).

39. T. Todorov, "Genres Littéraires," in *Dictionnaire encyclopédique des sciences du langage* (Paris: Editions du Seuil, 1972), pp. 197-201.

40. Elizabeth W. Bruss, "L'Autobiographie considérée comme acte littéraire," *Poétique* 17 (1974), pp. 14-26. See also her book *Autobiographical Acts: The Changing Situation of a Literary Genre* (Baltimore: Johns Hopkins University Press, 1976).

41. See John R. Searle, *Speech Acts: An Essay in the Philosophy of Language* (London: Cambridge University Press, 1969).

42. H. R. Jauss, "Littérature médiévale et théorie des genres," *Poétique* 1 (1970), p. 79.

43. For the analysis of the narrative, the "Discours du récit" by G. Genette (in *Figures, essais III* – English translation: *Narrative Discourse: An Essay in Method*, trans. Jane E. Lewin (Ithaca, N.Y.: Cornell University Press, 1980) – provides a good working instrument, which can be completed as far as temporal questions go, by *Le Temps* by H. Weinrich (Paris: Editions du Seuil, 1973).

For the analysis of contents, an example was furnished by M. J. Chombart de Lauwe in her study on the mythical image of the child, *Un monde autre, l'enfance* (Paris: Payot, 1971). The author studies this myth by classifying the contents of the childhood narratives written during the nineteenth century. She treats in the same way both autobiographies and novels, which, she claims, present no notable differences in the point of view in which she envisions them.

44. On the diary, see Alain Girard, *Le Journal intime* (Paris: P.U.F., 1963); on autobiography, see my study *L'Autobiographie en France*; on the personal French novel, no complete study has appeared since the already outdated books by Joachim Merlant, *Le Roman personnel de Rousseau à Fromentin* (Paris: Hachette, 1905), and by Jean Hytier, *Les Romans de l'individu* (Paris: Les Arts et le Livre, 1928). On other areas like memoirs, or correspondence, in the nineteenth century, there exists no complete study.

45. Ferdinand Brunetière, "La Littérature personnelle" (1888), in *Questions de critique* (Paris: Calmann-Lévy, 1897), pp. 211-52.

46. H. R. Jauss, "Littérature médiévale et théorie des genres," p. 79.

47. Paul Valéry, *Cahiers* (Paris: Gallimard, Bibliothèque de la Pléiade, 1974), vol. 2, p. 1167.

48. It is the object, for example, of the series "Lectures" published by Armand Colin in the collection U2. Two recent works provide an inventory of the readings that have been done of Rousseau: Raymond Trousson, *Rousseau et sa Fortune littéraire* (Bordeaux: Ducros, 1971), and Jean Roussel, *Jean-Jacques Rousseau en France après la Révolution* (Paris: A. Colin, 1973).

49. For example, Roger Fayolle, *Sainte-Beuve et le dix-huitième siècle* (Paris: A. Colin, 1972).

50. To encompass this "topos," I have proceeded with an analysis of a rather reduced critical corpus (six issues of *Le Monde des livres*, from August 16 to September 27, 1973), that time of year when publishers, returning from vacation, get back to the business of publishing, especially new novels that might be eligible for one of the literary prizes awarded in September or October), but which already presented an impressive number of variations on this single theme, that the book that is presented is more or less directly an autobiography of its author. It is true that most of the publisher's blurbs set the critic off in this direction. But the topos can even be applied to novels, where nothing invites such a reading attitude. In my corpus the two extreme examples were the novels of Jarry, presented as a "singularly subverted: dreamed rather than lived" autobiography (whereas it is undoubtedly more the fictional contract that is subverted here by the reader), and a utopian book, *Nais-*

sance d'une île, by François Clément, "who expends so much care and love in telling us this adventure that one would think it was autobiographical!"

51. In the 1950s, oral autobiography developed from real oral situations, those of conversations intended for the radio; the transcription from the oral to the written was, then, a secondary phenomenon. What characterizes the intensive development of oral autobiography in recent years is, on the contrary, that the oral process is set in motion from the outset *in order to produce a book*; the public will never have been either witness or guarantor of the initial orality, and will not always know very well how the text it is reading was produced. "Taped autobiography" would merit a special study, emphasizing the variations that it can bring to the genre: in the testimony register, to give a voice to all those who have not mastered writing, and who would never have been able to get published (example: *Louis Lengrand, mineur du Nord*, Paris: Editions du Seuil, 1974); in the literary register, to attempt to substitute for the written style the expressivity of the *voice* (examples: Françoise Giroud, *Si je mens . . .* Paris: Stock, 1972; and Romain Gary, *La Nuit sera calme*, Paris: Gallimard, 1974, whose style could be compared to that of *La Promesse de l'aube*, 1960); on the technical level, to emphasize the presence of public opinion in questionnaire form which from implicit becomes explicit, through the go-between of the interlocutor.

52. Thanks to the "series," the editor assures the public of buyers-readers, to whom he guarantees conformity of the product to a certain "list of specifications," and among whom he exploits or arouses the attitudes of reading. On the other hand, the series incites authors to respond to forms of traditional or new demand. Current autobiographical production could not be studied outside these collective contracts, which moreover touch different publics: political or military memoirs in the series of Plon, Fayard, and other publishers; witness series ("Témoins," by Gallimard; "Témoigner," by Stock; "Témoignages," by Mâme, etc.); the mythology of the "Lived" ["*Vécu*"], in particular by Laffont; the confessions and professions of faith created in series ("Idée fixe," by Julliard; "Ce que je crois," by Grasset); autobiographies that have been taped by journalists ("Les Grands Journalistes," by Stock) or political figures; and so on.

53. Lejeune, *L'Autobiographie en France*, p. 105.

54. Renée Balibar, *Les Français fictifs* (Paris: Hachette, 1974), p. 178.

55. Etienne Balibar and Pierre Macherey, "Présentation" of the work by Renée Balibar, *Les Français fictifs* (see note 54). One part of this presentation was published in *Littérature* 13 (February 1974), under the title "Sur la littérature comme forme idéologique. Quelques hypothèses marxistes."

56. Postscript (1987). The two projects that I had come up with in 1975 have remained, for the moment, at the project stage. As will be seen in the next chapter, it is another angle that I finally used to explore the relationships between autobiography and social history.

Chapter 8. Autobiography and Social History in the Nineteenth Century

1. A more systematic exposé of the bases of this study will be found in "La Cote Ln 27," *Moi aussi* (Paris: Editions du Seuil, 1986), pp. 249-72. Four sections of the inventory have already been published: the merchants, manufacturers, and financiers, right here; the schoolteachers ("Les instituteurs du XIXe siècle racontent leur vie," *Histoire de l'éducation* 25 [January 1985], pp. 53-104); the criminals ("Crime et testament. Les autobiographies de criminels au XIXe siècle," *Cahiers de sémiotique textuelle*, Université de Paris X, no. 8-9, 1986, pp. 73-98); and the homosexuals ("Autobiographie et homosexualité en France au XIXe siècle," *Romantisme* 56 [1987], pp. 79-100).

2. Michel Ragon, *Histoire de la littérature prolétarienne en France* (Paris: Albin Michel, 1974). For an inventory of the autobiographies of militant workers in the nineteenth century, see Pierre Ponsot's introduction to the *Mémoires* of Jean-Baptiste Dumay (Paris: Maspero, P.U.G., 1976). For the workers, see no. 105 (October–December 1978) of *Mouvement Social*, "Travaux de femmes dans la France du XIXe siècle," presentation by Michelle Perrot. On a more general level, see the confusing but useful index by Paul Feller, *Nécessité, Adolescence, Poésie, ébauche d'un catalogue bio-*

bibliographique des auteurs ayant, des l'adolescence, gagné leur vie du travail de leurs mains (Paris: Le Musée du soir, 1960).

3. Pierre Guiral and Guy Thuillier, *La Vie quotidienne des domestiques en France au XIXe siècle* (Paris: Hachette, 1978), p. 14.

4. *Moi, Pierre Rivière . . . , un cas de parricide au XIXe siècle présenté par Michel Foucault* (Paris: Gallimard/Julliard, 1973); Xavier Thiriat, *Journal d'un solitaire* (Remiremmont: Librairie de Mme Leduc, 1868); *Vie de Mélanie, bergère de la Salette, écrite par elle-même. Son enfance (1831-46)* (Paris: Mercure de France, 1912).

5. In *Les Livres de raison (1328-1870)*, exhibition of November 16, 1954, at the Maison des Chambres d'Agriculture, you will find references and some excerpts from family record books by nineteenth-century farmers.

6. Discovered in 1910 by Daniel Halévy, published in 1932 by Emile Guillaumin, the narrative by Henri Norre, *Comment j'ai vaincu la misère*, is a pioneer's autobiography. He shows what you can do with courage and some of the methods of modern farming: "Without the help of anyone and through a very difficult time, I have attained the goal I set for myself almost forty years ago: to feel myself secure from want, to be king in my home."

But we find, well before Norre, "exemplary" autobiographies of rural entrepreneurs. For example, J. C. Potel-Lecouteux, proprietor-farmer in Créteil, *Quarante ans de travaux agricoles (de 1822 à 1863)* (Paris: Imprimerie E. Martinet, 1863), 16 pp.

7. For a synthesis of social history on these categories, see also Guy P. Palmade, *Capitalisme et capitalistes français au XIXe siècle* (Paris: A. Colin, 1961), and Louis Bergeron, *Les Capitalistes en France (1781-1914)* (Paris: Gallimard/Julliard, 1978). Louis Bergeron cites numerous autobiographical fragments originating in letters or unpublished accounts.

8. See, by contrast, the section "Businessmen, Financiers, Industrialists" in the inventory that Richard G. Lillard discusses in *American Life in Autobiography* (Stanford, Calif.: Stanford University Press, 1956), pp. 29-37.

9. For a presentation of these different mentalities, see Werner Sombart, *Le Bourgeois* (Paris: Petite Bibliothèque Payot, 1966).

10. Thus the correspondence of Alfred Motte-Grimonprez, cited by Louis Bergeron, *Les Capitalistes en France*.

11. One example, among many others: *Emile Guimet, 1er janvier 1860-1er janvier 1910. Cinquantenaire* (BN, 4 Ln27 59255), exchanges of discourse between Emile Guimet and his employees.

12. For example, the *Dictionnaire biographique des grands négociants et industriels, contenant toutes les notabilités du commerce et de l'industrie avec leur portrait, leurs noms et prénoms, la date et le lieu de leur naissance, leur famille, leurs débuts, leurs fonctions successives, leur adresse, leurs découvertes, inventions, productions, spécialités, les récompenses obtenues aux concours et expositions, les perfectionnements apportés à leur commerce et à leur industrie, leurs titres, leurs oeuvres, leurs écrits, etc. et toutes les indications bibliographiques qui s'y rapportent.*

This dictionary, begun in 1895 by Henry Junger in anticipation of the World's Fair of 1900, clarifies for those who are interested: "The biographies that we propose to write, according to the notes people will want to give us, will be of the most rigorous accuracy. The judgments made on the men and their works will be brief, but we will put the greatest sympathy at the disposal of all." This dictionary, one among many others, contains 120 rather developed reviews that are visibly due, essentially, to the models.

13. For a formalized presentation of the "roman à thèse" (didactic novel), see Susan Suleiman, "La Structure d'apprentissage. Bildungsroman et roman à thèse," *Poétique* 37 (February 1979).

14. Narcisse Faucheur, *Mon Histoire. . . .* , pp. 5-6. See Appendix 7.

15. Ibid., p. 361.

16. Ibid., p. 383.

17. Pierre Ameline, "Les Mémoires d'un travailleur bas-normand (première moitié du XIXe siè-

cle," published by Gabriel Désert in the *Annales de Normandie* 19 (March 1969), pp. 59–77, and 19 (June 1969), pp. 155–78. On his plan of suicide, see p. 71.

18. Prosper Delafutry, *Les Mémoires d'un travailleur* (Paris: L. Sauvaitre, 1887), 142 pp.

19. Xavier-Edouard Lejeune, *Calicot*, edited and introduced by Michel and Philippe Lejeune (Paris: Arthaud-Montalba, 1984), pp. 217–18.

Chapter 9. The Autobiography of Those Who Do Not Write

1. Annie Mignard, "L'un écrit, l'autre signe"; François Maspero, "Qui est le 'nègre'?" *La Quinzaine Littéraire* (June 16–30, 1977).

2. Doesn't a *translated* text have two authors? But quite obviously, insofar as there exists an original published text, the translator finds himself in a hierarchically dependent situation. While it might be a true art, translation has been for some time, and remains, a poorly paid and relatively thankless occupation (the mention of the name of the translator on the cover of the book is not the general rule). The position of the writer is in many aspects similar to that of the translator, with just one difference, but an enormous one: in the writer's case, *the original text does not exist*. The writer does not transmit the text from one language to another, but draws the text from a "before-text."

3. See, for example, "Celui qui raconte n'est pas toujours celui qui écrit," by Jean-Claude Lamy, *France-Soir*, October 10, 1975; "L'Ecrivain-fantôme," statement, by G. W. (Ghost Writer!), *Les Nouvelles Littéraires* (March 3–10, 1977), in the dossier "Ecrire au magnétophone" realized by Karine Berriot; "Les nègres en littérature," survey by Jean-Marc Théolleyre, *Le Monde*, July 8, 1977 (with the response of Charles Ronsac in *Le Monde* of July 29, 1977).

4. *Hack [faiseur]*: "He who usually works for someone else. This theater has its hacks. This bookseller has his regular hacks. That minister is very happy to have such a good hack. We often suspect a female author of having a hack." *Cleaner [teinturier]*: "He who goes over, corrects the writings of another. Voltaire was the King of Prussia's cleaner for a long time. There is no female author whom jealous men do not suspect of having a cleaner" (*Dictionnaire national* by Bescherelle, 1861). The word "ghostwriter" *[nègre]* (which [in French] implies not only the idea of a work, but that of the *exploitation* of the worker) progressively replaced at the end of the nineteenth century the other two words that had fallen into disuse.

5. See the reviews in *Le Globe*, with regard to the memoirs of Madame du Barry (April 15 and July 11, 1829), those of a "woman of quality" on the court of Louis XVIII (July 15, 1829), and those of Cardinal Dubois (October 14, 1829). See also Jean Tulard, *Bibliographie critique des mémoires sur le Consulat er l'Empire* (Paris: Droz, 1971), p. viii. In fact the cleaners work either in apocryphal autobiography or in collaborative autobiography (according to written notes or confidences of living models, who signed the book, like Bourienne, or Constant, the valet of Napoleon).

6. *Le Globe*, Ocotber 14, 1829.

7. See "Genèse du texte," *Littérature* 28 (December 1977); and Jean-Louis de Rambures, *Comment travaillent les écrivains* (Paris: Flammarion, 1978).

8. "Les nègres en littérature," *Le Monde*, July 8, 1977. The repeated use of the expression "the author" in a text that describes the work of composition and of writing, of which this "author" must be totally unburdened, might appear strange, but it is surely intentional: it is a way of putting the ghostwriter back in his place.

9. Martin Gray, *Au nom de tous les miens* (Paris: R. Laffont, 1971), preface by Max Gallo.

10. One could be tempted to define this genre as a "heterobiography in the first person," which would be a case exactly the inverse of that of "autobiography in the third person." One who pretends to be two; two who pretend to be only one. But symmetry established in this way is deceiving: the pretense does not have the same function in the two cases, and especially is not situated on the same level.

In autobiography in the third person, the narrator seems to speak of himself as if he were someone else, or as if he were speaking about someone else; the reader must remain aware of this game for the text to keep its meaning. In collaborative autobiography, the writer speaks of the model as if it were he, by constructing his role as autodiegetic narrator; the reader must forget this game for the text to keep its meaning. In *Au nom de tous les miens*, I cannot attribute the "I" of the narrator to Max Gallo, even though I know that it is he who wrote it. It is no longer a matter of a figure of enunciation within the text (and decipherable from the contract), but of a disposition of contract, midway between the contract of fiction that governs a novel in the first person and the referential contract that introduces a reported discourse. The narrator of the story, while still being reconstituted by someone else, is no less real since it is he who signs the book. Max Gallo finds himself caught between two apparitions of Martin Gray, upstream, as signing author at the beginning of the credits, downstream, as supposed narrator of the written narrative.

11. This was the principle adopted by Claude Glayman for his series "Les Grands Journalistes" (Stock), launched by Françoise Giroud with *Si je mens . . .* (1971). But even if the answers were reworked, the book kept the form of the conversation, which is also the case for *La Nostalgie n'est plus ce qu'elle était*, and explains the misapprehension of Anne Gaillard (see below, note 13).

12. Christiane Rochefort, *Ma vie revue et corrigée par l'auteur*, from conversations with Maurice Chavardès (Paris: Stock, 1978). While a self-portrait, this book is also a parody of the "livre-entretien" (book-conversation) and a lampoon against the genre itself (pp. 9–31).

13. On May 10, 1977, Anne Gaillard and Jean-Edern Hallier accused Simone Signoret of not having written her own book herself—in spite of the preface by Maurice Pons, however explicit it might be. Prosecuted, both of them were forced to pay a fine, both damages and interest. This affair, like that of Annie Mignard, reveals two things: first, that all legal affairs or "polémiques de presse" [press polemics] in which scandal occurs have to do with "badly chosen" cases. Anne Gaillard was obviously wrong, and the case of Annie Mignard seems rather doubtful. The point is that when the causes are "well chosen," there is no scandal: the editor or author concerned sees to it that no scandal breaks out. On the other hand, those who have seen in this type of allegation ("she did not write the book she is signing") an error and not a libel are rare: on the level of presuppositions (ideology of the author), everyone agrees. At the time of the Gaillard affair, very few journalists went back as far as that presupposition, to declare that this had barely any importance (see note 20).

Simone Signoret next told in a second book (*Le Lendemain elle était souriante . . .* Paris: Editions du Seuil, 1979) how she had written the first.

14. See the suggestive book by François Flahaut, *La Parole intermédiaire* (Paris: Editions du Seuil, 1978).

15. "The quality of author belongs, save proof to the contrary, to the one or ones under whose name the work comes out" (Law of March 11, 1957, article 8). It is thus the signature that proves authenticity. In the course of the trial that she brought against Anne Gaillard, Simone Signoret did not have to prove that she had written the book. It was up to Anne Gaillard to prove the contrary, something she would have had great difficulty in doing, even if Simone Signoret had not written one single line.

16. The cases I am examining here fall under the category of collaborative works: "A collaborative work is one to which several physical people have contributed. The work of collaboration is the common property of the coauthors" (articles 9 and 10 from the Law of March 11, 1957). But the law does not determine what is collaboration giving access to the status of coauthor, and what is not, and until now jurisprudence has not gone into any detail about the specifics of the law. The law, on the other hand, has solved the problem in the case of cinematographic works by listing the different persons who ought to be considered coauthors of a film (article 14).

17. On this point, see E. P. Goldschmidt, *Medieval Texts and Their First Appearance in Print* (1943; New York: Biblo and Tannen, 1969). On the subsequent evolution, see Lucien Febvre and Henri-Jean Martin, *L'Apparition du livre* (1958; Paris: Albin Michel, 1971), pp. 233–42 and pp. 367–68.

It is interesting to follow not only the evolution of practices and legislation, but also that of the theory of law. In Pierre Recht, *Le Droit d'auteur, une nouvelle forme de propriété. Histoire et théorie* (Paris: Duculot, 1969), is found a review (and a critique) of the personalist and individualist theories upon which one attempted to base the "droit d'auteur" [author's right] in the nineteenth century.

18. See Pierre Bourdieu, "La Production de la croyance, contribution à une économie des biens symboliques," *Actes de la recherche en sciences sociales* 13 (February 1977), pp. 3–44.

19. Even when the collaboration is not hidden, it is minimized. Especially, in these matters, the public is reduced to believing (or not believing) exactly what one wants to tell them, because the public obviously has no way to evaluate the work of the writer. The public is unaware, and will always be unaware, of what the initial contribution of the model consisted. It is unlikely that a publisher ever gives access to this type of information: if one had recourse to a writer, it is precisely because what the model was capable of producing was not presentable. As for ghostwriters, they are *de facto*, bound by a sort of professional secrecy. Consequently suspicion can continue to surround even an admitted collaboration.

20. "All things considered, only the result counts finally: consumers are indifferent to the processes of fabrication: they want especially to be satisfied with the product being proposed to them . . . Above all the work must be interesting. It matters little if someone held the hand of the person who signed." Georges Vittel summarizes here and justifies the reaction of the general public (*Le Hérisson*, December 29,1977). And if that person signs what he has not written, it is because it is he who provided the initial capital: "There is nothing scandalous here. These books would not exist without their authors and there would be some hypocrisy to say that one was deceived about the merchandise, when the book is bought on the theme that it develops, the personality that it allows to be discovered or the story it tells." (F. Gilles, *Le Journal quotidien Rhône-Alpes*, December 25, 1977.)

21. An excellent survey of this field of notoriety is provided by skimming through the catalog of some 2,000 Radioscopies (live radio programs, an hour a day, each day a different guest is asked to recount his or her life story) realized by Jacques Chancel since 1969. Thirty-one headings cover practically every domain in which one can achieve and become socially interesting. "Radioscopy" is, of course, one instance of *consecration*: it supposes an already constituted notoriety, which it helps to increase. Only three headings contain some interviews based upon ethnological curiosity, the interest in those whom Chancel calls in a revealing manner "anonymous" ("Testimony and Documents," "Artisans," "Agriculture"). Still, most of these "anonymous" witnesses are no longer so when they arrive in Radioscopy; they come here as *author* of the book that has just drawn them out of anonmyity (thus Martin Gray, Louis Lengrand, Nicole Gérard, Emilie Carles, and many others).

22. Consequently facsimiles of handwritten signature are sometimes used on the jackets or covers of books.

The signature of the book by the model doesn't inevitably imply that the writing proceeds as if the author had written it. In many of these books, the wording allows the oral origin of the narrative to come through, and tries to pluralize the attraction of the written narrative and of the voice recorded by an interviewer. The reference "récit recueilli par" [story gathered by] serves to make this mixture of techniques believable.

23. The share of the author's rights accorded the model is variable. In the best of cases the writer and the model share equally (for example, Maurice Catani and Mohamed, for the *Journal de Mohamed*, Paris: Stock, 1973). But the arrangements can be less favorable to the model. It has even happened that his share is reduced to nothing.

24. It is interesting to examine, for example, the presentation of Emilie Carles's book, *Une soupe aux herbes sauvages* (1978). Emilie Carles, daughter of peasants, who became a schoolteacher but remained a peasant, could have been treated like Mémé Santerre or Gaston Lucas, ethnologically. But at the same time that she is a witness of peasant France, she is a militant pacifist and ecologist. A schoolteacher, she belongs to the world of writing. She will sign, then, "her" book, directly, as a hero, even though it is not she who wrote it ("conversations gathered by Robert Destanque").

25. Agricol Perdiguier, *Mémoires d'un compagnon* (1853); Martin Nadaud, *Mémoires de Léonard, ancien garçon maçon* (1895), republished recently under the title *Léonard, maçon de la Creuse* (Paris: Maspero, 1976); Joseph Benoit, *Confessions d'un prolétaire*, finished around 1871, published in *Ed. sociales* in 1968; Jean-Baptiste Dumay, *Mémoires d'un militant ouvrier du Creusot* (1841-1905), published by Maspero and Les Presses Universitaires de Grenoble in 1976. In the Introduction of the last book (pp. 12-15), Pierre Ponsot inventories the autobiographies of militant workers in the nineteenth century.

26. *Moi, Pierre Rivière, ayant égorgé ma mère, ma soeur et mon frère*, a case of nineteenth century parricide presented by Michel Foucault (Paris: Gallimard/Julliard, 1973). Pierre Rivière's autobiographical memoir had been published in part in a dossier relating the affair, in the *Annales d'hygiène publique et de médecine légale* in 1836. At the time of the two publications, it is the crime that is the center of interest (or, for Foucault, the discourse on the crime), and not the "ethnographic" testimony, uninteresting in 1836, left out with some regret by Foucault in 1973.

27. On the reception of *La Vie d'un simple*, which was subtitled *Les Mémoires d'un métayer*, and which was often taken for an authentic ethnological document, see R. Mathe, *Emile Guillaumin, l'homme de la terre et l'homme de lettres* (Paris: Nizet, 1966), pp. 217-22.

28. *Catalogue de l'histoire de France* (Bibliothèque impériale, 1865), vol. 9, chap. 15, Biographie française. All the printed matter on a real individual (whether it concerns biography or autobiography) is grouped in the Bibliothèque Nationale under the same call number, Ln 27.

29. See "Autobiography and Social History in the Nineteenth Century," chapter 8 of this volume.

30. Any society can define itself by the biographical models that it diffuses. The *Catalogue de l'histoire de France*, in section 3 (*Biographies spéciales*) of chapter 15 (*Biographie française)* lists in this way the categories of lives that inspired the biographers of the nineteenth century: French saints and religious celebrities, clergy, men of state and administrators, parliamentarians, magistrates and barristers, army, scholars and men of letters, artists, doctors, manufacturers, artisans and financiers, members of different orders, medal of valor, members of diverse associations, convicts, women of France (from saints to courtesans), young French men and women (edifying lives). We could compare the list of categories used in the catalog of *Radioscopies* by Jacques Chancel, in order to see both the continuity and the emergence of new legitimate roles.

31. Pierre Bourdieu, 'La Paysannerie, une classe objet," *Actes de la recherche en sciences sociales* 17/18 (November 1977), p. 4. The continuation of this development can be applied particularly well to autobiography.

32. For the image of the peasant in literature, see Paul Vernois, *Le Roman rustique de George Sand à Ramuz, ses tendances et son évolution* (Paris: Nizet, 1962); for that of the worker, Louis Chevalier, *Classes laborieuses et Classes dangereuses* (Paris: Plon, 1958).

33. See *La Parole ouvrière 1830/1851*, texts collected and presented by Alain Faure and Jacques Rancière (Paris: Editions 10/18, 1976).

In *L'Atelier* (March 31, 1843), an article entitled "Si les ouvriers doivent se permettre d'écrire?" puts the workers on guard against the temptation of individual promotion in the governing circuit and favors, on the contrary, the anonymous and collective production of texts published not in the form of books, but in workers' newspapers and magazines. The testimony will therefore take more the form of the *enquête* [survey] than that of the personal narrative.

34. On the genre of the narratives of fugitive slaves, see Stephen Butterfield, *Black Autobiography in America* (Amherst: University of Massachusetts Press, 1974), pp. 9-89, and the clarification by Benjamin Quarles, "Relation de la vie de Frederick Douglass," *Dialogue* 2 (1977), pp. 42-52.

35. Norbert Truquin, *Mémoires et Aventures d'un prolétaire à travers la révolution* (1888; Paris: Maspero, 1977). A commited "socialist" but not affiliated with any group, Truquin devised his memoirs as a "work of propaganda": "It is urgent that all those who work and suffer from the vices of the social organization count only on themselves to get out of trouble and create a better present and future through solidarity. It is essential then that each one among them brings his stone to the

common edifice, by publishing his notes, his notebooks, his memoirs, in a word all the documents that can contribute to destroying the inequities of the old world and to hastening the social revolution" (p. 273). His testimony, precise, gripping, argued, is the model of what could be expected of a popular autobiography in the nineteenth century. It has nonetheless remained for a long time without any effect. In the mid-1940s, Michel Ragon tried in vain to have it republished.

36. The memoirs of Nadaud, of Benoit, of Dumay present the same profile: the narrative of adolescence has a frankly "ethnographic" aspect, centered on group life and the portrayal of working conditions (masons from Creusot, silk-workers from Lyon, metallurgists from Creusot); the sequel to the narrative belongs rather to the genre of political memoirs with an apologetic function, centered on the personal action of the militant.

37. Michel Ragon, *Histoire de la littérature prolétarienne en France. Littérature ouvrière, littérature paysanne, littérature d'expression populaire* (Paris: Albin Michel, 1974).

38. Ibid., p. 19.

39. Ibid., pp. 205-6.

40. Ibid., p. 11.

41. In particular in the last two chapters on the worker writers and the peasant writers.

42. Michel Ragon, *Histoire de la littérature prolétarienne*, p. 11.

43. Louis Lengrand and Maria Craipeau, *Louis Lengrand, mineur du Nord* (Paris: Editions du Seuil, 1974), pp. 183-84. For an overview of this problem, see the work by René Kaès, *Les Ouvriers français et la culture*, survey, 1958-61 (Paris: Dalloz, 1962), in particular, pp. 114-76, on reading; and pp. 203-12, on the attitude regarding history.

44. Constant Malva, *Ma nuit au jour le jour* (Paris: Maspero, 1978), p. 194 (letter to René Bonnet, May 28, 1937).

45. *Ma nuit au jour le jour* is the journal kept by the author for one year (from May 1937 to May 1938). Some excerpts were published in 1947 by *Les Temps Modernes*. The entire book was published in Belgium only in 1952.

46. Thus the narrative of a peasant childhood published at the author's expense by Marie-Juliette Barrie, *Quand les bananes donnent la fièvre* (Paris: La Pensée universelle, 1973).

47. It is one of the problems that one asks oneself while reading the beautiful book by Louis Oury, *Les Prolos* (Paris: Denoël, 1973).

48. Published in 1974 by the Ecomusée du Creusot.

49. Georges Navel's *Travaux* (1948) is differentiated from other narratives of working life by the writing, inspired by Verlaine, and especially by the picaresque aspect of the narrative. Far from being rooted in an occupation or a region, and domesticated by a family to support, Navel led a roving life that allowed him to practice most of the manual occupations (from factory work to seasonal agricultural labor). His book is at the same time the story of a search for the meaning of life, guided by the love of nature, of freedom, and of solidarity. It is an often painful, disappointing search, certain passages of the book calling to mind *Voyage au bout de la nuit*, but with a more committed and warmer anarchism. *Travaux* knew some success in 1948 and was republished in 1969 by Stock, then in 1979 in the "Folio" series.

50. The Maspero series "Actes et mémoires du peuple" republishes or publishes different testimonies of militants, thus repeating, on the autobiographical level, the biographical work undertaken since 1948 by Jean Maitron for his *Dictionnaire biographique du mouvement ouvrier français*. In Germany, in the same way, some copious anthologies-indexes published in 1974-75 have inventoried the corpus of workers' autobiographies, to give back to the present workers a class memory. See a presentation of these anthologies by Jérôme Radwan, 'Perspectives nouvelles sur un genre méconnu: l'autobiographie ouvrière,' *Allemagnes d'Aujourd'hui* (March-April 1976), pp. 73-84.

51. The proceedings of this meeting have been published in *Ethnologie française* 8, no. 4 (1978). Following this meeting, a French Association of Sound Archives was established in February 1979,

which unites the conservators of sound archives and the researchers who set up recording resources for their works.

52. On the history and the project of the series "Terre humaine" (Plon), see the long interview by Jean Malaurie in the *Magazine Littéraire*, September 1975.

53. On the history and the problematic of the "life story" in sociology, see the mimeographed account by Daniel Bertaux, *Histoires de vie—ou récits de pratique?*, methodology of the biographical approach in sociology, March 1976, 232 pp., and the book by Jean Poirier, Simone Clapier-Valladon and Paul Raybaud, *Les Récits de vie. Théorie et pratique* (Paris, P.U.F., 1983).

54. See Louis M. Starr, "Oral History," in *Encyclopedia of Library and Information Science* (New York: M. Dekker, 1977), vol. 20, pp. 440–63. On the most recent developments of oral history in Great Britain, see Raphaël Samuel, "L'Histoire orale en Grande-Bretagne," *Bulletin du centre de recherches sur la civilisation industrielle*, Ecomusée du Creusot (November 1977), pp. 15–23.

55. On the birth of oral history in France, see the discussion by Philippe Joutard, "Historiens, à vos micros! Le document oral, une nouvelle source pour l'histoire," *L'Histoire* 12 (May 1979), pp. 106–12, and his book *Ces voix qui nous viennent du passé* (Paris: Hachette, 1983).

56. Ephraïm Grenadou and Alain Prévost, *Grenadou, paysan français* (Paris: Editions du Seuil, 1966; new edition, 1978, in the series "Points"). Grenadou was a great success. He went on to television; journalists poured into his village; some Prévost-Grenadou radio conversations were broadcast in 1967, and the book itself was published in serial form in *Rustica* (in other words, reverberated toward the milieu of origin). But this success has remained isolated and has aroused hardly any imitation for the moment.

A good panorama of this first generation of published life stories is given by the survey in *Le Monde*, "La littérature au magnétophone," April 12, 1969.

57. Sélim Abou, *Immigrés dans l'autre Amérique*, autobiographies of four Argentinians of Lebanese origin (Paris: Plon, 1972), series "Terre humaine," foreword.

58. Daniel Bertaux, *Histoires de vie*. Bertaux does not mention Michel Ragon's study, which does not enter into his field—just as Michel Ragon does not mention the works of sociologists who collect "proletarian" narratives.

59. L'Ecomusée du Creusot, in collaboration with the Institut national de l'audiovisuel, puts together audiovisual life stories (see *Bulletin du Centre de Recherches sur la Civilisation Industrielle* 1 [June 1978], pp. 40–41).

60. Quite obviously, these written narratives take into account the curiosity of the investigator, of his questions: he remains the addressee, and will be able to use that curiosity.

I am talking here about *oral* surveys, which involve people who have no practice in writing. One other case, completely different, might present itself: that of a written survey, by questionnaire, which awakens in the subjects being questioned, once the pen is in hand, the desire to answer through a narrative of their life as a whole. Jacques Ozouf has thus, by launching a vast survey with 20,000 schoolteachers from "la Belle Epoque," awakened the autobiographical vocation of 300 of them. They sent him texts, relatively short but often exciting, and documents, from which he has drawn a very lively historical picture, *Nous, les maîtres d'école, autobiographies d'instituteurs de la Belle Epoque* (Julliard, "Archives" series, 1967). But he addressed himself, in writing, to specialists of writing, completely competent in history and composition. By publishing his book, he played a part in consolidating and perpetuating the memory of this social group, since the people being surveyed were at the same time readers.

Ozouf's practice, at the beginning involuntary, recalls that of the "autobiography competition" that has developed in Poland since 1921 at the instigation of sociologists and diverse cultural institutions (see Janina Markiewicz-Lagneau, "L'Autobiographie en Pologne, ou de l'usage social d'une technique sociologique," *Revue Française de Sociologie* [October–December 1976]). This call to the writing and *reading* of autobiographical texts (some of the stories were published) results in the investigation not being content to divert the memory of the groups studied, but it stimulates memory. It is a kind of intervention and can allow a class consciousness to develop. It doesn't seem that in France, at the time of proletarian literature, or since, such a technique has ever been used.

61. *Les Nouvelles Littéraires*, January 26–February 1, 1978, dossier compiled and presented by Jean-Pierre Rioux.

62. Certain researchers allege, however, the individual function of "psychotherapy" and the social function of intervention that the investigation can have; but this effect is not the aim of the investigation, and it is sometimes neither foreseeable nor verifiable by the person who sets it in motion. See Jacques Gutwirth, "L'Enquête en ethnologie urbaine," *Hérodote* 9 (January–March 1978), pp. 38–55.

63. The two books were badly received by African criticism (see *Révolution africaine*, December 7, 1973, and *L'Algérien en Europe*, January and March, 1974), which finds that these two émigrés are not representative and that the publication of their discourse serves to denigrate their country. These monologues are too different from the image that the spokesmen for the Algerian community want to present of it. Against these criticisms, and those of the large French press (Tahar Ben Jelloun, in *Le Monde*, December 6, 1973, and Claude Jannoud in *Le Figaro*, January 5, 1974), Maurice Catani has tried to defend their ethnological status (in *Vivre en France*, April 1974). Rejected by the Algerians who read, and by the left, the two narratives (which, after all, their system of presentation makes difficult to read) didn't find success among the general public either.

64. At the beginning of *Un couple ouvrier traditionnel*, Jacques Caroux-Destray explains himself on this point. He knows well that it is not his "models" who will read him. Rather, he wants to bear witness in their name, by making himself echo their speech. And he should especially have been read by those who were in the same social position as he—he had recently left the working class. The book hardly made any news in the press of the Communist party, undoubtedly because it did not give an optimistic enough image of the working class, and because it painted candidly its alienation.

65. Interview in *Le Figaro*, June 27, 1966.

66. What the people of the country read, then, is the *listening* that the existence of the book manifests as much as the speech whose tenor they already know on the whole.

67. *Le Mouvement Social* 97 (October–December 1976), p. 163.

68. It is undoubtedly rather paradoxical to read as an autobiography of the author this book that wants first and foremost to be considered a document on the world of his parents. But the awkwardness with which he seeks to remain in the background forces the reader to feel the extraordinary tension of this divided "I," quartered between two worlds and two languages. In the Preface, a dramatic and allusive language imposes on the reader an autobiographical reading. The Afterword, which tries to theorize the alienation of parents, shows a young student who is not yet mastering the theoretical instrument he has just acquired. "Gilles's" monologue represents an undoubtedly rare case of solitary self-interview on tape, whose recomposition is cut by fragments of personal journals. Four discourses with different strategies and addressees, four facets of a broken I, around a silence, the absence of the impossible discourse to address his parents directly.

69. "Mémé Santerre is the staggering story of hunger, of poverty, of cold, a story of opppression, of war, and of death. And nevertheless, happiness radiates in this existence: Mémé Santerre, is above all the story of a love that transfigured everything, of a love that even death could not conquer, and which justifies an unalterable optimism and serenity" (description of the book on the cover).

70. It is sometimes the second home which puts the writer or journalist in touch with his model. Alain Prévost had bought the old rectory of Saint-Loup; Grenadou was one of his neighbors. Mother Denis, whose biography was later written by Serge Grafteaux, was "discovered" by one of his "neighbors" of Carteret, who was working in Paris in advertising.

71. Benoît Verhaegen, *Introduction à l'histoire immédiate* (Paris: Duculot, 1974), pp. 192–93.

72. But one can think that the evolution of the video recorder will parallel that of the tape recorder in the last twenty years, and that it will become more widely used.

73. See note 59. From each life story (which covers hours of tape and was realized in the course

of lengthy conversations with the models), there has been drawn, both for local interest and for television, an average footage of fifty minutes. But this is only an initial utilization of this very rich material.

Chapter 10. Teaching People to Write Their Life Story

1. The book by Claude Bonnafont (no. 21) is rather a compilation in book form than a practical guide written by someone who has personal experience in keeping a diary. I mentioned the book by Charles de Ribbe, published a century ago, for historical reasons. In his very stimulating *Ecrire*, Jean Guénot offers advice about all literary genres except for autobiography. The other texts mentioned are not guides but exemplify pedagogical practices in different fields.

This inventory was done in 1981. It would certainly be much larger today (1987). Here are some examples of what could be added. Some new "how to" guides: Lois Daniel, *How To Write Your Own Life Story. A Step by Step Guide for the Non-Professional Writer* (Chicago: Chicago Review Press,1980); Ruth Kanin, *Write the Story of Your Life* (New York: Dutton, 1981); Wilson Ketterer, *How to Write and Sell a Book of Your Intimate Thoughts and Adventures* (Albuquerque, New Mexico: American Classical College Press, 1982); Earlynne Webber, *Your Life Story – How to Write, Print, Publish and Sell It Yourself* (Beaumont, Texas: Echo Publishing, 1986); and so on. Some new reports of pedagogical experiences: Marilyn B. Smith, "The Time of Their Lives: Teaching Autobiography to Senior Adults," *College English*, November 1982; Nicole Fialeyre, 'L'Autobiographie en 5ème" and Catherine Barbier, "Autoportrait: entrer dans la chair du sujet," *Le Français aujourd'hui* 65 (March 1984).

2. "Each person is an unrecognized book. Writing professionals at your service to correct, revise, or edit the book that you carry within you," says the advertisement for SOS Manuscripts (11, rue Boyet-Barret, 75014 Paris). See the article by Thierry Gaudillot, "La clinique de l'écriture," *Le Monde dimanche*, 7 June 1981.

3. Suggestions made by Editions Fleurville of Paris, which manufactures and sells such books.

4. "J'étais une fois" (Paris: Editions du Temps retrouvé). The client first has several hours of conversation with an interviewer (the equivalent of what used to be "posed" sittings for a portrait). Then the conversation is transcribed and put in care of a professional writer, who puts it into the form of a narrative. Once it is accepted by the client, the text is printed, possibly with illustrations, in a very small edition – which recent technology allows without an exorbitant cost. The copies are not put on the market but are sent to the client, who does what he or she wants with them. For a presentation of this undertaking, see *Gé-Magazine* 10 (September 1983), pp. 11–12.

5. See my study of the pitfalls of vanity press publication, "L'autobiographie à compte d'auteur," *Moi aussi* (Paris: Editions du Seuil, 1986), pp. 292–309.

6. See my essay on the teaching of autobiography, "Par où commencer?", *Moi aussi*, pp. 224–45.

7. Paul Le Bohec has commented on this practice in *Les Co-biographies dans la formation*, Documents de l'éducateur, 182–83 (Cannes: Coopérative de l'enseignement laïc, 1985), 48 pp. His method, which was elaborated during the seventies, is similar to methods developed in the early eighties by different groups: methods like that of the Germinal group (see *La Groupe familial* 96, July–August 1982, but this exercise does not operate on the basis of writing), that of different practitioners of "permanent formation" (see *Education permanente* 72–73, March, 1984), or, in Québec, that of Gaston Pineau (*Produire sa vie; autoformation et autobiographie* [Québec: St. Martin's, 1983]).

8. These autobiographies were immediately published, in Hackney itself, by Centerprise, the cultural center that houses the workshop. The history of this undertaking is told in *Local Publishing and Local Culture* (London: Centerprise, 1977).

9. *Glossaire: j'y serre mes gloses* is a poetic game invented by Leiris in 1925 in the framework of the activities of the surrealist group. *Le Glossaire* was reprinted in the volume entitled *Mots sans mémoire* (Paris: Gallimard, 1969), then further elaborated in *Langage Tangage* (Paris: Gallimard, 1985). Here are two examples from it. The first can only fascinate: "*Psychanalyse: lapsus canalisés*

au moyen d'un canapé-lit" ("Psychoanalysis: slips canalized by means of a sofa-bed"). The second can be only an entrance (hermetic to others) into the personal history of the "player": *"Père: perpétuel pet de reptile" ("Father: perpetual reptile fart").* I have presented this game in *Sub-Stance* 11–12 (1975), pp. 116–30.

Epilogue

1. "Epilogue" is the final section of Lejeune's analysis of the first three chapters of *L'Age d'homme* by Michel Leiris. In *Lire Leiris, autobiographie et langage* (Paris: Klincksieck, 1975), pp. 175–85. —Ed.

Publications of Philippe Lejeune

Publications on Autobiography

Books

1971. *L'Autobiographie en France*. Paris: A. Colin.

1974. *Exercices d'ambiguïté, lectures de 'Si le grain ne meurt'*. Paris: Lettres Modernes.

1975. *Lire Leiris, autobiographie et langage*. Paris: Klincksieck. (Grand Prix de la Critique Littéraire, 1976.)

——. *Le Pacte autobiographique*. Paris: Editions du Seuil.

1980. *Je est un autre, l'autobiographie de la littérature aux médias*. Paris: Editions du Seuil.

1984. Xavier-Edouard Lejeune. *Calicot*. Edited and introduced by Michel and Philippe Lejeune. Paris: Montalba.

1986. *Moi aussi*. Paris: Editions du Seuil.

Bibliography of Studies in French on Personal Literature and Life Stories. (Biennual bibliography taking into account, from a multidisciplinary perspective, studies in French that deal with the following genres: autobiography, journal, correspondence, self-portrait, memoirs, witness accounts, biography, oral and audiovisual life stories; preceded by a thematic inventory.)

1982–83. *Cahiers de Sémiotique Textuelle* 3 (1984).

1984–85. *Cahiers de Sémiotique Textuelle* 7 (1986).

Inventory of Autobiographies Written in France in the Nineteenth Century (1789-1914). (The program of this Inventory is described in "La Cote Ln 27. Pour un répertoire des autobiographies écrites en France au XIXe siècle," in *Moi aussi*, Paris: Editions du Seuil, 1986, pp. 249-72. Each section deals with a distinct social or professional category; a general study precedes the inventory itself.)

Section I. *Commercial, Industrial, and Financial Lives*

"Autobiographie et histoire sociale au XIXe siècle." *Revue de l'Institut de Sociologie*, 1-2 (1982), pp. 209-34 (inventory, pp. 226-34). (See Chapter 8 of the present volume).

Section II. *Lives of Teachers*

"Les instituteurs du XIXe siècle racontent leur vie." *Histoire de l'éducation* 25 (January 1985), pp. 53-104 (inventory pp. 83-104).

Section III. *Lives of Criminals*

"Crime et testament. Les Autobiographies de criminels au XIXe siècle." *Cahiers de Sémiotique Textuelle* 8-9 (1986), pp. 73-98 (inventory, Section III, 1 [1789-1880], pp. 87-98).

Section IV *Lives of Homosexuals*

"Autobiographie et homosexualité en France au XIXe siècle." *Romantisme*, 56 (1987), pp. 79-100 (Inventory, pp. 95-100).

Articles

(Only articles that have not been reprinted in book form or that are not part of the Inventory are mentioned here.)

1974. "Le Dangereux Supplément. Lecture d'un aveu de Rousseau." *Annales* 4, pp. 1009-22.

1976. "Le Peigne cassé." *Poétique*, 25, pp. 1-30 (Rousseau).

———. "Stendhal et les problèmes de l'autobiographie." In *Stendhal et problèmes de l'autobiographie* (Symposium of 1974), Grenoble: Presses de l'Université de Grenoble, pp. 21-36.

1978. "Ça s'est fait comme ça." *Poétique* 35, pp. 269-304. (Study of a sequence of the film *Sartre par lui-même*.)

1980. "Grammaire de l'interview." Conversation with Jean-Luc Hennig. *Libération*, August 2, 1980.

1985. Article "Autobiographie" for *Dictionnaire des Littératures*, Larousse, vol. 1, pp. 124-25.

1986. "Les Bricoleurs du moi." *La Croix*, June 22-23, 1986, p. 20.

———. "Les Souvenirs de lecture d'enfance de Sartre." In *Lectures de Sartre*,

texts collected and presented by Claude Burgelin, Lyon: Presses
Universitaires de Lyon, pp. 51–87.
——. Foreword to Marie-France Terry. *En passant par la rue haute, Des
anciens racontent Saint-Ouen l'aumône.* Editions du Valhermeil. (Oral
history of the city.)
——. "Friselis. Chronique de lecture." *Romance Studies* 9 (Winter 1986), pp.
7–19. (On *La Fête des pères* by François Nourissier.)
1987. "Cinéma et autobiographie: Problèmes de vocabulaire." *Revue Belge du
Cinéma* 19 (Spring 1987), pp. 7–13.
——. "Wanted: autobiographies!", *L'Histoire* 101, June 1987, pp. 82–83.
——. "Le récit de vie, un nouveau genre?" *Le Français aujourd'hui* 79, sep-
tember 1987, pp. 59–66.
1988 "L'autobiographie existe-t-elle?" In *Biographie et autobiographie au
XXe siècle*, actes du 20ème congrès de l'A.G.E.S., Montpellier 16–17
May 1987, *Cahiers de l'Institut détudes Germaniques* (Université Paul
Valéry, Montpellier III 5, 1988, pp. 81–94.
——. " 'Cher cahier . . . ' " *Le Magazine littéraire* 252–253, April 1988,
pp. 45–46.
——. "L'ère du soupçon." In *Le récit d'enfance en question*, Actes du col-
loque de Nanterre, 16–17 January 1987, *Cahiers de sémiotique tex-
tuelle* 12, 1988, pp. 41–65.
——. "Peut-on innover en autobiographie?" In *L'Autobiographie*, Les Belles
Lettres, series "Confluents psychanalytiques," pp. 67–100.
——. "L'autobiocopie," in Actes du colloque *Autobiographie et biographie*,
Heidelberg, 25–27 May 1988.
——. "Le bourreau Véritas" followed by "Genèse de W ou le souvenir d'en-
fance," *Cahiers Georges Perec* 2, (Université Paris VII), pp. 101–55.
——. "L'écriture privée. Projet d'enquête sur le journal personnel," *Bulletin
du Cedref* (Centre d'études et de recherches féministes).

Translations

Italian Translations
1986. *Il Patto Autobiografico.* Bologne: Il Mulino.
(Followed by an afterword written for that edition.)

English Translations
1975. "Glossaire." *Sub-Stance*, 11–12, pp. 116–30.
(Two excerpts from *Lire Leiris* and from *Le Pacte*, on Michel Leiris.)
1977. "Autobiography in the Third Person." *New Literary History* 9 (Au-

tumn 1977), pp. 27–50. (Original publication of the study that appeared in French in *Je est un autre*, 1980.)

1982. "The Autobiographical Contract." In *French Literary History Today, A Reader*, edited by T. Todorov, Cambridge: Cambridge University Press, pp. 196–222. (Translation of the first chapter of *Le Pacte*, 1975.)

1984. "Women and Autobiography at Author's Expense." *New York Literary Forum* 12–13, pp. 247–60, reprinted in *The Female Autograph* (Chicago: University of Chicago Press, 1987), pp. 207–18. (Original text, in part reprinted in *Moi aussi*, 1986.)

1986. "Making Ripples: A Reader's Chronicle." *Romance Studies* 9 (Winter 1986), pp. 21–34. (Translation of "Friselis," published after the French text.)

Polish Translations

1975 "Pact autobiograficzny," *Teksty* 5 (1975), pp. 31–49.

Publications on Other Subjects

1968. *L'Ombre et la lumière dans "Les Contemplations"*. Paris: Archives des Lettres Modernes.

1969. "L'Enseignement de la 'littérature' au lycée au siècle dernier." *Le Français aujourd'hui* 4, pp. 26–37

1971. "Ecriture et sexualité." *Europe* (February–March), pp. 113–43 (on Proust).

1977. "Les Carafes de la Vivonne." *Poétique* 31, pp. 283–305. (Reprinted in the volume *Recherche de Proust*, Paris: Seuil, 1980.)

———. "Introduction" to *Poétique* 30, "Enseignements," edited in collaboration with Jean Verrier.

1979. 'La Côte-Verte et le Tartaret." *Poétique* 40, pp. 475–86. (On *Germinal*.)

1985. "Colette Vivier a toujours dix ans." Conversation with Colette Vivier (1979), *Trousse-Livres* 60 (May 1985), pp. 18–19.

1988. "Maupassant et le fétichisme." In *Maupassant Miroir de la Nouvelle*, Saint-Denis: Presses Universitaires de Vincennes, pp. 91–109.

Index

Index

Theory and History of Literature

Philippe Lejeune teaches French literature at the Université de Paris-Nord. He has also taught at Yale University and at the Université de Lyon. Lejeune has published seven books and many articles on autobiography. His most recent books are *Moi aussi* (1986) and *Je est un autre* (1980); he contributes to *Poétique* and *Cahiers de Sémiotique textuelle*.

Katherine Leary is an assistant professor of French and chair of the department of French at Salve-Regina, The Newport College, and previously served as a lecturer at Tufts University. Leary received her Ph.D. in comparative literature from the University of Minnesota.

Paul John Eakin is a professor of English at Indiana University, and he has served as Senior Fulbright-Hays Lecturer in American Literature at the Université de Paris (1972–73) and the University of Athens (1978–79). Eakin is the author of *The New England Girl: Cultural Ideals in Hawthorne, Stowe, Howells, and James (1977)* and *Fictions in Autobiography: Studies in the Art of Self-Invention* (1985), and his work has appeared in *American Literature, South Atlantic Quarterly, Prospects, New Literary History,* and other journals.

For Reference

Not to be taken from this room